Designing Digital Systems
With
SystemVerilog

Dr. Brent E. Nelson
Department of Electrical and Computer Engineering
Brigham Young University
Provo, UT, 84602
brentnelson@ieee.org

May 24, 2018

Version 1.1

Contents

1 Introduction to Digital Systems Design   **13**
1.1   Digital vs. Analog 13
1.2   Positional Number Systems 13
1.3   Digital vs. Analog Continued 14
     1.3.1   Analog vs. Digital Data Storage 16
     1.3.2   Analog vs. Digital Data Processing 17
     1.3.3   Analog vs. Digital - A Summary 17
1.4   Combinational vs. Sequential Digital Circuits 17
1.5   Chapter Summary 18

2 Number Systems and Binary Encodings   **19**
2.1   Positional Number Notation 19
     2.1.1   Conversion from Decimal to Other Bases 20
2.2   Hexadecimal (Base-16) Numbers 21
2.3   Binary-Coded Decimal 22
2.4   Other Codes 22
     2.4.1   ASCII Codes 23
     2.4.2   Gray Codes 23
2.5   Chapter Summary 24
2.6   Exercises 25

3 Signed Number Representations, Negation, and Arithmetic   **27**
3.1   Addition of Unsigned Numbers 27
     3.1.1   Overflow in Unsigned Addition 27
3.2   Signed Numbers: Sign-Magnitude 28
     3.2.1   Negating Sign-Magnitude Numbers 28
3.3   Signed Numbers: 2's Complement 28
     3.3.1   Sign-Extension 29
     3.3.2   Negating a 2's Complement Number 29
     3.3.3   Adding 2's Complement Numbers 30
     3.3.4   Subtracting 2's Complement Numbers 31
3.4   Signed Numbers: 1's Complement 32
3.5   Summary — Number representations 32
3.6   More on Overflow and Underflow 33
     3.6.1   Detecting and Handling Overflow and Underflow - Some Ideas 33
3.7   Chapter Summary 34
3.8   Exercises 35

4   Boolean Algebra and Truth Tables   **37**
   4.1   Introduction to Boolean Algebra and Truth Tables   37
   4.2   Truth Tables for Arbitrary Functions   38
   4.3   Converting Truth Tables to Boolean Equations   39
   4.4   Converting Boolean Functions to Truth Tables   40
   4.5   Boolean Identities and Theorems   41
       4.5.1   Single-Variable Theorems   41
       4.5.2   Two-Variable Theorems   42
       4.5.3   Commutative, Associative, and Distributive Theorems   42
       4.5.4   The Simplification Theorems   43
       4.5.5   The Consensus Theorems   43
   4.6   Summary of the Boolean Theorems   44
   4.7   Chapter Summary   44
   4.8   Exercises   45

5   Logic Gates   **47**
   5.1   Basic Gate Types   47
   5.2   Transistors - The Building Blocks of Gates   48
       5.2.1   Building An Inverter Using FET's   49
   5.3   Other 2-Input Gates   51
       5.3.1   NAND Gates   51
       5.3.2   NOR Gates   51
       5.3.3   An Exclusive-OR Gate   51
       5.3.4   An Equivalence Gate   52
   5.4   Multi-Input Gates   52
   5.5   Alternative Gate Symbology   53
   5.6   Multi-Level Logic   56
       5.6.1   Speed of Operation   56
       5.6.2   Circuit Area   57
       5.6.3   Speed and Area Comparisons   57
       5.6.4   Factoring and Multiplying Out   58
   5.7   Chapter Summary   59
   5.8   Exercises   60

6   Boolean Algebra - Part II   **63**
   6.1   Inverting a Function - DeMorgan's Rules   63
   6.2   Sum-of-Products and Product-of-Sums Forms   64
   6.3   Canonical Forms - Minterm Expansion and Maxterm Expansion   66
   6.4   Boolean Minimization   68
       6.4.1   What is a Minimal Form for an Expression?   68
       6.4.2   Minimization By Applying Boolean Theorems   69
       6.4.3   Proving Equalities Using Boolean Theorems   70
   6.5   Incompletely Specified Functions and Boolean Minimization   71
   6.6   Summary of Boolean Minimization   72
   6.7   Chapter Summary   73
   6.8   Exercises   74

7   Gates - Part II   **75**
   7.1   NAND-NAND and NOR-NOR Logic   75
   7.2   Functionally Complete Logic Sets   77
   7.3   Gate Symbology — Matching Bubbles   78
       7.3.1   Bubble Matching and Reconvergent Fanout   80
   7.4   Chapter Summary   80

7.5 Exercises 81

8 An Introduction to Gate-Level Design Using SystemVerilog   **83**
8.1 Three Important Rules Regarding Designing using an HDL For Digital Systems Design 84
8.2 Levels of Design Abstraction in SystemVerilog 84
8.3 Basic Structural SystemVerilog Design 85
    8.3.1 Structural Gate Instantiations are Concurrent Statements 86
8.4 Declaring Wires in SystemVerilog 87
8.5 CAD Tool Design Flow 89
8.6 Chapter Summary 89
8.7 Exercises 90

9 Gate-Level Arithmetic   **91**
9.1 A Hardware Adder 91
9.2 An Adder/Subtracter Module 93
9.3 Chapter Summary 94
9.4 Exercises 94

10 Higher Level Building Blocks: Multiplexers, Decoders, and Lookup Tables   **95**
10.1 Introduction 95
10.2 Multiplexers 95
    10.2.1 A 4:1 Multiplexer 97
10.3 Multi-Bit Wires in Schematics 98
10.4 Using Multiplexers for Logic 99
10.5 Decoders 101
10.6 When to Use Multiplexers and Decoders 102
10.7 Read-Only Memories (Lookup Tables) 104
10.8 Chapter Summary 105
10.9 Exercises 106

11 Continuing on With SystemVerilog - Hierarchical Design, Constants, and Multi-Bit Signals   **107**
11.1 Creating Hierarchy Via Structural Instantiation 108
    11.1.1 Semantics of Module Instantiation 109
11.2 Specifying Constants in SystemVerilog 109
11.3 Accessing Bits of Multi-Bit Wires in SystemVerilog 110
11.4 More on Naming - Modules, Instance Names, and Wires 110
11.5 Hierarchical Design Flow 111
11.6 Chapter Summary 111

12 Karnaugh Maps   **113**
12.1 Truth Tables to KMaps 113
12.2 Three-Variable KMaps 116
12.3 Minterm and Maxterm Expansions and KMaps 117
    12.3.1 Circling More Than Two 1's 118
12.4 Four-Variable KMaps 119
12.5 Plotting a Boolean Equation on a KMap 121
12.6 Deriving Product of Sum Expressions from KMaps 122
12.7 Solving a KMap With Don't Cares 122
12.8 Finding Optimal Solutions Using KMaps 123
12.9 A Worked Example — A BCD to 7-Segment Converter 126
12.10 Chapter Summary 127
12.11 Exercises 128

13 Gate Delays and Timing in Combinational Circuits   **129**
 13.1 Introduction 129
 13.2 Basic Gate Delays 129
 13.3 Critical Path Analysis 130
 13.4 Levels of Detail in Timing Analysis 131
 13.5 Input Glitches, Timing, and Gate Behavior 132
 13.6 A Pulse Generator 134
 13.7 False Outputs 135
  13.7.1 False Outputs and Hazards: Summary 137
 13.8 Gate Delay Variations 137
  13.8.1 Gate Delay Variation: Summary 138
 13.9 Chapter Summary 138
 13.10 Exercises 140

14 Dataflow SystemVerilog   **143**
 14.1 A Basic 2:1 MUX 143
 14.2 Dataflow Operators 144
  14.2.1 Bitwise vs. Logic Operators 145
  14.2.2 Reduction Operators 145
  14.2.3 Concatenation and Replication Operators 145
  14.2.4 Operator Precedence 146
  14.2.5 Matching Wire Widths 146
 14.3 Example - a 2:4 Decoder 147
 14.4 Parameterization in Dataflow SystemVerilog 148
  14.4.1 Mixing Dataflow and Structural SystemVerilog Design 149
 14.5 SystemVerilog and Arithmetic 149
 14.6 Chapter Summary 150
 14.7 Exercises 150

15 Latches and Flip Flops   **151**
 15.1 Bistability and Storage: The SR Latch 152
 15.2 The Gated Latch 155
 15.3 The Master/Slave Flip Flop 157
  15.3.1 Rising-Edge Triggered Flip flop 161
 15.4 Timing Characteristics Of Flip Flops 163
 15.5 Flip Flops With Additional Control Inputs 165
 15.6 A Note on Timing Diagrams 166
 15.7 A Note on Metastability 167
 15.8 Chapter Summary 169
 15.9 Exercises 170

16 Registers and RTL-Based Design   **173**
 16.1 Flip Flop-Based Registers 173
  16.1.1 Loadable Registers - First Attempt 174
  16.1.2 Loadable Registers - The Correct Method 175
 16.2 Shift Registers 178
 16.3 Mini Case Study: An Accumulator-Based Averaging Circuit 179
 16.4 An Introduction to Register Transfer Level (RTL) Design 180
  16.4.1 The Loadable Register of Figure 16.4 181
  16.4.2 The Clearable Up Counter of Figure 16.7 181
  16.4.3 The Shift Register of Figure Figure 16.9 181
  16.4.4 The Averaging Circuit of Figure 16.11 181
  16.4.5 More Complex Examples of RTL 182

16.5 Chapter Summary 183

16.6 Exercises 183

17 Behavioral SystemVerilog for Registers 185

17.1 Introduction to Behavioral SystemVerilog 185

17.2 The *always_ff* Block 185

17.3 Shift Register Design Using Behavioral SystemVerilog 187

17.4 The Semantics of the *always_ff* Block 188

17.5 Reset Problems With Registers 191

17.6 Chapter Summary 193

17.7 Exercises 193

18 Modeling Combinational Logic Using Behavioral SystemVerilog 195

18.1 Combinational *always* Blocks 195

    18.1.1 The Use of *case* Statements in *always_comb* Blocks 198

18.2 The Problem With Latches in *always_comb* Blocks 199

18.3 Avoiding Latches When Using *case* Statements 202

    18.3.1 Summary: Avoiding Latches in *always_comb* Blocks 203

18.4 Mapping SystemVerilog Programs to a Specific Technology 204

18.5 Chapter Summary 205

18.6 Exercises 205

19 Memories 207

19.1 Introduction 207

19.2 Register Files 207

19.3 Register File Design Using Behavioral SystemVerilog 209

19.4 Multi-Ported Register Files 210

19.5 Multi-Ported Register File Design using SystemVerilog 211

19.6 Multi-Ported Register Files With Bypass 212

19.7 Larger Memories 213

19.8 Read-Only Memories (ROM) 214

19.9 Consulting Tool Documentation 216

19.10 Chapter Summary 217

19.11 Exercises 217

20 Simple Sequential Circuits: Counters 219

20.1 A Two-Bit Binary Counter 219

20.2 A Two-Bit Gray Code Counter 221

20.3 A Counter Example With An Incomplete Transition Table 222

20.4 Counters With Static Output Signals 223

20.5 Delay Characteristics of Counters 225

    20.5.1 Moore Output Delay Characteristics of Counters 226

20.6 Counters With Additional Inputs 227

20.7 Mealy (Dynamic) Outputs 227

    20.7.1 Mealy vs. Moore Outputs 229

20.8 Counter Design Using Behavioral SystemVerilog 229

20.9 Chapter Summary 231

20.10 Exercises 232

21 State Graphs **233**
21.1 An Example State Graph 233
21.2 State Graphs For Counters With Inputs 234
21.3 State Graphs For Counters With Multiple Inputs 235
21.4 Design Procedure Using State Graphs 236
21.5 Representing Counter Outputs in State Graphs 236
    21.5.1 Moore (Static) Outputs 236
    21.5.2 Mealy (Dynamic) Outputs 237
21.6 Properly Formed State Graphs 237
21.7 Chapter Summary 239
21.8 Exercises 240

22 Finite State Machines **241**
22.1 A Simple State Machine - A Sequence Recognizer 242
    22.1.1 A Continuous '011' Detector - Moore Version 244
    22.1.2 A Continuous '011' Detector - Mealy Version 245
22.2 Finite State Machine Example - Car Wash Controller 247
    22.2.1 Implementation Details 248
    22.2.2 A Car Wash With Two Different Wash Settings 249
22.3 Resetting State Machines 250
22.4 Completeness and Conflicts in State Graphs Revisited 251
22.5 Chapter Summary 252
22.6 Exercises 253

23 State Machine Design Using SystemVerilog **255**
23.1 SystemVerilog Features for Coding State Machines 255
23.2 State Machine Coding Styles 258
    23.2.1 A Defensive Coding Style for Finite State Machines 259
23.3 Chapter Summary 261
23.4 Exercises 261

24 Asynchronous Input Handling **263**
24.1 Asynchronous Inputs and Metastability 263
24.2 An Example Asynchronous Input Problem 264
24.3 Synchronizing Asynchronous Inputs - The Easiest and Preferred Approach 265
24.4 Hazard Free Design Combined With Adjacent State Encodings - Another Approach (Advanced Topic) 266
    24.4.1 Adjacent State Encodings - A Partial Solution 266
    24.4.2 False Outputs and Hazards 267
    24.4.3 The Complete Solution 268
24.5 Chapter Summary 269
24.6 Exercises 270

25 Field Programmable Gate Arrays (FPGAs) - An Introduction **271**
25.1 Lookup Tables - Universal Function Generators 271
    25.1.1 Mapping Larger Combinational Circuits to LUTs 272
    25.1.2 Mapping Gate-Level Circuits to LUTs 273
25.2 FPGA Logic Elements 274
25.3 Global FPGA Architecture 276
    25.3.1 A Mapping Example 277
25.4 Configuring an FPGA Device 278
    25.4.1 Configuring a LUT 278
    25.4.2 Configuring the Fabric 279
25.5 More Advanced FPGA Architectures 280

25.5.1 Configurable Input/Output 280
25.5.2 Configuration Technology 280
25.5.3 Carry/Cascade Chains 281
25.5.4 Programmable Interconnections 281
25.5.5 Segmented and Hierarchical Routing 281
25.5.6 Clustered LEs 282
25.5.7 Embedded Functional Units 282
25.6 FPGA vs. ASIC Technology 283
25.7 Chapter Summary 284
25.8 Exercises 285

26 Case Study - Debouncing Switches and Detecting Edges   287
26.1 Debouncing a Switch 287
26.1.1 Design of the Debouncer Using SystemVerilog 289
26.2 A One-Shot (Also Known as Pulse Generator) 291
26.3 Exercises 294

27 Case Study: A Soda Machine Controller   295
27.1 Step 1 - Understand the Complete System Requirements and Organization 295
27.1.1 Understanding the Coin Mechanism 295
27.1.2 Understanding the Dispense Module 298
27.1.3 Understanding the User Interface 299
27.2 Step 2: Determine a System Architecture 300
27.3 Step 3 - Design the System Parts 301
27.3.1 Design of the Timer Subsystem 301
27.3.2 Design of the Keypad Interface Subsystem 302
27.3.3 Design of the Central Control Subsystem 304
27.3.4 Design of the Accumulator 305
27.3.5 Design of the Central Control Subsystem State Machine 308
27.3.6 A Complete and Conflict-Free State Graph 311
27.3.7 Implementing the State Machine Using SystemVerilog 311
27.3.8 Asynchronous Inputs, Adjacent State Encodings, and Glitch-Free Outputs 313
27.4 Summary 313
27.5 Exercises 313

28 Case Study: The Design of a UART   315
28.1 UART Protocol Design 315
28.1.1 Protocol Summary 317
28.2 Designing the UART 318
28.3 Design of a UART Transmitter 318
28.3.1 Host-UART Handshaking 318
28.3.2 The Transmitter Datapath 320
28.3.3 The Transmitter Control Section 321
28.3.4 An Alternate Transmitter Coding Style 324
28.4 Design of a UART Receiver 327
28.5 Summary 329

29 Tri-State Drivers and Buses   331
29.1 SystemVerilog Design for Bus Structures 335
29.2 Summary 336

30 SystemVerilog vs. Verilog **337**

30.1 SystemVerilog vs. Verilog 337

30.2 Data types 337

    30.2.1 The *logic* Variable Type 337

    30.2.2 Enumerated Types 338

30.3 Enhanced *always* Blocks 338

30.4 Verilog, SystemVerilog, and VHDL Interoperability 338

30.5 Moving Forward 338

A ASCII Table **339**

Author's Forward

This textbook is different from typical textbooks I have used in the past. Mainly it is much shorter than others. It was written to provide exactly the content to be covered in a first university course on digital systems design. It is expected that, in such a course, all topics in this text will be covered, in addition to a set of laboratory exercises. I have observed that students often conclude that the *trick* in a course (for the students) is to divine just *what* of all the material in a large book is actually the important material. The most commonly asked question in some classes seems to be "Is this going to be on the test?". Virtually everything in this text will appear on the tests in courses I teach. Read the chapter summary and list of desired skills at the end of each chapter. They are there to eliminate the guesswork mentioned above, as far as is possible. If you are comfortable that you have the desired skills listed at the end of each chapter, you are on track. If not, they will provide you a guide on what you might be lacking.

Some may fault this book because it omits numerous topics that they feel are an important part of digital design. When deciding what to include and not to include, I have tried to avoid content bloat. I have used my lecture notes and lecture schedule as a guide — if I spend time in class lecturing on a topic, then I considered including it in this text. If I couldn't fit it into my course schedule, I left it out.

This is an introductory text. There are a number of others texts available (some quite large and quite expensive) which are more comprehensive than this but which go far beyond what can be achieved in a first university course on digital design.

Some may also fault this book because they would like a more full treatment of the SystemVerilog language. The main purpose of this text is the fundamentals of digital design — it is not primarily a book on Verilog or SystemVerilog. That said, the way we teach the course at Brigham Young University is to include significant labs each week where students design and implement digital systems and test them on FPGA development boards. Thus, there is a need for them to learn sufficient Verilog or SystemVerilog so they can accomplish that.

The amount of SystemVerilog included in this text is much more than adequate to satisfy that purpose. But, the book should not be viewed as a SystemVerilog reference guide. There are many such books on the market, and those books (or simply the web) can be used for additional detail as needed. That said, there is nothing in the assignments or examples given in this book which cannot be readily designed using the SystemVerilog language as taught in its pages.

This book has short chapters. Each chapter tries to introduce a topic to be covered in a lecture or, at most, two. The short chapters closely follow the organization of the course lecture slides we use. The hope is that this close match between textbook and course content will help you learn the material more easily.

Finally, thanks to students at BYU for their feedback over the years on the text. And, an extra thanks to Ken McGuire for his careful work in proof reading this SystemVerilog version of the text!

Changes for This Revision

This book is actually the third version of a previous book I wrote called "Designing Digital Systems". That book contained 3 small appendices of tutorial material on the Verilog language. This book is a major rewrite of that book with a number of sections of dated material removed. Importantly, starting with this version of the text SystemVerilog is the HDL of choice and is now incorporated throughout the body of the book. As a result I have given it a new name and am using 1.0 as its version number.

Brent Nelson
Department of Electrical and Computer Engineering Brigham Young University Provo, Utah May 2018 (Version 1.0)

Chapter 1

Introduction to Digital Systems Design

This text deals with the design of digital systems. The purpose of this chapter is to introduce the notion of digital systems in preparation for the remainder of the text. The main concepts you should get from this chapter include an understanding of a few of the differences between digital and analog systems.

1.1 Digital vs. Analog

It is often said that we live in a digital world, but what does that really mean? What is the opposite of or alternative to digital? In its simplest form, a digital system is one that manipulates and stores binary values. A binary value can have only one of two different values: TRUE or FALSE. The values TRUE and FALSE are often represented by 1 and 0 respectively. We use the term *bit* (short for *binary digit*) to refer to a single value consisting of either a 1 or a 0. Using a single binary value you can represent notions such as ON vs. OFF, HIGH vs. LOW, HUNGRY vs. NOT-HUNGRY, etc.

The physical representation of a binary value in a digital system might be done using a voltage on a wire. In this case a high voltage could correspond to a 1 (TRUE) and a low voltage could correspond to a 0 (FALSE). The digital system would then contain circuits to operate on those voltages (values) to do computations.

In contrast, an *analog* value is one that can take on any value from a continuous range. An example of an analog quantity might be the representation of the current temperature, which could take on any value from the continuous range of -120 to +120 degrees, and would be mapped to the range of 0V to 2.4V. In this case, each 0.01V change on the wire voltage might correspond to a 1 degree change in temperature. Clearly, this quantity could represent the temperature much more accurately than a single bit would be able to. The temperature could (conceivably) take on any real number while in the digital case, the temperature would be represented simply as one of two different quantities such as HOT vs. NOT-HOT (COLD) where the dividing line between HOT and COLD might be arbitrarily set at 80 degrees.

The reader may be inclined to conclude that analog values can more accurately represent information than digital values. This is true when the digital value is a single bit, but to represent a wider range of values a binary word can be created from multiple bits, thereby providing accuracy comparable to that achievable with an analog representation. To better understand this, a review of positional number systems is in order.

1.2 Positional Number Systems

In elementary school we all learned the notion of a positional number system. We all know that the number 735 can be interpreted as follows:

$$735 = 7 \times 10^2 + 3 \times 10^1 + 5 \times 10^0$$

That is, the digits of the number 735 can be interpreted as being applied to powers of the base (10 in this case). Further, in base 6 the following is true:

$$325_6 = 3 \times 6^2 + 2 \times 6^1 + 5 \times 6^0 = 108 + 12 + 5 = 125_{10}$$

The positional number system can be applied to any number base. In the case of binary data the number base used is base 2. This has the interesting property that the only available digits are 0 and 1. This corresponds exactly to our definition of binary values above. The interpretation of a base 2 number follows exactly from the examples given above:

$$1101_2 = 1 \times 2^3 + 1 \times 2^2 + 1 \times 2^0 = 8 + 4 + 1 = 13_{10}$$

The largest quantity a 4-bit binary number can represent is 15 (1111) and the smallest is 0 (0000). The range of values that a number can represent can be enlarged by simply adding more bits. Thus, an 8-bit binary number can represent values in the range $0 - 255$ and a 12-bit number can represent values in the range $0 - 4,095$. The result is that by adding additional bits to a binary word we can create a way of representing information just as accurately as analog values do.

1.3   Digital vs. Analog Continued

At this point you are prepared to now understand a few of the differences between analog and digital. A first difference has to do with how values are represented. In an analog world, the current temperature might be represented by a voltage on a wire as discussed above. Alternatively, the voltage might be represented by some other physical quantity such as the amount of current flowing through a wire, the pressure in a vacuum, or the strength of a magnetic field. In each case, a continuously variable physical quantity is used to represent the analog value.

In a digital world the current temperature would be converted to a binary number to represent it. For example, a binary value of 1000011 would represent the number 67 in base 10, and could be used to represent the fact that the current temperature was 67 degrees. It would require 7 wires in this case to represent the current temperature in the system, each of which would contain either a 1 (a high voltage) or a 0 (a low voltage).

To further motivate the difference between analog and digital storage and processing of information let us consider an example from the the area of photography, particularly the process of taking and processing a black and white picture using both analog and digital means.

Many of the earliest photographs were taken using a simple camera as shown in Figure 1.1. A sheet of light-sensitive paper (film) was placed at the back of a box. A pinhole was then opened in the front of the box. The light penetrating the box through the pinhole would strike the film at the back of the box and an image would be formed. The photographic paper, being coated with light-sensitive chemicals (the emulsion), would record an analog image of the scene. Emulsion in the areas on the photographic paper which received light would undergo a chemical change and those areas not receiving light would not. Developing the photo consisted of using chemicals to wash away the parts of the emulsion which were thus chemically changed while leaving behind the other emulsion (or vica versa). The result was what we call a black-and-white photograph.

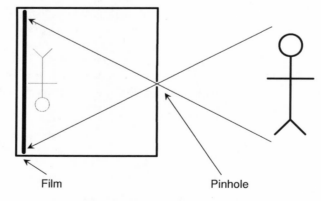

Figure 1.1: Basic Analog Camera

This description of the photographic process is still not quite complete since it has described the emulsion as either being completely chemically altered by light striking it or not (a digital concept!). In actuality, the amount of chemical change experienced by any *area* of the emulsion layer is in proportion to the intensity of light it is exposed to and thus we perceive it as a gray-scale image with shades ranging from black through various shades of gray all the way through white. This is an example of recording analog data - the concentration of emulsion remaining in any area on the developed film is essentially a continuous function of the amount of light exposure received by that portion of the film[1].

Once an image is captured on a piece of film, what can then be done with it? If the film base were transparent then light could be projected through it and a copy of the image could be created on a second piece of film. In the process various filters could be placed between the original and the copied image to effect a change such as blurring or contrast enhancement. The entire process, however, is an analog process — essentially continuous physical quantities (light intensity, chemical concentrations) are used to store and manipulate the original data (the image). An important consideration with analog processes is that they are sensitive to variations such as chemical intensity, lens aberrations, and even dust particles or scratches on the filter surface.

In contrast, consider the process of taking a digital photograph as shown in Figure 1.2. A camera lens is used to focus the light from a scene onto a silicon detector (a sensor circuit). The sensor surface is divided into a 2-dimensional grid of locations called *pixels* or picture-elements. The light intensity at each pixel (an analog quantity) is sensed and converted to a multi-bit binary number. As an example, the pixel intensities might be represented by 8-bit binary numbers with 0 (00000000 in binary) representing black and 255 (11111111 in binary) representing white.

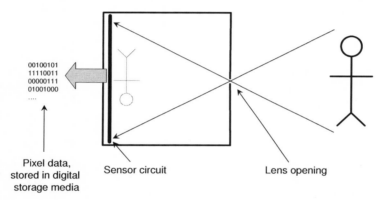

Figure 1.2: Basic Digital Camera

The digital photograph then, is simply a listing of the light intensities at each and every pixel location. These intensity values (binary words) are transmitted from the sensor circuit to a digital storage circuit and can then be stored on a computer. The 'GIF' file format is an example of such a file format and essentially contains a list of the light intensities at each pixel location, each represented as one or more binary words. To view the picture, the pixels on a computer monitor are used to display the pixel intensities stored in the GIF file. When we view such a computer display we 'see' the original image.

This is an example of *digital quantization* of two kinds. First, the image itself is *spatially quantized* or sampled. That means that a finite set of pixel locations are chosen and the image intensities *only* at those locations are recorded. If the number of pixels is large enough (the spatial sampling rate is high enough) we see no visible degradation in the final image. If the number of pixels is small (the spatial sampling rate is low) we then see a 'blocky' image.

---

[1] At the atomic level, even photographic emulsion has spatial quantization effects (called *grain*) and also sensitivity limitations. Nevertheless, it is common to view the intensities stored on the film as continuous analog values both spatially and in intensity.

An example of this is shown in Figure 1.3 which is made up of an 8-by-8 array of pixels and might be used as a pointer icon in a windows-based operating system. The effects of spatial quantization are very evident. A 64-by-64 pixel version of the pointer would look much better (have less blockiness). In a 1,024-by-1,024 pixel version the blockiness would likely not be visible.

Figure 1.3: An 8 × 8 Image

The second kind of quantization that occurs in this process relates to quantization of the intensity values. In a real image the intensity at any given pixel location can take on any continuous value from a range of values. By choosing an 8-bit binary word to represent each pixel intensity we are limiting the intensities that we can represent to 256 different values. If the quantization is fine enough (there are enough different intensity values) we don't perceive a difference between the recorded image and the original image. But, if the quantization of the intensities (brightness values) is coarse enough we see artifacts in the image which indicate to us it is a digitally captured image. This can be seen in the image of Figure 1.4 which is an image which has been quantized to both 8-bit intensities (256 different brightness values) and to 3-bit intensities (only 8 different brightness values).

(a) 8-Bit Intensities   (b) 3-Bit Intensities

Figure 1.4: Wendy Quantized to Both 8-bits Per Pixel and 3-bits Per Pixel

1.3.1 Analog vs. Digital Data Storage

Next, consider the storage of images. A photographic image often will fade over time due to gradual chemical changes in the emulsion and film. While the rate of fading varies with the film type, long term changes in the emulsion, film, and paper are inevitable. Analog photos are thus not completely permanent.

In contrast, once the pixel intensities have been recorded as binary data in a GIF file it should be possible to preserve the exact image (the pixel intensities) indefinitely. We are careful to say 'should be possible' in that new digital media is constantly being introduced and it can be difficult to find equipment to read old-format digital media (try to find a 5.25" floppy drive nowadays). Independent of that, however, if the 1's and 0's of the original data can be retrieved from the media, that original image can be precisely reproduced (stated more correctly, the originally sampled and quantized version can be precisely reproduced).

Further, consider the process of making copies. A copy of a digital image (the GIF file) can be bit-for-bit exact and so there is no limit to the number of identical digital copies which can be made. In the case of analog copies, the copying process itself may introduce changes due to imperfections in the lenses used, in the chemicals used to develop the copies, or in any one of a number of other parts of the copying process. The result is that n-th generation analog copies may differ noticeably from the original.

1.3.2 Analog vs. Digital Data Processing

Continuing on with our digital photo example, processing an analog photo (to alter its color in the case of a color photo) can be done by projecting it through a lens or filter of some kind and recording the new image on film. In the case of a digital image, the contents of the GIF file (or a copy) can be altered by a computer program. Users of the popular Adobe Photoshop program are aware of the many, many changes that can be made to a digital photo in this way including: sharpening, color changing, contrast enhancement, blurring, etc. Further, parts of various images can be combined into one via cutting and pasting. All of this done by manipulating the binary data from the GIF file representation of the image.

1.3.3 Analog vs. Digital - A Summary

In summary, digital representations of data have a number of benefits over analog representations for storage, duplication, transmission, and processing. Does this mean there is no longer a need for analog circuits? Absolutely not. The world we live in is largely an analog world and analog techniques are needed to deal with it. That said, a general trend over the past few decades has been to increasingly design systems which convert these analog quantities into equivalent digital representations, and which then store and manipulate the resulting values using digital rather than analog techniques. As will be shown in the remainder of this text, digital circuits are readily designed and built to operate on digital (binary) data and which can manipulate, store, and retrieve binary data.

1.4 Combinational vs. Sequential Digital Circuits

The above discussion focused on the use of digital techniques for recording, manipulating, and storing data. Another important use of digital systems is for control circuits. For example, consider the creation of a machine to control a car wash. The machine must react to the insertion of coins into its coin box, it must sequence the car wash pumps in order to properly spray the car, apply soap, rinse the car, etc. Further, it must time these various steps since each takes a different amount of time. Finally, it must flash lights to communicate with the user. A digital system is a good way of implementing such a controller.

Digital circuits can be divided into two broad categories — *combinational* circuits and *sequential* circuits. Combinational circuits are the simpler of the two and are circuits whose outputs are a simple and direct function of their inputs at all times. A typical problem which could be solved using a combinational circuit would be a cooling fan control circuit for a computer:

> Create a circuit whose output is TRUE any time the current temperature in the computer case is HOT or any time the CPU power is turned ON.

This would be a circuit with two inputs and one output, each of them 1-bit wide. The first input would represent the temperature in the computer case (HOT=1 vs. NOT-HOT=0). The second input would signify whether the power to the CPU was ON or OFF (ON=1, OFF=0). This circuit would ensure that any time the case was hot the fan would be turned on (even if the CPU was not being powered). It would do this by asserting its output to be TRUE (high) in this case. It would also ensure that the fan was on any time the CPU was receiving power by asserting its output. The first part of this textbook is devoted to the design and implementation of combinational circuits such as this — they continuously monitor their inputs and continuously update their outputs in response.

In contrast, a sequential digital system is one which possesses some form of memory. At each time instant it makes a decision on what to generate for its outputs based not only on the current value of its inputs (the presence of a coin in a coin slot for example), but also on its current state (what step it is at in the process it is performing). For a car wash controller that is required to perform 5 steps to complete a car wash, we would say that the sequential machine would have 5 *states*.

By querying the value of its state, such a sequential machine can determine what action to perform in response to changes on its inputs. For example, consider our hypothetical car wash controller. The action it should take when a coin is inserted into its coin box is different depending on what state it is in. If it were in the IDLE state it would interpret that action as a request to start the car wash and thus start the 5-step process to wash the car. If it were in a state indicating it was in the middle of the car wash's rinse cycle, it would interpret the insertion of a coin as a mistake by the customer and generate the necessary outputs to return the coin to the user. It is only by using this notion of state that we can design a sequential system such as this 5-step car wash controller.

The design of sequential circuits has, as a prerequisite, the ability to design and implement combinational circuits. Thus, sequential circuit design is postponed until you have mastered combinational logic design. By the end of this text, you will have enough knowledge to design and build complex digital systems for a variety of uses. These digital systems will contain both combinational and sequential parts.

In order to actually implement a digital circuit you have a few options. One is to purchase individual transistors or logic gates and flip flops and wire (solder) them together on a printed circuit board. This was the state of the art decades ago. Now, all digital design of consequence is doing using computer-aided design tools (CAD tools). Some time ago, design was done using graphics-based CAD tools to draw schematics which represented the desired circuit design. Those schematics were then implemented onto physical silicon circuits either by hand or by automated means.

Now, the state of the art is to describe a digital circuit using a Hardware Description Language (HDL). This is a specialized programming language designed just for this purpose. That HDL circuit description can then be *simulated* using a simulation program to determine whether it performs the desired functionality. Only when the designer is satisfied that it does perform the desired functionality, would that HDL-based circuit design be implemented onto actual physical circuits. This conversion from HDL to physical circuits is now always automated. Thus, in addition to being a textbook on digital circuit design, this text also introduces one such HDL, SystemVerilog, and teaches how to use it to implement all of the circuits the textbook includes.

1.5 Chapter Summary

This chapter has commenced our discussion of digital systems by introducing the notion of binary values, binary number representations, and the use of binary data to represent real-world quantities. Further, a few words about analog vs. digital and combinational vs. sequential circuits were provided. At this point, rather than further delay beginning our study of digital systems design with more overview and examples, let's move on to the next chapter and begin to lay the foundational elements necessary to design and build real digital systems.

Chapter 2

Number Systems and Binary Encodings

An understanding of how values can be coded using binary data is an important prerequisite to beginning a study of digital systems design. This chapter reviews the concept of positional notation for representing numbers. The use of base-2 or binary is then reviewed. Other methods for using binary data to encode numerical or other data are then presented. These other methods are specifically those commonly used in the design and creation of digital systems.

2.1 Positional Number Notation

In elementary school we all learned the notion of a positional number system. We all know that the number 735 can be interpreted as follows:

$$735 = 7 \times 10^2 + 3 \times 10^1 + 5 \times 10^0$$

That is, the digits of the number 735 can be interpreted as being applied to powers of the base (10 in this case). In base 6 the following is true:

$$325_6 = 3 \times 6^2 + 2 \times 6^1 + 5 \times 6^0 = 108 + 12 + 5 = 125_{10}$$

Note that when the base is not base-10, a subscript is often used to ensure it is clear what the base is. Positional notion also allows for digits to the right of the decimal point:

$$73.502 = 7 \times 10^1 + 3 \times 10^0 + 5 \times 10^{-1} + 2 \times 10^{-3}$$

and

$$52.1_8 = 5 \times 8^1 + 2 \times 8^0 + 1 \times 8^{-1} = 40 + 2 + 1/8 = 42.125_{10}$$

The following is an illegal number: 524_4. Can you see why? In the case of a base 4 number the only available digits are $\{0, 1, 2, 3\}$. Likewise, in a base 6 number the only available digits are $\{0, 1, 2, 3, 4, 5\}$. In general, the digits in a positional number are in the range $\{0, ..., n - 1\}$ where n is the base.

In the case of binary data the number base used is base 2. This has the interesting property that the only available digits are $\{0, 1\}$, which corresponds exactly to our definition of binary values from the previous chapter. The interpretation of a base 2 number follows exactly from the examples given above:

$$1101_2 = 1 \times 2^3 + 1 \times 2^2 + 1 \times 2^0 = 8 + 4 + 1 = 13_{10}$$

When discussing binary values, a binary digit is often called a *bit* and the value 1011_2 can be said to have four bits.

The largest quantity a 4-bit binary number can represent is 15 (1111_2) and the smallest is 0 (0000_2). The range of values that a number can represent can be enlarged by simply adding more bits. Thus, an 8-bit binary number can represent values in the range $0 - 255$ and a 12-bit number can represent values in the range $0 - 4,095$. This is easily demonstrated by writing out the largest number possible for a given number of bits (all 1's) and then doing the conversion to decimal as shown in the examples in this chapter. In the general case, a k-bit binary value can represent numbers in the range from 0 to $2^k - 1$.

2.1.1 Conversion from Decimal to Other Bases

Conversion from decimal to other number bases can be done using a method reminiscent of long division. As an example, consider the problem of converting 112_{10} to base 6 as shown in Figure 2.1.

```
        112
       -108        (3×6²)
          4
       -  0        (0×6¹)
          4
       -  4        (4×6⁰)
          0


     Result = 304₆
```

Figure 2.1: Conversion Between Base-10 and Base-6

Here, the first step is to determine the highest power of 6 that is less than 112. This is 6^2 (36). It can be seen that 3×6^2 (108) is less than 112 and so that quantity is subtracted from 112. The next step is to determine whether 6^1 is less than the remainder of 4. In this case it is not. It is then seen that 6^0 is less than the remainder and so 4×6^0 is subtracted. The final answer (304_6) is obtained by collecting the coefficients used at each step.

This same procedure can be used to convert between numbers of any base, including numbers which include fractional parts (digits to the right of the radix point). For example, Figure 2.2 shows two conversions from decimal to binary.

```
    113                              12.625
  -  64    (1×2⁶)                  -  8        (1×2³)
    49                               4.625
  -  32    (1×2⁵)                  -  4        (1×2²)
    17                               0.625
  -  16    (1×2⁴)                  -  0        (0×2¹)
     1                               0.625
  -   0    (0×2³)                  -  0        (0×2⁰)
     1                               0.625
  -   0    (0×2²)                  -  0.500    (1×2⁻¹)
     1                               0.125
  -   0    (0×2¹)                  -  0        (0×2⁻²)
     1                               0.125
  -   1    (1×2⁰)                  -  0.125    (1×2⁻³)
     0                               0.000


  Result = 1110001₂              Result = 1100.101₂
```

Figure 2.2: Two Different Conversions Between Base-10 and Base-2

A number of interesting shortcut methods for hand conversions to and from binary have been developed over the years which you may find in other sources.

2.2 Hexadecimal (Base-16) Numbers

In addition to binary, base-16 numbers are often used in digital systems design. Base-16 is also referred to as *hexadecimal*, or *hex* for short. In the case of hex, we need additional digits beyond $0 - 9$. For base-6 numbers we use 6 different digits $(0 - 5)$, and for base-10 numbers we use 10 digits $(0 - 9)$. For base-16 we need 16 digits — what should be used for the other digits? The convention chosen is to use the letters A-F for these. Table 2.1 shows the digits used in hexadecimal notation and the decimal equivalent for each digit.

Table 2.1: Hexadecimal Digits

Digit Symbol	Decimal Equivalent
0	0
1	1
2	2
3	3
4	4
5	5
6	6
7	7
8	8
9	9
A	10
B	11
C	12
D	13
E	14
F	15

Using Table 2.1 as a guide, the following is true:

$$1A2F_{16} = 1 \times 16^3 + 10 \times 16^2 + 2 \times 16^1 + 15 \times 16^0 = 4096 + 2560 + 32 + 15 = 6,703_{10}$$

Additional examples include:

$$FF_{16} = 15 \times 16^1 + 15 \times 16^0 = 255_{10}$$

$$BEEF_{16} = 11 \times 16^3 + 14 \times 16^2 + 14 \times 16^1 + 15 \times 16^0 = 48,879_{10}$$

The key point is that there is no difference between base-16 and any other base — the only complication is the need to remember the additional digits possible in a base-16 number.

There is a reason that base-16 is commonly used in digital systems. A 32-bit value in binary requires a 32-digit word like this:

$$0100000000000000000000000000000_2 = 1 \times 2^{30} = 1,073,741,824_{10}$$

Thus, when using 32-bit binary, one is required to keep track of 32 digits' worth of information. Base-16 has the interesting characteristic that, since 16 is a power of 2, it is possible to simply take groups of 4 binary digits and write down the base-16 representation by inspection. An example is shown in Figure 2.3 for a 16-bit binary value.

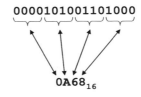

Figure 2.3: Conversion Between Hexadecimal and Binary

Each group of 4 binary digits (bits) is replaced by its base-16 equivalent. To demonstrate that the conversion shown in the figure is correct, one can simply do the conversion to base-10 and compare the results:

$$0000101001101000_2 = 1 \times 2^{11} + 1 \times 2^9 + 1 \times 2^6 + 1 \times 2^5 + 1 \times 2^3 = 2,664_{10}$$

$$0A68_{16} = 10 \times 16^2 + 6 \times 16^1 + 8 \times 16^0 = 2,664_{10}$$

When doing conversions between binary and hex, it may be the case that the number of binary digits is not a multiple of four. In this case 0's should be added to the left end of the number before doing the conversion:

$$100011_2 = 00100011_2 = 23_{16}$$

Another important point is that the process is reversible — to convert a hex value to binary, each hex digit is simply replaced by its 4-digit binary equivalent. This is shown here (spaces have been added to the binary number to show the groups of four bits):

$$FADE27_{16} = 1111\ 1010\ 1101\ 1110\ 0010\ 0111_2$$

Experienced digital designers and programmers, through experience, acquire the ability to freely convert between hex and binary and to even do hex arithmetic in their heads. Be patient and you will acquire this ability to a certain extent.

A similar process can also be used to convert between base-8 (octal) and binary. Here, 3-bit groups of binary digits are used instead of 4-bit groups. A perceived disadvantage of octal is that bits are left over when converting 8-bit, 16-bit, and 32-bit values, and so we will not use octal in this text (however, it was heavily used in the past and so you may encounter it in the future).

2.3 Binary-Coded Decimal

Another commonly used code is binary-coded decimal or BCD for short. This arises when a digital system is representing data in binary but which is most easily viewed as being in decimal (base-10). For example, consider the binary value 1111_2 which is equivalent to 15_{10}. An alternate representation for this would be: $0001\ 0101_{BCD}$ (a space has been added to emphasize that the leftmost four digits represent a 1 and the rightmost four digits represent a 5). Other examples include:

$$263_{10} = 0010\ 0110\ 0011_{BCD}$$

$$007_{10} = 0000\ 0000\ 0111_{BCD}$$

BCD usually requires more binary digits than a positional binary representation would. This can be seen by comparing the following number in positional notation with the 12 bits required for BCD:

$$263_{10} = 100000111_2$$

Nevertheless, in many digital systems designs, it is sometimes advantageous to represent decimal numbers this way. We will see instances later in this text where BCD is used.

2.4 Other Codes

As should be obvious by now, binary values consisting of 1's and 0's can be viewed as representing many different things. When presented with an 8-bit binary quantity, it is impossible by simply looking at the bits to determine what it is intended to represent — is it an 8-bit binary number (using positional powers-of-2)? — is it a 2-digit BCD quantity? Other ways of interpreting binary data are also possible. For example, in a study of computer architecture you will learn that the instructions a computer executes are encoded and stored as binary data. Two other ways of representing information in binary are introduced in this section.

2.4.1 ASCII Codes

The ASCII code is commonly used to represent text. The term ASCII stands for American Standard Code for Information Interchange. It is a 7-bit code which can be used to represent text (all of the punctuation, numeric digits, upper and lower case letters). For example, in ASCII, the letter 'A' is represented as 41_{16} (hex 41) while a period '.' is represented as $2E_{16}$.

The 7-bit ASCII standard allows for 128 different values. The characters mentioned above (punctuation, digits, and upper/lower case letters) do not use up all 128 values. The ASCII standard also defines certain values which may be interpreted by printers and CRT terminals as control information. Thus, an ASCII table will also contain codes for CR (carriage-return), LF (linefeed), ESC (escape), etc..

Since the basic unit of data storage and transfer in computers is based on bytes (8 bits), the 7-bit ASCII code is often extended to be 8-bits long. This results in a total of 256 values and allows for the inclusion of 128 more symbols.

Computer terminals and other equipment are often designed to accept ASCII codes and display the corresponding textual symbols. A digital system generating binary information for such use would be required to generate that data using the ASCII coding standard. Table A.1 in Appendix A shows the portion of the ASCII encoding for printable text.

2.4.2 Gray Codes

Gray codes are a method used to encode binary values but have the important characteristic that two *adjacent* values in the code can only differ by a single bit. For example, Table 2.2 shows a gray code for values between 0 and 7. Note that going from 3 to 4 only requires changing a single bit and that going from 1 to 2 only requires changing a single bit (wrapping around - going from 7 back to 0 - also requires changing only a single bit).

Gray codes are not unique. There are numerous ways of creating a 3-bit gray code and Table 2.3 shows another one (compare to the code in Table 2.2). In the end, a code is called a gray code simply when its adjacent values differ by exactly one bit. Gray codes will show up in numerous places later in this text and further motivation for their use will be given there.

Table 2.2: A 3-Bit Gray Code

Decimal Value	Gray Code
0	000
1	001
2	011
3	010
4	110
5	111
6	101
7	100

Table 2.3: Another 3-Bit Gray Code

Decimal Value	Gray Code
0	111
1	011
2	010
3	110
4	100
5	000
6	001
7	101

2.5 Chapter Summary

This chapter has introduced a number of ideas related to positional number systems and the encoding of information using bits. The key points to understand from this chapter include:

1. Positional number systems are based on the idea of multiplying the digits of the number by powers of the base value according to their position in the number.

2. This idea works for both digits to the left of the radix point and for digits to the right of the radix point.

3. This idea works for any base desired.

4. A knowledge of positional number systems makes it possible to easily convert between bases.

5. A base-K number can only contain digits from 0 through $K - 1$.

6. For bases greater than 10, additional digit symbols must be employed.

7. Base-16, also known as hexadecimal or hex, uses the characters A-F to represent the additional required digits.

8. Converting between binary and hexadecimal is trivial and so hexadecimal is an oft-employed shorthand for binary values.

9. Other coding methods can be used for text or other data. In the end, these other coding methods are simply agreed-upon ways of assigning binary codes for other uses.

10. Commonly used alternative codes are ASCII and BCD.

11. Gray codes have the important property that adjacent values in the code differ by exactly one digit (bit).

The skills that should result from a study of this chapter include the following:

1. The ability to convert from any base to any other base.

2. The ability to quickly convert from binary to hexadecimal or octal and back.

3. The ability to convert from decimal to BCD and back.

4. The ability to create a gray code with a desired number of bits.

2.6 Exercises

2.1. Convert the following value to base-2, base-3, base-8, and base-16: 242_{10}.

2.2. Convert the following value to base-2 and base-5: 71.93. Take your answer to no more than 6 places to the right of the radix point. Truncate if necessary.

2.3. Convert the following value to base-2: 17.522_{10}. Take your answer to only 2 places to the right of the radix point and round if necessary.

2.4. Convert the following value to hexadecimal: 11001001001000000111_2.

2.5. Convert the following value to binary: $DEAF.BEE_{16}$. Take your answer to no more than than 8 places to the right of the radix point and truncate if necessary.

2.6. Repeat the previous problem but take your answer out to as many places as is necessary.

2.7. Convert the following value to binary: $DEAF.BEE_{16}$. Take your answer to no more than than 8 places to the right of the radix point and <u>round</u> if necessary. Base your rounding on what you learned in grade school on when to round up and when to round down.

2.8. Convert the following number to octal: $5A6F_{16}$.

2.9. Convert the following number to BCD: 422_{10}.

2.10. Convert the following number to BCD: 00100101_2.

2.11. Convert the following number to binary: 000101010010_{BCD}.

2.12. Create a 2-bit gray code.

2.13. Create a 3-bit gray code different from those shown in the body of this chapter.

2.14. Get on the WWW and find an ASCII table. Write out the hex equivalent of the message "*Hello, world.*$\backslash n$" where $\backslash n$ is interpreted as a CR (carriage-return) followed by a LF (linefeed). For this, assume that each character is represented by an 8-bit quantity (if the ASCII table you have found lists 7-bit codes, append a '0' to the left of the code to get an 8-bit code).

Do not include codes for the quotes around the string. Clearly show what codes you used for CR and LF.

Chapter 3

Signed Number Representations, Negation, and Arithmetic

The concept of representing numbers using binary encodings was presented in Chapter 2. That chapter, however, only showed non-negative number representations (another word for non-negative numbers is *unsigned* numbers). Digital systems are often required to manipulate values which can be signed (negative, zero, or positive). In addition, arithmetic on binary numbers is often required. The major methods used for encoding signed numbers are introduced in this chapter. Addition and subtraction of numbers using a variety of these representations is also introduced, and the advantages and disadvantages of each are described.

3.1 Addition of Unsigned Numbers

Addition of unsigned numbers follows directly from grade-school arithmetic as shown in Figure 3.1. The top row of

$$
\begin{array}{ll}
\begin{array}{c}
\scriptstyle 0\ 0\ 0 \\
0011 \\
+\ 0100 \\
\hline
0111
\end{array} &
\begin{array}{l}
(3_{10}) \\
(4_{10}) \\
(7_{10})
\end{array}
\end{array}
\qquad
\begin{array}{ll}
\begin{array}{c}
\scriptstyle 0\ 1\ 0 \\
0011 \\
+\ 0010 \\
\hline
0101
\end{array} &
\begin{array}{l}
(3_{10}) \\
(2_{10}) \\
(5_{10})
\end{array}
\end{array}
\qquad
\begin{array}{ll}
\begin{array}{c}
\scriptstyle 1\ 1\ 1 \\
0011 \\
+\ 0111 \\
\hline
1010
\end{array} &
\begin{array}{l}
(3_{10}) \\
(7_{10}) \\
(10_{10})
\end{array}
\end{array}
$$

$\qquad$ (a) No carries $\qquad\qquad\qquad$ (b) With carries $\qquad\qquad\qquad$ (c) With more carries

Figure 3.1: Unsigned Arithmetic Examples

each figure shows how the carry propagates from column to column. In part (a) of the figure, no carries result from adding each of the columns. In parts (b) and (c) of the figure, carries are generated and must be carried over to the next column precisely as in base-10 arithmetic (remember that $1 + 1 = 2 = 10_2$ and that $1 + 1 + 1 = 3 = 11_2$).

3.1.1 Overflow in Unsigned Addition

Overflow can occur in unsigned addition. The addition of a 4-bit number to a 4-bit number can generate an answer too large to be represented by a 4-bit result. An obvious example is $1111_2 + 0001_2 = 0000_2$. The problem here is that there is an additional carry-out of the leftmost position which is dropped. This indicates that overflow has occurred. If a 5-bit result is acceptable, that bit can simply be used as the most significant bit (MSB) of the result: $1111_2 + 0001_2 = 10000_2$. If the result must be 4-bits wide, however, we would say that overflow has occurred. How this is handled in a digital system depends on a number of factors and will be dealt with later.

3.2 Signed Numbers: Sign-Magnitude

When doing arithmetic by hand, writing a negative number is as simple as prepending a '-' to the number. Thus, -6 is "negative six". When doing binary arithmetic the same can be done. In this case, an additional bit (the sign bit) is prepended to the number. If that bit is a '0' then the remainder of the number is interpreted as a positive number. If that bit is a '1' then the remainder of the number is interpreted as a negative number:

$$0011_{SM} = +(011_2) = +3$$

$$1011_{SM} = -(011_2) = -3$$

This is an intuitive and easy to understand way to represent positive and negative numbers in binary. This method is called "sign-magnitude" because the bits of the number can be broken into two parts — the leftmost bit is the sign and the other bits represent the magnitude of the number.

Unfortunately it has at least two problems. The first is that zero can be represented two different ways which complicates its use:

$$0000_{SM} = +(000_2) = +0$$

$$1000_{SM} = -(000_2) = -0$$

The second problem is that adding and subtracting sign-magnitude numbers is a bit complex. This can be shown using base-10 numbers and a few of the rules you learned in grade school:

$$5 + (-2) = 5 - 2 = 3$$

$$5 - (-2) = 5 + 2 = 7$$

$$-5 - 1 = -(5 + 1) = -6$$

Thus, whether you add or subtract the magnitudes of the numbers depends not only on the operation requested ($+$ or $-$) but also on whether each number is positive or negative itself to begin with. Thus, the creation of an adder for sign-magnitude numbers actually requires the creation of an adder/subtracter since, at times, a subtraction is really what is required.

3.2.1 Negating Sign-Magnitude Numbers

Negating a sign-magnitude number is trivial and is done by *inverting* the sign bit. That is, if the sign bit is a '0' change it to a '1'; if the sign bit is a '1' change it to a '0':

$$-5 = 1101_{SM} \overset{negate}{\rightarrow} 0101_{SM} = +5$$

3.3 Signed Numbers: 2's Complement

A different interpretation of the bits in a binary value makes it possible to represent both signed and unsigned numbers in a way that has advantages over sign-magnitude. This representation is called 2's complement and can be illustrated by the following examples:

$$1111_{2c} = -1 \times 2^3 + 1 \times 2^2 + 1 \times 2^1 + 1 \times 2^0 = -8 + 4 + 2 + 1 = -1_{10}$$

$$1011_{2c} = -1 \times 2^3 + 1 \times 2^1 + 1 \times 2^0 = -8 + 2 + 1 = -5_{10}$$

$$0111_{2c} = 1 \times 2^2 + 1 \times 2^1 + 1 \times 2^0 = 4 + 2 + 1 = +7_{10}$$

$$1000_{2c} = -1 \times 2^3 = -8$$

Here it can be seen that the most significant bit of the value (the MSB) is given a negative weight. All the other bits have a positive weight as before. A little thought will show that a number with a leading '0' will always be positive in 2's complement and a number with a leading '1' will always be negative.

However, to determine the value of a negative number you must use the method shown above - a 2's complement negative number is *NOT* the same as a sign-magnitude negative number:

$$1111_{SM} = -7$$
$$1111_{2c} = -1$$
$$1111_{SM} \neq 1111_{2c}$$

3.3.1 Sign-Extension

An interesting feature of 2's complement numbers is that replicating the most significant bit of a number (to make the number wider) does not change its numeric value:

$$0011_{2c} = 00011_{2c} = 00000000011_{2c} = 3_{10}$$

This also works for negative numbers:

$$10011_{2c} = 110011_{2c} = 1111111110011_{2c} = -13_{10}$$

Interestingly, according to our definition of 2's complement numbers:

$$1_{2c} = 111_{2c} = 1111111_{2c} = 111111111111111111_{2c} = -1_{10}$$

Extending a number in this way is called *sign-extension* and is valid for both positive and negative 2's complement numbers. The reverse (removing bits) is valid as long as the "original sign bit" is left behind:

$$-4_{10} = 1111100_{2c} = 100_{2c} \neq 00_{2c}$$

3.3.2 Negating a 2's Complement Number

To negate a 2's complement number you invert all the bits and add '1'. The following shows how to determine the value of -5 in 2's complement — it starts with +5 in binary, inverts the bits, and adds 1:

$$+5_{10} = 0101_{2c} \overset{invert}{\to} 1010_{2c} + 1 = 1011_{2c} = -5_{10}$$

The process is reversible as well:

$$-5_{10} = 1011_{2c} \overset{invert}{\to} 0100_{2c} + 1 = 0101_{2c} = +5_{10}$$

An interesting case is negating zero:

$$0000_{2c} \overset{invert}{\to} 1111_{2c} + 1 = 0000_{2c} = 0_{10}$$

Another interesting case is shown here:

$$-8_{10} = 1000_{2c} \overset{invert}{\to} 0111_{2c} + 1 = 1000_{2c} = -8_{10} \ ???$$

In this case, negating -8_{10} results in -8_{10} which is surely incorrect. What happened? It turns out that in 2's complement there are more negative numbers than positive. That is, -8_{10} can be represented by a 4-bit 2's complement value but $+8_{10}$ cannot be. The range of values representable by 4-bits is $-8 \to +7$. The range of values representable by 5-bits is $-16 \to +15$ and so on. This range is easily determined for any number of bits since the most negative number in a 2's complement representation is $1000 \cdots 0$ and the most positive number is $0111 \cdots 1$. This assymetry of positive vs. negative numbers (there is one extra negative number) is an interesting feature of 2's complement but rarely causes problems (as long as you remember that it exists).

3.3.3 Adding 2's Complement Numbers

Addition of 2's complement numbers proceeds identically to that for unsigned numbers at the bit level as shown in Figure 3.2 and Figure 3.3. In these figures, a series of additions are performed which are no different on a bit-by-bit basis than would be done if the numbers were being interpreted as unsigned values.

```
  0 0 0                    1 1 1                    1 1 1
  0011    (3₁₀)            1011    (−5₁₀)           1111    (−1₁₀)
+ 0100    (4₁₀)          + 0101    (5₁₀)          + 0111    (7₁₀)
  0111    (7₁₀)            0000    (0₁₀)            0110    (6₁₀)
```

| (a) No carries | (b) With carries | (c) With carries |

Figure 3.2: 2's Complement Addition Examples

```
  1 1 0                    1 1 1                    1 0 0 0
  1011    (−5₁₀)           1011    (−5₁₀)           1011    (−5₁₀)
+ 1110    (−2₁₀)        + 1101    (−3₁₀)         + 1100    (−4₁₀)
  1001    (−7₁₀)           1000    (−8₁₀)           0111    (+7₁₀)  ??
```

| (a) No problem | (b) No problem | (c) Overflow - wrong answer |

Figure 3.3: More 2's Complement Addition Examples

An incorrect result occurs in Figure 3.3(c) where $-5_{10} + -4_{10} = -9_{10}$. This cannot be represented by a 4-bit number. The proper answer is $10111_2 = -9_{10}$ which is a 5-bit result. However, the addition shown in the figure only produced a 4-bit result, and so we say that overflow occurred.

It may seem from the example of Figure 3.3(c) that simply using the final carry-out from the leftmost bit position as the most significant bit (MSB) of the result will work — the final carry out in this particular example is a '1' and that could be used to provide the MSB of the result ('10111'). While it works in this particular case **it will not work in general**. A case where it will not work is shown in Figure 3.4(a). In this example, adding -8 to $+7$ should result in an answer of -1, but using the final carry out as the MSB gives an incorrect result ($+15$). The correct procedure is to **first** sign-extend the operands by one bit and then perform the addition. This is shown in Figure 3.4(b) where the correct result $-8 + 7 = -1$ is shown.

```
  0 0 0 0                      0 0 0 0
  1000    (−8₁₀)              11000    (−8₁₀)
+ 0111    (7₁₀)            +00111    (7₁₀)
  01111   (+15₁₀)  ???        11111   (−1₁₀)
```

| (a) No sign-extension - wrong answer | (b) With sign-extension |

Figure 3.4: 2's Complement Addition Overflow Problems

3.3.4 Subtracting 2's Complement Numbers

Subtraction of 2's complement numbers can be done in a similar way. Figure 3.5 shows subtraction in the absence of borrows between bit columns for both positive and negative numbers.

$$
\begin{array}{ll}
\texttt{0111} & (7_{10}) \\
-\ \texttt{0100} & (4_{10}) \\
\hline
\texttt{0011} & (3_{10})
\end{array}
\qquad\qquad
\begin{array}{ll}
\texttt{1011} & (-5_{10}) \\
-\ \texttt{0001} & (-1_{10}) \\
\hline
\texttt{1010} & (-6_{10})
\end{array}
$$

(a) Positive Numbers (b) Negative Numbers

Figure 3.5: Subtraction of 2's Complement Numbers

What about when borrows are required? Note that $0 - 1 = -1 = 11_{2c}$ and that $0 - 1 - 1 = -2 = 10_{2c}$ — notice how these 2-bit quantities are themselves 2's complement representations. Consider the subtraction that happens in Figure 3.6. Consider column A (the rightmost column). Here, we have $0 - 1 = -1 = 11_{2c}$, which generates a difference of 1 with a borrow to column B.

$$
\begin{array}{ll}
\texttt{D C B A} & \\
\texttt{0\ 0\ 1\ 1} & \\
\texttt{0100} & (4_{10}) \\
-\ \texttt{0011} & (3_{10}) \\
\hline
\texttt{0001} & (1_{10})
\end{array}
$$

Figure 3.6: 2's Complement Subtraction With Borrows

In column B, we now have $0 - 1 - 1$ where the second 1 is the borrow bit from column A. The result is $0 - 1 - 1 = -2 = 10_{2c}$. We thus write the 0 of that quantity as the difference column B and use the leftmost bit (the 1) as the borrow into column C.

In column C we have $1 - 0 - 1 = 0 = 00_{2c}$. The rightmost of those 0's is the difference bit for the column and the leftmost of those 0's is the borrow into column D. The process continues on until we reach the leftmost column. And, as will be seen later when we learn how to build adder and subtracter circuits, this formulation of representing each column's result as a 2-bit number leads to a very straightforward implementation for a subtraction circuit.

Underflow is analogous to overflow (which we saw above in relation to adding 2's complement numbers). Preventing this can be done in the same way as we saw above — first sign extend the numbers and then do the subtraction.

3.4 Signed Numbers: 1's Complement

An alternative to 2's complement is known as 1's complement. A 1's complement number is negated by simply inverting all the bits of the number. For example:

$$9_{10} = 01001_{1c} \overset{invert}{\rightarrow} 10110_{1c} = -9_{10}$$

When doing addition in 1's complement, the final carry-out on the left end must be carried around and used as the carry-in on the right end. While this has no parallel to arithmetic you may have done in the past, it is correct. An example of adding 5 and -3 in 1's complement is shown in Figure 3.7.

$$
\begin{array}{rl}
\text{1 1 0 0} & \\
0101 & (5_{10}) \\
+ \ 1100 & (-3_{10}) \\
\hline
0001 & \\
\hline
0010 & (+2_{10})
\end{array}
$$

Figure 3.7: 1's Complement Addition

Why not use a 1's complement representation instead of 2's complement? After all, 1's complement is clearly easier to negate than 2's complement. For one reason, 1's complement has two different zero representations:

$$
\begin{aligned}
0000_{1c} &= +0 \\
1111_{1c} &= -0
\end{aligned}
$$

Another reason is that 1's complement addition, while possible, takes twice as long as 2's complement addition due to the end-around-carry.

For this and a variety of other reasons, 2's complement is the representation method of choice for the vast majority of all modern digital systems (including computers). The remainder of this text will focus exclusively on 2's complement representations of signed numbers.

3.5 Summary — Number representations

In summary, numbers can be represented in at least 5 different ways: unsigned, sign-magnitude, 2's complement, 1's complement, and BCD. Only sign-magnitude, 2's complement, and 1's complement can represent negative numbers — the others (unsigned and BCD) can only represent positive numbers.

Table 3.1 shows a collection of 8-bit values and their numerical representations in each of these formats. Note that not all bit patterns are legal BCD quantities as shown in the table.

Table 3.1: Some 8-Bit Quantities and their Values

Bit Pattern	Unsigned	Sign-Mag	2's Comp	1's Comp	BCD
1111 1111	255	-127	-1	-0	—
1000 0000	128	-0	-128	-127	80
1111 0000	240	-112	-16	-15	—
0111 1111	127	127	127	127	—
0000 0001	1	1	1	1	01

Unsigned number representations are used in digital systems when only non-negative values are needed. When negative values are required as well, 2's complement is most commonly used due to the relative simplicity of adding, subtracting, and multiplying 2's complement values. Sign-magnitude and BCD are used less frequently. The author has never encountered the use of 1's complement arithmetic in a digital circuit. While that does not imply it is never used it *may* serve to show that its use is not widespread.

3.6 More on Overflow and Underflow

We talked above about how adding two numbers can result in overflow. In particular, adding two k-bit numbers can result in a value which requires k+1 bits to represent. This is true regardless of whether they are unsigned, sign-magnitude, or 2's complement. The same is true when subtracting where underflow can occur.

As discussed above, in some cases it may look as if the final carry-out or borrow-out from the leftmost column could be used as the MSB of the result. While this may be true for unsigned arithmetic, *it is not true* for 2's complement addition and subtraction.

For 2's complement arithmetic, the correct method is to first sign-extend the operands to the width of the desired result and then to do the addition or subtraction. The bits computed this way will be correct and overflow or underflow *cannot* occur.

3.6.1 Detecting and Handling Overflow and Underflow - Some Ideas

There is always the option of adding or subtracting two k-bit values and keeping only a k-bit result — this is precisely what most computers do. In light of this, two obvious questions include: (1) how can overflow and underflow be detected? and (2) what should be done when they do occur?

First, if two k-bit positive numbers are added together and the k-bit result looks negative (has a '1' MSB) you can be assured that overflow occurred. Similarly, adding two negative numbers and obtaining what looks like a positive result indicates that overflow occurred. Finally, adding a positive and a negative number can *never* result in overflow, even if only a k-bit result is computed.[1] For subtraction, similar considerations apply but the situation is mostly reversed.

Handling Overflow or Underflow

The question may be asked regarding what should be done in a digital system when overflow or underflow does occur? The answer to that is very much dependent on the application. When designing a digital system which performs binary arithmetic, it is up to the designer to do one of the following: (a) ensure that it does not occur (by making the result have enough bits, as in our sign-extension example), (b) design circuitry to detect and react to it if it does occur, or (c) ignore it. In this text, we will choose a combination of (a) and (c), depending on the application.

---

[1] Overflow detection can, and often is, done differently than what is described here by comparing the carry-in and carry-out values for the most significant column of the addition. One of the homework problems at the end of the chapter will lead you through discovering how that is done.

3.7 Chapter Summary

This chapter has introduced various methods for representing negative binary numbers and discussed some of their advantages and disadvantages. It has also shown how the addition and subtraction of unsigned and 2's complement numbers is done. Overflow and underflow were also discussed and a number of methods for detecting and preventing them presented.

The key high-level points to master from this chapter include the following:

1. Addition of binary numbers occurs identically to addition of numbers in other bases — the digits in a column are added, the result recorded, and any carries propagated to the next more significant columns.

2. Overflow can occur during addition. This occurs when the result of adding two k-bit values is too large to represent using a k-bit number.

3. Subtraction of binary numbers occurs similarly to subtraction in other bases. The digits in a column are subtracted, the result recorded, and any borrow propagated to the next more significant column.

4. Sign-magnitude numbers have a single bit (the MSB) which signifies whether the magnitude (the remaining bits) should be multiplied by -1 to obtain the value.

5. Sign-magnitude numbers are more difficult to add due to the different cases which must be considered.

6. Sign-magnitude numbers have two different zero representations.

7. 2's complement numbers are positional numbers like unsigned numbers. The only difference is that 2's complement numbers apply a negative weight to the MSB of the number to arrive at its equivalent value.

8. Sign-extension consists of replicating the MSB of a 2's complement number as many times as desired to increase the width (number of bits) of the number.

9. Sign-extension does not change the value of a 2's complement number.

10. Sign-extension works only for 2's complement numbers. Zero-extension (adding 0's to the left end) is how an unsigned number is made wider.

11. Sign-extending the operands to a 2's complement add or subtract operation by at least one bit guarantees that overflow and underflow will never occur.

12. Removing most significant bits from a 2's complement value will not change its number as long as the "original sign bit" is left intact.

13. A 2's complement number can be negated by inverting all the bits and adding a '1'.

14. This is reversible (works for both positive and negative numbers).

15. 2's complement representations are asymmetrical (there is one more negative value than positive value). Thus, negating a k-bit 2's complement value may result in a value which cannot be represented by k bits.

16. 2's complement is the most common representation of numbers in computers.

The skills that should result from a study of this chapter include the following:

1. The ability to add and subtract unsigned numbers.

2. The ability to interpret 2's complement numbers.

3. The ability to convert a 2's complement number to base-10.

4. The ability to negate 2's complement and sign-magnitude numbers.

5. The ability to sign-extend 2's complement numbers.

6. The ability to add and subtract 2's complement numbers.

7. The ability to detect overflow and underflow when adding 2's complement numbers.

8. The ability to negate 1's complement numbers.

3.8 Exercises

3.1. Convert the following to unsigned binary, add the numbers together in binary, and check your result by converting it back to base-10: $4 + 5 = ?$. Use four bits for your operands and result.

3.2. Repeat the above for $8 + 5 = ?$.

3.3. Repeat the above for $12 + 15 = ?$ but use five bits for the result.

3.4. Does zero-extending the operands in the previous problem give a different answer from using the final carry-out as the MSB of the result? Do it both ways to determine this.

Produce a "proof" (a nice tight argument will do) that this is always true for unsigned addition.

3.5. Repeat the three additions from the previous problems but for 2's complement. Use four bits for the operands if possible, use five bits if needed.

In each case first do the addition and compute a result with the same number of bits as the operands.

Then, determine which operations overflowed and repeat those after first sign-extending the operands by one bit position.

3.6. Do the problem directly above but do a subtraction instead and check for underflow instead of overflow.

3.7. Do the following addition using 2's complement and 4-bit numbers: $-8 + 7 = ?$. Try using the most significant carry-out as the MSB for a 5-bit result. Show why it doesn't work. Repeat by first sign-extending the operands to be 5-bit values and then compute a 5-bit result.

3.8. Add the following 2's complement 4-bit numbers to give a 4-bit result: $-8 + 5 = ?$.

3.9. Repeat the above problem for $-1 + -1 = ?$.

3.10. Repeat the above two problems but do subtraction instead.

3.11. Overflow in 2's complement addition can also be detected by looking at the carry-in and carry-out values associated with the most significant bit when doing addition. Create some test cases which do and don't overflow for both positive and negative numbers, and determine how you could detect whether overflow occured by simply examining those two bits.

Chapter 4

Boolean Algebra and Truth Tables

We continue our study of digital systems design by examining Boolean Algebra - the basic method of describing and manipulating combinations of binary values. After that we turn our attention, in the next chapter, to the circuits which implement the computations described by Boolean Algebra.

4.1 Introduction to Boolean Algebra and Truth Tables

Boolean algebra is named after George Boole, the 19th century mathematician who developed it. It is an *algebra* over the values TRUE and FALSE. In developing this, Boole was not pursuing a method to reason about and design digital systems but rather was studying formal logic. Later, Claude Shannon pioneered the use of Boole's algebra to describe and manipulate binary variables with the goal of describing digital switching systems. Today, Boolean Algebra is the foundation upon which the specification and design of digital systems rests.

In Boolean Algebra, we map TRUE to the value 1 and FALSE to the value 0. A variable or constant whose range is taken from the set $\{0, 1\}$ is called a boolean variable or boolean constant.

Because it is an algebra, Boolean Algebra further includes operators for operating on the values 0 and 1. These operators include AND, OR, and NOT. The results of applying these operators to boolean values are fairly intuitive. For example, the expression "X AND Y" will be TRUE only when X is TRUE <u>and</u> Y is TRUE. The expression "X OR Y" is TRUE whenever X is TRUE <u>or</u> Y is TRUE. Finally, if X is TRUE then "NOT X" is FALSE and if X is FALSE then "NOT X" is TRUE.

Since boolean variables can take on only one of two values, it is possible to describe a boolean function by exhaustively enumerating all possible combinations of its input values and the corresponding output values. This is in direct contrast to conventional high-school algebra where enumerations are generally not useful. An enumeration in this respect can be done using a *truth table*. For example, the function of the AND operator can be described using the truth table of Figure 4.1(a).

A	B	A · B		A	B	A + B		A	A'
0	0	0		0	0	0		0	1
0	1	0		0	1	1		1	0
1	0	0		1	0	1			
1	1	1		1	1	1			

| (a) AND | (b) OR | (c) NOT |

Figure 4.1: The AND, OR, and NOT Operators

The arguments of the AND operator are shown on the left side of the truth table (A and B), and the result is shown on the right. The AND operator is often represented using the • symbol and so the AND of A and B is $A \bullet B$. There are four possible combinations of values for the A and B arguments: (00, 01, 10, and 11). The only case where $A \bullet B$

is TRUE is when *all* of the function's inputs are true. In all other cases, $A \bullet B$ is FALSE. This matches precisely the word definition given previously.

Similarly, the function of an OR operation is TRUE whenever *any* of its inputs are TRUE as shown in the truth table of Figure 4.1(b). Here, the $+$ symbol is used to represent the OR operator, and $A + B$ is TRUE any time either A or B is TRUE. Once again this matches the word definition given previously.

Finally, the NOT operator is shown in Figure 4.1(c). It negates or *inverts* its argument. When writing boolean expressions a number of symbols have traditionally been used for the NOT operator. Examples of this include A' and $\bar{A}$. In this text, an apostrophe will be used. Thus, A' is the same as NOT A and $\bar{A}$.

4.2 Truth Tables for Arbitrary Functions

Truth tables can be used to describe any binary (boolean) function beyond simple AND, OR, and NOT. For example, the truth table of Figure 4.2 shows a function which is TRUE when its inputs are equal to one another.

A	B	F
0	0	1
0	1	0
1	0	0
1	1	1

Figure 4.2: The Equivalence Function

There are two cases where the function is TRUE. The first case is the top row of the truth table and represents the case when both inputs are FALSE (A' $\bullet$ B'). The second case is the bottom row of the truth table and represents the case when both inputs are TRUE (A $\bullet$ B). In the other two cases the function is FALSE. A boolean expression representing this could be written as: $F = A' \bullet B' + A \bullet B$. Thus, an equation taken from a truth table is simply the OR of the rows with TRUE outputs.

As another example, consider the function shown in Figure 4.3. This function is only TRUE in a single case — when A is TRUE and B is FALSE. The function is FALSE for the other three cases. This would be written as: $F = A \bullet B'$.

A	B	F
0	0	0
0	1	0
1	0	1
1	1	0

Figure 4.3: Another Boolean Function

Finally, consider the function shown in Figure 4.4. In this truth table, the function is always TRUE. Following our methodology of listing the *product terms* corresponding to TRUE outputs for the function, this would be written as $F = A' \bullet B' + A' \bullet B + A \bullet B' + A \bullet B$. However, another way to write this would be: $F = 1$ (F is always TRUE).

A	B	F
0	0	1
0	1	1
1	0	1
1	1	1

Figure 4.4: A Trivial Boolean Function

Note that in the equations written for these functions, an implied precedence of operators was used. The order is that NOT has the highest precedence, followed by AND, and then OR. This is similar to the precedence of multiply before add found in conventional arithmetic. If a different interpretation than the default precedence is desired, parentheses can be used.

Truth tables can be created for functions with more than two inputs. In this case the process is the same as above: (1) Enumerate all possible combinations of the function's inputs and then (2) for each such combination (row in the truth table) specify the function's output value. For a k-input function there are 2^k possible combinations and thus there will be 2^k rows in the truth table.

A 3-input function is shown in Figure 4.5. This function is TRUE any time at least two of its inputs are TRUE. A boolean equation representing it could be written as: $F = A' \bullet B \bullet C + A \bullet B' \bullet C + A \bullet B \bullet C' + A \bullet B \bullet C$.

A	B	C	F
0	0	0	0
0	0	1	0
0	1	0	0
0	1	1	1
1	0	0	0
1	0	1	1
1	1	0	1
1	1	1	1

Figure 4.5: A 3-Input Function

4.3   Converting Truth Tables to Boolean Equations

From these examples it should be clear how to construct a boolean equation from a truth table. For each row which has a TRUE output (a '1'), write down the AND of the input values which it corresponds to. A careful examination of the previous figures will show how this is done in each case (begin by examining Figure 4.3 since there is only one product term). These product terms are then OR-ed together to form the final result.

The AND symbol ($\bullet$) is often omitted for clarity and so the function of Figure 4.5 could be written like this: $F = A'BC + AB'C + ABC' + ABC$. Additional examples of converting truth tables to boolean equations are shown in Figure 4.6. In each case, the number of *product terms* in the boolean equation is equal to the number of rows in the truth table which contain a '1' in the output column.

A	B	F
0	0	1
0	1	1
1	0	0
1	1	1

(a) $F = A'B' + A'B + AB$

A	B	F
0	0	0
0	1	1
1	0	1
1	1	0

(b) $F = A'B + AB'$

A	B	F
0	0	1
0	1	1
1	0	1
1	1	0

(c) $F = A'B' + A'B + AB'$

Figure 4.6: Some Additional Examples

4.4   Converting Boolean Functions to Truth Tables

Converting a boolean equation to a truth table is a relatively straightforward process. For example, consider the function: $F = A'B + AB$. This corresponds to a truth table with two rows that are TRUE (the '01' row and the '11' row). The corresponding truth table is shown in Figure 4.7. To ensure you understand how this is done, go back and review the previous figures and ensure you see how to map both directions (truth table $\rightarrow$ equation as well as equation $\rightarrow$ truth table.)

A	B	F
0	0	0
0	1	1
1	0	0
1	1	1

Figure 4.7: Truth Table for $F = A'B + AB$

A more interesting problem is mapping the following function to a truth table: $F = A + A'B$. In this equation, the first product term does not contain a B in either inverted or non-inverted form. Thus, the process is a bit different and results in the truth table shown in Figure 4.8.

A	B	F	
0	0	0	
0	1	1	} A'B
1	0	1	} A
1	1	1	

Figure 4.8: Truth Table for $F = A + A'B$

Here, the A term corresponds to <u>all</u> rows for which A is TRUE. This includes the '10' row as well as the '11' row. The term $A'B$ corresponds to the '01' row. As another example, consider the 3-variable function shown in Figure 4.9 and its truth table.

	A	B	C	F	
	0	0	0	0	
	0	0	1	0	
	0	1	0	0	
BC {	0	1	1	1	
	1	0	0	0	
	1	0	1	0	
	1	1	0	1	} AB
BC {	1	1	1	1	

Figure 4.9: Truth Table for $F = AB + BC$

Here, the product terms overlap. That is the '111' row is covered by both AB as well as BC.

4.5 Boolean Identities and Theorems

As with regular algebra, boolean algebra has an associated set of identities and theorems. These are useful for doing algebraic manipulations on boolean expressions, usually with the goal of simplifying those expressions. A set of commonly used boolean identities and theorems are introduced in this section.

4.5.1 Single-Variable Theorems

$$A \bullet 0 = 0$$

This first theorem can be proven using a truth table as shown in Figure 4.10. This is done by listing the possible combinations of A in the truth table and AND-ing them with a '0'. Using the truth table of Figure 4.1(a) as a guide, the output column values can be determined. The resulting output column (all 0's) shows that indeed $A \bullet 0 = 0$.

A	0	A·0=0
0	0	0
1	0	0

Figure 4.10: Proof for $A \bullet 0 = 0$

In like manner, the following identity can be proven as shown in Figure 4.11.

$$A \bullet 1 = A$$

A	1	A·1=A
0	1	0
1	1	1

Figure 4.11: Proof for $A \bullet 1 = A$

Similarly, the following can be shown to be true:

$$A + 0 = A$$

$$A + 1 = 1$$

An additional set of theorems include the following which are proven in Figure 4.12

$$A' \bullet A = 0$$

$$A' + A = 1$$

A'	A	A'·A=0
1	0	0
0	1	0

(a) $A' \bullet A = 0$

A'	A	A'+A=1
1	0	1
0	1	1

(b) $A' + A = 1$

Figure 4.12: Proofs for Additional Theorems

4.5.2 Two-Variable Theorems

The following theorem is useful for simplifying boolean expressions:

$$A + A'B = A + B$$

When presented with a boolean expression, you can simplify it (reduce the number of terms and variables it contains) by applying this theorem. An expression with fewer terms and variables is preferable to one containing more terms and variables since it will often result in a smaller circuit. The proof of the theorem $A + A'B = A + B$ is shown in Figure 4.13.

A	B	A'B	A+A'B	A+B
0	0	0	0	0
0	1	1	1	1
1	0	0	1	1
1	1	0	1	1

A+A'B = A+B

Figure 4.13: Proof for $A + A'B = A + B$

In this figure, additional columns are added to the truth table to build up the proof, piece-by-piece, using the basic definitions of AND, OR, and NOT. In the end, the columns labeled $A + A'B$ and $A + B$ contain the same combination of 0's and 1's. This shows that the two expressions have the same output for all possible input combinations and, are therefore, equivalent.

This theorem can also be used for simplifying more complex expressions using variable substitution:

$$(N + M + K') + (N + M + K')' \bullet WXY = (N + M + K') + WXY$$

where $(N + M + K') \rightarrow A$ and $WXY \rightarrow B$. A similar theorem which is easily proven using a truth table is given by:

$$A(A' + B) = AB$$

4.5.3 Commutative, Associative, and Distributive Theorems

Theorems similar to the commutative and associative laws hold true in Boolean Algebra:

$$A \bullet B = B \bullet A$$

$$(A \bullet B) \bullet C = A \bullet (B \bullet C)$$

$$A + B = B + A$$

$$(A + B) + C = A + (B + C)$$

These are easily extended to more than three variables. Boolean algebra also has *two* theorems similar to the distributive law:

$$A(B + C) = AB + AC$$

$$A + BC = (A + B)(A + C)$$

These distributive laws are proven in Figure 4.14.

A	B	C	B+C	A(B+C)	AB	AC	AB+AC
0	0	0	0	0	0	0	0
0	0	1	1	0	0	0	0
0	1	0	1	0	0	0	0
0	1	1	1	0	0	0	0
1	0	0	0	0	0	0	0
1	0	1	1	1	0	1	1
1	1	0	1	1	1	0	1
1	1	1	1	1	1	1	1

A	B	C	BC	A+BC	A+B	A+C	(A+B)(A+C)
0	0	0	0	0	0	0	0
0	0	1	0	0	0	1	0
0	1	0	0	0	1	0	0
0	1	1	1	1	1	1	1
1	0	0	0	1	1	1	1
1	0	1	0	1	1	1	1
1	1	0	0	1	1	1	1
1	1	1	1	1	1	1	1

(a) $A(B + C) = AB + AC$ (b) $A + BC = (A + B)(A + C)$

Figure 4.14: Proofs for Distributive Theorems

4.5.4   The Simplification Theorems

Two of the most useful theorems for simplification of boolean expressions are these:

$$AB' + AB = A$$

$$(A + B')(A + B) = A$$

While the first can be proven using a truth table, it can also be proven using previously introduced theorems:

$$AB' + AB = A(B' + B) = A(1) = A$$

The second of these theorems can also be proven by *multiplying it out* and then applying the other theorems:

$$
\begin{aligned}
(A + B')(A + B) &= AA + AB + B'A + B'B \\
&= A + AB + AB' + 0 \\
&= A + A(B + B') + 0 \\
&= A + A + 0 = \\
&= A
\end{aligned}
$$

4.5.5   The Consensus Theorems

The final theorem which will be introduced is the consensus theorem:

$$AC + A'B + BC = AC + A'B$$

where the 3rd term in the left hand side expression is redundant and can be eliminated. A companion theorem is:

$$(A + C)(A' + B)(B + C) = (A + C)(A' + B)$$

While the consensus theorems are correct theorems, identifying opportunities to apply them when simplifying boolean expressions can be difficult.

4.6 Summary of the Boolean Theorems

A set of useful boolean theorems is summarized in Table 4.1. Note the symmetry in the table — for every theorem in the left half of the table a corresponding theorem (its *dual*) is listed in the right half of the table. This table summarizes the set of boolean theorems which will be used throughout the remainder of this text.

Table 4.1: Some Useful Boolean Identities and Theorems

$A \bullet 0 = 0$	$A + 1 = 1$
$A \bullet 1 = A$	$A + 0 = A$
$A \bullet A' = 0$	$A + A' = 1$
$A + A'B = A + B$	$A(A' + B) = AB$
$AB = BA$	$A + B = B + A$
$(AB)C = A(BC)$	$(A + B) + C = A + (B + C)$
$A(B + C) = AB + AC$	$A + BC = (A + B)(A + C)$
$AB' + AB = A$	$(A + B')(A + B) = A$
$AC + A'B + BC = AC + A'B$	$(A + C)(A' + B)(B + C) = (A + C)(A' + B)$

4.7 Chapter Summary

The basics of Boolean Algebra have been introduced in this chapter. It has been shown that every boolean expression has a corresponding truth table and that every truth table can be reduced to a boolean expression. A set of theorems, useful for simplifying boolean expressions, was introduced. Proofs using truth tables were also introduced.

   The key high-level points to master from this chapter include the following:

1. Boolean algebra is an algebra over the set $\{0, 1\}$ and the operators AND, OR, and NOT.

2. The boolean operators can be described by simple truth tables.

3. A truth table is an enumeration of all possible input combinations and the corresponding function output.

4. Truth tables for arbitrary boolean functions can be easily created.

5. For every truth table there is a corresponding boolean equation relating the truth table output to its inputs.

6. For every boolean equation there is a corresponding truth table.

7. Truth tables can be used to prove or disprove the truthfulness of a proposed equality.

8. A set of boolean theorems exist which can be used to simplify boolean expressions.

9. This set of boolean theorems can also be used to prove or disprove a proposed equality.

The skills that should result from a study of this chapter include the following:

1. The ability to create a truth table from a simple word description of a boolean function for any number of inputs.

2. The ability to write the boolean equation corresponding to a truth table.

3. The ability to create a truth table from a boolean equation.

4. The ability to prove or disprove a proposed equality using a truth table.

5. The ability to understand and apply the boolean theorems presented in this chapter.

4.8 Exercises

4.1. Draw the truth table for a 3-variable function whose output is TRUE any time an odd number of its inputs is TRUE.

4.2. Draw the truth table for a 4-variable function whose output is TRUE any time an even number of its inputs is TRUE. For purposes of this problem, zero is an even number.

4.3. Draw the truth table for a 4-variable function whose output is TRUE any time its inputs, when interpreted as the bits of a 4-bit unsigned binary number, is a multiple of 3 (consider 0 to be a multiple of 3).

4.4. For each of the problems above, write the boolean equation for the function by reading it off the truth table.

4.5. Prove that the following identity is TRUE using a truth table: $AC + A'B + BC = AC + A'B$. This theorem has a name. What is its name?

4.6. Prove that the following is TRUE by *multiplying it out* and then simplifying: $(A+BC)(A+DE) = A+BCDE$

Chapter 5

Logic Gates

The goal of a course in digital systems design is to learn how to design, implement, and test digital circuits which perform a desired function. This chapter introduces a set of circuits called *logic gates* which implement the basic boolean operators given in the previous chapter. With a knowledge of the basic gate types, you can draw circuit schematics to implement any boolean equation.

5.1 Basic Gate Types

Figure 5.1(a) shows the symbol used for an AND gate. The shape of the symbol denotes the AND function. The inputs are on the left and output is on the right. This is a 2-input AND gate. Figure 5.1(b) shows the symbol for a 2-input OR gate. The key characteristic of the OR symbol that differentiates it from the AND symbol is the curve on the left side and the more pointed right hand side. Figure 5.1(c) shows the symbol for a NOT gate (usually called an *inverter*).

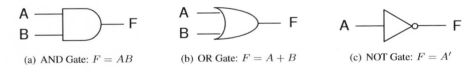

(a) AND Gate: $F = AB$ (b) OR Gate: $F = A + B$ (c) NOT Gate: $F = A'$

Figure 5.1: Basic Gates

The schematic shown in Figure 5.2 shows how the function: $F = AB' + C$ would be implemented using gates. As shown, wires (denoted as lines) are used to convey intermediate values between gates.

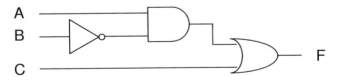

Figure 5.2: Schematic for: $F = AB' + C$

Figure 5.3 shows another example where optional parentheses in the boolean equation of the caption are used to emphasize the gate level structure.

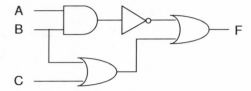

Figure 5.3: Schematic for: $F = (AB)' + (B + C)$

5.2 Transistors - The Building Blocks of Gates

Gates are built out of transistors. A simple n-type field-effect transistor is shown in Figure 5.4. This symbol indicates that this is a *field-effect transistor* and that it has three *terminals* labeled the *gate*, the *drain*, and the *source*. Because it is a field-effect transistor, it is often called a 'FET'.

One way to think of a transistor is as a switch that can be turned *on* or *off*. In part (b) of the figure, the transistor has been *turned on* due to a high voltage (3 volts) on its gate. As a result, electrical current is allowed to flow between the drain and source. The direction it flows will depend on the voltages of the drain and source — current always flows from a point of higher voltage to a point of lower voltage. In part (c) of the figure, a low voltage (0 volts) has been applied to its gate. As a result no current is allowed to flow between the drain and the source (regardless of the voltages on the drain and source terminals), and we say that the transistor has been turned off[1].

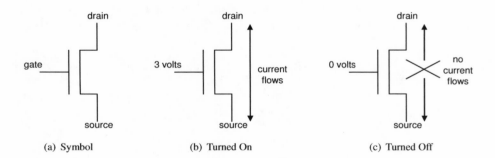

Figure 5.4: An n-type Transistor

---

[1] In this example, we are using 0 volts for a low voltage and 3 volts for a high voltage, but the exact voltages used by any particular technology will vary.

Another type of FET is the p-type transistor shown in Figure 5.5. The first difference in the symbol is the circle on the gate terminal. This indicates that a <u>low</u> voltage on the gate terminal will turn it on. This is the opposite of how the n-FET works. This is shown in parts (b) and (c) of the figure. The second difference is that the source of a p-FET is usually drawn on top in a schematic (the opposite of n-FET's).

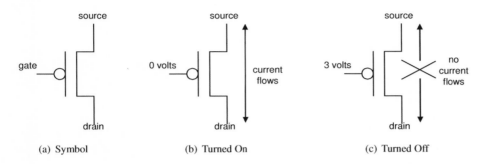

(a) Symbol (b) Turned On (c) Turned Off

Figure 5.5: A p-type Transistor

5.2.1 Building An Inverter Using FET's

An inverter can be easily built out of transistors as shown in Figure 5.6. Here an n-FET and a p-FET are wired together in series. The same signal (V_{in}) is wired to the gates of both transistors. The source of the p-FET is wired to V_{cc} which is the power supply wire in the circuit. The source of the n-FET is likewise wired to GND (stands for "ground") which has a voltage of 0 volts. The output of the inverter is wired between the drains of the transistors.

Part (b) of the figure shows what happens when $V_{in} = 3\ Volts$. This input voltage causes the p-FET to turn OFF and the n-FET to turn ON. The n-FET will now connect the output of the inverter to GND (0 volts). Thus, a high voltage on the input produces a low voltage on the output. In similar fashion part (c) of the figure shows that a low voltage on the input turns on the p-FET and turns off the n-FET, thus connecting the output with V_{cc} (3 $Volts$).

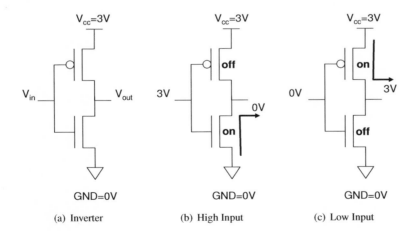

(a) Inverter (b) High Input (c) Low Input

Figure 5.6: An Inverter (NOT Gate)

A truth table for this behavior is shown in Figure 5.7(a) where, instead of '1' and '0' values, the voltages have been listed. A simple mapping of $3\ Volts \rightarrow 1$ and $0\ Volts \rightarrow 0$ leads to the truth table of part (b) of the figure which is precisely the truth table for an inverter as seen previously.

Vin	Vout
0V	3V
3V	0V

(a) Voltage Table

Vin	Vout
0	1
1	0

(b) Truth Table

Figure 5.7: Truth Tables for FET-Based Inverter

Although beyond the scope of this text, n-FET and p-FET transistors can be used to design essentially any circuitry you will see in this book. Consult any of a number of excellent textbooks on transistor level electronics or digital integrated circuit design for details.

5.3 Other 2-Input Gates

5.3.1 NAND Gates

A NAND gate is a common 2-input gate. A truth table and symbol for this circuit is shown in Figure 5.8. The reason for the name can be seen from the truth table by noting that the output column is the inverse of the truth table for an AND gate. The name NAND is shorthand for NOT-AND. Thus, the symbol for a NAND gate is an AND gate symbol with an inverted output (the circle) as shown in Figure 5.8. The correct way to read the symbol is that it *is a gate whose output is FALSE when all of its inputs are TRUE.*

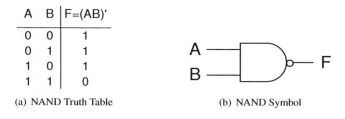

A	B	F=(AB)'
0	0	1
0	1	1
1	0	1
1	1	0

    (a) NAND Truth Table   (b) NAND Symbol

Figure 5.8: NAND Gate Truth Table and Symbol

An interesting point to note with respect to NAND gates is this: in all gate technologies available today constructing a 2-input NAND gate is less costly than constructing a 2-input AND gate. That is because an AND gate must be constructed from a NAND gate followed by an inverter due to the way field effect transistors operate. To achieve the smallest and least costly circuit designs possible, techniques for making use of NAND and NOR gates in preference to AND and OR gates have been developed. These will be outlined in a future chapter.

5.3.2 NOR Gates

Another commonly used 2-input gate is a NOR gate as shown in Figure 5.9. The name NOR implies NOT-OR. An examination of the truth table for this gate shows that it is the inverse of an OR gate. The correct way to read the gate-level symbol is that it *is a gate whose output is FALSE when any of its inputs are TRUE.*

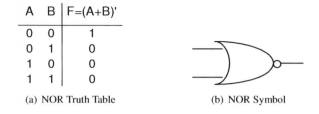

A	B	F=(A+B)'
0	0	1
0	1	0
1	0	0
1	1	0

    (a) NOR Truth Table   (b) NOR Symbol

Figure 5.9: NOR Gate

5.3.3 An Exclusive-OR Gate

The truth table for a gate called "exclusive-or" or XOR is shown in Figure 5.10. The name exclusive-or means that one (but not both) of the inputs must be TRUE for the output to be TRUE. The symbol used for XOR in boolean equations is the $\oplus$ symbol like this: $F = A \oplus B$.

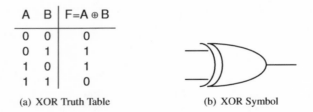

(a) XOR Truth Table   (b) XOR Symbol

Figure 5.10: XOR Gate

There are two very different ways to think about the function of this gate:

1. The gate output will be TRUE whenever the two inputs are different from one another.

2. The gate output will be TRUE whenever an ODD number of the gate's inputs are TRUE.

When thinking about 2-input XOR gates, the first definition makes the most sense. However, XOR gates are not limited to just two inputs. In the case that an XOR gate has more than two inputs, the second definition is preferred — its output will be TRUE when an odd number of its inputs are TRUE. The XOR gate is commonly used for building adder circuits and also for computing parity in data communications circuits as will be seen later in this text.

5.3.4 An Equivalence Gate

A function was introduced in the last chapter whose output was TRUE whenever its inputs were equal. This is called an "equivalence gate". It is a common function whose truth table is shown in Figure 5.11. A careful examination of this truth table will show it to be the inverse of the truth table for the XOR gate, and so this gate is sometimes called an XNOR gate (NOT-XOR). There are two different symbols for equivalence gates commonly in use as shown in Figure 5.11. As with the XOR gate, there are two ways of thinking about this gate's function. The first is that its output is TRUE when both inputs are the same. The second is that its output is TRUE when an even number of its inputs are TRUE. Using the second definition allows you to extrapolate the behavior of XNOR gates with more than two inputs. As with XOR, the XNOR gate is useful for computing parity in data communications circuits.

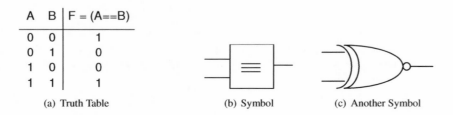

(a) Truth Table   (b) Symbol   (c) Another Symbol

Figure 5.11: Equivalence (XNOR) Gate

5.4   Multi-Input Gates

The 2-input AND, OR, NAND, NOR, XOR, and XNOR gates seen previously can be extended to include more inputs. The function of such gates follows from the textual descriptions for these gates given previously. For example, Figure 5.12 shows a 3-input NAND gate. As with a 2-input NAND gate, its output is FALSE when all of its inputs are TRUE.

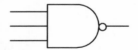

Figure 5.12: A 3-Input NAND Gate

Figure 5.13 shows symbols for a number of gates with more than two inputs. By now you should be able to determine their functions by inspection.

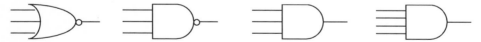

Figure 5.13: Multi-Input Gates

It is possible, in theory, to create gates with any number of inputs desired, but physical realities associated with transistors prevent this. For example, wide gates can be very slow to function and take up significant silicon area.

We will focus (somewhat arbitrarily) on gates with 4 or fewer inputs in this text, realizing that wide gates can always be constructed from a collection of narrower gates. Figure 5.14 shows how a 12-input AND function would be implemented with such narrower gates. Similar techniques can be used for other boolean functions.

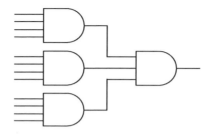

Figure 5.14: A 12-Input AND Function

5.5 Alternative Gate Symbology

This is an important topic that many people ignore. Don't ignore it! The schematic symbols shown for representing gates are not the only symbols in common use. For example, consider the schematic symbol shown in Figure 5.15(a). This is a NOR gate. One way to understand how this gate works it to simply memorize its truth table. Another way is to remember that it is simply the NOT of an OR. A third way (the recommended way) is to learn to read the symbol and understand what it means. When applying this third method, we find that this is a gate *whose output is FALSE when any of its inputs is TRUE*. It is understood that its output is TRUE otherwise. Thus, the bubble on the output indicates that we are interested in when the output is FALSE rather than when it is TRUE. Further, the gate shape (OR) tells us that we are interested in the OR condition of the inputs (as opposed to the AND condition).

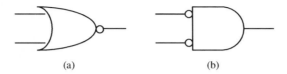

(a)   (b)

Figure 5.15: NOR Gate Symbols

An alternate symbol for a NOR gate is shown in Figure 5.15(b). A reading of the symbol indicates that *the output of the gate is TRUE when all of its inputs are FALSE*. A careful examination of these two English statements indicates that they describe exactly the same function (and the same truth table) — one statement specifies when the output is FALSE and the other specifies when the output is TRUE.

Figure 5.16 shows two different symbols for a NAND gate. The textual description of part (a) is that the output is FALSE only when *all* of the inputs are TRUE. The textual description of part (b) is that the output is TRUE when *any* of the inputs is FALSE. These are just two different ways of describing the same function.

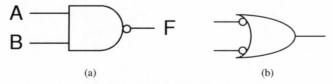

(a)   (b)

Figure 5.16: NAND Gate Symbols

Further examples of alternate gate symbols are shown in Figures 5.17 and 5.18.

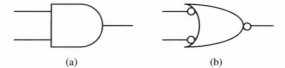

(a)   (b)

Figure 5.17: AND Gate Symbols

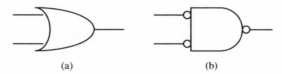

(a)   (b)

Figure 5.18: OR Gate Symbols

Can you now see the pattern? To convert a gate symbol from AND to OR, follow these steps:

1. Redraw the symbol to be an OR symbol.

2. If the output on the original gate is non-inverted (no bubble there), then add one to the new gate. If there is a bubble there, remove it.

3. For each input on the original gate, if there is no bubble there add one to the new gate. If there is a bubble there remove it.

This same procedure can be used to convert from an OR to an AND symbol. In summary, the steps are to *convert the symbol and invert all inputs and outputs.*

Figure 5.19 shows two alternative symbols for an inverter. The left-hand symbol can be read as *the output is FALSE when the input is TRUE*. The right-hand symbol can be read as *the output is TRUE when the input is FALSE*. Both correctly describe the operation of an inverter.

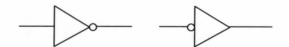

Figure 5.19: Inverter Symbols

Why Use Alternative Gate Symbols?

The decision on which symbol to use when drawing a schematic is based mainly on readability and understandability of your design. For example, consider the following problem statement:

Design a function whose output is TRUE only when all its inputs are FALSE.

Based on the words chosen to describe the function (especially the word "all"), an AND gate symbol is most appropriate. The resulting gate symbol to use would be the gate shown in Figure 5.15(b). An example of such a problem statement might be:

Turn on the sprinkler system if it is not raining, and if it is not the weekend.

Alternatively, given the following problem statement, what symbol is most appropriate?

Design a function whose output is FALSE when either of its inputs is FALSE.

The function this is describing is an OR function but with bubbles on both inputs and outputs. The proper symbol to use is the one from Figure 5.17(b). By using the proper symbol, you make your schematics more accurately reflect the function they are to perform, making it easier for others to understand your designs, and for you and others to maintain your designs long after they are completed.

Mixed Symbols

Another collection of schematic symbols can often be used as a shorthand to simplify the drawing of schematics. For example, the function $F = AB'$ can be drawn as in Figure 5.20(a). Reading the gate symbol yields the following: *F is TRUE when A is TRUE and B is FALSE* which is precisely what the boolean equation says. The actual schematic used to implement this function is shown in part (b) of the figure. You can use bubbles as needed when drawing schematics to avoid drawing inverters, and to make your schematics more readable. Just remember that such gates usually will not exist for your use but must be built from AND, OR, NAND, NOR, and NOT gates.

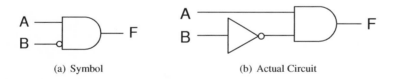

(a) Symbol   (b) Actual Circuit

Figure 5.20: $F = AB'$

So, just what gates are actually available for constructing digital systems? NOT, AND, OR, XOR, NAND, and NOR gates will always be available (at least). A given technology library may contain other gates as well, so check your library documentation. A little creativity will enable you to draw schematics using alternate symbols and do the necessary conversions when actually implementing the design using the available gates. The net result will be significantly more readable schematics of your designs.

5.6 Multi-Level Logic

The examples of boolean equations seen so far have all been implemented with two levels of logic, usually a level of AND gates followed by a level of OR gates. This is called two-level logic and has the advantage of being fast. An example of two-level logic is shown in Figure 5.21. The time from when any input changes until the output changes is $t_{AND} + t_{OR}$, where t_{AND} is the time it takes for an AND gate to react to a change on one of its inputs and t_{OR} is the time it takes for an OR gate to react to a change on one of its inputs.

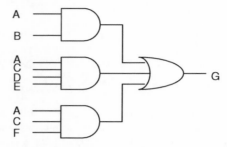

Figure 5.21: Two-Level Logic Implementation of $G = AB + ACDE + ACF$

An equivalent boolean expression for G is:

$$AB + ACDE + ACF = A[B + C(DE + F)]$$

which results in the gate-level representation shown in Figure 5.22. Thus, we have two different gate-level schematics which implement the same boolean function. Which is preferable? While the exact answer depends on the area and speed characteristics of the specific technology being used, a number of general observations can be made.

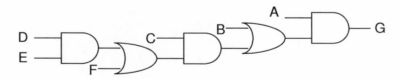

Figure 5.22: Multi-Level Logic Implementation of $G = A[B + C(DE + F)]$

5.6.1 Speed of Operation

The first consideration is speed of operation. When an input changes, how soon is that change reflected on the output? The slowest delay through the circuit of Figure 5.21 would consist of the delay through the middle AND gate plus the delay through the OR gate[2]. One rough estimate of speed is to simply count the levels of logic along the slowest path (the maximum number of gates between the output and any input). Using this as a metric, the circuit of Figure 5.21 has two gate delays while the circuit of Figure 5.22 has five gate delays.

A more accurate representation of delay would be to write the delay as a sum of the actual gate delays. In this case the delay in Figure 5.21 is $t_{circuit} = t_{AND4} + t_{OR3}$ where t_{AND4} is the delay through a 4-input AND gate and t_{OR3} is the delay through a 3-input OR gate. The delay through the circuit of Figure 5.22, on the other hand, would be written as $t_{circuit} = t_{AND2} + t_{OR2} + t_{AND2} + t_{OR2} + t_{AND2}$. Which circuit is faster depends on the relative delays of the gates used. Most likely, the two-level implementation of Figure 5.21 will be faster for the following reason: while it is true that a 4-input AND gate is slower than a 2-input AND gate, the difference is likely not enough to compensate for the difference in number of logic levels in these example circuits (2 vs. 5).

---

[2]The middle AND gate was identified as a part of this slowest path through the circuit because a 4-input gate will generally be slower than a 3-input or 2-input gate.

5.6.2 Circuit Area

The second consideration when comparing implementations is circuit area. An integrated circuit is built on a flat wafer of silicon; transistors and wires occupy space on that silicon wafer. A gate with 12 transistors will consume more silicon area than a gate with 4 transistors. The less area a circuit occupies, the cheaper it will be to manufacture.

One rough measure of circuit area is to count the number of gates in the circuit. Figure 5.21 contains four gates while Figure 5.22 contains five gates.

Another indicator of area is to count the total number of gate inputs. A 2-input NAND gate requires four transistors to build while a 3-input NAND gate requires six transistors. Thus, there is a correlation between circuit area and the number of inputs required by all the gates in the circuit. In the case of Figure 5.21, there are a total of 12 gate inputs $(2 + 4 + 3 + 3)$. In the case of Figure 5.22, there are a total of 10 gate inputs $(2 + 2 + 2 + 2 + 2)$. Therefore, it would seem that the multi-level circuit of Figure 5.22 requires fewer transistors and therefore less area.

5.6.3 Speed and Area Comparisons

Related to both speed and area is a consideration of the largest gate required. In the case of Figure 5.21, a 4-input AND gate is required. In the case of Figure 5.22, all of the gates are 2-input gates.

One way to make a gate faster is to make its transistors physically larger. This, however, makes the the gate significantly larger. A 4-input gate will either make the circuit slow (its transistors have not been increased in size) or large (its transistors have been increased in size). As a result, an implementation with "narrower gates", meaning fewer inputs per gate, may be preferable. This could argue in favor of the circuit of Figure 5.22.

Table 5.1 summarizes these comparisons between the two circuits, both of which implement the same boolean function. The two-level circuit would seem to be superior based on levels of logic, delay, and gate count. The multi-level circuit would seem to be superior based on the total number of gate inputs and the largest gate. Without consulting the actual delays and sizes for the gates in the technology being used, it would be difficult to say exactly which of the two implementations would be smaller, and which would be faster. What can be said, however, is that two-level implementations are often larger and faster while multi-level implementations are often smaller and slower. So, which to choose when implementing a design? As always, it depends. In this case, it depends on the speed you desire your system to operate at. In general, you should always choose the smallest circuit possible that will meet the performance (speed of operation) requirements. Making the circuit any larger than that will (a) use more silicon and therefore cost more and (b) probably use more power. As will be seen in a later chapter, one of the advantages of HDL-based CAD tools is that they do this selection automatically, freeing you as the engineer from needing to worry about it as much as if you were doing all the circuit optimization yourself.

Table 5.1: Comparison of Circuits of Figures 5.21 and 5.22

	Two-Level Circuit	Multi-Level Circuit
Levels of Logic	2	5
Delay	$t_{AND4} + t_{OR3}$	$3 \times t_{AND2} + 2 \times t_{OR2}$
Gate Count	4	5
Gate Inputs	12	10
Largest Gate	4 input	2 input

5.6.4 Factoring and Multiplying Out

Given a boolean function to implement, it is possible to manipulate the function algebraically to convert it between two-level and multi-level forms. For example, the following shows how the two-level circuit in the example above can be converted to a multi-level form by factoring it (factoring is defined as applying the distributive theorem $AB + AC \rightarrow A(B + C)$):

$$
\begin{aligned}
AB + ACDE + ACF &= A[B + CDE + CF] \\
&= A[B + C(DE + F)]
\end{aligned}
$$

The first step of this conversion also shows that there is an intermediate three-level logic form of this same function which is $G = A[B + CDE + CF]$. The circuit for this is shown in Figure 5.23.

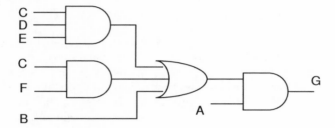

Figure 5.23: Another Form of The Circuit From Figure 5.21

Conversely, a multi-level form can always be converted to two-level form by *multiplying it out*:

$$
\begin{aligned}
A[B + C(DE + F)] &= A[B + CDE + CF] \\
&= AB + ACDE + ACF
\end{aligned}
$$

which also shows the intermediate three-level implementation possible.

5.7   Chapter Summary

The key high-level points to master from this chapter include the following:

1. The boolean operators AND, OR, and NOT have corresponding digital circuits called gates.

2. Gates can be built from n-type and p-type field effect transistors, also known as FET's.

3. An n-FET turns on when a high voltage is applied to its gate input. A p-FET turns on when a low voltage is applied to its gate input.

4. NAND and NOR gates are also commonly used and readily built using FET's.

5. AND and OR gates must usually be built using NAND and NOR gates followed by inverters.

6. XOR and XNOR gates are useful gates for building adder circuits and for computing parity functions.

7. Gates with more than two inputs can be built. However, the larger the number of inputs, the slower and/or larger the resulting gate will be.

8. When a problem statement implies the use of an alternate symbol (based on how it is stated), an alternate symbol should be used.

9. Mixed symbols containing arbitrary collections of bubbles on the inputs and outputs can be used to simplify the drawing of schematics.

10. A boolean function need not always be implemented as a two-level network of gates. Factoring an AND-OR equation can often lead to a multi-level network of gates with different speed and area characteristics.

11. Determining the optimum number of logic levels to employ to implement a boolean function depends on the technology being used. Common metrics used for evaluating circuits for speed and area include: levels of logic, total gate delay, gate count, total input count, and maximum gate width/size.

The skills that should result from a study of this chapter include the following:

1. Given a truth table or boolean equation, be able to draw a schematic which represents it.

2. Given a gate-level schematic, be able to write the equivalent boolean equation for the function it implements.

3. Know the truth tables and symbols for all the common gates: AND, OR, NOT, NAND, NOR, XOR, XNOR. Know the alternate symbols as well.

4. Know when to use alternate symbols.

5. Be able to convert a schematic with conventional symbols to one which uses alternate symbols.

6. Understand the issues associated with gates containing large numbers of inputs.

7. Given an equation, be able to implement it as a two-level network of gates by first multiplying it out.

8. Given an equation, be able to implement it as a multi-level network of gates by first factoring it.

5.8 Exercises

5.1. Create an inverter (NOT gate) using a single 2-input NAND gate.

5.2. Create an inverter (NOT gate) using a single 2-input NOR gate.

5.3. Create an AND gate using only NAND gates.

5.4. Create an AND gate using only NOR gates.

5.5. Draw the gate-level schematic for this equation: $F = (AB' + A'B)'$. Use only AND, OR, and NOT gates.

5.6. Write the boolean equation for the circuit shown in Figure 5.24. Write it using parentheses so that the structure of the equation exactly matches the structure of the circuit.

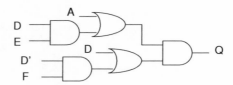

Figure 5.24: Circuit A

5.7. How many levels of logic does the circuit of Figure 5.24 have?

5.8. Write a 2-level AND-OR equation for the circuit shown in Figure 5.24. This will require that you do some algebraic manipulations first. Draw the resulting circuit.

5.9. Write the truth table for the circuit shown in Figure 5.25(a).

5.10. Write the truth table for the circuit shown in Figure 5.25(b).

5.11. Write the truth table for the circuit shown in Figure 5.25(c).

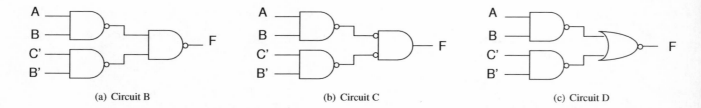

(a) Circuit B   (b) Circuit C   (c) Circuit D

Figure 5.25: More Circuits

5.12. Evaluate the circuit of Figure 5.24 using the metrics of Table 5.1. Do this by summarizing its levels of logic, delay, etc.

5.13. Create a two-level network of gates which implements the following equation: $F = (AB + CD)E$. Evaluate it using the metrics of Table 5.1.

5.14. Create a multi-level network of gates which implements the following equation: $F = (AB + CD)E$. Evaluate it using the metrics of Table 5.1.

5.15. Draw a single gate implementing this function: *the output is false when any of the inputs are false*. Draw a truth table for this function.

5.16. Draw a single gate implementing this function: *the output is true when the first two inputs are both false and the third input is true*. Draw a truth table for this function.

5.17. Prove or disprove the following proposed boolean theorem: $A \oplus (B \oplus C) = (A \oplus B) \oplus C$. Hint: using a truth table is one way (and often the easiest way) to construct such a proof.

5.18. Prove or disprove the following proposed boolean theorem: $A(B \oplus C) = AB \oplus AC$.

Chapter 6

Boolean Algebra - Part II

6.1   Inverting a Function - DeMorgan's Rules

The following theorems form the basis of what are called DeMorgan's rules:

$$(AB)' = A' + B'$$

$$(A + B)' = A'B'$$

These are easily proven using truth tables and show how to complement a boolean expression. In either case, the complement is created by changing the logic function to its dual (AND to OR and OR to AND) and inverting all the variables. If the expression involves constants these should be inverted as well:

$$[A(1)]' = A' + 0$$

$$(A + 0)' = A'(1)$$

The process is also reversible. That is: $(A')' = A$ as shown here:

$$(A + 0)' = A'(1) \rightarrow [A'(1)]' = A + 0$$

DeMorgan's rules can be applied to more complex expressions such as this:

$$[AB + C]' = [(AB) + C]' = (AB)'C' = (A' + B')C'$$

Placing parentheses around AND terms in the original expression ensures that the implied precedence of AND over OR is retained in the inverted expression. A larger example follows:

$$
\begin{aligned}
[(AB + 0)D + 1(B + C')']' &= [((AB + 0)D) + (1(B + C')')]' \\
&= ((AB + 0)D)'(1(B + C')')' \\
&= ((AB + 0)' + D')(0 + (B + C')) \\
&= ((AB)' \bullet 1 + D')((B + C')) \\
&= (A' + B' + D')(B + C')
\end{aligned}
$$

You will find many uses for DeMorgan's rules throughout the remainder of this text.

6.2 Sum-of-Products and Product-of-Sums Forms

DeMorgan's gives rise to an alternate way of converting a truth table to a boolean equation. Figure 6.1(a) shows the standard method for writing a boolean equation — the 1's in the output column are noted and the product term for each written down. The result is an equation of the form: $F = term_1 + term_2 + \cdots$ where each *term* (also known as a *product term*) corresponds to one row of the truth table. Figure 6.1(b) shows an alternate method. This consists of noting the 0's in the output column and writing the product term for each. The result is an equation of the form: $F' = term_1 + term_2 + \cdots$. This indicates *when F is FALSE* rather than when F is TRUE. Applying DeMorgan's rule to the equation converts it to an equation of the form: $F = sum_1 \bullet sum_2 \bullet \cdots$.

A	B	F		
0	0	0		
0	1	1	X	A'B
1	0	0		
1	1	1	X	AB

F = A'B + AB

(a) Sum-of-products (SOP) Form

A	B	F		
0	0	0	X	A'B'
0	1	1		
1	0	0	X	AB'
1	1	1		

F' = A'B' + AB'

F = (A + B)(A' + B) (by DeMorgan)

(b) Product-of-sums (POS) Form

Figure 6.1: Deriving SOP vs. POS Forms from Truth Table

As the figure shows, both approaches (mapping the 1's or mapping the 0's) lead to valid equations representing F, but one results in a sum-of-products (SOP) form and the other results in a product-of-sums (POS) form. To reiterate, to compute a POS form from a truth table do the following:

1. Write $F' = \cdots$ by writing the product term for each '0' in the truth table output. In this case the result is $F' = A'B' + AB'$.

2. Apply DeMorgan's rule to convert that to an equation of the form: $F = \cdots$. In this case the result is $F = (A + B)(A' + B)$.

Figure 6.2 shows how these SOP and POS equations are implemented using gates. A SOP realization maps directly to a layer of AND gates followed by an OR gate (known as an AND-OR configuration). Conversely, a POS realization maps to an OR-AND configuration. Both SOP and POS are valid representations for functions. In the case shown, neither one is particularly better than the other. However, for certain functions there may be differences in the number of gates required.

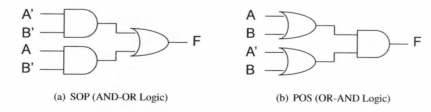

(a) SOP (AND-OR Logic)   (b) POS (OR-AND Logic)

Figure 6.2: Schematics of SOP and POS Forms

Figure 6.3 shows such a case where the POS form is simpler. You should work to become equally at home working with SOP and POS forms. Once you have mapped a number of truth tables to POS form using the method above, you will likely figure out there is a shortcut method and that you do not need to first write the $F' = \cdots$ equation and then apply DeMorgan's rules. Rather, you will learn to do it by inspection.

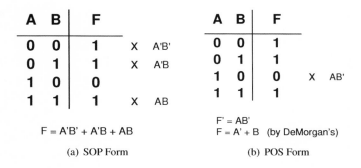

Figure 6.3: Another SOP vs. POS Example

In summary, an expression is said to be in SOP form when it can be implemented by a layer of AND gates followed by a single OR gate. Conversely, POS forms can be implemented by a layer of OR gates feeding a single AND gate.

6.3 Canonical Forms - Minterm Expansion and Maxterm Expansion

In mathematics, a *canonical form* is a function written in the standard or conventional way. A common result of using canonical forms is that it is trivial to determine whether two expressions are equal when written in canonical form (when written in canonical form they are equal if they are precisely the same — if not, they are not equal).

As we saw previously, applying boolean theorems to an expression allows for simplifying that expression. Thus, the following is true:

$$AB' + AB = A(B' + B) = A(1) = A$$

This series of equalities shows four different (yet equivalent) forms for the expression $AB' + AB$. It is often desirable to write boolean expressions in canonical form but only one of the four forms above could be considered canonical. Which one is it?

There are actually two canonical forms often used for boolean expressions. The SOP canonical form is called a *minterm expansion*. To derive a minterm expansion we first write the truth table, taking care to order the rows by increasing binary value for the inputs (000 followed by 001 followed by 010 and so on). We then number the rows with their decimal equivalent as shown in Figure 6.4. Here, the first row is minterm $m0$, the second row is minterm $m1$, and so on. The minterm expansion is simply the OR condition of the TRUE minterms and can be written in a number of different ways. The first is to simply write out the boolean equation as we did in Figure 6.1(a) and Figure 6.3(a). The second is to use a shorthand notation and write it out as a sum of minterms. The third is to write it as a summation. All three methods are shown in Figure 6.4.

A	B	F	
0	0	1	m0
0	1	1	m1
1	0	0	m2
1	1	1	m3

$$F = A'B' + A'B + AB$$
$$F = m0 + m1 + m3$$
$$F = \Sigma m(0, 1, 3)$$

Figure 6.4: Creating a Minterm Expansion

Just what is a minterm? A minterm is a product term which contains all input variables in either normal or complemented form. For a function of the variables A, B, and C, the following are minterms: $A'B'C$, $AB'C'$, and the following are not: AB, $A'B$, $A'C'$. There is thus a one-to-one correspondence between minterms and the rows of a truth table. By looking at the minterm name it is possible to determine the input combination which it represents. For example, $m6$ is ABC' and the binary equivalent of 6 is '110'. The pattern '110' indicates which variables should be complemented in the minterm (C in this case), and which should not (A and B in this case).

A minterm expansion is the canonical form for a sum-of-products (SOP) expression, and therefore uniquely specifies the expression. Another way to look at this is to consider that a minterm expansion is just another way of writing a truth table. Neither form contains more information than the other — they are equivalent. One is in table form, one is in equational form.

A *maxterm expansion* is the canonical form for POS expressions. This is shown in Figure 6.5. The rows are numbered with their maxterm number, and the final equation is created by writing out the product of the maxterms. The maxterms correspond to the 0's in the truth table output column.

A	B	F	
0	0	1	M0
0	1	1	M1
1	0	0	M2
1	1	0	M3

$$F = (A'+B)(A'+B')$$
$$F = M2 \cdot M3$$
$$F = \Pi M(2, 3)$$

Figure 6.5: Creating a Maxterm Expansion

Determining the sum that a maxterm represents is a bit more complicated than for minterms. Note that $m0' = M0$. That is, maxterm 0 can be formed by writing out minterm 0 and then inverting it using DeMorgan's rules. Thus, $m0 = A'B'C'$ and $M0 = A+B+C$. This form for the maxterms can be seen from Figure 6.5, where $M2 = (A'+B)$ and $M3 = (A' + B')$.

The minterms which a given function contains are mutually exclusive with the maxterms it contains — the minterms are the '1' outputs for the function and the maxterms are the '0' outputs. If a function contains minterm m_2 you can be certain it does *not* contain maxterm M_2. Thus, converting from a minterm expansion to a maxterm expansion is trivial, and can be done by looking at which minterms it contains and putting all the other terms into its maxterm expansion. A similar method can be used to convert from a maxterm expansion to a minterm expansion.

Although minterm and maxterm expansions are canonical or standard forms for specifying boolean expressions, they do not usually lead to the minimum size circuit implementation — the boolean theorems can almost always be applied to reduce the complexity of such an expression. Nevertheless, minterm and maxterm expansions do provide useful and standard ways to specify expressions which are more compact and easier to write than truth tables. For that reason they will be used frequently throughout the remainder of this book.

6.4 Boolean Minimization

We have seen in previous examples that a given expression can be written in a number of ways such as:

$$AB' + AB = A(B' + B) = A(1) = A$$

We have also seen that there is a direct correspondence between the structure of the expression and the resulting gate-level implementation. An implementation that requires fewer gates is almost always preferable — it will cost less to produce, it will consume less power, it will usually run faster. Thus, there is a desire when designing digital systems to derive minimal cost solutions. The process of attempting to find such a minimal cost solution is known as *minimization*, and there are a number of ways it can be accomplished. In this section we discuss using the boolean theorems introduced previously as one way. We introduce other methods for doing so in a later chapter.

6.4.1 What is a Minimal Form for an Expression?

Before introducing boolean minimization techniques, a discussion of what constitutes a minimal form is in order. In general, it is difficult to say precisely what the minimal form of an expression is without considering the actual circuit technology which will be used to implement it. Given two equivalent forms of an expression, one may be minimal when implemented in *Technology A*, while the other is the minimal form when implemented in *Technology B*. The reasons for this lie in how various technologies implement gates.

30+ years ago much design was done using a family of circuits known as TTL (transistor-transistor-logic). TTL refers to a circuit technology based on a type of transistors called bipolar transistors. Using these transistors, a complete family of logic circuits were created and used for digital design on printed circuit boards. One such family was known as the '7400 Series' and was introduced in the 1960's. A typical chip from the family was the 7402 which contained four 2-input NOR gates. Designs were created by soldering chips to a printed circuit board and wiring them together. A typical chip might contain four 2-input AND gates while another chip might contain four 2-input NOR gates or eight inverters. If you needed one inverter, you had to use a chip containing eight inverters (and the seven remaining inverters would go unused in your design). A a result, *the number of individual chips which had to be soldered onto the board* determined the final cost of the product, rather than the number of gates. TTL logic minimization was thus often done in a way to minimize the number of chips on the board. While minimizing chip count is *similar* to minimizing gate count, the two are slightly different. If a chip containing four 2-input NAND gates only used two of its NAND gates, one of the remaining two NAND gates might be used as an inverter rather than add another chip containing eight inverters to the design. Thus, with TTL, it was not uncommon to see logic implemented using gates that otherwise would not have been used for that purpose — the goal was to minimize chip count, not gate count.

On the other hand, 30 years ago a technology called nMOS was the predominant integrated circuit implementation technology. It consisted solely of n-type transistors. Because it did not rely on individual chips to implement the design but rather a collection of transistors on a silicon chip, the goal was to minimize the number of transistors required. In nMOS technology, NOR gates are superior to NAND gates (they are smaller and faster) and so nMOS designers worked to reduce their boolean equations to NOR-gate-only forms, avoiding NAND gates whenever possible. Additionally, NOR and NAND gates were always preferable to OR and AND gates (which had to be implemented using NOR and NAND gates followed by inverters).

Today's predominant technology is known as CMOS, which stands for complementary metal-oxide-semiconductor. CMOS contains both n-type and p-type transistors. Due to the differences in how n- and p-type transistors operate, however, CMOS NAND gates are often preferable to CMOS NOR gates[1].

In summary, what is considered a "minimal" form for an expression depends on the target technology. Therefore, when asked to minimize a function, your response should be "what is the minimization criteria"?

We will use *literal count* as the minimization criteria in this text. In a boolean expression, every appearance of a variable in either complemented or uncomplemented form is called a literal. The expression: $A'B + ABD + A$ has six literals. Minimizing literal count is easy to do and gives good results for many technologies.

---

[1]N-type transistors may be as much as three times as fast as similar p-type transistors. The reason is that n-type transistors rely on the movement of electrons through the silicon for their operation while p-type transistors rely on the movement of "holes" for their operation (a hole is the absence of an electron in the silicon crystal lattice). This difference in *mobility* between electrons and holes accounts for the performance difference between the transistor types. For speed reasons, it is preferable to place n-type transistors in series in a gate (as in NAND gates) rather than p-type transistors. Thus, NAND gates are often preferred over NOR gates in CMOS.

For example, consider this:

$$F = AB' + AB + C = A + C$$

The final form $(A + C)$ is preferable to $AB' + AB + C$ because it has two literals as opposed to five. Literal count is related to transistor count for CMOS gates. A 2-input NAND gate requires four transistors, and a 3-input NAND gate requires six transistors. The same is true for NOR gates. Thus, minimizing literal count will often minimize the circuit area required.

6.4.2 Minimization By Applying Boolean Theorems

A straightforward application of the boolean theorems from Chapter 4 can simplify an expression as in the following example:

$$A'B' + AB' = (A' + A)B' = (1)B' = B'$$

The first step in simplifying an expression is to determine which, if any, theorems can be used for simplification. The challenge when applying the theorems is to know when to apply which one because the order of application of the theorems can lead to different overall solutions. A little experience with boolean minimization will help you understand the various strategies to apply. The remainder of this section consists of a set of boolean minimization examples, complete with explanations.

Example 1

$$A'C + AB + BC \quad = \quad A'C + AB \qquad \text{By the consensus theorem}$$

Example 2

$$
\begin{aligned}
A'B + AB' + AB &= A'B + AB' + AB + AB & AB = AB + AB \\
&= A'B + AB + AB' + AB & \text{Commutative theorem} \\
&= (A' + A)B + A(B' + B) & \text{Distributive theorem} \\
&= (1)B + A(1) & A' + A = 1 \\
&= B + A
\end{aligned}
$$

The first step in Example 2 is to recognize that an additional AB term needs to be added to the equation so that the distributive law can be applied twice. An alternate solution is:

$$
\begin{aligned}
A'B + AB' + AB &= A'B + A(B' + B) & \text{Distributive theorem} \\
&= A'B + A & B' + B = 1 \\
&= B + A & A + A'B = A + B
\end{aligned}
$$

The alternate approach is possible because $A'B + A = A + B$ is one of the boolean theorems. Nevertheless, there will be times when duplicating terms is necessary to obtain a smaller solution.

Example 3

$$
\begin{aligned}
(A'B + AB)' &= (A + B')(A' + B') & \text{DeMorgan's} \\
&= AA' + AB' + A'B' + B'B' & \text{Multiply it out} \\
&= 0 + (A + A')B' + B' \\
&= B' + B' \\
&= B'
\end{aligned}
$$

Example 4

$$(X + Y + Z)NM + X'Y'Z' \quad = \quad X'Y'Z' + NM$$

This example looks much harder than it is. By noting that $X'Y'Z' = A$, $NM = B$, and $X + Y + Z = A'$, you can directly apply the following theorem: $A'B + A = A + B$. Thus, while multiplying it out is a good idea at times, carefully looking for such mappings will often allow you to directly reduce the equation using a single theorem.

6.4.3 Proving Equalities Using Boolean Theorems

A problem related to minimization is proving or disproving an equality. In conventional algebra, a set of rules indicate legal operations which can be applied to both sides of an equation without changing it. The techniques available in boolean algebra for this purpose are much more limited. Various methods for proving boolean equalities are given below.

Method 1: Construct a Truth Table for Both Sides

While this may not be viewed as an elegant solution method, it does work (for small numbers of variables). If the truth tables for two expressions are equal, the expressions themselves must be equal.

Method 2: Convert Both Sides to a Minterm or Maxterm Expansion

This method entails *undo-ing* any minimization that may have been done to both sides of the equality. For example, consider a 3-variable expression. If the term AB appears, it can be replaced by $ABC' + ABC$ since $ABC' + ABC = AB(C' + C) = AB$. Further, if B appears, it can be replaced by $A'BC' + A'BC + ABC' + ABC$. In both cases, the term is replaced by all the minterms it represents.

This process is shown in the example below. Between the first and second rows each term on the left hand side is replaced by the minterms it represents. In the third row this is repeated for the right hand side. Finally, the terms are all written using minterm notation and then reordered to show that the two sides are equivalent.

$$
\begin{array}{rcl}
AC + A'B + AC' & ?=? & BC' + BC + AB' \\
\underline{AB'C + ABC} + \underline{A'BC' + A'BC} + \underline{AB'C' + ABC'} & ?=? & BC' + BC + AB' \\
AB'C + ABC + A'BC' + A'BC + AB'C' + ABC' & ?=? & \underline{A'BC' + ABC'} + \underline{A'BC + ABC} + \underline{AB'C' + AB'C} \\
AB'C + ABC + A'BC' + A'BC + AB'C' + ABC' & = & A'BC' + ABC' + A'BC + ABC + AB'C' + AB'C \\
m5 + m7 + m2 + m3 + m4 + m6 & = & m2 + m6 + m3 + m7 + m4 + m5 \\
m2 + m3 + m4 + m5 + m6 + m7 & = & m2 + m3 + m4 + m5 + m6 + m7
\end{array}
$$

A similar process can be used to convert each side to a maxterm expansion to prove or disprove equality.

Method 3: Manipulate One Side So That It Equals The Other

This method consists of applying the boolean theorems to one side to make it equal the other. This may involve simplifying using $AB' + AB = A$ or a similar theorem, multiplying it out as in $A(B + C) = AB + AC$, or factoring as in $AB + AC = A(B + C)$.

Method 4: Perform the Same Operation on Both Sides

This method is similar to conventional algebra where the same operation can be performed on both sides to simplify the equation. However, *only a few operations can be applied to both sides*. In particular, only reversible operations can be applied to both sides. The operations of AND and OR are not reversible. OR-ing the same term on both sides of an equation is not permissible because OR has no inverse operation (neither does AND). NOT <u>is</u> reversible, however, and so taking the complement of both sides of an equation is an acceptable manipulation as shown here:

$$
\begin{array}{rcll}
[A + (B' + C')(B' + C)](A' + C) & ?=? & (A' + C)(A + B') & \\
A'(BC + BC') + AC' & ?=? & AC' + A'B & \text{Inverted version of previous line} \\
A'B + AC' & = & A'B + AC' &
\end{array}
$$

The first step taken in this example is to apply DeMorgan's rules to invert both sides. Simplification follows to reduce the left side to resemble the right side. Inversion is the only operation we have discussed that can legally be applied to both sides of an equation.

6.5 Incompletely Specified Functions and Boolean Minimization

The case often arises in digital design where a boolean function is not completely specified. An example of this is shown in Figure 6.6. Here, circuit block N1 generates three bits of information which is then processed by circuit block N2. Further, it is known that circuit N1 will never generate ABC=101 and will never generate ABC=111 (maybe circuit N1 is a binary code converter and the output code is designed to never contain 101 and 111). How should the truth table for circuit N2's operation be written?

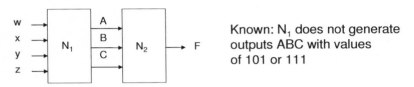

Figure 6.6: An Incompletely Specified Function

Figure 6.7(a) shows the truth table with ?'s for the unknown locations. What should go into those locations? Remember that since circuit N1 will *never* generate those input combinations to circuit N2, it really doesn't matter. It would be acceptable for N2 to output 0's in these two cases; it would be acceptable for N2 to output 1's in these two cases. *Any output value is acceptable* — in the end it just doesn't matter.

The correct way to write the truth table is shown in Figure 6.7(b). Here, × symbols are used to denote that we don't care what the output is in those two cases. An × in a truth table output is known as a *don't care* value.

A	B	C	F
0	0	0	1
0	0	1	1
0	1	0	0
0	1	1	1
1	0	0	0
1	0	1	?
1	1	0	1
1	1	1	?

(a) Truth Table

A	B	C	F
0	0	0	1
0	0	1	1
0	1	0	0
0	1	1	1
1	0	0	0
1	0	1	X
1	1	0	1
1	1	1	X

(b) Correct Truth Table

Figure 6.7: A Truth Table for an Incompletely Specified Function

How should the function of this truth table be written? One way is to write it using minterm or maxterm notation like this:

$$F = m0 + m1 + m3 + m6 + d5 + d7 = \sum m(0, 1, 3, 6) + \sum d(5, 7)$$

This indicates that rows 0, 1, 3, and 6 contain 1's and that rows 5 and 7 contain don't cares. Using maxterm notation it would be written like this:

$$F = M2\ M4\ D5\ D7 = \Pi M(2, 4)\Pi D(5, 7)$$

The next question is how to write a minimized expression for the function? If the × symbols are replaced by 0's then a minimized version of the function is shown in Figure 6.8(a). On the other hand, if the × symbols are replaced by 1's then the solution is shown in Figure 6.8(b). There are two other solutions which are possible — these are shown in Figure 6.9 for a total of four different solutions to this truth table. Since we don't care about the function's output for input combinations 101 and 111, all four of these solutions are valid. To find the minimal solution for a function in the presence of don't cares a whole family of truth tables must be created, which represent all the possible mappings of the × symbols to 0's and 1's. The smallest boolean function resulting from solving these truth tables then becomes the minimal implementation. This example shows that there *can* be a difference in which truth table gives the smallest result. In this case, mapping both don't cares to 1's leads to the smallest solution. For other incompletely specified functions a different mapping may lead to the smallest solution. Because evaluating all such possible mappings can be difficult to do using the method shown in the figure, we will learn in a later chapter how to easily and systematically investigate all such possible mappings to arrive at the optimal solution.

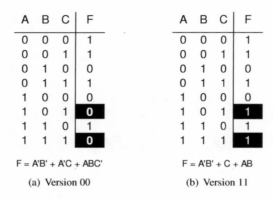

Figure 6.8: Two Solutions for Problem of Figure 6.7(b)

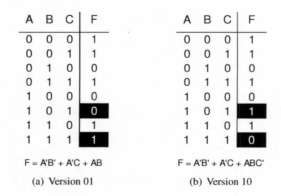

Figure 6.9: Two More Solutions for Problem of Figure 6.7(b)

6.6 Summary of Boolean Minimization

Expressions can be simplified by repeatedly applying the boolean theorems introduced previously. Doing hand minimization this way is fraught with problems because it is often not obvious in which order the theorems must be applied to result in the very simplest result. For simple expressions, however, the techniques introduced here are adequate. A graphical method of minimizing expressions (which can be shown to find optimal two-level solutions) is introduced in a later chapter.

6.7 Chapter Summary

Concepts that should be clear before moving on to the next chapter include the following:

1. DeMorgan's rules can be applied to take the inverse of a function.

2. Two major forms for boolean expressions exist: sum-of-products (SOP) and product-of-sums (POS).

3. Every truth table has a corresponding SOP expression as well as a corresponding POS expression.

4. A minterm is a product term where every variable appears in either normal or complemented form.

5. A maxterm is a sum term where every variable appears in either normal or complemented form.

6. In a minterm or maxterm expansion, the minterm or maxterm numbers correspond to the row numbers from the truth table.

7. Minterm and maxterm expansions are canonical forms and uniquely specify a given function.

8. For a given function, the set of minterms and maxterms it contains are mutually exclusive (the minterms are the '1' outputs and the maxterms are the '0' outputs). This simplifies the conversion from a minterm to a maxterm expansion or from a maxterm to a minterm expansion.

9. Boolean theorems can be applied to minimize a boolean expression.

10. What constitutes a minimal form of a boolean expression is dependent upon the technology used to implement it.

11. Literal count is a reasonable minimization criteria since input count directly relates to transistor count for many technologies and input count on gates is closely related to literal count.

12. A boolean equality can be proven by converting both sides to either minterm or maxterm expansion form and comparing.

13. A boolean equality can be proven by manipulating both sides of the equation until they are equal.

14. The only operation we have discussed that can be legally applied to both sides of an equality is NOT (apply DeMorgan's).

15. When a function is incompletely specified it will have don't care symbols in its truth table.

16. Don't care's can be mapped to any desired value to get the smallest circuit possible. Doing so may require the creation of a whole family of truth tables.

The skills that should result from a study of this chapter include the following:

1. The ability to take the inverse of a complex boolean expression using DeMorgan's rules.

2. The ability to obtain a SOP boolean equation from a truth table by inspection.

3. The ability to obtain a POS boolean equation from a truth table by inspection.

4. The ability to create an equivalent minterm expansion from either a truth table or a boolean expression.

5. The ability to create an equivalent maxterm expansion from either a truth table or a boolean expression.

6. The ability to convert a minterm expansion of an expression to a maxterm expansion of that expression.

7. The ability to simplify a boolean expression using boolean theorems.

8. The ability to prove or disprove a proposed boolean equality using the boolean theorems, by converting to a minterm or maxterm expansion, or by constructing truth tables.

6.8   Exercises

6.1. Write the minterm expansion for the function shown in Figure 6.10.

A	B	C	F
0	0	0	1
0	0	1	1
0	1	0	0
0	1	1	1
1	0	0	0
1	0	1	1
1	1	0	1
1	1	1	0

Figure 6.10: Sample Truth Table

6.2. Write the maxterm expansion for the function in the previous problem.

6.3. Take the inverse of following expression (do not further minimize):[(AB+C'+0)(A'+B'(D+C))]

6.4. Convert the following minterm expansion to a minimized boolean equation: $F = \sum m(0, 1, 4, 7)$.

6.5. Convert the following minterm expansion to an equivalent maxterm expansion: $F = \sum m(0, 1, 4, 7)$.

6.6. Write the minterm expansion for the following function: $F = A + A'B' + BC'$.

6.7. Write the maxterm expansion for the following function: $F = A + A'B' + BC'$.

6.8. Minimize the expression of problem 6.1 using boolean theorems.

Chapter 7

Gates - Part II

7.1 NAND-NAND and NOR-NOR Logic

Consider the following:

$$AB + CD = (AB + CD)'' \quad \text{Legal since } A'' = A$$
$$= ((AB)'(CD)')' \quad \text{Apply one of the complements using DeMorgan's}$$

From this we see that $AB + CD = ((AB)'(CD)')'$. Figure 7.1 shows the gate-level implementations of each of these forms of the same expression. This figure shows that two levels of NAND gates are equivalent to AND-OR logic for this expression.

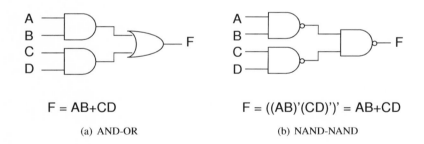

F = AB+CD

(a) AND-OR

F = ((AB)'(CD)')' = AB+CD

(b) NAND-NAND

Figure 7.1: AND-OR vs. NAND-NAND Logic

Using the alternative gate symbols introduced previously in Chapter 5, the preferred way to draw this circuit is shown in Figure 7.2. It is preferred since it emphasizes that it is an AND-OR type of function.

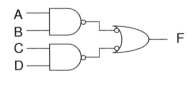

F = ((AB)'(CD)')' = AB+CD

Figure 7.2: Preferred Symbols for NAND-NAND Logic

It can be shown graphically that NAND-NAND is *always* equivalent to AND-OR as shown in Figure 7.3. First of all, adding two inverters in series does not change a value ($A'' = A$). Thus, two inverters can be placed on each of the intermediate wires without changing the logic function. Second, the inverters can be pulled into the gates themselves, resulting in the circuit show on the right side of the figure. Regardless of whether the derivation is carried out algebraically or graphically, the end result is the same: NAND-NAND logic is <u>always</u> equivalent to two-level AND-OR logic.

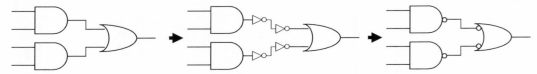

Figure 7.3: Graphical Derivation of NAND-NAND

If it is possible to use NAND gates instead of AND and OR gates, is it a good idea to do so? There are a number of reasons why it might be. First, as already mentioned, NAND gates are simpler, less costly, and faster than AND and OR gates in many technologies. Using NAND gates may result in a better implementation (cheaper, faster, lower power). Second, in the case where a circuit is built out of discrete gate chips (as with TTL), only having to keep NAND gates on hand is a benefit.

A similar conversion of OR/AND logic can be done to obtain NOR/NOR logic:

$$
\begin{aligned}
(A+B)(C+D) &= ((A+B)(C+D))'' && \text{Legal since A''=A} \\
&= (A+B)' + (C+D)')' && \text{Apply one of the complements using DeMorgan's}
\end{aligned}
$$

Figure 7.4(b) show a NOR-NOR circuit which implements this.

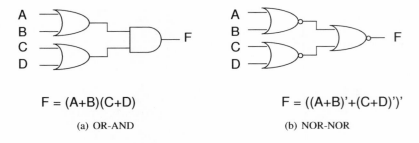

F = (A+B)(C+D)

(a) OR-AND

F = ((A+B)'+(C+D)')'

(b) NOR-NOR

Figure 7.4: OR-AND vs. NOR-NOR Logic

There is a preferred way of drawing NOR-NOR logic schematics as well as shown in Figure 7.5. The preferred symbology emphasizes that the function being performed is OR-AND. This same structure can be derived graphically in a manner similar to that done for NAND-NAND logic above.

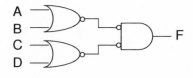

F = ((A+B)'+(C+D)')' = (A+B)(C+D)

Figure 7.5: Preferred Symbols for NOR-NOR Logic

The net result is that two layers of NOR gates are equivalent to OR-AND logic. As with NAND-NAND logic, NOR-NOR logic has the advantages of usually being faster than logic built from AND and OR gates, and only requiring a single gate type to be available.

7.2 Functionally Complete Logic Sets

A *functionally complete set* is a set of gates which can implement any possible boolean expression. The set {NOT, AND, OR} forms a complete set — there is no truth table that can be created which cannot be implemented using NOT, AND, and OR gates. We have seen that NAND-NAND can implement AND-OR logic. Does that mean that NAND gates alone can implement any possible truth table? Not quite. What is lacking is the ability to invert values. To show that NAND gates can implement any possible boolean expression (they are functionally complete in other words) we need to demonstrate that a NAND gate can also implement the NOT function. Two ways of doing so are shown in Figure 7.6.

A —[NAND]o— F = A'   '1' —[NAND]o— F = ((1)A)' = A'
                           A —

Figure 7.6: Using a NAND as a NOT

NAND gates alone are thus functionally complete — they can implement any truth table which can be constructed. An alternative method of demonstrating this is to simply show that NAND gates can be used to build all three of the basic building blocks (*i.e.* AND, OR, and NOT). We have just shown that a NAND can be used to build a NOT gate. Further, it is obvious that a NAND and a NOT together form an AND gate. All that is left to do is to show that NAND gates can be used to build an OR gate. Figure 7.7 shows how this is done.

Figure 7.7: Building an OR Gate from NAND Gates

A similar procedure can be used to demonstrate that NOR gates alone are functionally complete. First, NOR gates can be used to perform the NOT function as shown in Figure 7.8. Second, a NOR and an inverter can be used to perform the OR function. Third, NOR gates can be used to build an AND gate. The derivation for this parallels that for NAND shown above.

A —[NOR]o— F = A'   '0' —[NOR]o— F = (0+A)' = A'
                          A —

Figure 7.8: Using a NOR as a NOT

The net result is that any boolean expression can be implemented using nothing but NAND gates or nothing but NOR gates. You may wonder why determining whether a set of gates is functionally complete is important? An anecdote from the author's graduate school days helps illustrate why. When I was a graduate student, I attended a talk in which a researcher presented a new silicon circuit technology which had a number of important advantages over the conventional silicon technology of that time (nMOS). The talk focused on how to construct extremely high-density and high-speed AND-OR array structures using this new technology. The claim was that this was a superior way of creating logic circuits. Late in the talk, the question was asked about how inversion (NOT, NAND, or NOR) could be constructed using the technology. The answer was that the researcher did not know how to do so — he only knew how to construct AND and OR gates. The audience's interest in the technology changed markedly at that point — without the ability to construct inverters the technology was not viewed as useful — it did not provide a functionally complete set of gates.

7.3 Gate Symbology — Matching Bubbles

This is an important topic that many people ignore. Don't ignore it! Chapter 5 discussed that the choice of which gate symbol to use for a function is often determined by the logic function being performed. For example, the function *"F is true when A is true and B is true"* should be drawn using the AND gate of Figure 7.9(a), and the function *"F is false when A is false or B is false"* should be drawn using the AND gate of Figure 7.9(b). In both cases the gate used is really an AND gate. However, one symbol matches one way of stating the function and the other symbol matches the other way of stating the function. By using symbols which match your idea of what function is being performed, you make your schematics clearer (easier to understand). Although this is a stylistic issue, it is an important consideration. A schematic drawn with the incorrect version of the symbol is considered by many to be an incorrect schematic.

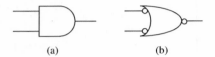

(a)   (b)

Figure 7.9: Two Symbols for an AND Gate

Continuing on with this discussion of schematic drawing, two ways of drawing NAND-NAND logic were shown above in Figure 7.1(b) and Figure 7.2. It was further stated, with respect to those figures, that the form shown in Figure 7.2 was preferable. The reason given was that it emphasized that the AND-OR function was being performed, thus making the schematic more understandable.

This leads to a general strategy for drawing schematics which is sometimes called "bubble matching", or "polarized mnemonics" (in this text we will use the term "bubble matching"). In bubble matching, the gate symbols used are chosen in such a way that if the output of a gate has a bubble on it (it is a NOR, NAND, or NOT gate) and drives the input of another gate, that gate input also has a bubble on it — the bubbles *match*. Conversely, if the output of a gate has no bubble on it (it is an AND or OR gate), then it can only drive gate inputs without bubbles. This makes schematics easier to understand as in the NAND-NAND example above. To someone reading the schematic, the bubbles can be considered to "cancel each other out" and the function is more readily apparent.

The circuit of Figure 7.10 shows a circuit drawn with and without bubble matching applied. In part (a) of the figure the function being performed is unclear without some boolean manipulations:

$$
\begin{aligned}
F &= ((AB)'(C+D)')' \\
&= AB + (C+D) \\
&= AB + C + D
\end{aligned}
$$

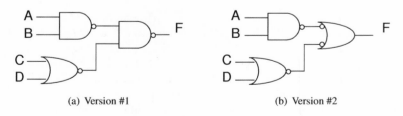

(a) Version #1   (b) Version #2

Figure 7.10: Bubble Matching

In contrast, the function in part (b) of the figure can be read by inspection (while mentally canceling the matching bubbles):

$$F = AB + (C + D) = AB + C + D$$

While this example is relatively trivial, larger examples show the benefit in significant ways. It may sometimes take a little thought to get the bubbles to match when formulating a schematic in this way. An example is shown in Figure 7.11, where converting the output NAND gate to its alternate form doesn't solve the problem.

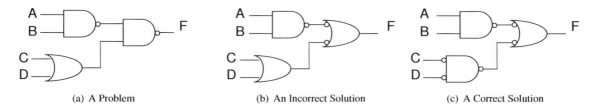

(a) A Problem   (b) An Incorrect Solution   (c) A Correct Solution

Figure 7.11: More Difficult Bubble Matching

To finish the bubble matching process in this figure, the lower OR gate of part (b) of the figure must also be converted to its alternate form. This is shown in part (c) of the figure. All interior bubbles are now matched and the function is easily written by inspection (don't forget to include the bubbles on the C and D inputs):

$$F \quad = \quad AB + C'D'$$

You can push the bubbles to either the inputs or outputs in this process. Figure 7.12(a) shows a circuit which can be bubble-matched in one of two different ways. The first way is to modify the upper-left NOR gate to use its alternate symbol, as shown in Figure 7.12(b). From this the function can be readily read off by inspection: $F' = A'B'(C + D)$ (don't forget the final output bubble implies a function in terms of F'). The second method is to replace the lower left gate *and* the output gate by their equivalent symbols as shown in Figure 7.12(c). From this the function can be read by inspection: $F = A + B + C'D'$. To verify that these two representation are equivalent, simply apply DeMorgan's rule to the first to remove the complement on F. Doing so directly results in the second form:

$$(A'B'(C + D))' = A + B + C'D'$$

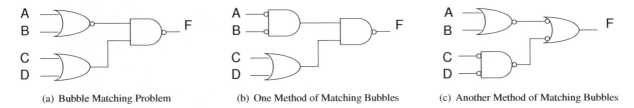

(a) Bubble Matching Problem   (b) One Method of Matching Bubbles   (c) Another Method of Matching Bubbles

Figure 7.12: Two Ways of Matching Bubbles

In summary, you can do bubble matching in one of two ways as shown above. Once this is done, it is relatively straightforward to read the function from the schematic. The choice of which method to use (inverted output or non-inverted output) will depend on the problem statement as discussed above — if the problem statement specifies when the output is FALSE, use the inverted output form — if the problem statement specifies when the output is TRUE, use the non-inverted form.

7.3.1 Bubble Matching and Reconvergent Fanout

An interesting question is whether it is always possible to do bubble matching on an arbitrary circuit consisting of gates. The answer is yes, except in one case. It is the case of reconvergent fanout, an example of which is shown in Figure 7.13. In this circuit, the quantity $(AB)'$ drives two different gates. It is the converging of those two different quantities, at the OR gate, that gives rise to the term *reconvergent fanout*. When bubble matching, either the output gate *will* have bubbles on its inputs and the middle NAND gate *will not*, or the output gate *will not* have bubbles on its inputs and the middle NAND gate *will*. A little thought will show that, for this circuit, there is no combination of gate symbols which will allow the interior wires to be bubble matched on both ends. Nevertheless, bubble matching should be done whenever possible to improve the readability of schematics.

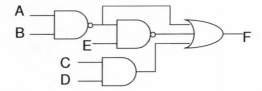

Figure 7.13: Bubble Matching and Reconvergent Fanout

7.4 Chapter Summary

Concepts that should be clear before moving on to the next chapter include the following:

1. NAND-NAND logic is equivalent to AND-OR logic (SOP form).

2. NOR-NOR logic is equivalent to OR-AND logic (POS form).

3. A functionally complete logic set is a set of logic functions which can implement any truth table that can be created.

4. NAND gates alone are functionally complete as are NOR gates.

5. When drawing schematics, you should take care to use gate symbols which match the problem statement to help make your schematics clearer.

6. Bubble matching is the process of drawing a schematic in such a form that bubbles on wire always match.

7. By doing bubble matching, the resulting schematic is easier to understand. Usually, the logic function being implemented can be written by inspection.

8. For every schematic, there are usually two forms which can be derived by bubble matching. The first has a non-inverted output. The second has an inverted output. Use the version that matches the problem statement.

The skills that should result from a study of this chapter include the following:

1. The ability to implement circuits using only NAND gates or only NOR gates.

2. The ability to determine whether a given set of functions form a logically complete set.

3. The ability to draw schematics which match the problem statement.

4. The ability to do bubble matching in a way which results in a correctly bubble-matched schematic.

5. The ability to read a bubble-matched schematic and write, by inspection, the function being performed.

6. The ability to do bubble matching in such a way that the final output is non-inverted or inverted.

7.5 Exercises

7.1. Implement the schematic of Figure 6.2(a) using only NOR gates.

7.2. Implement the schematic of Figure 6.2(a) using only NAND gates.

7.3. Implement the schematic of Figure 6.2(b) using only NOR gates.

7.4. Implement the schematic of Figure 6.2(b) using only NAND gates.

7.5. Assume you have been given the assignment to design a function to determine whether the value of a 4-bit boolean value is equal to zero. A 4-bit value is zero if all of its individual bits are zero. The output of this function should be TRUE when the value of the 4-bit value is zero. Draw a single-gate which implements this function. Use the correct symbol and justify your answer.

7.6. Assume you have been given the assignment to design a function to determine when the value of a 4-bit unsigned boolean value is not equal to fifteen. The output of this function is FALSE when the value of the 4-bit value is equal to fifteen and TRUE otherwise. Draw a single-gate schematic which implements this function. Use the correct symbol and justify your answer.

7.7. Bubble match the schematic of Figure 7.14 to have a non-inverted output. Then, write the logic function the circuit implements by inspection.

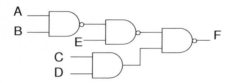

Figure 7.14: Problem Circuit

7.8. Bubble match the schematic of Figure 7.14 to have an inverted output. Then, write the logic function the circuit implements by inspection.

7.9. Use DeMorgan's to verify that your answers to the previous two problems are equivalent.

Chapter 8

An Introduction to Gate-Level Design Using SystemVerilog

At this point in your studies, you should be adept at drawing and understanding gate-level schematics since these are the ways that designs have been represented in the previous chapters. Historically, schematics were a popular mechanism for describing logic. Computer-aided design tools (CAD tools) called *schematic editors* were used to enable engineers to draw the schematics representing the desired circuit. However, if you were to use such tools long enough for reasonably sized designs, you would quickly begin to realize, that schematic-based design has significant limitations.

Hardware descriptions languages (HDL's) are similar in some ways to programming languages, but were designed expressly for the purpose of describing digital circuits. HDL-based design looks and feels somewhat like software development. With software, you enter your program code, compile it, and execute it. With an HDL, you enter your HDL code, compile it, and simulate it. When you are done simulating (and have convinced yourself that your design will operate as desired) you then *synthesize it to a gate-level circuit* using a CAD tool specifically designed for that purpose. Such a tool is called a *synthesizer* and is able to take a text-based description of a design (written in an HDL) and from it generate a description of the needed gates, flip flops, and wires that implement that design. In the process, a synthesizer will perform a number of design optimizations (such as logic minimization), relieving the designer from having to do them and thus greatly improving the designer's productivity. For example, synthesizers can make tradeoff decisions regarding how to implement various circuit structures. For example, there are a number of different ways to implement an addition circuit with names like *ripple carry* and *carry look ahead*. Some of these are fast but require many gates while others are slower but require less circuitry. A synthesizer, when needing to implement an adder might choose between the various options it knows about and choose the *smallest* version that is fast enough to meet the required *speed* of operation.

Hardware Description Languages first appeared in the 1980's. The two most popular HDL's today are Verilog and VHDL. Both have similar capabilities for describing hardware. Verilog is considered by many to be a bit simpler to learn and use than VHDL.

Both Verilog and VHDL are *standardized* languages, meaning their language specifications have gone through a standards development process sponsored by the IEEE. Commercial CAD tools are available which help engineers use these languages to design circuits.

Languages often go through multiple revisions over the years as new features are added. In the past decade a revision of the Verilog language, called SystemVerilog, was released and is now supported by commercial CAD tools. The use of SystemVerilog is the subject of this text. Once you know SystemVerilog, you should also be able to understand older designs written in previous versions of Verilog.

Many books have been written on Verilog and SystemVerilog and the reader is referred to them if a more detailed treatment than what is provided here if desired. Some may object to the basic treatment provided here since the language is so extensive — however, the goal is to get you up and working with SystemVerilog in this introductory digital design course as soon as possible rather than providing a detailed reference on SystemVerilog.

It is important to remember that, for purposes of this text, the differences between SystemVerilog and Verilog are very slight. The vast majority of what is presented herein is simply standard Verilog. The SystemVerilog-specific language features introduced here were selected to help you as a beginning designer avoid many of the common coding errors that designers make when first learning Verilog. The list is fairly short and mainly includes: the *logic* type, the *always_comb* and *always_ff* enhancements to *always* blocks, enumerated types, and enhancements to *case* statements.

8.1   Three Important Rules Regarding Designing using an HDL For Digital Systems Design

There are three extremely import things you need to understand and remember as you begin to learn to design using an HDL such as SystemVerilog. If you will learn and internalize these concepts, you will avoid some serious errors that beginners often make when starting out.

1. You must remember that when designing using an HDL, you are *not* writing a computer program which will be compiled and then executed sequentially like C or Java. Rather, you are describing a set of hardware building blocks and their interconnections.

2. You must remember that when designing using an HDL, you are *not* writing a computer program which will be compiled and then executed sequentially like C or Java. Rather, you are describing a set of hardware building blocks and their interconnections.

3. You must remember that when designing using an HDL, you are *not* writing a computer program which will be compiled and then executed sequentially like C or Java. Rather, you are describing a set of hardware building blocks and their interconnections.

Now that it has been repeated to you three times, I hope you will remember it. It is crucial to your understanding. As you learn to write SystemVerilog I also encourage you to constantly think about just what circuit structure is going to result from a particular piece of SystemVerilog code. The sooner you do that the sooner you will be able to engineer circuits which do what you want, at the speeds you want, with the minimum number of gates.

8.2   Levels of Design Abstraction in SystemVerilog

SystemVerilog supports the description of hardware at a number of different levels of abstraction. The lowest level of abstraction is called *structural design*, where the circuit is described by listing the gates it contains and how they are interconnected. The following statement represents an AND gate in SystemVerilog:

```
and(q, a, b, c);
```

Signal q is the output and a, b, and c are the inputs. A full circuit can be designed this way by listing the desired gates. Interconnections between gates are implied by the signal names in each gate statement.

The next higher level of abstraction in SystemVerilog is called *dataflow design*, and allows the use of C-like expressions to specify logic. The following dataflow statement would implement a 3-input AND function in SystemVerilog:

```
assign q = a & b & c;
```

which states that signal q is to be assigned (thus the *assign* keyword) the value derived from AND-ing together signals a, b, and c.

The third level of design abstraction in SystemVerilog we will discuss is called *behavioral verilog*. Below is a behavioral way of specifying the design of a 2:1 MUX selector circuit. The *always_comb* keyword states that a section of combinational logic circuitry is to be described. This block of circuitry will react any time any of the *sel*, *a*, or *b* signals change value. When one of them does change value, the *if-then-else* logic then specifies what the circuit is to do.

```
always_comb
   if (sel)
      q = b;
   else
      q = a;
```

The attraction of both dataflow and behavioral SystemVerilog coding is that much of the detailed work of mapping your HDL design to a specific set of gates and memory elements is done for you by the SystemVerilog *synthesis* tool, which converts the more abstract circuit descriptions you enter into an optimized design. By relieving you of a tremendous amount of detailed work, CAD tools can greatly improve your productivity. In the balance of this chapter we introduce structural SystemVerilog design as an easier way to enter digital designs than schematics. The other levels of SystemVerilog design will be introduced later in this text.

8.3 Basic Structural SystemVerilog Design

A structural SystemVerilog design is simply a textual listing of the gates and wires making up a circuit. Figure 8.1 is a simple gate-level circuit and Program 8.3.1 is the structural SystemVerilog design for it.

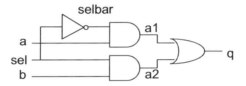

Figure 8.1: A Simple Gate Level Circuit

Program 8.3.1 SystemVerilog Code for Circuit of Figure 8.1

```
module mux21(
      // Define the types and directions of the ports
      output logic q,
      input logic sel, a, b
      );

   // Declare some internal signals
   logic selbar, a1, a2;

   not(selbar, sel);
   and(a1, selbar, a);
   and(a2, sel, b);
   or(q, a1, a2);

endmodule
```

Verilog and SystemVerilog are case-sensitive ("module" is different from "MODULE"). In general, all SystemVerilog keywords are lower-case. The first line in Program 8.3.1 declares that a module named "mux21" is being described.

The module has four wires connected to its input and output ports. The inputs are named *sel*, *a*, and *b*. The output is named *q*. These all have the data type of *logic*. Three additional signals named *selbar*, *a*1, and *a*2 are declared which are internal to the module (they don't enter or exit the module on ports). Four gate instantiations are then provided which define the logic for the module.

In the figure, each gate corresponds to one line in the body of the SystemVerilog program. The calling convention for a gate is:

```
gateType(output, input1, input2, ..., inputk);
```

SystemVerilog contains the following built-in gates for your use: *not*, *buf*, *and*, *or*, *nand*, *nor*, *xor*, and *xnor*. These are called built-in gates because they are built into the language — they are always available for your use.

With the exception of the *not* and *buf* gates, all of them take an arbitrary number of inputs. Just what is a *buf* gate? It is a non-inverting inverter — that is, it takes a single input signal and outputs a non-inverted version of that signal. You may use a *buf* where you simply want to rename or duplicate a signal — logically the output wire of a *buf* has the same value as the input wire but they are distinct signals!

8.3.1 Structural Gate Instantiations are Concurrent Statements

The various gate instantiations in Program 8.3.1 are *concurrent* statements (as opposed to *sequential*) statements. This means they do not execute in order but rather are structural declarations of a collection of circuit elements. Another word for such a listing of gates and interconnections is called a *netlist*. Thus, the ordering of the gates in Program 8.3.1 could be listed in any order desired as shown in Program 8.3.2.

Program 8.3.2 Equivalent SystemVerilog Code for Circuit of Figure 8.1 - Statements Have Been Re-Ordered

```
module mux21(
        // Define the types and directions of the ports
        output logic q,
        input logic sel, a, b
        );

    // Declare some internal signals
    logic selbar, a1, a2;

    // Declare the gates in any order desired
    and(a2, sel, b);
    not(selbar, sel);
    or(q, a1, a2);
    and(a1, selbar, a);

endmodule
```

8.4 Declaring Wires in SystemVerilog

There were seven wires in Program 8.3.1 (sel, a, b, q, $selbar$, $a1$, and $a2$). Four of these inputs to or outputs from the module and were thus declared as a part of the module definition header. Three were local wires: $selbar$, $a1$, and $a2$ — this means that they don't enter or exit the module through its ports but rather are used to internally wire together the circuitry inside the module.

Input and output wires to a module must be declared in SystemVerilog. A compilation error will result if you fail to declare them. The declaration of local wires is optional, however. This can lead to very difficult-to-find problems. Mis-spelling a local wire name in your design will not generate a compilation error - your circuit just won't work because it will be wired up differently than you had intended. Finding such errors can be very difficult. An example is shown in Program 8.4.1.

Program 8.4.1 Incorrect SystemVerilog Code Due to Wire Name Mis-Spelling

```
module mux21(
        output logic q,
        input logic sel, a, b);

    logic a1, a2;

    not(selbar, sel);
    and(a1, selbar, a);
    and(p2, sel, b);
    or(q, a1, a2);

endmodule
```

Figure 8.2 shows the circuit corresponding to Program 8.4.1. Can you see where an undeclared wire has been used? If you were to enter such a typo in your design and not notice, it may take a lot of debugging in a simulator to find this problem. So, take care to ensure that mis-spellings don't result in mis-wired circuits of this kind.

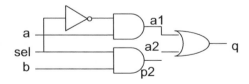

Figure 8.2: Circuit of Program 8.4.1

To avoid the problem of Program 8.4.1, you can prefix your designs with a *macro* which causes the SystemVerilog compiler to issue a warning or error if an undeclared net name is used in your design. This is shown in the top line of Program 8.4.2, telling the compiler that there is no default type of net in this design and therefore an undeclared net is an error. Note that the first character on the line is *not* a normal single quote — it is a back-quote, found on the same key as the tilde on many keyboards[1]. With this included, compiling Program 8.4.2 will generate an error, thereby warning you of the design flaw in your SystemVerilog code.

---

[1]Note, there is a difference of opinion within the design community about whether this feature of SystemVerilog (not needing to declare wires before using them) is a good thing or a bad thing. Some think it leads to hard-to-find bugs in SystemVerilog code (and can even lead to latent bugs in *completed* designs). Others feel that all the extra typing required to always declare signals before using them leads to even more bugs in designs.

Program 8.4.2 Adding a Macro to Detect Undeclared Net Names

```
`default_nettype none    // Force error on undeclared net names

// Note that the module definition syntax here is different from the
// rest of the text.  This is an older syntax for module definitions.
module mux21(q, sel, a, b);
  output logic q;
  input logic sel, a, b;

  // Declare local signals
  logic selbar, a1, a2;

  not(selbar, sel);
  and(a1, selbar, a);
  and(a2, sel, b);
  or(q, a1, a2);

endmodule
```

As noted in the program's comments, the use of this macro requires the use of an older-style of Verilog module definition. Otherwise, compilers will throw errors. The full explanation for why this is the case is beyond our scope here. To use this style of module definition, you re-declare the module's inputs and outputs with their directions and types *after* the module statement while just listing the input and output signal names in the module statement.

For the remainder of this text, module definitions will be shown using the newer form. However, if you choose to use the macro as in Program 8.4.2, then you MUST use the older module definition syntax to avoid compiler errors.

What is the author's recommendation in this regard? I feel that the small amount of additional typing required to use the older style module declarations is well worth the trouble for the troubleshooting that the macro provides.

8.5 CAD Tool Design Flow

The use of SystemVerilog CAD tools to do digital design entails a number of steps as shown in Figure 8.3. The first step is to create a design by entering a text file containing the design ("mux21.sv" in the figure). The next step is usually to simulate the design using a simulation program. This will verify that the design operates as intended. In order to do a simulation, however, the design must first be *compiled*. This process is similar to compiling a C or Java program — the compiler reads the input text file and checks it for syntactical errors (missing semicolons, etc). An intermediate format of the compiled design is generated if there are no syntactical errors. This intermediate form can then be simulated by a simulator program.

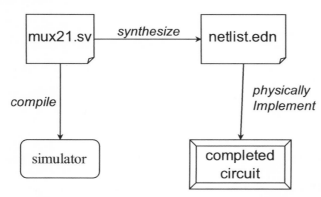

Figure 8.3: SystemVerilog-Based Design Flow

The next step in the development process is to convert the SystemVerilog code into a hardware design. As mentioned previously, a synthesizer is used for this purpose. The synthesizer reads the SystemVerilog source file and converts it to an intermediate form. Unlike the compiler, however, the synthesizer program's main goal is to determine the smallest set of gates and other circuit elements which will implement the design. The result of synthesis is some form of *netlist*. A netlist is a file containing a listing of the set of circuit elements the synthesizer has determined are required to implement the original SystemVerilog design. A common netlist format is EDIF (Electronic Design Interchange Format).

Ultimately, the netlist must be converted into a description of a physical circuit which can be constructed. This step may be done in a number of ways and using a number of CAD tools, depending on the technology being targeted (custom silicon integrated circuit, FPGA, etc), but the end result is always a set of computer files which can be used to physically realize the circuit.

In the case of an FPGA (see Chapter 25), the FPGA vendor will provide tools which will *map*, *place*, and *route* the circuit elements for your design onto an FPGA chip. The result of that process is a *bitfile*, or set of configuration bits. These bits, when downloaded into an FPGA chip will customize that chip to perform the function of the design. In contrast, in the case of a custom integrated circuit the result is the creation of a set of geometric mask data which is then used in the fabrication of the integrated circuit in a semiconductor manufacturing plant.

8.6 Chapter Summary

This chapter has presented the basics of gate-level SystemVerilog design using a simple example or two. By following the examples given, you should be able to use SystemVerilog to describe any logic gate-based circuit you desire to design.

In addition to what has been presented here, there is a significant amount of tool-specific information you need to know to successfully use a SystemVerilog CAD tool system to actually compile, simulate, and synthesize a design. Consult your instructor, TA, or tool documentation for details on how to perform those steps.

The key points with regard to SystemVerilog-based design include:

1. Every SystemVerilog module is declared within a module definition. This specifies the module name, its port names, and the directions and widths of those ports.

2. Wires local to a module may be declared. However, their declaration is optional, which may result in subtle design errors. Using the `` `default_nettype=none `` macro will cause the compiler to require the declaration of local wires. To use it, however, you must then use the old-style Verilog module definition syntax.

3. SystemVerilog is case-sensitive.

4. A SystemVerilog design is not a sequential program which is executed line-by-line like a program, but rather it is a specification of a circuit structure. It is more like a textual schematic than a computer program in this sense.

The skills that should result from a study of this chapter include the following:

1. The ability to understand the simple SystemVerilog circuits shown in the code examples in this chapter.

2. The ability to combine circuits you have already designed into higher-level circuits.

3. The ability to draw the resulting schematic of any simple SystemVerilog design (which uses the constructs introduced thus far).

8.7 Exercises

For all of the problems below, enter the designs using SystemVerilog. Enter the code and do enough of a compilation to complete a syntax check of your code to ensure that it is syntactically correct (you need not fully simulate it, however). How you do that will depend on the particular CAD tools you are using. If you are running the SystemVerilog from the command line, a simple *vlog filename.sv* will be sufficient.[2]

8.1. Design the circuit of Figure 5.21.

8.2. Design the circuit of Figure 5.22.

8.3. Design the circuit of Figure 5.23.

8.4. Design the circuit of Figure 5.24.

8.5. Design the circuit of Figure 5.21 but use the "default_nettype none" macro and older style of module definitions.

8.6. Design the circuit of Figure 5.22 but use the "default_nettype none" macro and older style of module definitions.

8.7. Design the circuit of Figure 5.23 but use the "default_nettype none" macro and older style of module definitions.

8.8. Design the circuit of Figure 5.24 but use the "default_nettype none" macro and older style of module definitions.

---

[2]However, when running from the command line you must always first create a work library for the compiler to operate with. This is done by first executing *vlib work* once from the command line in the directory where you intend to work. The *vlog* command will then put its compiled files in intermediate form into that work library.

Chapter 9

Gate-Level Arithmetic

The concept of representing numbers using binary encodings was presented in Chapter 2 and methods for performing arithmetic on those encodings was presented in Chapter 3. Now that you understand the basics of implementing logic functions using gates, this short chapter presents gate-level circuits which can be used to implement that arithmetic. Remember that here as well as in the rest of this text, unless otherwise specified, all arithmetic performed is done using either unsigned or 2's complement numbers.

The logical question to ask is how to tell what the number representation used is for a given example? There are two answers. The first is that it should be obvious from the context. The second is more interesting — the arithmetic circuits used for adding and subtracting unsigned numbers are identical to the arithmetic circuits used for adding and subtracting 2's complement numbers (this is likely another reason that 2's complement is the signed number representation of choice). Put another way, the bit-level computations for unsigned arithmetic are identical to those for 2's complement arithmetic.

9.1 A Hardware Adder

Consider the case of adding two 3-bit numbers together. One approach would be to write a 6-input, 4-output truth table (three bits each for A and B and four bits for the result). This is a very large truth table (64 rows). However, given enough time (and a knowledge of how to minimize 6-variable functions), you would be able to design a two-level logic circuit to implement it.

Another solution is called a *ripple-carry adder*. A block diagram for a 3-bit version of such an adder is shown in Figure 9.1. The circuit consists of three identical copies of a circuit called a *full adder*. A sum bit is produced at each bit position as well as a carry out bit to the next more significant position. These carry bits are the C's in the design. This circuit mimics how we do hand addition by propagating carries from one column to the next.

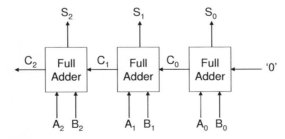

Figure 9.1: Block Diagram for a 3-bit Ripple-Carry Adder

91

A truth table for one stage or cell of such an adder is shown in Figure 9.2 along with the corresponding gate-level circuit. The truth table mirrors the information used in Chapter 3 to do hand addition. For example $0+1+1 = 2 = 10_2$ and $1 + 1 + 1 = 3 = 11_2$.

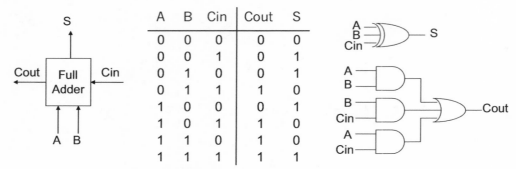

A	B	Cin	Cout	S
0	0	0	0	0
0	0	1	0	1
0	1	0	0	1
0	1	1	1	0
1	0	0	0	1
1	0	1	1	0
1	1	0	1	0
1	1	1	1	1

Figure 9.2: Full Adder Truth Table and Circuit

The design procedure for an n-bit adder would be to create a module (call it *fullAdder*) out of gates, and then replicate it as many times as needed (three times for a 3-bit adder, four times for a 4-bit adder, ...). This is called a ripple-carry adder because as the addition proceeds, carries ripple from less significant bit positions to more significant bit positions.

An n-bit adder constructed this way will contain many more than two levels of logic between the least significant input bits and the most significant output bits. The delay for such an adder will thus be a function of how many bits wide it is. The slowest path through a ripple carry adder is from the A_0 and B_0 inputs to the S_{n-1} output.

If the operands are unsigned, the final carry out can be used as the most significant bit of the result (adding two n-bit operands results in an $n + 1$-bit result). This was discussed in Chapter 3. Also as discussed there, if the operands are signed, you should first sign-extend both operands, and then use an $n + 1$-bit adder to compute the full result.

A subtracter can be designed in an almost identical manner. A full subtracter is a circuit which subtracts two bits from one another (taking into account any borrow from the column to the right) and which produces a difference bit and a borrow bit to the column to the left. The truth table for a full subtracter is shown in Figure 9.3 along with the block diagram of a 3-bit subtracter. The truth table mirrors the information used in Chapter 3 when doing hand subtraction such as $0 - 0 - 1 = -1 = 11_{2c}$ and $0 - 1 - 1 = -2 = 10_{2c}$.

A	B	Brin	BrOut	D
0	0	0	0	0
0	0	1	1	1
0	1	0	1	1
0	1	1	1	0
1	0	0	0	1
1	0	1	0	0
1	1	0	0	0
1	1	1	1	1

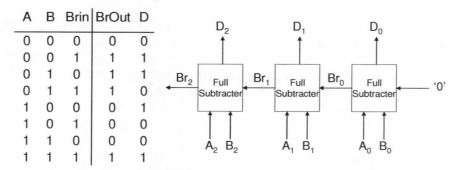

Figure 9.3: Full Subtracter Truth Table and 3-Bit Subtracter

9.2 An Adder/Subtracter Module

What if you want a circuit which can either perform an addition or a subtraction, depending on the value of a single-bit control signal? Remember that $A - B = A + (-B)$. Thus, negating B and adding it to A will accomplish a subtraction. The *equivalent of this* can be accomplished using the circuit of Figure 9.4, where $addSub\#$ controls whether the circuit is to add or subtract.

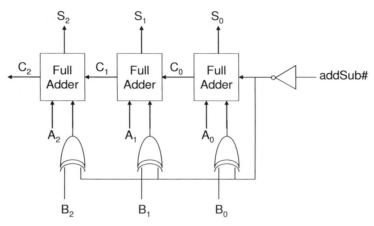

Figure 9.4: Adder/Subtracter Block

The key to understanding this circuit is to remember how to negate a 2's complement number such as B. This is done by inverting the bits of B and adding 1.

The adding 1 part is easy - it is the output of the inverter on the right which feeds into the initial carry in of the rightmost full adder. So, how about the inversion? If you were to examine the truth table for an XOR gate with inputs x and y, you could convince yourself that when $x == 0$ the output is y and when $x == 1$ the output is y'. Thus, an XOR gate is a conditional inverter, controlled by the x input. For example, consider what happens when $addSub\#$ = '1' (adding) as shown in Figure 9.5(a). The carry-in to the rightmost full adder is '0', and the 'B' inputs to the full adders are the original B_k signals. The circuit therefore computes $S = A + B$.

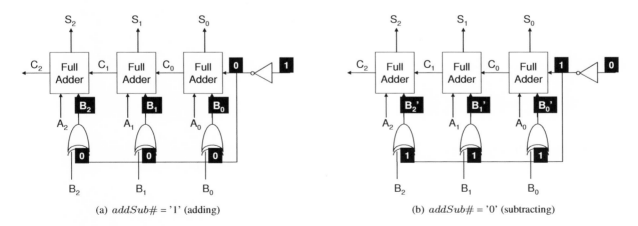

(a) $addSub\#$ = '1' (adding) | (b) $addSub\#$ = '0' (subtracting)

Figure 9.5: Two Adder/Subtracter Cases

Now consider part (b) of the figure where $addSub\#$ = '0' (subtracting). The carry-in to the rightmost full adder is now a '1', and the 'B' inputs to the full adders are the INVERSE of the original B_k signals. This accomplishes the negation and the +1. The circuit therefore computes $S = A + (-B) = A - B$.

9.3 Chapter Summary

This short chapter has introduced some basic gate-level logic circuits for adding and subtracting unsigned numbers and for adding and subtracting 2's complement numbers.

The key high-level points to master from this chapter include the following:

1. Adder and subtracter modules are easily designed using truth tables and gates.

2. An adder/subtracter can be created from an adder and some XOR gates.

The skills that should result from a study of this chapter include the following:

1. The ability to design adders, subtracters, and adder/subtracters of any width from gates.

9.4 Exercises

9.1. A previous chapter discussed detecting overflow in 2's complement addition by looking at the sign of both operands and the sign of the result. Derive the logic equation required to detect overflow this way and draw a gate-level schematic of the resulting overflow detection circuit.

9.2. Overflow in 2's complement addition can also be detected by looking at the carry-in and carry-out values of the most significant full adder in the addition circuit. Create some test cases which do and don't overflow for both positive and negative numbers, and determine what logic would be required to detect overflow in this manner. Write the logic equation for this and draw a gate-level schematic of the resulting overflow detection circuit. Is this significantly simpler than the result to the previous problem?

9.3. Show how to implement a sign-magnitude adder using circuits from this chapter.

9.4. Write the SystemVerilog code for a 1-bit full adder module.

9.5. Write the SystemVerilog code for a 1-bit full subtracter module.

Chapter 10

Higher Level Building Blocks: Multiplexers, Decoders, and Lookup Tables

10.1 Introduction

You now know enough to design and implement essentially any combinational logic function. Recall that a *combinational* circuit is one whose outputs depend only on the current state of its inputs. Logic gates are sufficient to implement any combinational circuit. As seen previously, a number of different sets of logic gates can be used including: AND-OR-NOT, NAND only, or NOR only.

Most digital designs use building blocks beyond simple gates to implement combinational circuits. These building blocks are built out of gates but, by creating higher-level building blocks, many design tasks are simplified. This chapter introduces three such building blocks: multiplexers, decoders, and lookup tables.

10.2 Multiplexers

Consider the following problems statement:

> Design a circuit which has 2 data inputs (A and B), one control input (S), and one output (F). The function to be performed is that when $S = 0$, F gets the value on A and when $S = 1$, F gets the value on B. In other words, S selects whether A should be sent to the output or B should be sent to the output.

The first step in solving this problem is to write a truth table as shown in Figure 10.1. When $S = 0$, the output indeed will get the same value that is on the A input. When $S = 1$, the output will get the same value that is on the B input.

S	A	B	F
0	0	0	0
0	0	1	0
0	1	0	1
0	1	1	1
1	0	0	0
1	0	1	1
1	1	0	0
1	1	1	1

$$F = S'A + SB$$

Figure 10.1: A Truth Table For a Multiplexer

The schematic for this circuit is shown in Figure 10.2(a) and follows directly from the minimized truth table equation. This circuit is so commonly used in digital systems design that it has a special name and its own symbol. It is called a *multiplexer* or MUX for short. Its function is to select between one of two different values and pass the selected value to the output. Its schematic symbol is shown in Figure 10.2(b). The major advantage of drawing the symbol rather than the schematic of part (a) is that it makes the schematic more readable — the schematic clearly indicates that the function being performed is a selection (or multiplexing) function.

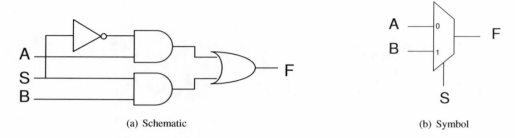

(a) Schematic   (b) Symbol

Figure 10.2: Multiplexer Schematic and Symbol

Various MUX symbols have been employed over the years. Two of these are shown in Figure 10.3. For this text we will use the MUX symbol shown in Figure 10.2(b). It has the advantage that the shape indicates selecting one from among multiple choices. We will choose to label the inputs with the S value they correspond to. As a result, there is never any question about which input is selected when S=0 vs. when S=1. This is true even when the symbol is rotated or mirrored when drawn in a schematic.[1]

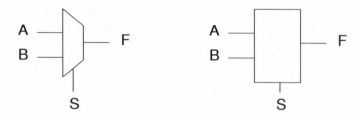

Figure 10.3: Other MUX Symbols

The form of the boolean equation for a MUX helps convey its function:

$$F = S'A + SB$$

When $S = 0$ the equation reduces to:

$$F = 1(A) + 0(B) = A$$

and when $S = 1$ the equation reduces to:

$$F = 0(A) + 1(B) = B$$

Thus, the selection is done merely by AND-ing the inputs with the select signal and its inverse.

---

[1]It is important to note here that the MUX symbol as shown here is simply a shorthand for a collection of NOT/AND/OR gates. There is no "MUX" gate — it *is* built out of gates or transistors like any other digital circuit.

10.2.1   A 4:1 Multiplexer

The notion of selection can be extended to select from among more than two candidates. Figure 10.4(a) shows a 4:1 MUX symbol. It requires two select bits because it is selecting from among four candidates. The two select bits form a 2-bit binary word (address) in the range $\{00, 01, 10, 11\}$:

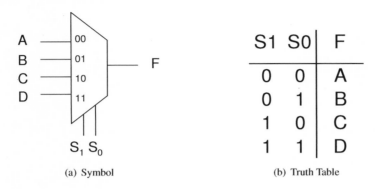

(a) Symbol   (b) Truth Table

Figure 10.4: A 4:1 MUX

A common way to describe the operation of a 4:1 MUX is with a symbolic truth table as shown in Figure 10.4(b). This truth table shows that when the select lines are 00 the output is A, when the select lines are 01 the output is B, and so on. The equation for a 4:1 MUX is:

$$F = S_1' S_0' A + S_1' S_0 B + S_1 S_0' C + S_1 S_0 D$$

This equation was arrived at, not by creating a truth table and solving a KMap (6 variables would be required), but rather by realizing that, as with the 2:1 MUX above, the selection is being done by AND-ing the inputs with various combinations of the select lines and their complements. After looking carefully at the pattern of S signals and their complements in the equation above, can you write the logic equation for an 8:1 MUX?

The equation for a 4:1 MUX could be turned directly into a gate-level schematic from the equation above. Or, Figure 10.5 shows a way to build a 4:1 MUX out of 2:1 MUX circuits. The only way to really understand why this circuit works is to simply set the S signals to various values and trace through what values appear on the output. You should do so.

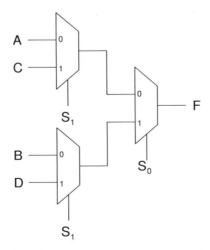

Figure 10.5: Building a 4:1 MUX out of 2:1 MUX Circuits

This same method can be used to create a MUX of arbitrarily large size out of smaller MUX blocks. When this is done we refer to it as a *MUX tree*.

10.3 Multi-Bit Wires in Schematics

The same boolean operation is often applied to all the bits of a multi-bit wire in a digital design. For example, consider the operation of selecting between two different 4-bit buses (a *bus* is a bundle of wires), using a MUX. One way to draw this would be to draw all four wires for each of the inputs and each of the outputs. This is tedious and clutters schematics. Figure 10.6 shows this schematic along with a shorthand way to draw it where the widths of the buses are shown. It is assumed that a four-bit bus named "A" will consist of the bits: $A_3 A_2 A_1 A_0$. Can you see why a single bit S wire is all this is needed in this schematic? Wherever possible, draw schematics using buses to make them more readable.

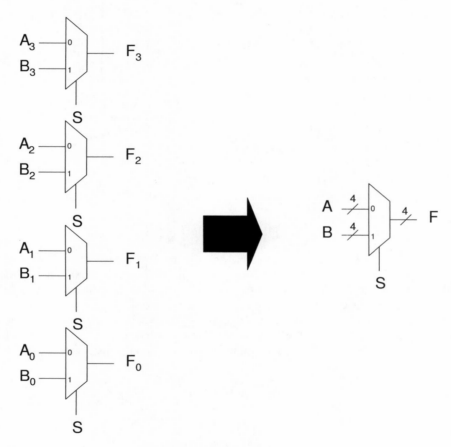

Figure 10.6: A Multi-Bit MUX

10.4 Using Multiplexers for Logic

An interesting use of multiplexers is to perform AND-OR logic. On the surface, this seems to have little to do with selecting between alternatives (which is what the multiplexer was designed for). Nevertheless, it shows the versatility of multiplexers, and offers some additional insights into ways of thinking about truth tables, KMaps, and boolean algebra.

Consider the truth table of Figure 10.7 and the corresponding circuit of the same figure. Note that the first four rows of the truth table correspond to the situation where $A = 0$, and that the last four rows correspond to $A = 1$. Now look at the circuit. When $A = 0$, the value on the upper MUX input is passed to the output. When $A = 1$, the value on the lower MUX input is passed to the output. Further, note that in the first four rows of the truth table that $F = 0$. Thus, a 0 has been wired to the upper MUX input. In the last four rows of the truth table, it turns out that $F = B + C$. Thus, the expression $B + C$ has been wired to the lower MUX input. In essence, we have divided the truth table into two different truth tables — one for the case where $A = 0$ and one for the case where $A = 1$. The solution to each of these *sub-truth tables* is wired to the MUX inputs.

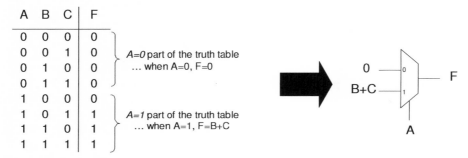

Figure 10.7: Using a Multiplexer for Logic

There is no reason why A must be the select input to the MUX. Figure 10.8 shows this same truth table redrawn so that B is the leftmost variable. The function for the top half is wired to the upper MUX input, the function for the bottom half is wired to the lower MUX input, and B is wired to the select input on the MUX.

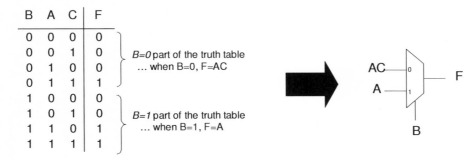

Figure 10.8: Using a Multiplexer for Logic - Second Version

Finally, consider Figure 10.9. Here, the truth table has been redrawn yet again to place C in the leftmost column, and a MUX with C as the select input used to implement the function.

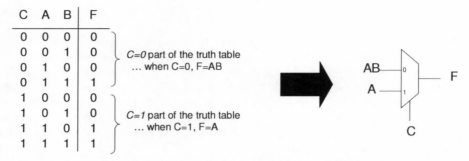

Figure 10.9: Using a Multiplexer for Logic - Third Version

Larger multiplexers can be used in a similar fashion to implement larger functions. Figure 10.10 shows such an example. In this case, the truth table is partitioned into four sections corresponding to $AB = 00$, $AB = 01$, $AB = 10$, and $AB = 11$. Each of these *sub-truth tables* is then solved, and the resulting functions fed into the corresponding MUX inputs. As before, the order of inputs can be changed to place different signals on the MUX select wires. Figure 10.11 and Figure 10.12 show two other versions with different input orderings for their truth tables (all of these implement the same function).

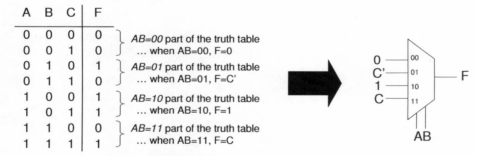

Figure 10.10: Using a 4:1 Multiplexer for Logic

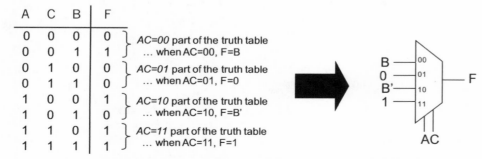

Figure 10.11: Using a 4:1 Multiplexer for Logic - Second Version

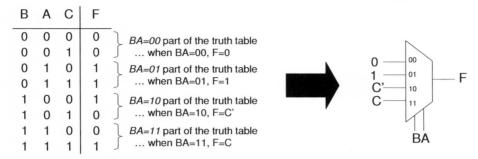

Figure 10.12: Using a 4:1 Multiplexer for Logic - Third Version

In summary, multiplexers can be used to perform arbitrary logic functions through a process related to what is known as *Shannon Decomposition*. They do this by allowing the truth table to be partitioned into a set of *sub-truth tables*. The solution to each of these *sub-truth tables* is then computed and then wired to the appropriate multiplexer input. Using multiplexers in this way is not of academic interest only — one use of this which we will see in later chapters is how to use this technique to partition and implement large truth tables using lookup table circuits.

10.5 Decoders

Another commonly used building block in digital systems is called a decoder. Consider the truth table shown in Figure 10.13(a). This truth table is different from others encountered thus far in that it has multiple outputs. This is simply a way of writing four different truth tables at once.

This circuit has two inputs and four outputs. The inputs can be thought of as forming a 2-bit address. When the input value (address) is 00, the first output is TRUE. When the input value (address) is 01, the second output is TRUE, and so on. Only one output will be TRUE for any input combination.

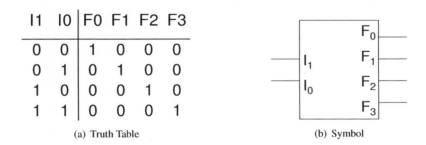

(a) Truth Table   (b) Symbol

Figure 10.13: A 2:4 Decoder

The logic equations for this truth table include the following:

$$F_3 = I_1 I_0$$
$$F_2 = I_1 I_0'$$
$$F_1 = I_1' I_0$$
$$F_0 = I_1' I_0'$$

A little thought will show that this is simply a minterm generator circuit. That is, $F_0 = m0$, $F_1 = m1$ and so forth. This is called a decode function and a circuit which implements it is called a *decoder*. This particular decoder is called a 2:4 decoder because it has two inputs and four outputs

A circuit symbol commonly used for a 2:4 decoder is shown in Figure 10.13(b). At times you may be confused about which output is asserted for which input combination. Remember, the two inputs form a 2-bit address ($I_1 I_0$)

in the range $\{00, 01, 10, 11\}$. The subscript on the output signal name *is* the value of the address which that output corresponds to. Thus, F_2 is asserted when $I_1 I_0 = 10$, F_3 is asserted when $I_1 I_0 = 11$, and so on.

Decoders can be designed with any number of inputs desired. If the decoder has k inputs,then it will have 2^k outputs. Figure 10.14 shows the symbol for a 3:8 decoder. As with the 2:4 decoder, only one output is TRUE at a time and the outputs are simply the minterms of the input combinations. Thus, when $I_2 I_1 I_0 = 011$, output F_3 will be asserted, and when $I_2 I_1 I_0 = 110$, output F_6 will be asserted. Can you write the output equations for a 3:8 decoder?

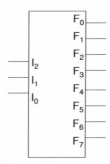

Figure 10.14: A 3:8 Decoder

Decoders find widespread use in digital systems. One example would be in selecting the function for an ALU. The word ALU stands for arithmetic logic unit. An ALU is found in all computers and typically performs the arithmetic and logic functions supported by the computer (ADD, AND, NOT, PASS, etc).

A table for a typical simple ALU is given in Table 10.1. Imagine that four different control signals are required to control the ALU. One signal tells the ALU that an ADD operation is to be performed, another tells the ALU that an AND operation is to be performed, and so on. For this problem, a 2:4 decoder is exactly the desired circuit. A truth table showing this is given in Figure 10.15.

Table 10.1: Functions for a Simple ALU

Code	Operation	Notes
00	PASS	Pass first operand through
01	ADD	Add two operands together
10	AND	AND two operands together
11	NOT	Invert first operand

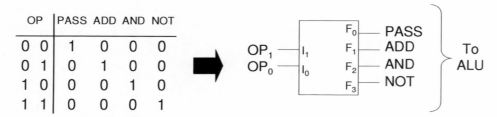

Figure 10.15: Using a Decoder as a Part of an ALU Control Circuit

10.6   When to Use Multiplexers and Decoders

Multiplexers and decoders are higher level building blocks which make the design process easier. That said, should you really use MUX and decoder circuits to implement arbitrary boolean functions as shown in this chapter? The answer (as always) is that it depends on the technology being used. Back in the days of TTL, designs were created by soldering chips onto printed circuit boards. Building a MUX out of NOT, AND, and OR gates took multiple chips, and therefore significant area on the board. TTL MUX and decoder chips were often used as a result, greatly saving on board area when used in a design. In particular, using MUX chips to help implement arbitrary logic functions by decomposing truth tables was widely used (both because it resulted in fewer chips on the board and also because it made hand implementation of large truth tables feasible).

On the other hand, when designing an integrated circuit from scratch the basic building block is a transistor. Any logic needed is constructed from transistors. Using a MUX or decoder for implementing arbitrary logic may cost extra transistors compared to implementing the same function using transistor-based NAND and NOR gates or other structures.

Finally, consider the modern-day use of logic synthesis CAD tools. These are computer programs which, given a description of the logic function to be performed, will generate an implementation optimized for the target technology. When using such a CAD tool, you may specify your design using multiplexers, decoders, gates, and other building blocks, but the CAD tool will *distill* that description down to the basic logic equations being implemented. It will then generate an implementation optimized for the target technology. As such, the manner in which your design was specified may be irrelevant and the final implementation generated by the CAD tool may bear little structural resemblance to the design you input. What does all this mean? To summarize:

- Any boolean function represented by a truth table can be implemented using AND, OR, NOT, NAND, and NOR gates. Thus, there is no need for any other kind of logic building block.

- Much of design is about abstraction. The use of higher-level building blocks helps designers think about the functions being performed at a higher level of abstraction. It also makes schematics easier to understand, and designs easier to maintain.

- For some technologies, these higher-level building blocks may simply be abstractions used to help improve the productivity of designers — they may simply be *macro cells* in a library which, when used in a design, are expanded by the CAD tools into their constituent gates.

- For other technologies, using these higher-level building blocks may actually result in a lower cost design. TTL design is a good example of this.

- Whether the availability of higher-level building blocks simply makes design easier or actually makes the final design smaller and therefore less costly depends on the target technology.

10.7 Read-Only Memories (Lookup Tables)

It may seem strange to include a section on read-only memories in a chapter on combinational circuits. The term "memory" conjures up thoughts about "storage" and "state". These are not issues associated with purely combinational circuits (combinational circuits are those whose outputs depend solely on the current values of their inputs). The reason that read-only memories (ROMs) are treated here is that they can be viewed as simply direct hardware realizations of truth tables and therefore are appropriate in a discussion of methods for implementing combinational circuits.

A ROM is a memory which can be read from but not written to. Clearly, at some point in the past it was written to, otherwise it would not contain any useful data. However, this was done before the ROM was put into use in a circuit, and so from the user's perspective the data stored in the ROM is non-volatile — it is permanently stored in the ROM.

Figure 10.16 shows a ROM along with a table denoting its contents. A ROM with k inputs will contain 2^k locations. Setting the inputs (the address) to a particular value will cause the ROM to output the data stored at that address (each ROM location contains a single bit). Setting all its inputs low will cause the ROM to output a '1' (from address 0), and setting all its inputs high will cause the ROM to output a '0' (from address 7). This is the memory-centric view of a ROM.

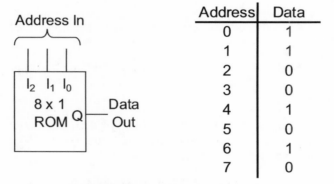

Address	Data
0	1
1	1
2	0
3	0
4	1
5	0
6	1
7	0

Figure 10.16: A Read-Only Memory

ROM blocks are not limited to having a single-bit output. Rather, each ROM location can be designed to hold as many bits as needed. Figure 10.17 shows such a ROM. Conceptually, you could think of this ROM as four individual ROMs, one for each bit of the output. Physically, however, such a ROM would be constructed as a single unit since doing so requires less circuitry than four separate ROMs would.

Address	Data
0	1101
1	0010
2	0000
3	1001
4	1011
5	1101
6	0000
7	0011

Figure 10.17: A ROM With a 4-Bit Output

The address/data table of Figure 10.16 can also be viewed as a truth table. This is shown in Figure 10.18. The addresses to the ROM are the inputs to the truth table (ABC), and the ROM output is the truth table output. If the ROM were initialized with the truth table contents for this function, the function could be implemented using just the ROM. This represents the logic view of a ROM.

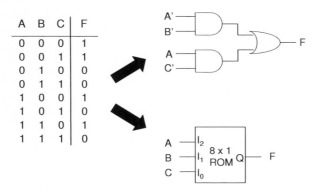

Figure 10.18: Using a ROM for Logic

Using a ROM in this way is no different from how many programs are written. A *lookup table* in programming terminology is usually an array which is initialized with a set of data values. During program execution, the lookup table is used to perform a mapping from input values to output values. If a program made heavy use of a hyperbolic tangent function ($tanh(x)$), it might make sense to initialize a large array to hold a table of $tanh(x)$ values. When needed during execution of the program, the table could be accessed (a simple array lookup) to evaluate the $tanh(x)$ function. This may be significantly faster than computing the $tanh(x)$ for every new value of x as needed during program execution. In this case, x would be used as the address into the $tanh()$ lookup table.

Using a ROM as a lookup table in a circuit is similar to this — the ROM holds the contents of the function to be evaluated (a boolean function in this case), and is used to *look up* the desired function output given the function's inputs. The function's inputs *are* the addresses used to index into the lookup table.

ROMs can be constructed to be high-speed and low cost in many technologies. CAD tools are available which take, as input, a truth table and output a ROM design which implements that function. In this case, no logic minimization is required — just fill out the truth table and let the CAD tool do the rest. Lookup tables are often referred to using the acronym "LUT".

10.8   Chapter Summary

This chapter has introduced a number of higher level building blocks. Key concepts from this chapter include the following:

1. A multiplexer (or MUX) performs a *select* operation — it selects from among a collection of inputs.

2. A MUX can be built from gates. However, using MUX symbols in schematics makes them more readable.

3. A MUX with a k-bit select signal will have 2^k inputs. Common sizes for MUXes include: 2:1, 4:1, 8:1, 16:1.

4. Larger MUX blocks can be built from smaller MUX blocks.

5. Drawing buses in schematics rather than individual wires helps to increase the readability of the schematic.

6. In addition to selection, multiplexers can be used for computing arbitrary logic functions.

7. A decoder is a minterm generator. It has k inputs and 2^k outputs, only one of which is asserted at any given time.

8. Read-only memories (ROMs) can be used as lookup tables (LUTs) to compute boolean functions.

The skills that should result from a study of this chapter include the following:

1. The ability to use MUX, decoder, and ROM blocks in a design..

2. The ability to write the logic function for and draw the gate-level schematic of any size MUX desired.

3. The ability to write the logic function for and draw the gate-level schematic of any size decoder desired.

4. The ability to use MUXes to implement arbitrary boolean functions.

5. The ability to use ROM blocks (LUTs) in designs.

10.9 Exercises

10.1. Implement an 8:1 MUX out of 4:1 MUX blocks.

10.2. For the following few problems, consider the following function: $F(ABCD) = \sum m(2, 5, 6, 7, 11, 13, 14, 15)$ Use a 2:1 MUX (A as the MUX select signal) to implement this function.

10.3. Use a 2:1 MUX (D as the MUX select signal) to implement the function from above.

10.4. Use a 4:1 MUX (AD as the MUX select signals) to implement the function from above.

10.5. Use a 16:1 MUX (ABCD as the MUX select signals) to implement the function from above.

10.6. Use a 4:16 decoder and some gates to implement the function from above.

10.7. Is the set of gates consisting of inverters and 2:4 decoders logically complete? If not, show why not. If so, show why.

10.8. Draw the gate level schematic for a 3:8 decoder using AND OR, and NOT gates.

10.9. Draw the gate level schematic for a 4:1 MUX using AND, OR, and NOT gates.

10.10. Show how to build an 8:1 MUX out of a 3:8 decoder, some AND gates, and a single OR gate.

10.11. Write the output equation for an 8:1 MUX.

10.12. Write the output equations for a 3:8 decoder.

Chapter 11

Continuing on With SystemVerilog - Hierarchical Design, Constants, and Multi-Bit Signals

In Chapter 8 it was stated that schematics were cumbersome for creating large designs but no real justification or elaboration was provided. So, just what are some of the reasons for that?

First, schematics can be cumbersome. Consider the task of designing a 2:1 MUX for selecting between two different 32-bit buses, as shown in Figure 11.1. You have two choices to design this circuit using a schematics editor. The first is that you might find a symbol for a 32-bit 2:1 bus MUX in the schematic library. If so, you could use it. If not, you must create one. This would entail inserting 32 different 2:1 1-bit MUXs into a design, pulling the individual bits out of the input buses to feed into those MUXs, and combining all 32 MUX outputs into a new 32-bit output bus. Depending on your schematic editor tool, this might be a time-consuming task. The first challenge with schematics, then, is that you are strongly affected by the availability of pre-defined building blocks in the schematic library. If the exact block you need is available in the library, you can use it but otherwise you have to build it. Since every circuit is slightly different, the number of building blocks required in your schematic library grows and grows and grows and you may find yourself constantly building slightly modified versions of existing blocks to use in your designs.

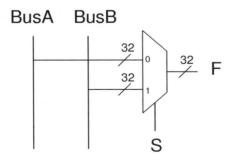

Figure 11.1: A 2:1 Bus MUX

Second, schematics are not parameterizable. If you create a 32-bit 2:1 MUX, you cannot use it on 39-bit buses - you will need a 39-bit 2:1 MUX for that. It would be very useful to have a way to design a 2:1 MUX which could take any width inputs, and produce that same width output. This is difficult to do with schematic editor tools. The second challenge of schematics is thus their lack of parameterizability — they are inflexible (non-parameterizable) circuit descriptions.

Finally, schematics provide few, if any, high level abstractions to help you efficiently design complex structures. In contrast, HDL's such as SystemVerilog provide a variety of abstractions to simplify your design work.

107

11.1 Creating Hierarchy Via Structural Instantiation

In Chapter 8 the gate-level design of a 2:1 MUX was presented in Program 8.3.1. Once a $mux21$ module has been created, it can be used anywhere as a building block in higher-level designs. Program 11.1.1 shows how to use three $mux21$ modules to create a 4:1 MUX (compare this code with Figure 10.5).

Program 11.1.1 Structural SystemVerilog Code for 4:1 MUX

```
module mux41(
      output logic q,
      input logic[1:0] sel,
      input logic a, b, c, d);

  logic tmp1, tmp2;

  mux21 M0(tmp1, sel[0], a, b);
  mux21 M1(tmp2, sel[0], c, d);
  mux21 M2(q, sel[1], tmp1, tmp2);

endmodule
```

This design has a number of new SystemVerilog syntax features over the previous one seen in Chapter 8:

1. This design is considered *structural* in that it is constructed by instancing previously-defined building blocks. While the 2:1 MUX design of Program 8.3.1 is built by structurally instancing logic gates, those gates are built into the SystemVerilog language. In contrast, here you are structurally instancing a module you previously designed.

2. The *sel* wire is defined to be two bits wide. The bits are numbered $sel[1]$ and $sel[0]$ where $sel[1]$ is the most significant bit. You access the bits of this wire using C-like array notation.

3. Since the *sel* input is two bits wide it is defined separately from the other inputs (which are one bit wide).

4. There is no need to break the port declarations up into separate lines as was done in this example — they could have been run into a single line so that the module statement was a single line.

5. The body of this module instances three copies of the previously defined $mux21$ module. When instantiating a previously-defined module, the calling convention is:

   ```
   moduleName instanceName(io1, io2, ..., iok);
   ```

   An *instanceName* is required. This is a unique identifier which is used for the instance name of the module being inserted. It is used to differentiate between the different copies of the $mux21$ in your design when you are viewing a representation of your design in a CAD tool.

When instancing a module, be sure to list the wires connected to its ports in the same order they were declared (when the *mux*21 module was originally declared in this case). Or, an alternative way to do this is to specify the parameters by name, as in Program 11.1.2. Here, each module port is listed by name along with the wire that is wired to that port. You don't need to rely on the order of the ports when you instance a module this way, but can list them in any order desired. This is obviously a safer way to design in that you need not remember the exact order of the originally declared ports.

Program 11.1.2 SystemVerilog Code for 2:1 MUX Using Named Port Associations

---

```
module mux41(
        output logic q,
        input logic[1:0] sel,
        input logic a, b, c, d);

    logic tmp1, tmp2;

    mux21 M0(.q(tmp1), .s(sel[0]), .a(a), .b(b));
    mux21 M1(.s(sel[0]), .a(c), .b(d), .q(tmp2));
    mux21 M2(.a(tmp1), .b(tmp2), .q(q), .s(sel[1]));

endmodule
```

11.1.1 Semantics of Module Instantiation

When you instance something like above, you are *structurally instantiating* a copy of that circuit module and inserting it into your design. A structural SystemVerilog design is thus <u>not</u> a program which is executed sequentially one line at a time like C or Java. Rather, it is a static collection of circuit instantiations (blocks). No order is implied between the blocks — they can be in any order you want. The module instantiations <u>imply</u> a structural circuit design.

11.2 Specifying Constants in SystemVerilog

There will be times when you need to specify a constant value as the input to a module in SystemVerilog. The general form for specifying a constant is:

```
#bits'base Value
```

An example would be:

```
4'b0001
```

which is a 4-bit value whose contents in binary are '0001'. Another example would be:

```
4'h1
```

which is the same as the previous example, but the value is specified in hex. Finally,

```
4'd1
```

is also '0001'. A few other constants include:

```
1'b0         // 0
1'b1         // 1
12'h0FF      // 000011111111
5'd11        // 01011
4'b00        // An error - must specify 4 bits
2'b00        // 00
5            // No width or base are given.  This will consist of 101 which
             // is then zero-padded on the left to be as wide as needed.
```

It turns out that there are variety of rules regarding constants in SystemVerilog which will not be detailed further here. They revolve around things such as (a) which parts of the syntax given above for constants are optional?, (b) how is the value to be interpreted if they are omitted? and (c) what happens if the width specifies more digits than the value specifies — what values are filled into the missing positions? Consult any of a number of on-line resources for answers to these questions.

11.3 Accessing Bits of Multi-Bit Wires in SystemVerilog

You declare a multi-bit wire like this:

```
logic[hi:lo] wireName;
```

Examples include:

```
logic[7:0] myByte;
logic[3:0] myNibble;
logic[15:0] busA, busB, busC;
```

Accessing the bits of multi-bit wires is more powerful than in C:

```
myByte[7]      // The most significant bit (MSB) of myByte
myNibble[0]    // The least significant bit (LSB) of myNibble;
myNibble[2:1]  // The middle two bits of myNibble
busA[11:8]     // Four bits taken out of the middle of busA
```

As shown, you can access a range of bits from a multi-bit wire, the result itself being a multi-bit wire. This is done using what is called *slice notation*. The order of the indices is always "more significant index" on the left, "less significant index" on the right. This is incorrect:

```
busB[3:9]  /* Incorrect */
```

These examples also show that C-style comments are allowed. Either double-slash "//" or "/* ... */" will work, and have the same semantics as in C (use "/* ... */" for multi-line comments).

11.4 More on Naming - Modules, Instance Names, and Wires

Using the same name for an instance name and a wire name will result in an error in SystemVerilog. This is shown in Program 11.4.1. Choose a convention and then follow it to ensure you don't have name clashes. One convention might be: (a) start all wire names with a lower-case letter, and (b) make instance names all upper-case.

Program 11.4.1 SystemVerilog Code With a Name Clash

```
...
myModule a1(a1, sel, b);   // Error - instance 'a1' clashes with wire name
myModule A2(a2, sel, b);   // OK - SystemVerilog is case-sensitive
...
```

11.5 Hierarchical Design Flow

When designing structurally using SystemVerilog, you most likely will start by defining the low level building blocks you desire. Our creation of a *mux*21 module above is one such building block (although in reality it is really too small of a building block to define as a module). Lower level building blocks are then combined into larger designs such as the *mux*41 above. A design hierarchy is created in the process. The top level of the design hierarchy is the final design.

The convention is to put each module definition in its own file. Lower level modules in the hierarchy need to be compiled first, before files that instance them are compiled. If you are using a GUI-based SystemVerilog development system, it will handle all this for you. If you want to compile from a command line, however, you would do a compilation like this (consult your tool documentation for the specific name of the compilation command):

```
vlog mux21.sv
vlog mux41.sv
```

The two commands compile the design files, starting with the lowest level modules in the hierarchy. If later you were to modify file "mux41.sv", you would only need to run the second of those two commands. Another option is to put all the files on the same command line like this so they all get recompiled any time you make a change and that "mux21.sv" gets compiled before "mux41.sv" does. This is:

```
vlog mux21.sv mux41.sv
```

11.6 Chapter Summary

This chapter has presented the basics of SystemVerilog hierarchical design using a set of simple examples. In addition, it described the use of multi-bit wires and also how to express constant values in SystemVerilog.

The key points with regard to SystemVerilog-based design include:

1. Once modules are defined, they can be instanced in other designs. The syntax is:

   ```
   myModule instanceName(io1, io2, ...);
   ```

2. Instance names are required when structurally instancing previously-defined modules.

3. There are two ways to instance modules in SystemVerilog. One lists the parameters in order, the other uses named port associations.

4. SystemVerilog supports the specification of constants like this: "4'b0100".

5. Multiple bits from a multi-bit bus can be accessed using what is called slice notation: "busA[11:8]".

6. Hierarchical design allows low level building blocks to be first defined and then used to build up more and more complex sub-circuits. The top level circuit in the hierarchy is the final design.

The skills that should result from a study of this chapter include the following:

1. The ability to understand the simple SystemVerilog circuits shown in the code examples in this chapter.

2. The ability to combine circuits you have already designed into higher-level circuits.

3. The ability to draw the resulting schematic of any simple SystemVerilog design (which uses the constructs introduced thus far).

Chapter 12

Karnaugh Maps

As was discussed earlier, minimizing a boolean equation using the boolean theorems can be difficult since it is sometimes unclear in what order the theorems should be applied to achieve the smallest result. This chapter presents a graphical technique known as Karnaugh Maps (KMaps for short) which makes it possible to obtain minimum solutions in a straightforward manner.

12.1   Truth Tables to KMaps

Consider the truth table shown in Figure 12.1 and note that there is a 1 in the first two rows. We know that this function can be simplified as follows:

$$F = A'B' + A'B = A'$$

A	B	F
0	0	1
0	1	1
1	0	0
1	1	0

F = A'

Figure 12.1: A Simple Truth Table With Adjacent "On" Minterms

This simplification is due to the application of what is often called the simplification theorem: $AB' + AB = A$. Another way to see this directly from the truth table, without resorting to boolean manipulations, is to observe that A'B' (00) and A'B (01) are adjacent in terms of gray code (they differ by exactly one bit). Any time we see the sum of two adjacent product terms (in terms of gray code), we can immediately apply the simplification theorem. Some additional examples include:

$$F = ABCD + AB'CD = ACD$$

and

$$F = A'B'C' + A'BC' = A'C'$$

113

It can be difficult to spot adjacent minterms in a truth table. In the truth table of Figure 12.2(a), the two TRUE minterms are adjacent in terms of gray code but are not physically adjacent in the table. Writing the truth table with its rows in gray code order makes it easier to see, as shown in Figure 12.2(b). Further, note that the top row and the bottom row are considered to be adjacent to one another in this re-ordered truth table.

A	B	F
0	0	0
0	1	1
1	0	0
1	1	1

F = B

(a) Normal Order

A	B	F
0	0	0
0	1	1
1	1	1
1	0	0

F = B

(b) Gray Code Order

Figure 12.2: Truth Tables With Rows Written in Different Orders

A different form of writing a truth table, known as a Karnaugh Map (KMap), is commonly used to simplify identifying adjacent minterms and maxterms. Figure 12.3 shows the truth table of Figure 12.2(a) rewritten in KMap form. The A variable is written across the top of the KMap and the B variable is written down the left side. By indexing into the KMap using A and B as the column and row indices, we see that the KMap is simply a different way of writing a truth table — in the end both contain exactly the same information. Further, note that if two squares are physically adjacent in a KMap they are adjacent in a gray code sense and thus the simplification theorem can be applied.

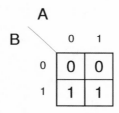

Figure 12.3: A KMap for the Truth Table of Figure 12.1

To apply the simplification theorem to the KMap of Figure 12.3, circle the two adjacent 1's and write down the resulting term. This is shown in Figure 12.4 where the circled 1's make up the expression: $A'B + AB$ which is equal to B. This can be seen graphically by noting that if B is TRUE it doesn't matter whether A is TRUE or FALSE — the output will be TRUE. Another way to do this is to look at the 1's that have been circled and find the variable that changes within the circled 1's. In this case it is the A variable. That variable is dropped from the expression leaving just B behind. In this example, A is irrelevant as long as B is TRUE.

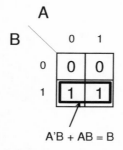

A'B + AB = B

Figure 12.4: Solving a KMap

Another truth table and KMap is shown in Figure 12.5, where three of the minterms are TRUE. Solving this KMap requires circling two groups of 1's (you cannot circle three 1's at once - you can only circle two at a time here). An algebraic equivalent to this KMap solution is given by:

$$
\begin{aligned}
F &= A'B + AB' + AB \\
&= A'B + AB' + AB + AB \\
&= (A' + A)B + A(B' + B) \\
&= B + A \\
&= A + B
\end{aligned}
$$

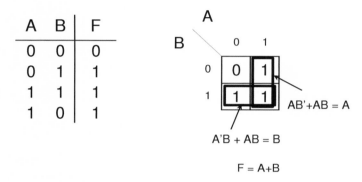

Figure 12.5: Solving Another KMap

Once again, for each pair of circled 1's, determine which variable changes and drop it. Clearly, the graphical method takes fewer steps than the algebraic method. In the end, however, all that is happening is that adjacent squares in the KMap are simplified using the simplification theorem: $AB' + AB = A$.

An irreducible KMap is given in Figure 12.6. This is the KMap for the XOR function. It contains no adjacent 1's and therefore cannot be reduced in any way — only individual 1's can be circled.

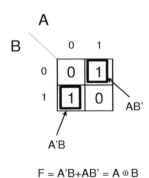

Figure 12.6: A KMap Which Cannot Be Reduced

12.2 Three-Variable KMaps

KMaps can be extended to more than two variables. Figure 12.7 shows a 3-variable KMap. As with 2-variable maps, adjacent squares in the map are adjacent in a gray code sense and thus the simplification theorem can be applied. Note the order of the rows in this KMap — these are written in gray code to ensure that the adjacency property is maintained. The minterm locations in the KMap are also labeled in this figure (the maxterm locations use the same numbering).

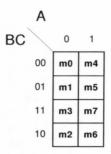

Figure 12.7: A 3-Variable KMap and Its Minterm Locations

A 3-variable KMap and its solution is given in Figure 12.8. The left half of the figure shows three different groups of 1's that could be circled. Two of these are shown using bold boxes and one is shown using a dashed box to make it easier to see. Note how two different groups of two 1's are circled to complete the solution shown on the right. Note also that the term $B'C$ is not needed (it is the term in the dashed box). The two 1's making it up are already covered by AB' and $A'C$. In this case the grouping $B'C$ is redundant and not needed.

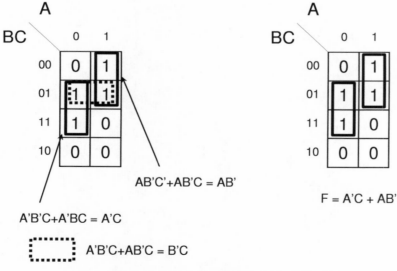

Figure 12.8: A 3-Variable KMap and Its Solution

Consider now the KMap of Figure 12.9. This shows something new — the top and bottom rows of the KMap are adjacent in a gray code sense and therefore 1's on the top row can be grouped together with 1's on the bottom row.

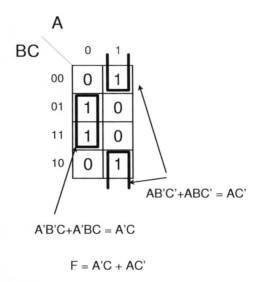

$$F = A'C + AC'$$

Figure 12.9: Another 3-Variable KMap and Its Solution

12.3 Minterm and Maxterm Expansions and KMaps

Mapping a minterm expansion to a KMap is a trivial task. Each minterm corresponds to one location in the KMap. An example of such a mapping is shown in the left half of Figure 12.10. Each minterm corresponds to a single '1' in the KMap; 0's are placed in the remaining KMap locations. Likewise, a maxterm expansion can be used to quickly fill in a KMap as shown in the right half of this same figure. Each maxterm corresponds to a '0' in the KMap; all the remaining locations are filled in with 1's.

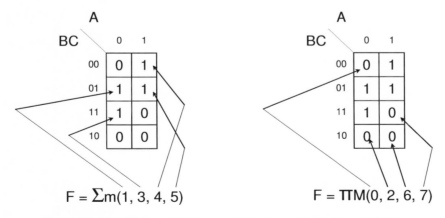

Figure 12.10: Mapping Minterm and Maxterm Expansions to KMaps

12.3.1 Circling More Than Two 1's

There are three basic rules in solving a KMap. The first is that only adjacent 1's can be circled. The second is that all 1's must be circled (at least once). The third is that 1's must be circled in power-of-2 groups. This is shown in Figure 12.11. Here, a group of four 1's are circled to result in the term *B'*, and a group of two 1's are circled to result in the term *AC*. Note that one of the 1's has been circled twice - this is perfectly acceptable. Also note that all of the 1's have been covered by at least one circle.

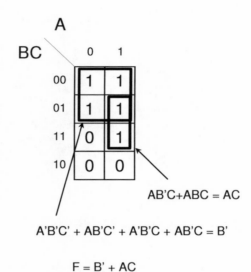

F = B' + AC

Figure 12.11: Circling Four 1's in a KMap

When circling four 1's at once, you are really applying the simplification theorem twice *in one fell swoop* as shown here:

$$
\begin{aligned}
F &= A'B'C' + AB'C' + A'B'C + AB'C \\
&= B'C' + B'C \\
&= B'
\end{aligned}
$$

Just as when circling two 1's, examine the circled terms to determine which variables change within the group of circled 1's, and drop them from the expression. In this case, however, two variables will be dropped. In Figure 12.11, it turns out that both *A* and *C* change within the group of four and so all that is left is *B'* for that group.

A final 3-variable KMap and its solution is shown in Figure 12.12. Here, two different groups of four 1's have been circled. Note how one of the groups (C') spans the top and bottom rows of the KMap.

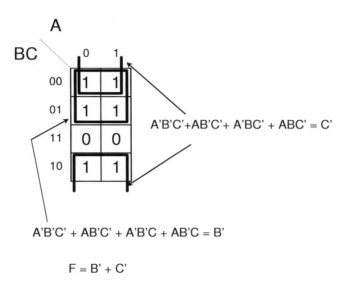

A'B'C'+AB'C'+ A'BC' + ABC' = C'

A'B'C' + AB'C' + A'B'C + AB'C = B'

F = B' + C'

Figure 12.12: A Final 3-Variable KMap

12.4   Four-Variable KMaps

The 3-variable map is easily extended to a 4-variable map as shown in Figure 12.13. As with the rows, the columns have been numbered using a gray code to ensure that adjacent locations in the map can be reduced using the simplification theorem. The minterm locations are marked in the figure.

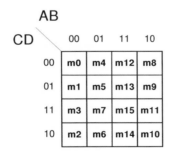

Figure 12.13: A Four-Variable KMap With Its Minterm Locations Marked

Larger groups of 1's can be circled in a 4-variable map as shown in the example of Figure 12.14, where a group of eight 1's has been circled (*D*). As with 3-variable maps, the top row and bottom row of the map are adjacent in the map. The leftmost and rightmost columns are also adjacent.

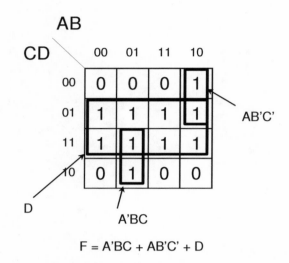

$$F = A'BC + AB'C' + D$$

Figure 12.14: A Four-Variable KMap and Its Solution

The four corners are also all adjacent as shown in Figure 12.15.

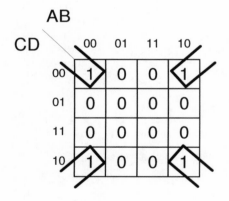

A'B'C'D' + AB'C'D' + A'B'CD' + AB'CD' = B'D'

Figure 12.15: Illustration of B'D'

Plotting minterm and maxterm expansions on a 4-variable KMap is straightforward. Minterms map to 1's on the map and maxterms map to 0's as shown in Figure 12.16 (compare to Figure 12.13 to get the minterm and maxterm location numbers).

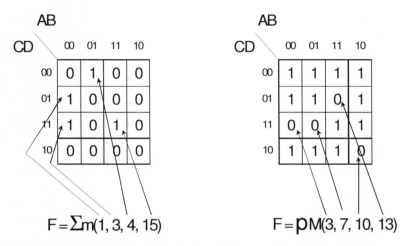

Figure 12.16: Mapping Minterm and Maxterm Expansions to KMaps

12.5 Plotting a Boolean Equation on a KMap

It is a straightforward operation to plot a boolean equation on a KMap. An example is shown in Figure 12.17 where each product term in the equation is mapped to its corresponding KMap locations. Note that a two-variable product term maps to two locations on a 3-variable KMap while a one-variable product term maps to four locations on such a map. A three-variable product term would map to a single location.

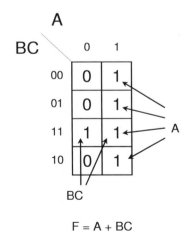

F = A + BC

Figure 12.17: Boolean Equations to KMaps

12.6 Deriving Product of Sum Expressions from KMaps

All of the examples so far have focused on deriving SOP expressions from KMaps. It is also possible to derive a POS expression from a KMap. An example is shown in Figure 12.18. Here, the function for F' (that's right: F') is written by circling the 0's in the map. The entire equation is then inverted to obtain a POS expression for F. With a little practice, you will learn how to read POS expressions directly from a KMap without first writing the equation for F' and then inverting.

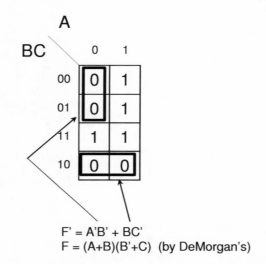

F' = A'B' + BC'
F = (A+B)(B'+C) (by DeMorgan's)

Figure 12.18: Product Of Sums (POS) From a KMap

12.7 Solving a KMap With Don't Cares

Don't care values can appear in KMaps just as they do in truth tables[1]. An example is shown in Figure 12.19. As mentioned previously, don't cares can be mapped to either 0's or 1's. They are trivially dealt with in KMaps — if circling an × leads to a larger group of 1's to circle, then do it. If not, then don't. The example of Figure 12.19 shows that the minimum solution in this case is found by circling one of the ×'s and not the other.

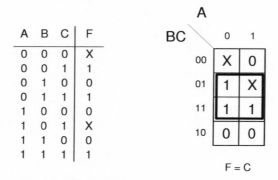

A	B	C	F
0	0	0	X
0	0	1	1
0	1	0	0
0	1	1	1
1	0	0	0
1	0	1	X
1	1	0	0
1	1	1	1

F = C

Figure 12.19: Don't Cares in KMaps - Circle Them When They Help - Ignore Them When They Don't

---

[1]Do you now understand that a KMap is nothing more than a truth table written in a different way? There is nothing that can be represented with a truth table that cannot be represented with a KMap.

12.8 Finding Optimal Solutions Using KMaps

The discussion in this chapter thus far has demonstrated the use of KMaps through a series of worked examples, where the minimum solution was relatively trivial to determine. In this section, we present a formal method for finding a minimum KMap solution. In all of the discussion which follows, SOP solutions are the focus. However, this discussion applies equally well to deriving POS solutions provided: (1) references to 1's are replaced with references to 0's, and (2) the technique shown in Section 12.6 is used to read groups of 0's off the KMap.

Definition An implicant is a group of 1's in a KMap which are adjacent to one another and can therefore be circled. An implicant can contain any power-of-2 number of 1's (1, 2, 4, 8, $\cdots$).

Definition A prime implicant is the largest implicant which can be created with respect to a given 1 in the map. Figure 12.20 shows examples of non-prime implicants (left hand side of figure). In each case, the implicant which has been created could be created from a larger group of 1's. Conversely, Figure 12.20 (right hand side) shows all of the prime implicants present in the KMap. It can be shown that any minimum solution will *only* contain prime implicants. Thus, whenever looking for implicants to circle (and possibly use in a solution) you should restrict your attention to only *prime implicants* and ignore the non-prime implicants.

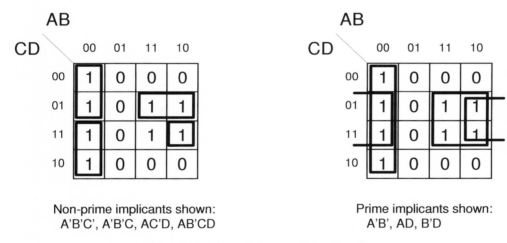

Non-prime implicants shown:
A'B'C', A'B'C, AC'D, AB'CD

Prime implicants shown:
A'B', AD, B'D

Figure 12.20: Non-Prime vs. Prime Implicants

Definition An essential prime implicant is a prime implicant which <u>must</u> be used in any minimum solution to the KMap. Figure 12.21(a) shows three prime implicants. Of these, two are essential. *Any* minimum solution to the KMap will include A'B' as well as AD. The reason is easy to see — if A'B' were left out then the A'B'C'D' (top left corner) and A'B'CD' (bottom left corner) locations in the map would not be covered. A'B' is *essential* to any solution — it is the only way to cover those two locations. Similarly, AD is essential. B'D (shown using dotted lines) is not essential — the minimum solution to this KMap doesn't necessarily require it to be present. The final solution to the problem in Figure 12.21(a) is: $F = A'B' + AD$.

This example of essential vs. non-essential prime implicants only tells a part of the story. Consider the KMap of Figure 12.21(b). Here, there are two essential prime implicants — they are the only way of covering certain 1's in the map. They are shown with heavy lines in the figure. Once they have been included in the solution there is still a single 1 that must be covered (A'BC'D). It can be covered in one of two ways. Either it can be covered by A'BD (shown with dashed lines), or it can be covered by A'C'D (also shown with dashed lines). In this case, *either* of these prime implicants can be included in the final solution. A common misconception is to believe that both A'BD and A'C'D are optional. This is incorrect. Neither is essential, but one or the other must be included in the final solution.

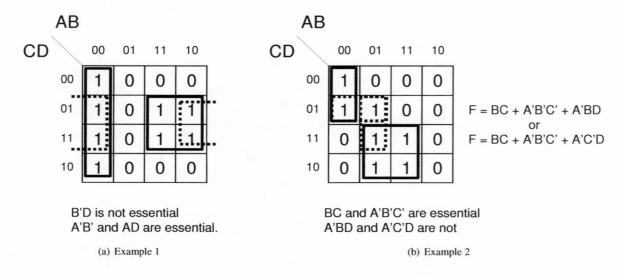

(a) Example 1   (b) Example 2

Figure 12.21: Essential vs. Non-Essential Prime Implicants

With these definitions in place we can articulate a KMap minimization technique which is guaranteed to find the minimum solution (minimum in terms of literal count). The steps of the algorithm are as follows:

1. Enumerate all prime implicants in the KMap.

2. Identify which are essential and which are not.

3. Add all essential prime implicants to the solution.

4. If there are still uncovered 1's in the map, choose a minimum set of non-essential prime implicants to cover the remaining 1's.

Step 1 of the algorithm requires that the largest groups of 1's possible be identified. One way to do this is to consider each 1 in the map in turn and identify the largest implicant it is a part of. A common error in this step is to neglect implicants which *wrap around* the KMap from top to bottom or from left to right. Remember also that the four corners in a 4-variable KMap are all adjacent.

Step 2 of the algorithm requires that you identify the <u>essential</u> prime implicants. This is most easily done by scanning the KMap for locations which are covered only once. Any such locations will indicate the presence of essential prime implicants. Mark these.

Once the essential prime implicants have been added to the solution, there may still be uncovered 1's in the map. Step 4 requires that you find a minimum set of non-essential primes to cover the remaining map locations. In Figure 12.21(a), once step 3 was done the solution was complete — the non-essential prime implicant B'D was not needed. In the example of Figure 12.21(b), a non-essential prime implicant was required and there was a choice to be made about which to include. It may be the case in more complex maps, that a collection of two or more non-essential prime implicants are required to finish covering the map. Choosing the minimum number of non-essential primes will minimize the solution in such a case. Finally, note that a given map may have multiple solutions, all with the same number of literals as was shown in Figure 12.21(b).

Finally, it is possible to create KMaps for expressions with more than four variables. The rules are the same for higher-order KMaps: logical adjacency must manifest itself as physical adjacency so as to make clear the possibilities for applying the simplification theorem. However, a 5-variable KMap requires three dimensions to represent and a 6-variable KMap requires four dimensions. Techniques have been developed to enable 5-variable and 6-variable KMaps solving to be done in 2-dimensions. However, such techniques will not be discussed further here.

12.9   A Worked Example — A BCD to 7-Segment Converter

A common digital circuit is one to convert a BCD code to the 7-segments required to light up an LED display. Figure 12.22(a) shows a 7-segment display where the various segments are turned on and off to display digits. Part (b) of the figure shows which segments would be turned on for the number "3", and part (c) shows which segments would be turned on for the number "7". In the remainder of this section, we use KMaps to derive the logic required to turn the middle segment on or off (it is the segment marked 'g' in the figure).

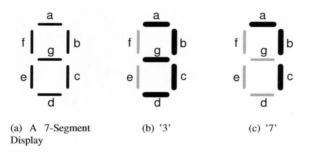

(a) A 7-Segment
Display

(b) '3'

(c) '7'

Figure 12.22: 7-Segment Display

The first step is to write a truth table for segment 'g'. This is shown in Figure 12.23(a). The inputs (B3-B0) make up the 4-bit BCD digit to be displayed. The output signifies for which input combinations segment 'g' in the display should be turned on. The truth table shows that it is turned on for the digits 2, 3, 4, 5, 6, 8, and 9. It is turned off for 0, 1, and 7. The large number of don't cares in the truth table arise because in a BCD code only the values 0-9 are used. By placing don't care symbols for the values 10-15, we enable the KMap minimization to result in a smaller solution.

B3	B2	B1	B0	g
0	0	0	0	0
0	0	0	1	0
0	0	1	0	1
0	0	1	1	1
0	1	0	0	1
0	1	0	1	1
0	1	1	0	1
0	1	1	1	0
1	0	0	0	1
1	0	0	1	1
1	0	1	0	X
1	0	1	1	X
1	1	0	0	X
1	1	0	1	X
1	1	1	0	X
1	1	1	1	X

(a) Truth Table

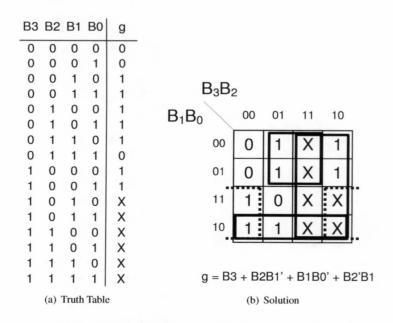

g = B3 + B2B1' + B1B0' + B2'B1

(b) Solution

Figure 12.23: Truth Table and KMap for Segment 'g'

The KMap solution is shown in Figure 12.23(b). The inclusion of the don't cares significantly reduces the logic. Without the don't cares, the solution would have been: $g = B3B2'B1' + B3'B2B1' + B3'B1B0' + B3'B2'B1$. This has 12 literals whereas the solution using don't cares has only 7 literals. This same approach can be used to derive equations for the remaining segments. This is a common laboratory exercise in digital systems courses, and one you will most likely encounter.

12.10 Chapter Summary

KMaps are the main method used for performing boolean minimization by hand. You should become very, very comfortable with their use since they will be used throughout the remainder of this text. In spite of this, it should be noted that in industrial digital design environments, essentially all boolean minimization is done using computer programs.

Concepts that should be clear before moving on to the next chapter include the following:

1. The sum of two product terms which are adjacent with respect to gray code can be merged into a simpler product term by application of the simplification theorem.

2. Finding adjacent terms in a truth table can be hard, especially for truth tables with more than two variables.

3. A KMap is a truth table drawn in a different form to make adjacencies easier to identify.

4. The rows and columns of a KMap are ordered in gray code order. This ensures that physical adjacency in the KMap implies logical adjacency of the product terms with respect to gray codes.

5. Minimizing a boolean function using a KMap consists of identifying groups of adjacent 1's in the KMap to apply the simplification theorem to.

6. A group of adjacent 1's in a KMap is called an implicant.

7. The size of an implicant must be a power of 2.

8. A prime implicant is the largest implicant that can be created with respect to a single 1 in the map.

9. An essential prime implicant is a prime implicant which any solution to the KMap must include.

10. Additional prime implicants may be required in a solution to completely cover a map.

11. The top row and bottom row of a KMap are logically adjacent. The leftmost and rightmost columns of a KMap are logically adjacent. The four corners of a 4-variable KMap are logically adjacent.

12. When circling 1's in a KMap, don't care values should be circled if they increase the implicant size. If they don't help, they can be ignored.

The skills that should result from a study of this chapter include the following:

1. The ability to convert a truth table to a KMap.

2. The ability to convert a minterm expansion or maxterm expansion to a KMap.

3. The ability to convert a boolean expression to a KMap.

4. The ability to convert a KMap to any of the following: truth table, minterm/maxterm expansion, boolean expression.

5. The ability to find the minimum SOP solution to a KMap.

6. The ability to find the minimum SOP solution to a KMap, taking into account don't cares.

7. The ability to find the minimum POS solution to a KMap.

8. The ability to find the minimum POS solution to a KMap, taking into account don't cares.

12.11 Exercises

12.1. Using a KMap, prove the SOP form of the consensus theorem (see Section 4.5.5 to refresh your memory of the consensus theorem). Does the KMap help illustrate why the third term is redundant?

12.2. Draw the KMap for a 4-input XOR function. Can you see why it cannot be reduced?

12.3. Find the minimum SOP solution to the following problem: $F(A, B, C, D) = \sum m(0, 2, 5, 7, 8, 10, 13, 15)$. If multiple minimum solutions exist, show all of them.

12.4. Find the minimum POS solution to the following problem: $F(A, B, C, D) = \Pi M(1, 3, 4, 6, 9, 11, 12, 14)$. If multiple minimum solutions exist, show all of them.

12.5. Find the minimum SOP solution to the following problem. If multiple minimum solutions exist, show all of them.

$$F(A, B, C, D) = \sum m(0, 1, 2, 3, 4, 5, 6, 7, 8, 9, 11, 13, 15).$$

12.6. Find the minimum POS solution to the previous problem. If multiple minimum solutions exist, show all of them.

12.7. Consider the following problem: $F(A, B, C, D) = \sum m(0, 1, 5, 6, 7, 10, 13) + \sum d(2, 4, 9, 14, 15)$. Identify all the prime implicants in its KMap. Then clearly mark (using color) the essential prime implicants.

12.8. Write the minimum SOP solution to the KMap above. If multiple minimum solutions exist, show all of them.

12.9. Repeat the problem above but find the minimum POS solution. If multiple minimum solutions exist, show all of them.

12.10. Consider the following problem: $F(A, B) = \sum m(0, 2, 3) + \sum d(1)$. Find the minimum SOP solution to this problem. If multiple minimum solutions exist, show all of them.

Chapter 13

Gate Delays and Timing in Combinational Circuits

13.1 Introduction

An important consideration of gate behavior has to do with how *fast* a gate will react to changes on its inputs. Knowing the *delays* associated with the gates in your design allows you to determine how fast the design will run. A design that can be clocked at a $100MHz$ rate should accomplish more computations per unit time than one that can only be clocked at $75MHz$. Thus, it is almost always in our interest to design the fastest circuits possible. To help with this task, this chapter provides an introduction to gate delays and timing analysis.

13.2 Basic Gate Delays

Figure 13.1 shows a stylized representation of the *timing* behavior of a CMOS inverter. When the input (V_{in}) rises, the output (V_{out}) falls, and when the input falls the output rises. This drawing also reflects *how long* it takes for the output to respond to changes on the input.

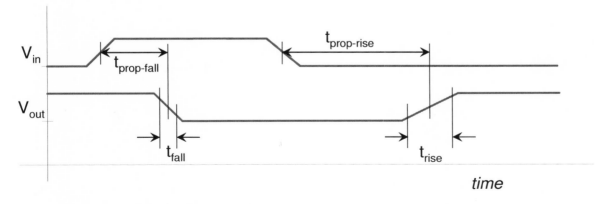

$t_{prop-fall}$ and $t_{prop-rise}$ are measured from 50% of input swing to 50% of output swing

t_{rise} is measured from 10% of output swing to 90% of output swing
t_{fall} is measured from 90% of output swing to 10% of output swing

Figure 13.1: Detailed Timing Characteristics of an Inverter

There are two delays of interest in this drawing. The first is called *propagation delay* or t_{prop}. It is defined as the time from when the input is at 50% of its input swing to when the output reaches 50% of its output swing. Designers normally call this the *delay* associated with the gate. In the figure, $t_{prop-fall}$ is the propagation delay associated with a falling transition on the output, and $t_{prop-rise}$ is the propagation delay associated with a rising transition on the output. Note that $t_{prop-rise}$ is not necessarily the same as $t_{prop-fall}$. This is generally true for most gates — their rising and falling delays are different due to how they are constructed from silicon.

The figure also shows another set of delays called *rise time* and *fall time*. Rise time (t_{rise}) is defined as the time required for the output to go from 10% of its output swing to 90% of its output swing. Fall time (t_{fall}) is defined similarly. For some purposes, rise and fall times are important quantities to consider in addition to propagation delays. However, for purposes of this text, we will focus exclusively on propagation delays because they best reflect the idea of circuit speed in the context of the question: *how fast will my circuit operate?*

13.3   Critical Path Analysis

What we would like is a simple number or two which tells us what we need to know about the delay characteristics of a circuit. Consider the circuit of Figure 13.2. The most common timing question about this circuit is simply "how fast will it run"? If an input were to change value, how soon would the output reflect the new result? For a circuit such as Figure 13.2, there may be a different delay associated with each input change. The time between a change on signal A and the resulting output change is likely much shorter than the time between a change on signal E and the resulting output change. Look at the circuit of Figure 13.2 until you understand why. When signal A changes, the output will react after only one AND gate's worth of delay. In contrast, a change on signal E will not be reflected on the output until after two AND gates' and one OR gate's worth of delay.

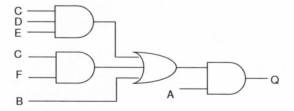

Figure 13.2: A Typical Circuit

We are usually interested in knowing the *longest time* we might need to wait. To determine this, we identify the *critical path* through the circuit. The critical path is defined as the slowest path between the inputs and outputs of the circuit.

Intuition tells us that the critical path will likely consist of three gate delays in Figure 13.2. Signals A and B are likely not on the critical path. The critical path will either be through the top left AND gate or the middle left AND gate. A 3-input gate will likely be slower than a 2-input gate and so the top left AND gate is likely on the critical path. However, we need to know the delays associated with all the gates in the circuit to determine the precise delay along the critical path.. We then add these three delays together to arrive at a final result. Figure 13.3 shows the circuit from above but with the critical path highlighted.

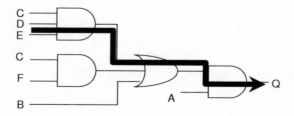

Figure 13.3: A Critical Path

Table 13.1 shows some sample delays for a hypothetical set of gates. We can compute the critical path delay through the circuit using this table of delays. In the worst case, once any of inputs C, D, or E changes, there is a delay of $5ns$ (5×10^{-9} seconds) until the output of the top left gate changes. Then, $6ns$ later, the output of the OR gate changes. Finally, $3ns$ after that, the output changes. The total delay through this circuit is thus $5 + 6 + 3 = 14ns$.

Table 13.1: Some Hypothetical Gate Delays

Gate Name	Delay
NOT	1ns
AND2	3ns
AND3	5ns
AND4	7ns
NAND2	2ns
NAND3	4ns
NAND4	6ns
OR2	4ns
OR3	6ns
OR4	8ns
NOR2	3ns
NOR3	5ns
NOR4	6ns

13.4 Levels of Detail in Timing Analysis

When doing timing analysis of a circuit, you must be clear about what you are attempting to accomplish. The analysis just completed is suitable for determining the *worst case delay* through the circuit. We chose the top left AND gate since it is slower than the middle left AND gate. In cases where both $t_{prop-rise}$ and $t_{prop-fall}$ are given and $t_{prop-rise} \neq t_{prop-fall}$, a worst case delay analysis might use the slower of the two as the basic gate delay. That way, no matter which gate outputs were rising and which were falling, the computed delay would represent the worst case delay.

However, there is nothing special about this kind of analysis. It may be that you want more detail in your analysis. In this case, you may choose to compute which gate outputs are rising and which are falling and use $t_{prop-rise}$ and $t_{prop-fall}$ values as necessary. This would provide a more accurate reflection of the delay through the circuit.

13.5   Input Glitches, Timing, and Gate Behavior

Consider the timing diagram for a 2-input AND gate as shown in Figure 13.4. Note that this is a stylized figure in that it doesn't show rise and fall times. When signals change, the rise and fall times are shown as $0ns$. This is a simplification which we will follow for the remainder of this text — we will focus only on propagation delay and ignore rise and fall times. This is a reasonable approximation for the kinds of timing analysis we will do (even though real gates have non-zero rise and fall times).

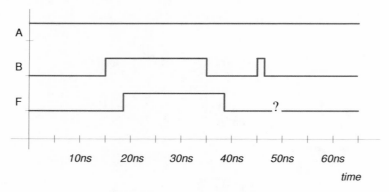

Figure 13.4: AND Gate Behavior

In Figure 13.4, input B changes at $t = 15ns$ and the output responds $3ns$ later. The input change at $t = 35ns$ further results in an output change at $38ns$. However, at $t = 45ns$ the input changes, but for a very short time (a time shorter than t_{prop} for the gate). What would the gate output response be in this case? One scenario would be that this short input *glitch* would be reproduced on the output as shown in Figure 13.5.

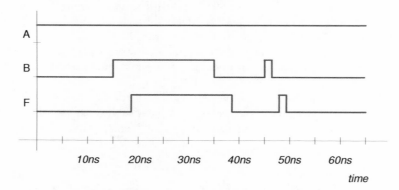

Figure 13.5: AND Gate Behavior - Version A

Another scenario would be that the input glitch would not cause any output change to occur. The gate would *filter out* the input glitch. This behavior is shown in Figure 13.6.

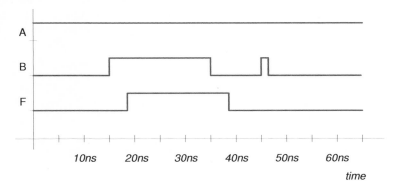

Figure 13.6: AND Gate Behavior - Version B

So, which behavior is the actual behavior? By now you should be able to guess that "the answer depends on the technology you are targeting" — this is a common theme in digital design. It also depends on the length of the glitch with respect to t_{prop} for the gate, the rise and fall times of the glitch, etc. It may be that the glitch would be propagated to the gate output in some instances, and the gate may filter it out in others. A third possibility also exists — a runt glitch may appear on the output. That is the output may glitch high for a short time but may not go all the way up to the voltage for a '1' signal.

A properly designed digital system will be designed to be immune from such issues, and thus it may not be important to determine the precise answer to this question. For purposes of this text, we will (perhaps somewhat arbitrarily) choose the version of Figure 13.5 to reflect gate behavior in the presence of input glitches.

13.6   A Pulse Generator

<u>Disclaimer:</u> The circuit discussed in this section, a pulse generator, is a good vehicle to further discuss the effects of gate timing and behavior. Its inclusion as an example in this section *should not* be taken as an endorsement of its use. Many people would not consider its use to be a part of a sound design discipline due to problems it presents in terms of verifying that the resulting design will work under all operating conditions. Nevertheless, it is used to further our discussion of gate delays.

Consider the circuit of Figure 13.7. A *static* or functional analysis will show that $F = A \bullet A' = 0$. Now, consider the timing diagram of the figure and note that F is not always FALSE. Can you see why? Due to the unequal delays between input A and the AND gate, there is a transitory time period where both AND gate inputs are TRUE. The width of the output pulse is a function of how long both AND gate inputs are true, which is dependent on the delay through the inverters. You can control the width of the output pulse by adjusting the number of inverters used (just make sure you include an odd number). Can you write the output pulse width as a function of the number of inverters?

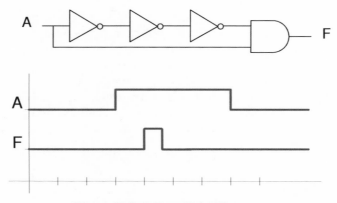

Figure 13.7: A Racy Pulse Generator

The reason for discussing this circuit is to underscore the notion that when the inputs to a combinational circuit change, there may be transitory values which appear on the circuit nodes before the network settles to a stable state (also known as its *steady state*). A realization that output pulses such as are found in Figure 13.7 do occur in real circuits is an important first step toward understanding the issues surrounding such "glitches" and how to design circuits immune to their effects in the real world.

13.7 False Outputs

The pulse on the output of the circuit just seen is known as a *false output*. That is, it is an output not predicted by the truth table for the circuit in question but which appears, nonetheless, due to the various gate delays in the circuit. As another example, consider the circuit and corresponding KMap of Figure 13.8. The solution is the standard KMap solution.

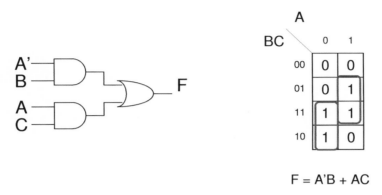

$$F = A'B + AC$$

Figure 13.8: A Sample Circuit

Now consider the timing diagram given of the circuit's operation as shown in Figure 13.9. Both inputs B and C are TRUE and so it shouldn't matter what the value of A is — the output should always be TRUE. The timing diagram shows different behavior, however. Signal F has a *false output*. It is called a false output because the truth table indicates that F should be TRUE during the entire period covered by the timing diagram. Thus, the momentary FALSE value on F is unexpected. False outputs fall under the general category of something called *hazards*.

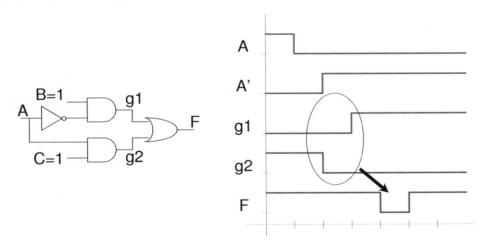

Figure 13.9: Timing Diagram Showing a False Output

To understand the reason for the false output, note that there is a short time period where both $A = A' = 0$. This is due to the delay through the inverter and so there will be a short time period where the outputs of both AND gates ($g1$ and $g2$) are low (circled in Figure 13.9). This is what gives rise to the false output.

The KMap of Figure 13.10 shows why this is happening. Each AND gate implements a prime implicant from the KMap. In the case being analyzed (*A* going from TRUE to FALSE), the circuit is moving from the right hand prime implicant to the left hand prime implicant in the KMap (the arrow shows the transition). The false output results because the *g*2 AND gate *turns off* **before** the *g*1 AND gate *turns on*.

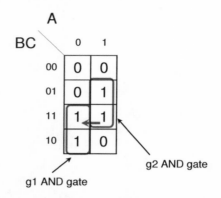

Figure 13.10: False Output Due to Moving Between Prime Implicants

One solution to this problem might be to try to adjust the delays of the AND gates to eliminate the problem (there are a variety of tricks which can be employed to do this). In general, trying to do such timing adjustment is fraught with problems. Your adjustment might work fine when the circuit is cold, but when it heats up and the gate delays change, the adjustment may no longer work. What we need is a solution that will work independent of the precise values of the gate delays.

Figure 13.11 shows a solution to the problem. Here, a redundant prime implicant is added to the solution to hold the output high while *A* transitions. The resulting circuit will have no false output since gate *g*3 will be on during the transition.

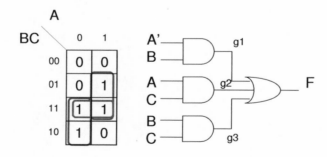

Figure 13.11: Redundant Prime Implicants Eliminate False Outputs

This overall method of adding redundant prime implicants to avoid hazards is known as *hazard-free design*.

Another example is shown in Figure 13.12. Multiple redundant prime implicants have been added in the right half of the figure to eliminate false outputs due to single-input changes.

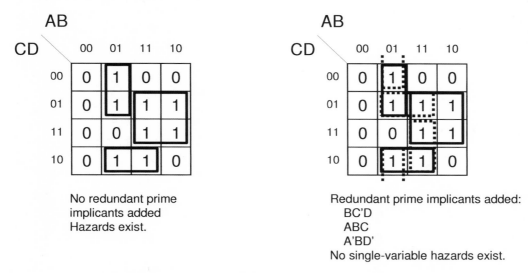

No redundant prime
implicants added
Hazards exist.

Redundant prime implicants added:
BC'D
ABC
A'BD'
No single-variable hazards exist.

Figure 13.12: Another Hazard-Free Design Example

13.7.1 False Outputs and Hazards: Summary

This section has shown how gate delays give rise to dynamic circuit behavior which produces outputs not predicted by truth tables or KMaps. The circuits we have seen in this regard perform as expected in a *static* sense but not in a *dynamic* sense, producing transitory false outputs.

False outputs and hazards are not necessarily bad. In fact, they occur all the time in real circuits and cause no harm. However, there will be specific times when a system design requires a signal without false outputs. Hazard-free design can eliminate false outputs in these cases when only a single input changes at a time. We will discuss (in later chapters) how and when to do hazard-free design, as well as other methods to deal with glitches and hazards in digital designs. Remember, however, that the hazard free technique just discussed will only prevent false outputs *in the case of single-input changes*. If multiple inputs to a function change at once, then the technique presented here will not be able to prevent false outputs.

13.8 Gate Delay Variations

In reality, actual gate delays are not characterized as neatly as this chapter might suggest. In particular, the delay through a gate is not a constant value but may vary according to a number of effects:

1. Gate delay is a function of temperature. The gate may run faster when it is cold and slower when it is hot. In this case you would want to use the delays associated with the circuit when hot to ensure that you compute the actual worst case (slowest) delay.

2. Gate delay is a function of the value of V_{cc} provided. Since no power supply or battery is perfect, a worst case analysis may need to take into account the possible variation in gate delay that the actual V_{cc} would result in.

3. Gate delay is a function of processing variations. Even a collection of seemingly identical gates (they are all fabricated on the same silicon integrated circuit for example) will all have slightly different delays due to manufacturing variations.

The net result is that the actual delay for a given gate may vary significantly from its *nominal value*. Data sheets for discrete gates thus always provide delay values in terms of a guaranteed minimum delay and a guaranteed maximum delay. Using these minimum and maximum delays you can determine the fastest your circuit might run and the slowest it might run.

The delay through a gate is also usually a function of how heavily loaded its output is. This is shown in Figure 13.13. The output wire of a gate connects to the inputs of other gates. In CMOS, those other gates (C through F in the figure) present a *capacitive load* to the driving gates (A and B in the figure). The heavier the load the longer it will take the driving gate to drive its output all the way up to V_{cc} or down to ground. In Figure 13.13, the effective gate delay for gate B (which is driving three other gates), will be longer than the effective gate delay for gate A (which is driving only one other gate).

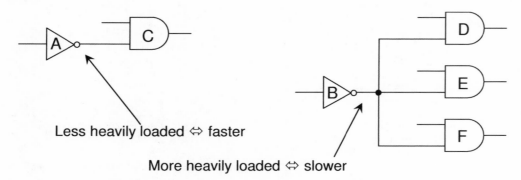

Figure 13.13: Effect of Capacitive Loading on Gate Delay

13.8.1   Gate Delay Variation: Summary

The point of all this is to show that doing a precise timing analysis of a circuit can be complex. The most common form of timing analysis performed on circuits is a *worst case timing analysis* (What is the slowest the circuit might run?). In this case, you should be sure to use the worst case delay values for the gates in your circuit.

13.9   Chapter Summary

This chapter has introduced gate delays and timing analysis. Concepts that should be clear before moving on to the next chapter include the following:

1. Propagation delay is defined as the delay from when the input is at 50% of its voltage swing until the output is at 50% of its voltage swing.

2. The propagation delay for when a gate output falls is not necessarily the same as the propagation delay for when the gate output rises. For simple worst case timing analysis, use the longer of the two delays.

3. Rise time is defined as the time from when the output is at 10% of its maximum voltage to when it is at 90% of its maximum voltage.

4. Fall time is defined as the time from when the output is at 90% of its maximum voltage to when it is at 10% of its maximum voltage.

5. For simple timing analysis, t_{rise} and t_{fall} are not used - t_{prop} is used instead.

6. The most commonly asked question regarding a circuit is its delay — that is, how long it takes its output to react to changes on its inputs.

7. When calculating total delay in a circuit, you must identify its critical path. This is defined as the slowest path from any input to the output.

8. Even though some delays through a circuit may be shorter than the delay along the critical path, always use critical path for determining the circuit delay since it will give the worst case (longest) delay.

9. When an input to a gate has a pulse width shorter than the propagation delay for the gate, the actual behavior is difficult to predict and will depend on a number of factors and characteristics of the technology being used.

10. Gate delays in a circuit give rise to false outputs which are transitory gate outputs not predicted by the truth table or boolean equation associated with the circuit.

11. False outputs can be eliminated using hazard-free KMap methods. The method shown in this chapter works to eliminate false outputs in the case of a single input change.

The skills that should result from a study of this chapter include the following:

1. The ability to determine the propagation delay to use for a gate from a detailed timing diagram of the gate's operation.

2. The ability to determine the critical path through a circuit.

3. The ability to create an accurate timing diagram of a circuit's operation given input waveforms.

4. The ability to detect and eliminate false outputs in circuits by adding redundant prime implicants.

13.10 Exercises

13.1. The figure below is a detailed timing diagram for a NAND-like gate. If you were interested in knowing how fast this gate would run for purposes of critical path analysis, what would you use for t_{prop}? Why?

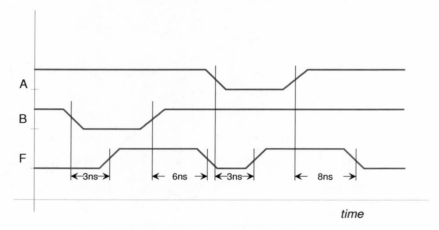

Figure 13.14: NAND Gate Timing

13.2. If you were doing a more detailed timing analysis which separated out $t_{prop-rise}$ and $t_{prop-fall}$, what would be reasonable values to use for each of these delays?

13.3. Determine what the critical path is through the circuit of Figure 13.15. To answer this question, redraw the circuit for your answer and draw a heavy line along the critical path. NOTE: inverters are often not drawn in schematics to simplify them. However, any signal that is complemented (A') has an implied inverter on it which *must* be accounted for in any delay calculations so draw them in when you redraw the circuit. Use the delays in Table 13.1 and be sure to give the total delay you calculated.

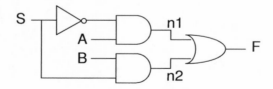

Figure 13.15: Sample Circuit

13.4. What is the function of the circuit shown in Figure 13.15?

13.5. For the circuit of Figure 13.15, complete the timing diagram of Figure 13.16. In your timing diagram, clearly label the time of each signal transition. Does the timing diagram contain any false outputs? Use the delays in Table 13.1.

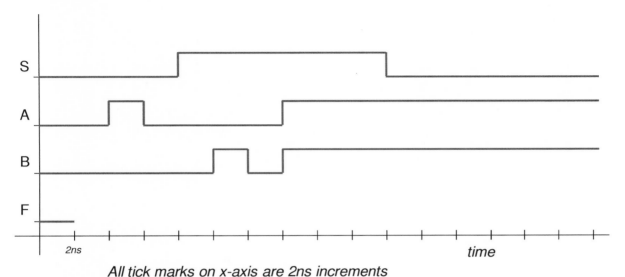

All tick marks on x-axis are 2ns increments

Figure 13.16: Timing Diagram for Sample Circuit

13.6. Determine what the critical path is through the circuit of Figure 13.17. To answer this question, redraw the circuit for your answer and draw a heavy line along the critical path. NOTE: inverters are often not drawn in schematics to simplify them. However, any signal that is complemented (A') has an implied inverter on it which *must* be accounted for in any delay calculations. Use the delays in Table 13.1 and be sure to give the total delay you calculated.

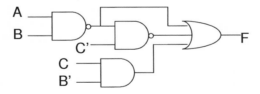

Figure 13.17: Sample Circuit #2

13.7. Consider the following function:

$$F(A, B, C, D) = \sum m(2, 3, 5, 7, 8, 9, 13, 15)$$

Draw a 4-variable KMap for this function. Then, do a conventional minimization of that KMap and implement the equation using gates. Finally, do a hazard-free minimization and implement those equations using gates. For each hazard, how many gates are added to the design?

Chapter 14

Dataflow SystemVerilog

This chapter introduces "dataflow" SystemVerilog design. This is the next higher level abstraction design style above gate-level structural design.

14.1 A Basic 2:1 MUX

Program 14.1.1 is the 2:1 MUX design from a previous chapter (the '~' operator is NOT, the '&' operator is AND, and the '|' operator is OR, all as in the C programming language). This design mimics the gate-level structure of a 2:1 MUX — the inverter, two AND gates and a single OR gate are readily apparent from the expression.

A more complex design might contain numerous *assign* statements to describe its logic. Each *assign* statement describes the gates required to compute one output signal. A full adder (which outputs both sum and carry-out signals would require two *assign* statements).

The semantics of dataflow SystemVerilog are that all dataflow statements execute all the time, reacting as needed to changes on their "inputs" (the signals specified on the right hand side of the assign statement), and continuously computing new "outputs" (the signal on the left hand side). When designing with dataflow SystemVerilog, you write designs such as Program 14.1.1, and a synthesizer converts them to equivalent gate-level circuits.

Program 14.1.1 SystemVerilog Code for 2:1 MUX

```
module mux21(
      output logic q,
      input logic sel, a, b);

   assign q = (~sel & a) | (sel & b);

endmodule
```

A second version of a 2:1 MUX is shown here as Program 14.1.2. This uses the C-like ? : operator and emphasizes the fact that a 2:1 MUX implements an if-then type of structure.

Program 14.1.2 SystemVerilog Code for 2:1 MUX - Version 2

```
module mux21(
       output logic q,
       input logic sel, a, b);

  assign q = sel?b:a;

endmodule
```

Importantly, this version has a significant advantage over Program 14.1.1. With minor adjustments to the declarations of the input and output wires, it will work for any width a, b, and q wires (provided they are all the same width). How this is done will be shown later in this chapter. In addition, a good rule of thumb is that if you can avoid truly gate-level design by leveraging higher level of constructs such as the ? : operator, you should always do so.

14.2 Dataflow Operators

The examples above show that C-like operators can be used on the right hand side of assign statements to form logic. Figure 14.1 summarizes the available operators.

Operator Type	Operator Symbol	Operation Performed	# of Operands	Comments
Arithmetic	*, /, +, -	As expected	2	* and / take LOTS of hardware
	%	Modulo	2	
Logical	!	Logic NOT	1	As in C
	&&	Logic AND	2	As in C
	||	Logic OR	2	As in C
Bitwise	~	Bitwise NOT	1	As in C
	&	Bitwise AND	2	As in C
	|	Bitwise OR	2	As in C
	^	Bitwise XOR	2	As in C
	~^	Bitwise XNOR	2	
Relational	<, >, <=, >=	As expected	2	As in C
Equality	==, !=	As expected	2	As in C
Reduction	&	Reduction AND	1	Multi-bit input
	~&	Reduction NAND	1	Multi-bit input
	|	Reduction OR	1	Multi-bit input
	~|	Reduction NOR	1	Multi-bit input
	^	Reduction XOR	1	Multi-bit input
	~^	Reduction XNOR	1	Multi-bit input
Shift	<<	Left shift	2	Fill with 0's
	>>	Right shift	2	Fill with 0's
Concat	{ }	Concatenate	Any number	
Replicate	{{ }}	Replicate	Any number	
Cond	?:	As expected	3	As in C

Figure 14.1: SystemVerilog Dataflow Operators

14.2.1   Bitwise vs. Logic Operators

The bitwise and logical operators are exactly as in C. Bitwise operators (&, |, and ~) operate on two operands in a bit-by-bit fashion. Conversely, the logical operators (&&, ||, and !) are used to combine the results of comparisons in logical ways. The following uses both kinds:

```
assign q = ((~a<4'b1101) && ((c&4'b0011)!=0)) ? 1'b0:1'b1;
```

This will invert the bits of a and determine whether the result is less than decimal 13. If it is, it will do a bit-wise AND between c and the constant '0011' and determine whether the result is non-zero. If it is, the expression will evaluate to FALSE (1'b0). Else, it will evaluate to TRUE (1'b1). Other than the use of SystemVerilog constants, the evaluation of this expression is identical to how it would be evaluated in C. By the way, the above could be recoded as:

```
assign q = ((~a<13) && ((c&3)!=0)) ? 0:1;
```

since SystemVerilog understands decimal numbers and will convert them to the needed number and pattern of bits as needed.

14.2.2   Reduction Operators

A collection of reduction operators exist which are in essence, single gates. They each take a multi-bit input and do the specified operation on all the bits of that input. For example:

```
assign z = &x;
```

is the same as:

```
assign z = x[2] & x[1] & x[0];
```

provided x is a 3-bit wire. Further,

```
assign z = ~|y;
```

is the same as:

```
assign z = ~(y[2] | y[1] | y[0]);
```

Consult the table of operators to see the full range of reduction operators available.

14.2.3   Concatenation and Replication Operators

Concatenation is the process of taking two or more wires and concatenating their bits into a wider wire. SystemVerilog provides { and } for concatenation:

```
logic[3:0] x, y;
logic[7:0] z, q, w, t;
assign x = 4'b1100;
assign y = 4'b0101;
assign z = {x, x};              // z is 8'b11001100
assign q = {2'b11, y, 2'b00};   // q is 8'b11010100
```

As many wires as desired can be concatenated together in a concatenation operation. A shorthand for {x, x} is {2{x}}. Thus, consider the following:

```
logic[1:0] a;
logic[7:0] b;
assign a = 2'b01;
assign b = {{2{a}}, {2{2'b00}}};   // b is 8'b01010000
```

This example uses a combination of concatenation and replication. The entire concatenation must be enclosed in curly braces. Further, each element in the concatenation is a *replication*. The basic replication syntax is that the item being replicated (a or 2'b00 in this case) must be enclosed in curly braces itself. Further, each entire replication must be encloses in curly braces as well. Thus, legal expressions are {2{a}} and {2{2'b00}} for the pieces and {{2{a}}, {2{2'b00}}} for the concatenation of the replications.

14.2.4 Operator Precedence

Operator precedence in SystemVerilog is similar to in C. Figure 14.2 shows this. As with programming languages, use parentheses to ensure you get what you want.

Higher precedence	
	Unary -, unary +, !, ~
	*, /, %
	+, -
	<<, >>
	<, <=, >, >=
	==, !=
	&, ~&
	^, ~^
	|, ~|
	&&
	||
	?:
Lower precedence	

Figure 14.2: SystemVerilog Dataflow Operator Precedence

14.2.5 Matching Wire Widths

Bitwise operators can only be applied to operands with the same width. Consider the following:

```
logic[3:0] a;
logic[2:0] b;
logic[3:0] q;
assign q = a & b;  // Error ---  a and b must be same width
```

Further, the result of a bitwise operator must be the correct width to receive the result. With this is mind, a 4-bit version of a 2:1 MUX could be written this way:

```
assign q = ({4{~sel}} & a) | ({4{sel}} & b);
```

The replicator operator is used to expand both ~*sel* and *sel* to each be 4-bits wide so they can be AND-ed with the individual bits of a and b.

14.3 Example - a 2:4 Decoder

A 2:4 decoder is easily done using dataflow SystemVerilog as shown in Program 14.3.1. As you can see it is a set of cascaded ? : operators which perform the equivalent of the corresponding *if-then-else* statements.

Program 14.3.1 SystemVerilog Code for 2:4 Decoder

```
module decode24(
        input logic[1:0] a,
        output logic[3:0] q
        );

    assign q = (a==2'b00)?4'b0001:
                (a==2'b01)?4'b0010:
                (a==2'b10)?4'b0100:
                4'b1000;
endmodule
```

A second, more compact version of this design is shown below in Program 14.3.2. This is an example where thinking not about gates but about bit manipulation can greatly simplify a logic design using SystemVerilog. Synthesizers are able to take such expressions and turn them into the required gates for implementation. This version may be considered a bit *too* terse, especially for someone first learning SystemVerilog. But, it is a valid implementation and will be turned into the necessary gates to implement the desired 2:4 decoder. Can you see why/how it works?

Program 14.3.2 SystemVerilog Code for 2:4 Decoder - Version 2

```
module decode24(
        output logic[3:0] q,
        input logic[1:0] a);

    assign q = (4'b0001 << a);

endmodule
```

14.4 Parameterization in Dataflow SystemVerilog

A powerful feature of dataflow SystemVerilog is that it allows for parameterized design. A parameterized design is one which can be used for any size operands. By learning to write parameterized modules, you make it possible to write a module just once and then use it in multiple applications.

A parameterized 2:1 MUX is shown in Program 14.4.1. Note that the *sel* wire is a single bit wide but that a, b, and q are parameterized according to the value of WID (where WID has a default value of 16). Also note that the keyword *parameter* is optional.

Program 14.4.1 SystemVerilog Code for a Parameterized 2:1 MUX

```
module mux21n #(parameter WID=16) (
        output logic[WID-1:0] q,
        input logic sel,
        input logic[WID-1:0] a, b
        );

   assign q = sel?b:a;

endmodule
```

Instancing a copy of $mux21n$ can be done in the normal way:

```
mux21n M0(q, sel, a, b);
```

and the value of WID will be assumed to be 16 (that was the default value of WID declared when $mux21n$ was defined). To create a 2:1 MUX for different size wires, just specify the value of WID you wish to use:

```
mux21n #(3) M0(q, sel, a, b);   // 3-bit version
mux21n #(4) M1(q, sel, a, b);   // 4-bit version
mux21n #(12) M2(q, sel, a, b);  // 12-bit version
```

One of the keys to making this work is writing the assign statement in the body of the module using the ?: operator. When coding this way, the logic works for any width of a, b, and q, as long as they are all the same width.

Careful planning often will allow you to define modules which can be re-used in many different places in a design. Re-use of circuit modules is a goal for many designers. It reduces the work required to complete a new design, and eliminates design errors by allowing you to re-use code across multiple designs. Use it whenever possible.

14.4.1 Mixing Dataflow and Structural SystemVerilog Design

There is no problem in mixing structural and dataflow constructs within a single module. What results, in the end, is a hardware design made out of gates. You may thus code in any mixture that is convenient, and which matches the design task at hand. For example, you could mix structural instantiations of $mux21$ modules with assign statements which generate other logic. An example is shown in Program 14.4.2 which is a 4-bit 2:1 MUX design but where the output is the reduction OR of the mux result.

Program 14.4.2 SystemVerilog Code Which Mixes Dataflow and Structural Design

```
module mixed(
        output logic q,
        input logic sel,
        input logic[3:0] a, b
        );

   logic[3:0] tmp;

   mux21n #(4) MYMUX(tmp, sel, a, b);
   assign q = |tmp;

endmodule
```

14.5 SystemVerilog and Arithmetic

Another advantage of dataflow SystemVerilog is that it provides arithmetic operators for use. The following will create as wide an unsigned adder as is needed (based on the widths of q, a, and b):

```
   assign q = a+b;
```

Most synthesis tools will attempt to choose the smallest adder circuit implementation which meets the timing constraints you give it. By using the '+' operator, you avoid specifying the specific gate-level adder circuit to use, and allow the synthesizer to make that determination. The alternative to specifying it this way would be to build your own adder out of gates. This is a more difficult task than using the '+' operator, and may actually give worse results than a synthesizer could provide[1].

Finally, there are a number of questions related to arithmetic that are not answered here. Some examples:

1. If a and b are not the same width, what does the synthesis tool generate for ciruitry?

2. What if q is too small or too large for the result?

3. If a and b are 8 bits wide and q is 9 bits wide, do you get the additional bit that results from bit growth?

4. How do you do signed arithmetic in SystemVerilog?

Understanding the answers to these questions is important to writing good SystemVerilog code. To get those answers you could experiment by writing some SystemVerilog code and looking to see what it generates (either in a simulator or in the resulting netlist) or go on-line and read to find the answers.

---

[1]There are a multitude of adder circuits which have been invented with names like ripple-carry, carry-lookahead, carry-save, and carry-select. The exact one that should be used in any instance is a function of the area and size requirements you have for your circuit, as well as the characteristics of the target technology. Synthesizers are designed to understand all of this and choose the smallest one that meets your timing requirements.

14.6   Chapter Summary

This chapter has discussed dataflow SystemVerilog. The key points include:

1. All dataflow SystemVerilog assignments must begin with the keyword *assign*.

2. Dataflow SystemVerilog allows for C-like expression syntax to describe the function to be performed.

3. Many SystemVerilog operators accept multi-bit wires as arguments. This simplifies the creation of multi-bit structures.

4. Dataflow SystemVerilog readily supports parameterized module creation. A parameterized module can take inputs of any width.

5. The use of arithmetic operators (+ for example) in dataflow SystemVerilog will cause most circuit synthesizers to select the smallest arithmetic circuit which meets the timing constraints specified when the synthesizer was run. This frees the designer from worrying about the details of how the adder should be constructed for a given technology.

The skills that should result from a study of this chapter include the following:

1. The ability to write any combinational circuit description using dataflow SystemVerilog.

2. The ability to create parameterized designs using dataflow SystemVerilog.

3. The ability to use any of the SystemVerilog operators in the creation of logic.

14.7   Exercises

14.1. Implement a 4:1 MUX using a single dataflow assignment statement involving only concatenation, replication, and the operators for AND, OR, and NOT.

14.2. Implement a 4:1 MUX using a single dataflow assignment statement and the ?: operator.

14.3. Repeat the previous 2 problems but parameterize your designs for any size operands.

14.4. Implement a 3:8 decoder using a single dataflow assignment statement.

14.5. Implement an 8-bit ALU using a single dataflow assignment statement. Your ALU should operate on 8-bit A and B inputs. It should also take in a 2-bit control code which implies the following functions: 00=PASS(A), 01=ADD, 10=AND, 11=NOT(A). Call the ALU output Q. Use the ?: operator.

14.6. Repeat the previous problem but make it parameterizable for any width operands.

14.7. Design a parameterized adder/subtracter. Its A and B inputs are of width 'WID' and its Q output is of width 'WID+1'. It adds its A and B operands when MODE=0 and subtracts them when MODE=1. To avoid overflow, first sign-extend each number by one bit as described in Chapter 3. Implement the sign-extensions as two separate dataflow assignment statements and then implement the adder/subtracter as a single dataflow assignment statement. Use some local wires for this design to simplify the logic.

14.8. Repeat the problem above but do it as a single *assign* statement.

14.9. Go on-line and answer one or more of the questions regarding arithmetic in Section 14.5 as directed by your instructor.

14.10. Devise a set of SystemVerilog coding experiments followed by simulation to answer one or more of the questions regarding arithmetic in Section 14.5 as directed by your instructor.

Chapter 15

Latches and Flip Flops

The circuits studied so far in this text have all been combinational. What this means is that in each case the circuit output is a function of only the current value of the inputs and nothing else. That is why truth tables have been used so extensively — they are able to capture the entire functionality of the circuit by simply listing the output that results from each input combination.

As useful as combinational circuits are, they cannot perform sequential processing and thus have limited usefulness by themselves. Consider a circuit designed to control a machine such as a copy machine. To copy a single-page document would require some number of steps such as:

1. Turn on lamp

2. Wait for signal indicating lamp has warmed up

3. Start motor to move scan arm

4. Start paper copy/roller mechanism

5. Wait for signal indicating that scan has completed

6. Turn off lamp

7. Update copy machine display to indicate completion.

The key component of a sequential circuit which could perform the above 6-step process is its ability to remember where it is in the process so that as signals arrive from the parts of the copier it can react appropriately. During certain steps user input from the console might be ignored. This *remembering* of the current state of the copy operation is implemented by sequential circuits using storage (memory). The focus of this chapter is on building storage elements and analyzing their behavior. We will learn how to use these storage circuits to construct sequential circuits in later chapters.

15.1 Bistability and Storage: The SR Latch

The kind of storage that will be studied in the following sections relies on the concept of bi-stability. A bi-stable circuit element is one that has two stable states.

An example of a simple bi-stable circuit is shown in Figure 15.1(a). Here, the R and S inputs are both low, the Q output is low and the Q' output is high. This is a stable state meaning that the circuit will remain in this state indefinitely unless one of the inputs changes. You can verify this by examining the inputs to the two NOR gates shown in the figure.

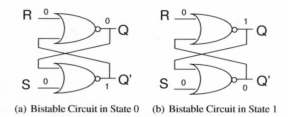

(a) Bistable Circuit in State 0   (b) Bistable Circuit in State 1

Figure 15.1: SR Latch With Two Stable States

Now consider the state of the circuit shown in Figure 15.1(b). It is the same structure but the Q output is now high and the Q' output is low. Once again, if you examine the inputs to the NOR gates, you will see that this is also a stable state.

This latch exhibits bi-stability. Once placed into one of the two states shown in the figure, it will stay there indefinitely. The only way it will change state is if one of the inputs changes to force it into the other state.

The latch in Figure 15.1(a) is said to be in the *reset* state — its Q output has been reset to a '0'. The latch in Figure 15.1(b) is said to be in the *set* state — its Q output has been set to a '1'.

Figure 15.2 shows the behavior of the latch in response to a pulse on the latch's S input. In part (a), the S input goes high. After the delay of the NOR gate, part (b) shows that the Q' output goes low. This value then wraps around to the top NOR gate and, after another NOR gate delay, the Q output goes high as shown in part (c). Finally, part (d) shows that when the S input goes back low no further output transitions occur. At this point, the latch has been set and will stay in that state until a pulse on its R input forces it into its other bi-stable state.

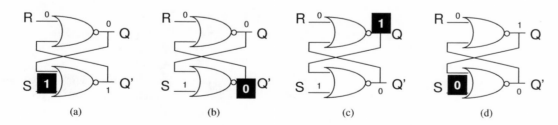

(a)   (b)   (c)   (d)

Figure 15.2: Setting an SR Latch

The timing diagram in Figure 15.3 shows the timing behavior of the latch. Points A-D in the timing diagram correspond to parts (a)-(d) of Figure 15.2. At point A (time $t = t_0$), the S input goes high which causes the lower NOR gate output (Q') to go low. This transition on Q' occurs after one NOR gate delay, or at time $t = t_0 + t_{NOR}$ (point B in the figure).

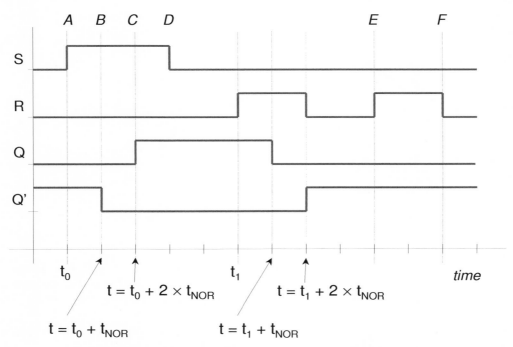

Figure 15.3: Timing Diagram for SR Latch Operation

With its two inputs now both low the top latch's output will change to a '1'. This is shown in the figure at point C which is at $t = t_0 + 2 \times t_{NOR}$. At this point, no further transitions will occur. The latch has reached a stable state with its Q output high and its Q' output low — the latch has been *set*.

Now consider point D in the timing diagram where the S input goes low once again. Since the bottom NOR gate still has a '1' input (from the Q wire), its output remains at a '0'. Thus, the circuit has returned to the same input combination as at point A in the figure ($S=R='0'$) but with different outputs.

In the next part of the timing diagram the R input goes high and then low to *reset* the latch. Note that R goes high and low again a second time but with no output change. There is no output change this second time because the latch was already in the reset state.

This circuit is called an SR latch. The S input sets it and the R input resets it. An SR latch can be used to store binary information. In the reset state, it is said that it has stored a '0'. In the set state, it is said that it has stored a '1'. A determination of what is stored in the latch can be made by examining the value on its Q output wire.

There is one input combination that has not yet been discussed. This is when $S=R='1'$. In this instance, both Q and Q' are '0'. Since neither output is '1', one might say the latch is neither set or reset. This is not generally considered a useful state, and so the combination $S=R='1'$ is usually avoided.

The behavior of an SR latch can be summarized in the form of a truth table. The behavior of the Q output depends on both the values of the S and R inputs, as well as on what is currently stored in the latch (the Q output's current value). The truth table thus *contains the current Q output as an input*. This is shown in Figure 15.4. Q represents the current state of the latch (the current value on the Q wire), and $Q+$ represents its next state (the value it will go to given the specified S, R, and Q values). Thus, the table summarizes the latch's transition behavior as a function of its inputs <u>and</u> current state. As a result, this table is often called a *transition table* rather than a truth table.

S	R	Q	$Q+$	Comment
0	0	0	0	No change
0	0	1	1	
0	1	0	0	Reset
0	1	1	0	
1	0	0	1	Set
1	0	1	1	
1	1	0	N/A	
1	1	1	N/A	

Figure 15.4: Truth (Transition) Table for SR Latch

The table completely summarizes the transition behavior of the latch. When $SR=='00'$, $Q+$ is simply the old value of Q. In this case there will be no transition on Q. When $SR='01'$, we see that $Q+ = '0'$ (the Q output transitions to a '0'). This is the reset transition. When $SR='10'$, we see that $Q+ = '1'$ (Q transitions to a '1'). This is the set transition. The input combination $SR='11'$ is marked as *N/A* to indicate that that input combination is not used.

A transition table is still a truth table and so a boolean expression for its output can be derived. The only difference is the output variable in the table expresses the output's *next state* value as a function of the inputs and of the output's *current state* value. Converting the table for the SR latch to a boolean equation yields the following (treating the N/A entries as don't cares):

$$Q+ = S + R' \bullet Q$$

This states that $Q+$ will be true (Q will transition to a '1') whenever $S='1'$ or whenever $R='0'$ *and* Q is already a '1'. This matches precisely the description of the latch's behavior given above.

15.2   The Gated Latch

The SR latch introduced above has the characteristic that it is constantly responding to its inputs. Each time one of its inputs changes, an output change is possible. Due to the presence of false outputs in the circuits which generate the *S* and *R* signals, this makes it difficult to use in most sequential systems designs. However, it can be augmented to make it more useful by controlling when it responds to input changes.

Consider the circuit in Figure 15.5. This is known as a *gated latch*. On the right of the figure you can see the SR latch from the previous section. Two AND gates have been placed between the latch and its inputs. These AND's form a gate that only allows the *S* and *R* inputs to reach the SR latch at certain times. In this context, the word *gate* refers to a gate which is periodically opened or closed to let something in. When the gate is open (*GATE*='1'), the inputs can affect the state of the latch via *GS* and *GR*. When the gate is closed (*GATE*='0'), the inputs cannot affect the state of the latch since *GS* and *GR* will each be forced to a '0'.

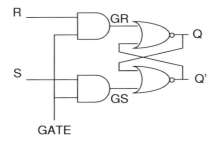

Figure 15.5: A Gated SR Latch

This behavior is shown in the timing diagram of Figure 15.6. Between points A and B in the timing diagram, the *GATE* signal is low and so *GS* and *GR* are low. During this time period the *S* and *R* inputs can transition repeatedly without any effect on the state of the latch.

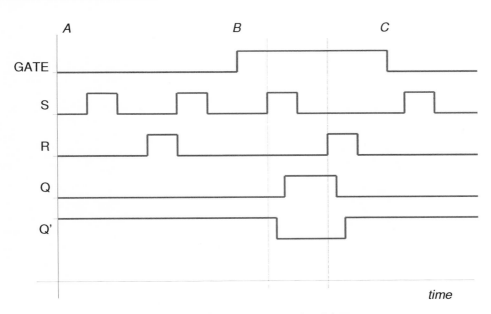

Figure 15.6: Gated SR Latch Timing Diagram

At point B, *GATE* → '1'. The *GS* and *GR* signals now follow the *S* and *R* inputs, and the circuit functions as a conventional SR latch (*S* sets it and *R* resets it). At point C, *GATE* → '0' once again, bringing *GS* and *GR* low as well. At this point, the latch simply retains its last stored value.

The gated latch only behaves as a latch when *GATE*='1'. At all other times, it ignores the values on its *S* and *R* inputs, and holds its old state value. This circuit is also sometimes known by the name of "transparent latch". This is because while the *GATE* input is high the AND gates are transparent (they pass the *S* and *R* values through unchanged). It is also sometimes known by the name of "loadable latch" since the *GATE* input acts as a load signal.

A variant of the gated SR latch is the gated D latch shown in Figure 15.7(a). An inverter has been added so that the two latch inputs are complements of each other. When *GATE*='1', the *Q* output takes on the value of the *D* input. When *D=GATE*='1', the latch will be set. When *D*='0' and *GATE*='1', the latch will be reset. At all other times it will hold its old value. A symbol for this latch is shown in part (b) of the figure.

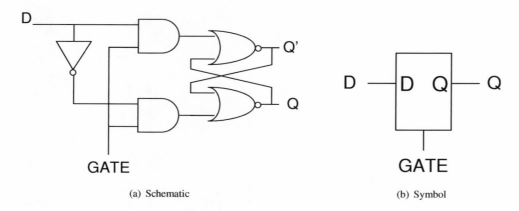

(a) Schematic   (b) Symbol

Figure 15.7: Gated D Latch

Figure 15.8 shows the operation of the gated D latch. When the *GATE* input is low (between points A and B), the latch ignores its *D* input. When the *GATE* input goes high (at point B), the latch output begins following the *D* input value. Once *GATE* goes low again, the latch simply retains its last state and ignores further transitions on the *D* input until *GATE* once again goes high.

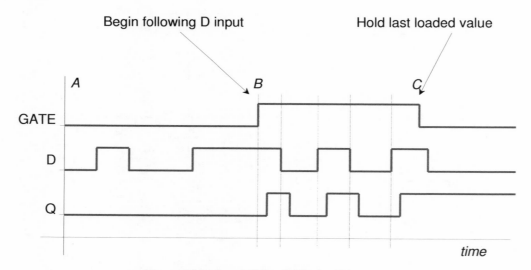

Figure 15.8: Gated D Latch Timing Diagram

A transition table can be created for the gated D latch as shown in Figure 15.9.

GATE	D	Q	$Q+$
0	0	0	0
0	0	1	1
0	1	0	0
0	1	1	1
1	0	0	0
1	0	1	0
1	1	0	1
1	1	1	1

Figure 15.9: Transition Table for Gated D Latch

Solving for $Q+$ yields the following equation:

$$Q+ = GATE' \bullet Q + GATE \bullet D$$

This states that the next state of the latch will be TRUE when either $GATE$ = '0' and the latch was already storing a '1' (maintain old value), or when $GATE$ ='1' and D = '1' (load new value).

15.3   The Master/Slave Flip Flop

The gated latch of the previous section is an improvement over the purely combinational SR latch in that it provides some control over when the latch can be loaded. In spite of this advantage, it still has limitations because it is transparent the entire time $GATE =' 1'$.

To understand the problems this may cause, consider the circuit shown in Figure 15.10. This is an attempt to build a circuit which toggles. A toggle circuit is one where the output inverts each time the latch is loaded. The intent with this design is that each time $GATE$ goes high and then low, the output toggles once from $0 \rightarrow 1$ or from $1 \rightarrow 0$.

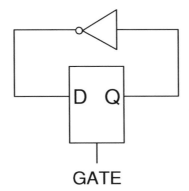

Figure 15.10: Oscillating Circuit Built from Gated D Latch

Figure 15.11 shows the operation of the latch and also that it does not work as expected. At point A, *GATE* → '1' resulting in Q → '1'. This value is then inverted and fed back into the latch input. Since *GATE* is still high, this new D value will cause Q → '0'. This will then be inverted and fed back to the input as a '1' and cause Q → '1' again. This will then be inverted again, and so on, and so on ... indefinitely. This is called an *oscillation* - the circuit output oscillates between a '0' and a '1'. The speed of oscillation depends on the delay through the circuit. At point B we see that *GATE* → '0' and the latch retains its last value.

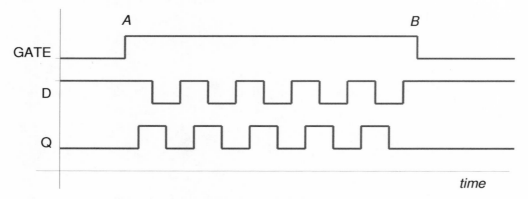

Figure 15.11: Timing Diagram for Oscillating Circuit

Using a gated latch in a feedback configuration (wrapping the output back to the input), leads to erroneous behavior *if the* GATE *input is held high too long.* A solution is to carefully control how long *GATE*='1' so that the gate circuit is closed by the time the inverted Q comes back around to the input. This is difficult to do in light of what we learned about gate delays in Chapter 13. A better solution is to use two gated latches as shown in Figure 15.12. The figure uses symbols to represent the two gated D latches rather than the detailed gate-level schematic shown above for each. This makes the logical operation of the circuit more readily apparent.

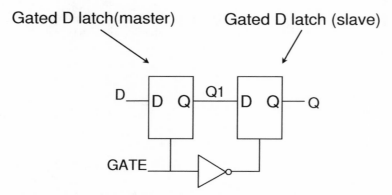

Figure 15.12: A Master/Slave D Flip Flop Built From Gated D Latches

The circuit in Figure 15.12 is called a master/slave flip flop. Note how the *GATE* signal fed to the slave latch is the inverse of that fed to the master latch. When *GATE*='1', the master loads and the slave does not. When *GATE*='0', the slave loads and the master does not. At no time do both load.

The behavior of this flip flop is shown in Figure 15.13 where the master and slave latch load (transparent) times are marked above the timing diagram. During the master period (*GATE*='1'), the master latch loads the D value (the contents of the master latch are reflected by the *Q1* signal in the timing diagram). When *GATE* → '0', the master turns off (quits loading) and the slave turns on, loading the master's value into the slave, and possibly changing the flip flop's output.

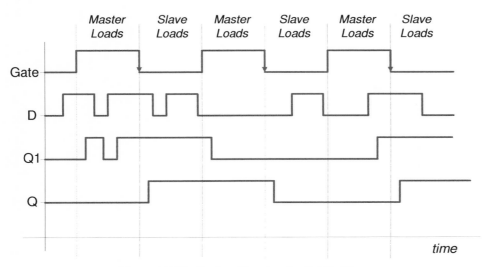

Figure 15.13: Timing Diagram for D Flip Flop

This is often called an *edge-triggered flip flop* since the output changes only when *GATE* goes from '1' → '0'. The *GATE* signal is usually called *CLOCK* or *CLK* to signify that it usually rises and falls in a regular, periodic manner[1]. In the figure, arrowheads have been placed on the clock edges which cause the slave to load (and therefore the output to change). This convention will be followed through the rest of this text to help make timing diagrams easier to understand.

Figure 15.14 shows the final schematic diagram of a falling-edge-triggered flip flop with the *GATE* signal relabeled *CLK*. The slave latch's input inverter has also been removed since the master gated latch produces both a *Q* and a *Q'* signal, and so the inverter is not required. This is the standard falling-edge-triggered D flip flop design which we will use for the remainder of this book.

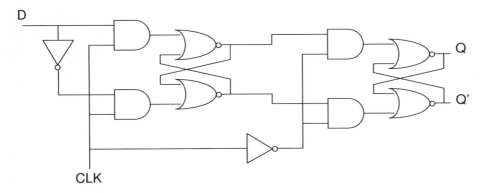

Figure 15.14: Falling Edge Triggered Master/Slave D Flip Flop

---

[1]To be precise, edge-triggered flip flops such as the historic TTL '7474 part were implemented using a different circuit than is shown here and had slightly different characteristics. For purposes of this text, however, we will use the term edge-triggered flip flop to describe this circuit since, in the end, the output changes in response to the clock edge.

Figure 15.15 shows the schematic symbol which is used to represent this circuit. The small triangle where *CLK* enters the flip flop signifies that the flip flop is edge-triggered. The bubble on the *CLK* input signifies that it is sensitive to the *falling edge* of the *CLK* rather than to the *rising edge*.

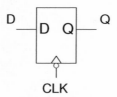

Figure 15.15: Falling Edge Triggered Master/Slave D Flip Flop Symbol

Figure 15.16 shows a toggle circuit built from such a master slave D flip flop along with its timing diagram. As can be seen, the oscillating behavior exhibited by the latch version of the circuit does not occur. Each transition of *CLK* from '1' → '0' results in exactly one change on the output of the flip flop. This is the desired behavior of the toggle circuit.

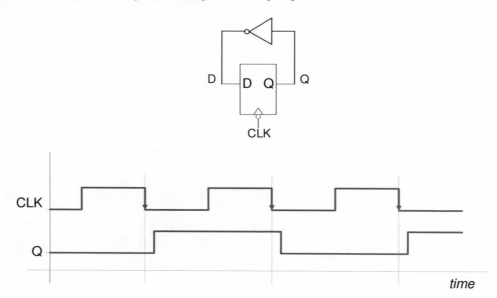

Figure 15.16: Toggle Circuit Built from Master/Slave Flip Flop

15.3.1 Rising-Edge Triggered Flip flop

It is also possible to build a flip flop sensitive to the rising edge of the clock. Figure 15.17 shows such a rising-edge-triggered D flip flop schematic. The only difference from Figure 15.14 is that an inverter has been added to the *CLK* line. This reverses when the master and slave latches load. The master loads when *CLK* = '0', and the slave loads (the output changes) when *CLK* $\rightarrow$ '1'.

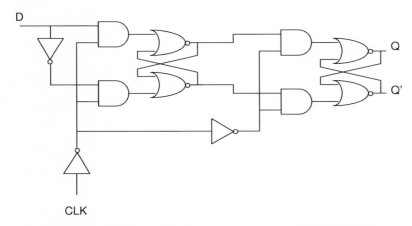

Figure 15.17: Rising Edge Triggered Master/Slave D Flip Flop

Figure 15.18 shows the schematic symbol for this. As above, the triangle on the *CLK* input signifies that the flip flop is edge triggered. The absence of the bubble on the *CLK* input signifies that the flip flop is sensitive to the rising edge of *CLK* rather than the falling edge.

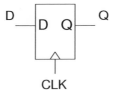

Figure 15.18: Rising Edge Triggered Master/Slave D Flip Flop Symbol

Figure 15.19 compares the behavior of these two different flip flops. As can be seen, the major difference is that one loads on the rising edge of the clock and the other loads on the falling edge of the clock.

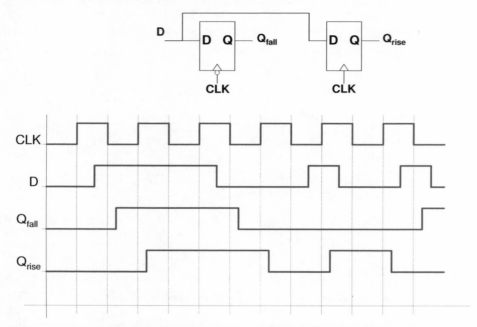

Figure 15.19: Timing Diagrams for Rising- and Falling-Edge Triggered Flip Flops

A transition table for an edge triggered D flip flop is shown in Figure 15.20. It shows that when the flip flop loads a new value, it loads the value present on the D input. The *CLK* input is not shown in the transition table since it is understood that the action described in the transition table happens on the edge of *CLK* (which edge of *CLK* the change occurs on is a function of the type of flip flop).

D	Q	Q+
0	0	0
0	1	0
1	0	1
1	1	1

Figure 15.20: Transition Table for D Flip Flop

From this transition table, the following next state function can be derived for the D flip flop:

$$Q+ = D$$

At this point we now have a variety of latches and edge triggered flip flops available for our use. The remainder of this book will focus on the use of rising edge triggered flips since they are the most commonly used. All examples shown could be easily modified to use falling-edge-triggered flip flops instead. However, most could not be easily modified to use SR latches or gated latches due to their different behavior with respect to clocking.

15.4 Timing Characteristics Of Flip Flops

The timing characteristics of flip flops are usually given in terms of three values. The first timing value is called t_{CLK-Q}. It is the time from when the clock edge occurs until the Q and Q' outputs stabilize. This delay can be determined by examining Figure 15.21. When the clock rises, it will take one inverter delay before the new clock value reaches the AND gates in the slave latch. Then, the two AND gates must react. Finally, it will take as long as $2 \times t_{NOR}$ for the Q and Q' outputs to stabilize. For the flip flop shown in Figure 15.21, the value for t_{CLK-Q} is $t_{CLK-Q} = t_{NOT} + t_{AND} + 2 \times t_{NOR}$. Once again, this is the delay between the edge of the clock and the flip flop's outputs stabilizing.

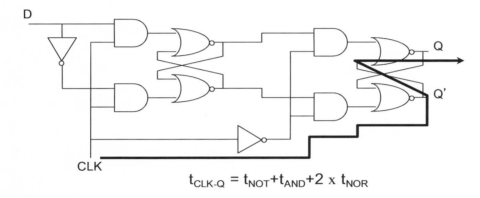

$$t_{CLK-Q} = t_{NOT} + t_{AND} + 2 \times t_{NOR}$$

Figure 15.21: Derivation of t_{CLK-Q} Delay For Falling Edge Flip Flop

The second timing value associated with a flip flop is its *setup time* or t_{setup}, as shown in Figure 15.22. There is a time delay between a D input arriving and the master latch being loaded. It is important that if a D input value is intended to be loaded on a clock edge, it must arrive early enough to do so. That is, it must arrive early enough to set the master latch contents before the clock edge occurs (actually, before the clock to the master latch goes away). Setup time, or t_{setup}, is a measure of how early that is. The value for t_{setup} for this flip flop is: $t_{setup} = t_{NOT} + t_{AND} + 2 \times t_{NOR}$. Any signal not arriving at least t_{setup} *before* the clock falls will not be loaded on that clock edge but rather will be loaded on the next clock edge after that. [2]

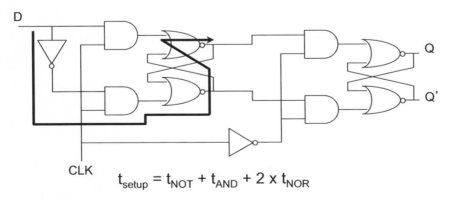

$$t_{setup} = t_{NOT} + t_{AND} + 2 \times t_{NOR}$$

Figure 15.22: Derivation of t_{setup} Time For Falling Edge Flip Flop

The answer is different in the case of the rising edge flip flop of Figure 15.17. Note that it is *the time at which the clock edge arrives at the the master latch's AND gates* which determines t_{setup}. Since the clock edge doesn't arrive at the input to the AND gates until t_{NOT} after the actual clock edge, this allows the D input to arrive later, reducing

---

[2]In actuality, the situation is much worse than this — see Section 15.7 for details.

t_{setup} by the delay of the inverter. Thus, for the flip flop of Figure 15.17 the value would be: [3]

$$t_{setup} = t_{NOT} + t_{AND} + 2 \times t_{NOR} - t_{NOT} = t_{AND} + 2 \times t_{NOR}$$

The third timing value associated with flip flops is *hold time* or t_{hold}. This is a measure of how soon after the clock edge the D input may change to a new value. To understand this, refer to Figure 15.23. The clock edge applied to the flip flop reaches the master latch's AND gates after a delay of t_{NOT}. It is thus not safe to change the D input value right after the clock edge. Rather, the old D value must be *held* on the D input until the clock to the AND gates is low. For the circuit of Figure 15.23, this hold time is t_{NOT}. To reiterate, this is to ensure that the AND gate clock has turned off before a new D value is applied.

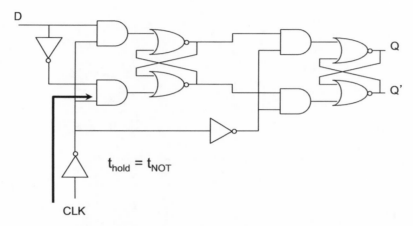

Figure 15.23: Derivation of t_{hold} Time For Rising Edge Flip Flop

By way of comparison, the value of t_{hold} for the falling-edge flip flop of Figure 15.14 is 0ns — there is no delay between the *CLK* input and the input to the AND gates of the master latch.

These three timing values are usually provided as a part of the documentation for a flip flop. To use a flip flop, one typically only needs to know the type of flip flop and these timing values. They are summarized in Figure 15.24 for a rising-edge flip flop.

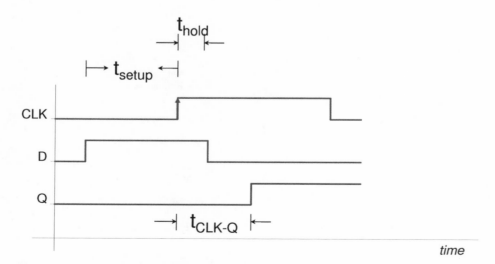

Figure 15.24: Timing Parameters Associated With Rising Edge Flip Flop

---

[3]This discussion has used a simplistic analysis of gate delays to determine t_{setup}. The actual answer depends on a much more detailed analysis of the construction and behavior of the transistors and gates making up the flip flop. Nevertheless, the analysis presented here results in a conservative value for t_{setup} and is sufficient for the purposes of this text.

15.5 Flip Flops With Additional Control Inputs

The flip flops discussed above have only two inputs: a *D* input and a *CLK* input. The *D* input can be considered a *data input*, while the *CLK* input is a *control input*. Additional flip flop control inputs are often provided in libraries of circuit elements. The purpose of these is to provide richer functionality for the flip flop, to make it easier to use in certain design contexts.

Consider the schematic shown in Figure 15.25. It is a conventional Master/Slave D flip flop but with a *CLEAR* signal. This *CLEAR* signal bypasses the gating logic to reset both the master and slave latches. When *CLEAR*='1', *Q*+ → '0' regardless of the value of either the *CLK* or *D* inputs. Asserting the *CLEAR* signal will thus immediately reset the flip flop. When *CLEAR*='0', the flip behaves as a normal D flip flop. The *CLEAR* signal is called an *asynchronous* input because the clearing action occurs independently of the clock. It is a simple matter to add additional logic for an asynchronous *PRESET* input as well (sets the flip flop to a '1').

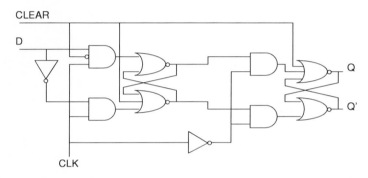

Figure 15.25: A Master/Slave Flip Flop With Asynchronous *CLEAR*

The flip flop shown in Figure 15.26 is a D flip flop with a synchronous clear. Its *CLEAR* signal only affects the gating logic, and thus any clearing it performs will be done on the clock edge. For this reason it is called a *synchronous* clear input. It is a simple modification to this circuit to add a synchronous *PRESET* signal.

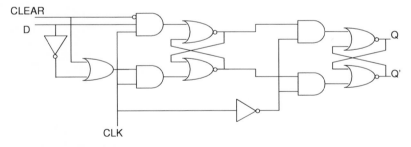

Figure 15.26: A Master/Slave Flip Flop With Synchronous *CLEAR*

The *CLEAR* signal has been designed, in these examples, to clear the flip flop when *CLEAR*='1'. This is called a *high asserted clear*. In many commercial circuit libraries, flip flops exist which cause the flip flop to clear when *CLEAR*='0'. This is called a *low asserted clear*. One should always consult the documentation for a flip flop to determine whether its additional control inputs are low asserted or high asserted.

The convention for indicating a low asserted signal is a bubble on the input. As an example Figure 15.27 shows two different symbols for D flip flops. The first one has a low-asserted clear. The second has a high-asserted preset and a low-asserted clear. It is not possible to tell from these schematic symbols whether they are asynchronous or synchronous control signals. The flip flop documentation must be consulted to determine that.

(a) Low-Asserted Clear   (b) Low-Asserted Clear, High-Asserted Preset

Figure 15.27: Various D Flip Flop Symbols

15.6 A Note on Timing Diagrams

In one case in this chapter, a detailed timing diagram reflecting the actual gate delays was shown (see Figure 15.3). In most other cases, the timing diagrams contained *approximate* timing (see Figure 15.16).. *Approximate* timing diagrams show that there are non-zero delays between signal transitions, but do not attempt to precisely quantify those delays. These are often used in the interest of simplifying the timing diagrams. Approximate timing is sufficient to show *cause-and-effect* between the various signals in the circuit diagrams. Detailed timing (as in Figure 15.3) is only used when it is needed to show exact gate delays.

15.7 A Note on Metastability

Up above we said that signals arriving too late (within the t_{setup} window) would not be loaded into the flip flop. In reality, it can be much worse than this — the behavior of a flip flop whose setup time has been violated is undefined. That is, the flip flop output may hang in an indeterminate state (between a '0' and a '1') for an arbitrarily long period of time if just enough energy is imparted to the latch by the late arriving signal.

To understand just how this can happen, consider when the D signal changes in Figure 15.17. Its new value and its inverse will then propagate through the two leftmost AND gates and start to change the latch value. If the setup time is violated, it is possible that the outputs of the two leftmost AND gates will return to 0 (in response to the clock's rising) *before the latch has finished transitioning completely to its the new state*. If this happens, one of three things might occur. First, the latch may flip back to its original state (likely if the latch was just starting to flip before the AND gates turned off). Second, it may continue its transition to its new state (likely if the latch was *mostly* flipped before the AND gates turned off). Third and worst of all, it may hang in an indeterminate state (with its outputs not fully settled one way or the other) for some amount of time.

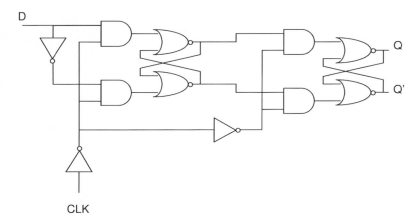

Figure 15.28: Rising Edge Triggered Master/Slave D Flip Flop (reproduced from Figure 15.17)

When this happens it can be said that the flip flop has entered a *metastable* region of operation and, while the flip flop is in the metastable state, its behavior is undefined. Importantly, when a flip flop goes metastable, it is impossible to place a bound on how long it will remain metastable.

Consider the physical example of rolling a ball up a hill, as shown in Figure 15.29. It is theoretically possible, but highly unlikely, that you could impart just the right amount of initial velocity to the ball so that it would stop at the top of the hill and balance there. The slope of the hill right at the top is 0 after all and so the ball perched at the top is a stable situation under ideal conditions. But, if this were to happen, it would be difficult to predict how long it would stay balanced — random movement of the air around the ball would likely be enough to eventually unbalance it, and send it back down one side or the other.

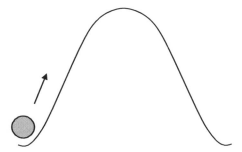

Figure 15.29: An Analogy for Metastability

The arrival of a signal during the setup time window for a flip flop is similar to rolling the ball up the hill. If just the right amount of energy is imparted to the input latch of the flip flop (the cross coupled NOR gates), that latching mechanism may hang between a '1' and a '0' state once the AND gates turn off. And, it is impossible to bound how long it would stay in this suspended state. It may move to the '1' state or to the '0' state relatively quickly and the rest of the system may not notice (it will resolve before the next clock edge). Or, it may take longer to resolve, feeding indeterminate values to circuit elements downstream.

The considerations regarding hold time are similar to those for setup time. Note in Figure 15.28 that the leftmost AND gates in the flip flop do not turn off immediately after the clock changes (they don't even receive the clock signal for an inverter delay after the clock changes). Considering the left half of the flip flop, it is thus possible for the following sequence of events to occur: (1) the clock signal rises, (2) the D input changes and starts to make its way through the AND gates and into the left latch's NOR gates, (3) the NOT gate output on the *CLK* line transitions to a low voltage, and (4) the AND gates finally turn off, preventing new values from entering the NOR gates of the latch. However, by this time, the D signal has already entered the latch and started to modify its contents. In essence the D signal changed *after* the clock changed but was able to *sneak* into the flip flop before its front end AND gates turned off. The result could be an error in the value stored in the flip flop or, as above, it could result in a metastability event.

In any case, intuition suggests that once metastability occurs, random perturbations in the circuit (thermal noise for example or other effects) will eventually cause a metastable latch to resolve to either the '1' state or the '0' state. But, as mentioned, if this *recovery time* is long enough the flip flop output may be misinterpreted by the remainder of the circuit and cause a logic error (a wrong answer).

As unlikely as it would be for a ball to sit perched on a hill for any appreciable amount of time, the probability of it happening is still non-zero. Similarly, the probability of a flip flop entering the metastable state and staying there for an appreciable amount of time may also be quite low (but it is non-zero for any time period you might choose). Modern integrated circuits are clocked at rates in excess of 4GHz (4×10^9 cycles per second). Over the course of a few minutes many, many opportunities for metastability may present themselves and so this is not merely an academic thought experiment.

The rate of circuit failures due to metastability has been the subject of much study over the years, and failure rates measured in hours or days have been observed when a flip flop's setup and/or hold times are violated at a high rate. Note that the discussion above states that when setup or hold times are violated the flip flop *may* go metastable (not *will* go metastable). That is, for a single setup or hold time violation the probability of metastability is very, very low.

Special flip flop designs have been created which are especially resistant to entering the metastable state or which are more likely to resolve quickly if they do. Running an asynchronous input through a series of such *hardened* flip flops (arranged as a shift register) can further reduce the probability of failure if the asynchronous input changes at a high enough frequency. An example of that would be when one clocked system was generating a signal used by another clocked system which was being clocked at a different clock rate. In this case, the rate at which the setup and hold times of the receiving flip flop were violated by the received signal could be very very high and, at those rates, mestability would be an issue. If the system were safety-critical that would be of even more concern. In contrast, if the asynchronous signal were changing at a very low rate (a push button operated by a human to dispense soda from a machine for example) then you would be able to safely ignore it — it would take an arbitrarily long time (forever in human terms) for metastability to occur and, if it did, the worst that could happen is that the soda machine would steal the customer's money.

What is the take-away of all this? There are two things you should focus on. First, you should pay attention to t_{setup} and t_{hold} when doing design and ensure that your design does not violate those time constraints. If your system has no asynchronous inputs (unlikely) then it can be designed in a way to avoid any chance of metastability. A part of the analysis done by CAD tools is to analyze the timing of a circuit (while ignoring asynchronous inputs) and (a) state the fastest rate it can be clocked while still avoiding setup time violations and (b) flag any places in the circuit where hold times are being violated (hold time violations are independent of clock rate). If you then fix the design to remove the hold time violations and clock the circuit below the max clock rate determined in (a) then you will have no possibility of metastability.

But, when there are truly asynchronous inputs, it is impossible to drive the probability of metastable behavior to zero. That is because with asynchronous inputs you cannot guarantee that neither t_{setup} nor t_{hold} are ever violated. In this situation, then, it is important that you consult the literature to understand how to compute MTBF, or mean time between failures due to metastability. Using that you can determine how this affects the reliability of your system and then take the appropriate steps to deal with it.

15.8 Chapter Summary

This chapter has introduced a number of ideas related to building storage elements, specifically latches and flip flops. The key high-level points to master from this chapter include the following:

1. Bi-stable circuits such as the SR latch are storage elements.

2. Latches hold their current state until input changes cause them to change state.

3. Latches continuously sample or react to their inputs.

4. Gated latches contain a gating circuit so that they only sample their inputs at certain times. Gated latches are also known as transparent latches or loadable latches.

5. Gated latches do not work in certain feedback configurations because they sample their inputs the entire time *GATE*='1'. Another way to say this is that they are transparent the entire time *GATE*='1'.

6. Master/Slave flip flops are made from two gated latches which operate with inverted *GATE* inputs. Either the master or the slave is loading at any time but not both.

7. A Master/Slave flip flop only changes its output state on the edge of its clock input. Thus, it is called an edge triggered flip flop.

8. Flip flops can be either rising-edge-triggered or falling-edge-triggered.

9. The timing behavior of flip flops is usually provided in the form of three values: t_{CLK-Q}, t_{setup}, and t_{hold}. These can be derived from the gate-level schematic diagram for the flip flop or from the data sheet associated with the flip flop.

10. Violating t_{setup} and t_{hold} can result in a flip flop going metastable.

The skills that should result from study of this chapter include the following:

1. The ability to draw the schematic (from memory) for any of the storage devices in this chapter.

2. The ability to draw an accurate timing diagram (approximate or detailed) of a circuit's operation given a schematic of the circuit and a specification of input waveforms for it.

3. The ability to determine precisely what kind of latch or flip flop a storage element is simply from the timing diagram of its operation.

4. The ability to write the transition table for any of the storage devices in this chapter.

5. The ability to write a transition table for a new storage element simply from a timing diagram of its operation.

6. The ability to derive the next state equation for $Q+$ for a storage element from either a timing diagram of its operation or its transition table.

15.9 Exercises

15.1. Below is a timing diagram for the SR latch of Figure 15.1. Fill in the output waveform. Reflect approximate timing. See Section 15.6 to remind you what is meant by *approximate timing*.

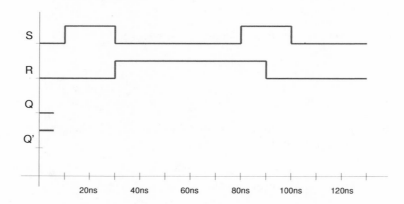

15.2. Repeat Problem 15.1 but with detailed timing. You may simply label each output signal transition in the timing diagram with the time it occurs. Delays of the various gates include: $t_{NOT} = 1ns, t_{AND} = 3ns, t_{NOR} = 2ns$.

15.3. Complete the timing diagram below for an SR latch. In this case, the circuit oscillates. Use $t_{NOR} = 2ns$ and accurately reflect the Q and Q' waveforms in the drawing (complete with timing).

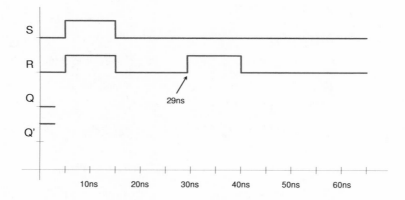

15.4. Write pseudo-code in the style of C or PASCAL or JAVA to describe the operation of an SR latch. For example, below is the outline of the pseudo-code you may start with:

```
// Return new Q output value as a function of its S/R inputs and
// current Q output value.
function srLatch(int S, int R, int Q) {
  return ...
}
```

15.5. Shown in the figure below is a storage circuit made from NAND gates instead of NOR gates. Experiment with values on the S and R inputs to determine how it works. Hint: start with $S=R='1'$. Write a transition table to summarize the operation of the gate.

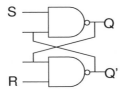

15.6. Below is a timing diagram for the circuit of Figure 15.7. Fill in the output waveform. Reflect approximate timing.

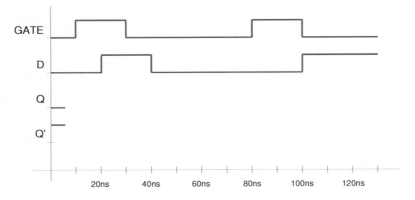

15.7. Repeat Problem 15.6 but with detailed timing. Use the following delays: $t_{NOT} = 1ns, t_{AND} = 3ns, t_{NOR} = 2ns$.

15.8. Build a gated D latch using cross coupled NAND gates instead of cross coupled NOR gates. Hint: draw them as OR gates with bubbles on the inputs. Then, modify the *GATE* logic to match up bubbles. Write a transition table for the resulting circuit.

15.9. Write pseudo-code in the style of C or PASCAL or JAVA to describe the operation of a gated D latch.

15.10. Write pseudo-code in the style of C or PASCAL or JAVA to describe the operation of a rising-edge-triggered D flip flop.

15.11. Below is a timing diagram for the circuit of Figure 15.18. Fill in the output waveform. Reflect approximate timing.

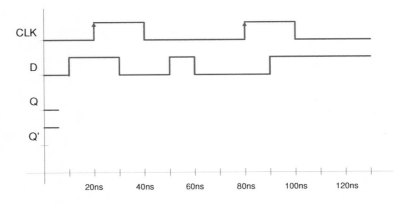

15.12. Repeat Problem 15.11 but with detailed timing. For your delays use the following: $t_{CLK-Q} = 2ns, t_{setup} = 4ns, t_{hold} = 3ns$. Which of these delays is actually needed in order to complete the timing diagram?

15.13. Design a rising-edge-triggered SR flip flop out of gated SR latches.

15.14. Below is a toggle circuit along with a timing diagram. Complete the associated timing diagram complete with detailed timing. Use the delays from Problem 15.12. Also, use $t_{NOT} = 2ns$.

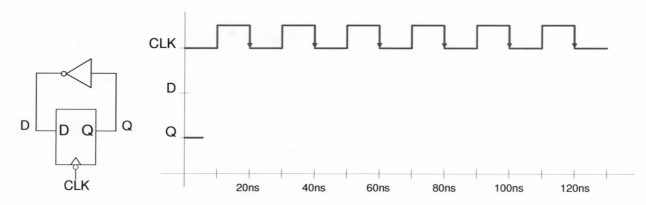

15.15. Discuss the problems associated with using flip flops with asynchronous clear or preset signals. In particular, address the following: (a) false outputs on the logic generating the asynchronous control signals and (b) timing issues associated with the asynchronous control signals.

Chapter 16

Registers and RTL-Based Design

If you were to think about the kinds of digital systems that can be created using only combinational logic you would conclude that the list is fairly small. Essentially all digital systems of any consequence are *sequential*, meaning they contain a mixture of combinational logic and flip flops. Why the word "sequential" to describe them? The reason is that with memory (flip flops) you now have the ability to perform sequences of operations, with the flip flops remembering both (a) partially computed results and (b) where in the sequence of operations the circuit currently is at.

To help motivate this, consider the task of computing the sum of 8 numbers. In software, there are two obvious ways to do this. The *combinational* or non-sequential way to do it would be with a statement of the form: $sum = a + b + c + d + e + f + g + h$. The *sequential* way to do it would be with a *for-loop* which accumulates the values into a single variable as in:

Program 16.0.1 C Program to Sequentially Sum 8 Values

```
sum = 0;
for (int i=0;i<8;i++)
   sum = sum + vals[i];
```

In this second version of the summation program there are two variables which store the *state* of the computation. The *sum* variable stores the computed sum as it is formed. This is an example of *data state*. The i variable stores a value which indicates the current iteration number, which indicates where we are in the computation. This is an example of *control state*. In a computer executing software, these variables' values are stored in memory. Hardware systems also require state, which is usually stored in the flip flops you have been introduced to.

A collection of flip flops which store information in a digital circuit is often called a *register*. Registers can be 1-bit wide or they can be many bits wide. In this chapter we introduce a few sample circuits based on registers. This helps to introduce the notion of RTL or Register Transfer Level design. This concept is perhaps the most important concept you will learn in this entire text since it forms the foundation for all digital systems design.

16.1   Flip Flop-Based Registers

A single D-type flip flop, such as shown in Figure 16.1(a), is a 1-bit register. It has the characteristic that it loads a new value on every single rising edge of the clock. The circuit shown in Figure 16.1(b) is a 4-bit register. It is simply four D-type flip flops in parallel and is said to store a 4-bit word. As with the 1-bit register, it loads a new value on every rising clock edge. The symbol shown in Figure 16.1(c) is a typical symbol for the 4-bit register from part (b) of the figure.

173

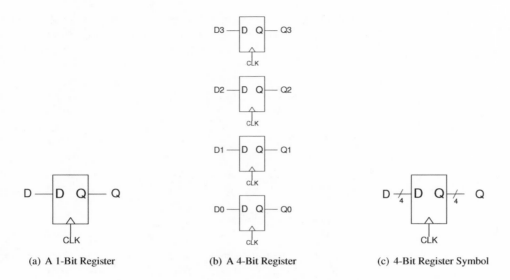

(a) A 1-Bit Register   (b) A 4-Bit Register   (c) 4-Bit Register Symbol

Figure 16.1: A 4-Bit Register Made from Flip Flops

16.1.1   Loadable Registers - First Attempt

The basic 1-bit register can be made more useful by adding logic to control when it loads. At first glance, it may seem that a simple way exists to control the loading of a flip flop by AND-ing a *LOAD* signal with the *CLK* signal as shown in Figure 16.2. When *LOAD*='0', the *GatedClock* signal will not transition high. This will inhibit the loading of the flip flop. While this may work in some cases, it introduces both glitches into the circuit as well as a timing dependency into the circuit, both of which are undesirable. As a result, DO NOT create a loadable register this way.

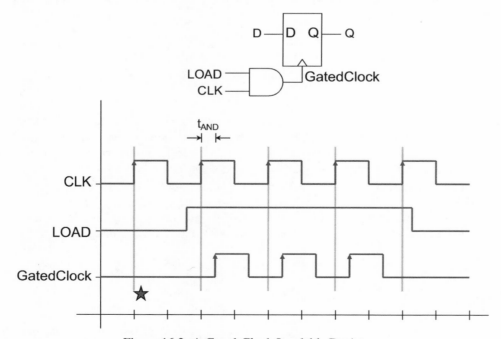

Figure 16.2: A Gated-Clock Loadable Register

Figure 16.2 shows that, due to the delay of the AND gate, when the flip loads, it does so one gate delay *after* the main clock edge (it loads on the rising edge of *GatedClock*). If the overall design contains other flip flops that are clocked by *CLK*, there is now the situation where different flip flops load at different times — some on the clock edge and some one gate delay later. The new outputs of these various flip flops now appear at different times as a result.

This situation where different flip flops receive the clock signal at different times is known as *clock skew* — the times the various flip flops load with respect to each other is *skewed*. To compensate for this requires that the designer perform a detailed timing analysis to ensure that these different flip flop load times do not result in a malfunctioning circuit. Doing so is a difficult and error-prone process.

Additionally, the flip flop is now sensitive to glitches on *LOAD*. To understand the problem, focus on the part of the timing diagram marked with a star symbol. We have previously learned that combinational logic outputs can glitch as gates turn on and off (see Section 13.7). And, high-going false outputs or glitches on *LOAD*, when AND-ed with *CLK* will cause the flip flop to erroneously load when you don't want it to. If glitches were to occur on *LOAD*, they would occur at the point marked with the star in the figure (immediately after the clock edge). Since *CLK* is also high at that point, the output of the AND gate would reflect the glitches on *LOAD* and the flip flop would erroneously load at that point in time.

As a result, for this text, we will adopt the absolute rule that all clock inputs to all flip flops must be tied to the same global clock signal. No logic is allowed to be done using the clock signal — the clock signal is simply directly wired to the clock input of all flip flops. This is called a *Globally Synchronous* design style and ensures that all registers in the system load in unison.

16.1.2 Loadable Registers - The Correct Method

The correct method for creating a register that loads only in response to a *LOAD* control input is shown in Figure 16.3. Here, the flip flop will load on every clock edge but a block of combinational logic selects whether the flip flop will load its existing value or whether it will load a new value. When *LOAD*='0', the flip flop loads its own current value (the value on its *Q* wire). When *LOAD*='1', the flip flop loads new data (the *DIN* value). This design has the property that the flip flop loads on the same clock edge as any other flip flop in the system — it simply loads its old value sometimes, and loads a new value at other times. The control over which it loads is provided by the *LOAD* signal. A truth table for the combinational logic is shown below the schematic.

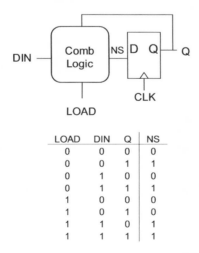

LOAD	DIN	Q	NS
0	0	0	0
0	0	1	1
0	1	0	0
0	1	1	1
1	0	0	0
1	0	1	0
1	1	0	1
1	1	1	1

Figure 16.3: A 1-Bit Loadable Register

Solving the truth table for signal NS (which stands for nextState) yields the following equation:

$$NS = LOAD' \bullet Q + LOAD \bullet DIN$$

which is simply the equation for a MUX.

Thus, this circuit can be implemented as shown in Figure 16.4. Looking at it this way makes perfect sense — when *LOAD* is true, signal *DIN* is selected and when *LOAD* is false, signal *Q* (the existing value stored in the register) is selected.

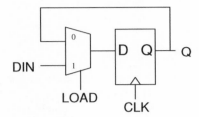

Figure 16.4: A 1-Bit Loadable Register

The above loadable flip flop design can be used to create n-bit loadable registers. Figure 16.5 shows a 4-bit loadable register.

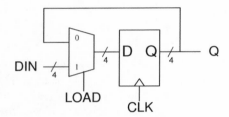

Figure 16.5: A 4-Bit Loadable Register

Importantly, the use of a MUX in front of a register allows essentially any combination of inputs to be selected and loaded into the register. Commonly used values to select between include:

- The register's current value (no-operation)

- Zero (clear the register)

- A data input value (load)

- Any other value desired

For example, the circuit of Figure 16.6 represents a clearable up-counter. When $CLR = 1$, the counter is loaded with all zeroes. Otherwise, the counter is loaded with its old value plus one (if the register's current value was '1011', after an increment it would have the value '1100').

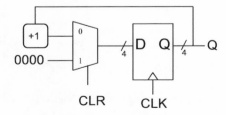

Figure 16.6: A 4-Bit Clearable, Counter

Another example is shown in Figure 16.7. When *CLR/INC*='10', the register loads all 0's which has the effect of clearing the register. When *CLR/INC*='01' the register loads its current value plus one. In all other cases, it loads its old value.

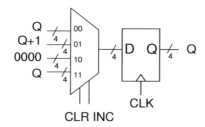

Figure 16.7: A 4-Bit Clearable, Up Counter

A table showing its functionality is given in Figure 16.8. Note the strong similarity between the structure of the truth table and the structure of the circuit.

CLR	INC	Q+
0	0	Q
0	1	Q+1
1	0	0
1	1	Q

Figure 16.8: Function Table for Circuit of Figure 16.7

16.2 Shift Registers

The term *shift register* is applied to circuits such as the one in Figure 16.9, where flip flops are wired in series. That is, the output of one flip flop is wired to the input of the next. All flip flops load new values on the clock edge — FF3 loads the value on the *SerialIn* input, FF2 loads the value of FF3, FF1 loads the value of FF2, and FF0 loads the value of FF1. Since all the flip flops are edge triggered and all are triggered on the same clock edge, the transfer of these values between flip flops happens in unison.

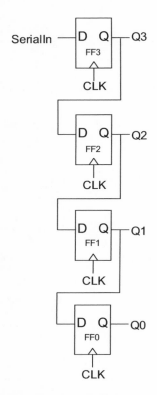

Figure 16.9: A Shift Register Made from Four D Flip Flops

Assume that the initial value stored in the shift register is '1011'. After the next clock edge its value will be 'S101', where 'S' is either a '0' or '1', depending on the value present on the *SerialIn* input. If *SerialIn* were held at a '0' value, the contents stored in the shift register would transition through the following sequence of values:

$$1011 \rightarrow 0101 \rightarrow 0010 \rightarrow 0001 \rightarrow 0000 \rightarrow 0000 \cdots$$

one per clock cycle. On the other hand, if the *SerialIn* input were held at a '1' value, the contents stored in the shift register would transition through the following sequence of values:

$$1011 \rightarrow 1101 \rightarrow 1110 \rightarrow 1111 \rightarrow 1111 \rightarrow \cdots$$

one per clock cycle. This is usually called a *serial-in, parallel-out* shift register since the input is shifted in serially, one bit at a time. At any given time, the four most recent input values are available on the *Q3-Q0* wires as a parallel, 4-bit word. Shift registers of any length desired can be created. Such shift registers are sometimes called *digital delay lines* because they can be used to delay a signal by some number of clock cycles. When used as a digital delay line the only output of interest is usually $Q0$, which in this case would be a 4-cycle delayed version of $SerialIn$.

A conditionally-shiftable shift register is shown in Figure 16.10. In this circuit, when *SHIFT*='0', the register loads its old value. When *SHIFT*='1', the register shifts (each flip flop loads its upper neighbor's value).

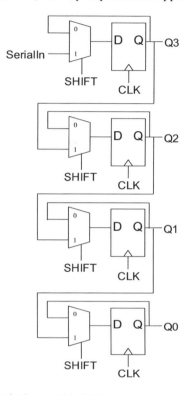

Figure 16.10: A 4-Bit Shift Register With Enable

16.3 Mini Case Study: An Accumulator-Based Averaging Circuit

As a final example of register-based design, consider the design of a circuit which, for each window of data samples it receives, will compute an average numerical value for the value of those data samples. Here is a more detailed description of the circuit's operation:

- The samples are 24-bits wide and arrive one per clock cycle.

- A control signal *init* is used to mark the first sample of each window.

- The windows are assumed to be 16 samples long.

A few considerations follow from this description:

- Taking the average of a window of 16 samples requires adding them all together followed by dividing by 16.

- An adder plus a register can do the adding of successive samples.

- A divide by 16 can be accomplished by shifting the sum right by 4 bit positions. Another way to accomplish this shift is to just throw away the bottom 4 bits in the signal returned from the module. Doing so will do the equivalent of an integer divide by 16, throwing away any remainder. This is much simpler than performing an actual long division (the design of which is beyond the scope of this entire textbook).

- If you add together sixteen 24-bit numbers, the result could conceivably grow to require 28 bits to represent the sum. To understand this, think about adding together 16 numbers, each of which are equal to $maxValue$, the maximum value that can be represented in 24 bits. The result will be $16 \times maxValue$ and will require 4 additional bits to represent it (Just as dividing by 16 eliminates 4 bits, multiplying by 16 adds 4 bits).

- The simplest way to accomodate this bit growth is to use a 28-bit register to hold the accumulated value, a 28-bit adder to do the addition, and to zero-pad each 24-bit sample by 4 additional 0's on the left so the widths line up.

- The *init* signal tells when a new window is starting. This same signal can be an output from the design to indicate that the current value stored in the register (before the next clock edge occurs) contains the window's accumulation value. Taking the top 24 bits of the register's output will be the computed average of the sample values from that previous window.

With this in mind, Figure 16.11 notionally represents a design that implements these design requirements. It is left to you to work through this design in your mind until you understand how it works and whether you agree it meets the design requirements. NOTE: the drawing of the output in this diagram may be a bit confusing. The output of the register is 28 bits wide and is fed back up into the adder as signal *sum*. Then, the 24 most significant bits (MSB's) of that register output are used as the primary output of the circuit (called *average*).

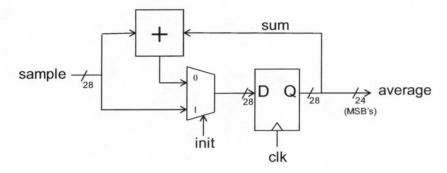

Figure 16.11: A Register-Based Averaging Circuit

16.4 An Introduction to Register Transfer Level (RTL) Design

If you go back and examine the circuit drawings in this chapter thus far, you may note that they all share a common structure. In each case, they consist of one or more flip flops (collectively called a register) with combinational logic and wires in front of the register. These logic gates and wires combine the current values stored in the register with additional inputs to compute new values to load into the register on the next clock cycle. A general diagram of this is shown in Figure 16.12. This is called the *Register Transfer Level (RTL) Structure*.

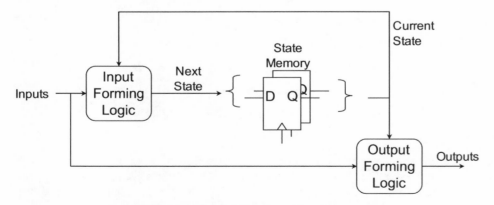

Figure 16.12: Register Transfer Level (RTL) Structure

Note that the term *state* shows up multiple times in this figure. An informal definition of state would be the information *stored* in the circuit (and thus information which will persist until changed). For the accumulator design above, for example, the state of the circuit is the current total accumulated value.

The outputs of the registers in a digital circuit form what is called the circuit's *current state* or CS. The inputs to the registers in a digital circuit form the *next state* or NS. That is, they represent what the new state stored in the register after the next clock edge.

The input forming logic (IFL) combines the current state of the register with any inputs to compute a new next state. On the next clock edge, those next state values will be loaded into the register, becoming the new current state. Thus, a computation in a digital circuit proceeds from one state to another, as new next state values are loaded into the registers of the circuit on successive clock edges.

Finally, the output forming logic (OFL) is combinational logic which generates outputs for the circuit. These outputs are boolean combinations of the current state and the inputs.

The term register transfer level (RTL) thus refers to a design abstraction we use when designing digital systems. It refers to the flow of digital signals between registers (the state registers) and the logical operations performed on those signals by the input forming logic.

Such an abstraction helps you as a designer in the design process. To design a circuit you first determine what *state* is required for the computation. You then determine, based on the computation you want performed, what logic and wiring you need between the registers to transform those CS values into NS values. You then implement the state with flip flops (registers) and you implement the input forming logic (IFL) with gates and wiring. The entire system works in synchrony with a global clock signal and the circuit progresses through a sequence of *states*, performing the needed computations as it goes.

To help illustrate this, let's take a few of the designs from earlier in this chapter and identify the various parts of the design and the computations performed by the input forming logic:

16.4.1 The Loadable Register of Figure 16.4

In this design, the register is the flip flop (the register will *always* be the flip flops). The current state is the output of the flip flop called Q (the current state will *always* be the output of the register). The next state is the input(s) to the register (the next state will *always* be the input(s) to the register). The IFL, using C-like notation, computes the following: $nextState = (LOAD == 1)?DIN : Q$.

16.4.2 The Clearable Up Counter of Figure 16.7

In this design, even though there are 4 flip flops we would say they constitute a single multi-bit register. The current state of the register is Q. The IFL performs the calculation shown in Figure 16.8 where $Q+$ is the next state value and Q is the current state value.

16.4.3 The Shift Register of Figure Figure 16.9

In this design, the state register is the 4 flip flops. The current state is the outputs of those flip flops ($Q3 - Q0$). In this case, however, the IFL is simply wires (no logic gates). The next state equation (using SystemVerilog concatenation syntax) would be: $nextState = \{SerialIn, Q[3:1]\}$.

16.4.4 The Averaging Circuit of Figure 16.11

As above, the register is the flip flops in this circuit and the current state is the output of the register (note in the diagram that this would be the 28-bits of register output, called *sum*). The IFL for the next state either selects the current sample value or the existing current state plus the current sample value. This circuit is different compared to the others in that it has a separate output which is not simply the register output. In this case, it is the 24 most significant bits of the *sum* signal and is called *average*. If you refer back to Figure 16.12 you will see a box labelled *output forming logic*. This is combinational logic and wiring which converts the current state into the desired output. In this case, the output forming logic (OFL) is simply the 24 most significant bits of the current state. In circuits we will see later, the OFL will contain actual logic and wiring.

16.4.5 More Complex Examples of RTL

In the above circuit examples, there was always one register and one block of IFL. In general, an RTL design will consist of *many* register/IFL/OFL combinations. For example, consider a modification to the averaging example given above where the *init* signal to the accumulator is generated by a separate counter circuit. For example, any time the counter circuit's output value is 0, then the accumulator should start a new accumulation window. The resulting circuit could be a combination of Figure 16.7 and Figure 16.11 as shown in Figure 16.13. In the combined circuit, the output of the counter is compared to 0000 and that signal used as the *init* for the averaging circuit. Here, there are two registers, each with their own IFL blocks and their own OFL blocks.

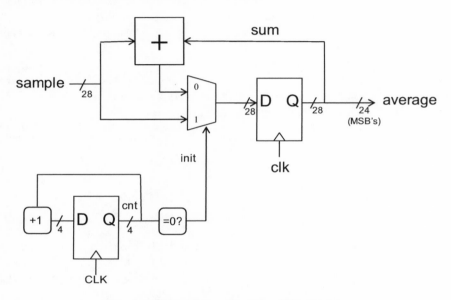

Figure 16.13: A More Complex RTL Design

As your digital designs grow in complexity and size you will start to visualize designs as collections of interconnected registers, IFL, and OFL. The rest of this text is devoted to helping you build up to that level of expertise by introducing additional types of modules you can combine into an RTL design.

16.5   Chapter Summary

This chapter has introduced the notion of registers. These are implemented using flip flops and logic to select what should be loaded into the flip flops on each clock edge. The chapter has also introduced the notion of RTL design, a way of modeling digital systems. Key concepts from this chapter include:

1. The timing problems associated with gated clock circuits were outlined. An alternative to gating clocks called Globally Synchronous Design was described. In it, all flip flops load new values at the exact same time.

2. The use of a MUX to select between various options for loading values into the register at the next clock edge is powerful. It enables the creation of a wide variety of useful circuits.

3. These useful circuits include:

   - Serial shift registers which simply transfer their contents one stage to the right or left on each clock cycle.
   - Bi-directional shift registers.
   - Loadable registers
   - Clearable registers
   - Incrementable registers (counters)

The major skill that should result from study of this chapter is the ability to design any of a variety of register circuits using flip flops and logic gates.

16.6   Exercises

16.1. Design a 4-bit shift register with the following functionality: shift-left, shift-right, clear, load-all-1's. Use a 2-bit control input to select between these options (00=shift-left, 01=shift-right, 10=clear, 11=load-all-1's).

16.2. Design a 3-bit up/down counter with the following functions: increment, decrement, no change, reset. Use a 2-bit control input to select between these options (00=increment, 01=decrement, 10=no change, 11=reset). You may assume you have an already-designed '+1' block available for your use as well as an already-designed '-1' block available for your use.

16.3. Design a 4-bit ring counter. This is a 4-bit shift register. When the control input is high, the register loads the value '1000', when the control input is low, the count sequence is: '1000' $\rightarrow$ '0100' $\rightarrow$ '0010' $\rightarrow$ '0001' $\rightarrow$ '1000' $\rightarrow \cdots$.

Chapter 17

Behavioral SystemVerilog for Registers

17.1 Introduction to Behavioral SystemVerilog

In the previous two chapters we learned how to use structural and dataflow SystemVerilog for the design of combinational circuits. This chapter introduces additional SystemVerilog constructs, called *behavioral* SystemVerilog, which allows for design at higher levels of abstraction than either structural or dataflow.

17.2 The *always_ff* Block

To describe sequential circuits (circuits containing flip flops or registers), SystemVerilog provides an *always_ff* block. With this block, flip flops and their input forming logic can be described in a compact structure.

The way to design the loadable register of Figure 16.4 using SystemVerilog is shown in Program 17.2.1. Here an *always_ff* block has been used to describe a register being loaded on the rising edge of the clock (a falling edge flip flop could be described by simply replacing the keyword *posedge* with *negedge*).

Program 17.2.1 SystemVerilog Code for a Loadable Register

```
module behavLoadableReg (
      output logic q,
      input logic clk, load, d);

   always_ff @(posedge clk)
     if (load)
       q <= d;

endmodule
```

A few things to notice about this example include:

- Since your intention is to create registered logic (one or more flip flops with their associated input forming logic), you use the *always_ff* keyword to start the circuit block description.

- The body of an *always_ff* block uses a variety of constructs (in this case an *if-then-else* statement), somewhat similar to that found in C or Java to describe the register's input forming logic.

- The implication of the *if-then-else* statement in Program 17.2.1 is that if *load* is false, then nothing will happen to the *q* signal. That is, *q will retain its previous value*, which is precisely what is desired for a loadable register. This is what makes *always_ff* so useful. Remember that in basic SystemVerilog *assign* statements you are

185

describing logic which will react to any changes on its inputs (and which must cover all input combinations). But with *always_ff* blocks you are specifying state changes which occur on clock edges. If the conditions in the *if-then-else* are not met then your registers will simply retain their previous values

- Assignments in a clocked *always_ff* block should <u>always</u> use the '<=' assignment operator. In contrast, you use the '=' assignment operator in dataflow SystemVerilog *assign* statements.

In the case of the code of Program 17.2.1, the *if-then* statement would be converted by a circuit synthesis tool into the MUX of Figure 16.4 and its inclusion inside a clocked *always_ff* block implies the register. Thus, with one construct (the *always_ff* block), you can describe a register as well as its input forming logic.

Additionally, with very little change, this loadable register can be converted to a parameterized version which allows for the use of any width inputs and outputs such as the design of Figure 16.5. The equivalent SystemVerilog program is shown in Program 17.2.2 — the only change required is the addition of width information for the *d* input and the *q* output. Note, however, that the actual specification of the logic for the register is identical in both programs (the *always_ff* block).

Program 17.2.2 SystemVerilog Code for a Variable-Width Loadable Register

```
module behavLoadableReg #(parameter WID=4) (
        output logic[WID-1:0] q,
        input logic clk, load,
        input logic[WID-1:0] d);

  always_ff @(posedge clk)
    if (load)
      q <= d;

endmodule
```

This method of parameterization of modules is a powerful mechanism to write reusable code. Some notes regarding this: (1) the keyword *parameter is optional* in the code above and (2) you can have multiple parameters declared inside the parentheses separated by commas.

When writing behavioral SystemVerilog, it is a simple matter to include additional control inputs to the IFL. For example, how would you code a loadable register which can also be cleared (set to all 0's)? Below is one example:

Program 17.2.3 SystemVerilog Code Fragment for a Clearable/Loadable Register

```
  always_ff @(posedge clk)
    if (clr)
      q <= 0;
    else if (load)
      q <= d;
```

Before proceeding, you should think about the following question: "what will the counter do when $clr = load = 1$?" Options might include (a) it will do nothing, (b) it will clear to all 0's, (c) it will load, (d) it will do something else.

A quick examination of the *if-then-else* statement makes it clear that the *clr* signal takes precedence and so the correct answer is (b). How might you code it to get (a)? The example below shows how:

Program 17.2.4 SystemVerilog Code Fragment for a Clearable/Loadable Register - Version 2

```
always_ff @(posedge clk)
  if (clr && !load)
    q <= 0;
  else if (load && !clr)
    q <= d;
```

The beauty of behavioral SystemVerilog is that you can code essentially whatever you, as the designer, want in the body of the block — the synthesis tools will convert that to input forming logic and place it in front of one or more flip flops to make a register.

17.3 Shift Register Design Using Behavioral SystemVerilog

Consider the circuit of Figure 16.9 where four flip flops in series form a shift register The SystemVerilog code is shown here:

Program 17.3.1 SystemVerilog Code for a 4-Stage Shift Register

```
module delay4 (
        input logic clk, SerialIn,
        output logic[3:0] Q);

  always_ff @(posedge clk)
  begin
    Q[3] <= SerialIn;
    Q[2] <= Q[3];
    Q[1] <= Q[2];
    Q[0] <= Q[1];
  end

endmodule
```

This *always_ff* block has four assignment statements and so the body of the block is wrapped in a *begin ... end* pair. Thus, the block actually actually describes four registers, each 1-bit wide.

This can be simplified by using vectors of bits and the concatenation operation as in Program 17.3.2. The assignment statement within the *always_ff* block simply throws away the LSB of *Q* and prepends the *SerialIn* input bit to the other bits on each successive clock edge. This is equivalent to the code above but is accomplished in one assignment statement.

Program 17.3.2 SystemVerilog Code for a 4-Stage Shift Register - Simplified Version

```
module delay4 (
        input logic clk, SerialIn,
        output logic[3:0] Q);

  always_ff @(posedge clk)
    Q <= {SerialIn, Q[3:1]};

  endmodule
```

This design could be easily modified to add a *shift* control signal to control which clock cycles the shifting should occur on as was shown back in Figure 16.10. This is shown in Program 17.3.3. It could be further modified to allow for bi-directional shifting, loading, or clearing, all in the spirit of the circuits of Chapter 16.

Program 17.3.3 SystemVerilog Code for a Controllable 4-Stage Shift Register

```
module delay4 (
        input logic clk, shift, SerialIn,
        output logic[3:0] Q);

  always_ff @(posedge clk)
    if (shift)
      Q <= {SerialIn, Q[3:1]};

  endmodule
```

17.4   The Semantics of the *always_ff* Block

The flip flop assignment statements in the *always_ff* blocks we have seen thus far have used the '$<=$' assignment operator (called a non-blocking assignment operator or NBA in SystemVerilog). The semantics of an *always_ff* block using '$<=$' assignment operators can be understood by the following:

- The names of register signals appearing on the right sides of '$<=$' statements refer to the current state values of those flip flops. For example, in the case of our shift register, the $q[2]$ expression in the statement $q[1] <= q[2]$ refers to taking the *current state* of the $q[2]$ register and making it the input (the *next state* of the $q[1]$ register.

- The signal appearing on the left side of the '$<=$' statement is the input to the flip flop (its next state value).

- There is no implied order of execution between '$<=$' statements in an *always_ff* block. That is, all assignment statements are considered to execute concurrently on the clock edge.

This last point is CRUCIAL TO UNDERSTAND. If the code in Program 17.3.1 were executed sequentially (meaning each statement was truly executed in order as in C or Java) it would not work as a shift register but, rather, after all the assignment statements the value of *serialIn* would have propagated all the way to $q[0]$ after one clock edge.

Another way to look at the code of Program 17.3.1 is to consider the 4 bits of Q to be 4 different registers, each with their own IFL (in this case a wire). As 4 different registers, they each operate independently. Thus, the following code is equivalent to that of Program 17.3.1:

Program 17.4.1 SystemVerilog Code for a 4-Stage Shift Register - Reordered Assignment Statements

```
module delay4 (
        input logic clk, SerialIn,
        output logic[3:0] Q);

   always_ff @(posedge clk)
   begin
     // The next 4 assignments can be in any order
     // and it will not change the circuit
     Q[2] <= Q[3];
     Q[0] <= Q[1];
     Q[3] <= SerialIn;
     Q[1] <= Q[2];
   end

endmodule
```

There is no ordering implied in the statements of an *always_ff* block — any order will work and the same logic will result. However, this is only true if you are using the non-blocking assignment operator ($<=$). Do NOT use blocking assignment operators ($=$), inside *always_ff* blocks.

As another example of how this is different from any other language you have ever encountered, consider the problem of swapping two values. In languages like C, you must use a temporary variable as in:

```
// C code to swap variables 'a' and 'b'
tmp = a;
a = b;
b = tmp;
```

Program 17.4.2 shows that this can be done without the temporary variable because the assignment statements are concurrent statements. This is a design containing two registers, whose outputs are *a* and *b*. When the *load* signal is true, they are each loaded with an input value but when the *swap* signal is asserted, the two registers swap their values on the clock edge.

Program 17.4.2 SystemVerilog Code for a Swapper Circuit

```
module swapper (
        input logic clk, load, swap,
        input logic[3:0] ina, inb,
        output logic[3:0] a, b);

    always_ff @(posedge clk)
      if (load)
      begin
        a <= ina;
        b <= inb;
      end
      else if (swap)
      begin
        a <= b;
        b <= a;
      end

endmodule
```

The circuit corresponding to Program 17.4.2 is shown in Figure 17.1. Can you see how the structure of the *if-then-else* statement is reflected in the use of MUX blocks? In particular, the first *if* clause results in a MUX directly in front of the flip flop. Later *if* clauses add additional MUXes in front of that MUX, thus enforcing the precedence implied by the *if-then-else* statement logic.

As a final note, note that when the body of an *if-then* statement contains more than one statement, you enclose the statements in a *begin ... end* pair. Similarly, when the body of an *always_ff* block has more than one statement in it, it is enclosed in a *begin ... end* pair as well.

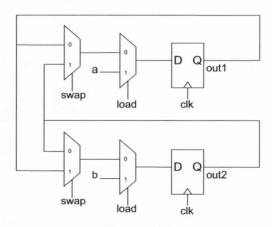

Figure 17.1: Circuit Corresponding to Program 17.4.2

17.5 Reset Problems With Registers

It has been said previously that the *logic* type is a 4-valued type consisting of '0', '1', 'X', and 'Z'. Because we are learning *digital* design, all of the circuits we are learning to use are designed specifically to limit their inputs and outputs to the values '0' (low voltage) and '1' (high voltage). In an advanced class (especially in a class on analog design or on VLSI design) you would learn to design circuits whose inputs and outputs can be any value between GND and Vcc. But, for purpose of simulating the designs shown in this book there are only two voltages that will occur — low (0) and high (1).

The value 'X' will never appear in a real circuit. It is included in SystemVerilog's signal types to reflect an *unknown* value. For example, if you were to wire up the outputs of two gates together (not possible with *logic* but possible with the *wire* type) and if those two gates were driving different values onto that wire, the logic simulator program would assign an 'X' value to the wire. In the simulation waveform viewer you would see that value and would understand that there was a problem in your circuit as a result.

A more common occurence of the 'X' value, however, happens on simulation startup. When an actual circuit is powered up, all the memory elements (flip flops) will load with either '0' or '1' values (but the actual values they will initialize to is unknown). Then, all the combinational logic circuits (gates) will update in light of those flip flop values. Thus, even though all the signal values in the circuit will be '0' or '1', it is unknown just what those various values will be. To reflect this, upon startup (and before you have applied any inputs to the circuit), the logic simulator will initialize all signals in the circuit to the 'X' value (including the values stored in flip flops).

In the case of circuits consisting only of combinational logic (gates), as soon as you drive real inputs into the circuit their outputs will transition to known logic values. However for circuits containing flip flops, these 'X' values will persist until those flip flops are explicitly loaded with binary values. Thus, if you fail to provide a way to either reset or load flip flops with known values, they will remain in the 'X' state indefinitely.

To better understand this, consider the circuit of Program 17.2.1 (which we saw previously). There, the flip flop will hold its previous value (an 'X') until the *load* signal is true. Similarly, the shift register of Program 17.3.1 will contain 'X' values until four clock cycles have passed and all four flip flops have loaded known values.

Next, consider Program 17.5.1 below. It represents a common mistake which you might make. It is a counter circuit — on each clock edge it adds 1 to the register's current value. Since the register initializes to 'XXXX', however, the register will never take on any other value since $XXXX + 0001 = XXXX$. If you fail to provide a clear or load signal on the counter to set it to a known binary value, you will never get it to begin counting.

Program 17.5.1 SystemVerilog Code for a Counter Which Will Never Count

```
always_ff @ (posedge clk)
  q <= q + 1;
```

As another example of this, consider the circuit schematic of Figure 16.13 and focus on the register in the lower left corner and its +1 circuit. This is exactly the problem shown in Program 17.5.1 — it is a counter with no reset signal and will never actually initialize to known binary values during simulation. At this point you may object and state that in the case of the circuit of Figure 16.13 all you want is a counter which will pass through 0 every 16 cycles to reset the accumulator. You may further state that the circuit shown in the figure will do that since the register will initialize to legal binary values. This may be true but (a) you need to be able to simulate the design and without a reset on the counter you cannot do so and (b) if you were to build the circuit you would want a way to test it (and an important part of testing actual circuits requires the ability to set them to a known state).

So, always ensure that circuits such as counters have a reset signal on them. A modification of Program 17.5.1 which reflects this is shown here:

Program 17.5.2 SystemVerilog Code for a Counter With a Reset Signal

```
always_ff @(posedge clk)
  if (reset)
    q <= 0;
  else
    q <= q + 1;
```

Alternatively, the register could have a load signal which will load it with a known signal as shown in Program 17.5.3. In this code, signal *dataIn* is assumed to come from logic which is being reset to known values so we can assume it will contain actual binary values instead of 'X' values during simulation.

Program 17.5.3 SystemVerilog Code for a Counter Which Loads From an External Signal

```
always_ff @(posedge clk)
  if (load)
    q <= dataIn;
  else
    q <= q + 1;
```

In summary, you should always take care to ensure that registers will get cleared or loaded with legal binary values. The appearance of 'X' values in your circuit during simulation is an indication of a problem in this regard (usually, that the circuit was never properly initialized). [1] Never ignore 'X' values in simulation.

---

[1] As mentioned just briefly, there are other instances where 'X' values can arise during simulation due to contention on wires which have multiple drivers attempting to drive them. However, if you use the *logic* type for all signals in your design it will not be possible to design such structures. That is one of the reasons the use of the *logic* type is recommended in this text. The alternative is to use *wire* and *reg* keywords for signals — these allow the creation of circuit structures which may result in contention (where multiple drivers are connected to a single wire). This may be due to a design error in your HDL code (a commmon problem beginners encounter). Or, it may also be on purpose where *tri-state drivers* are used to form a bus structure. However, the use of tri-state is not covered here. Our focus on the use of the *logic* type for signals means the only source of 'X' values during simulation will be due to uninitialized flip flops.

17.6 Chapter Summary

This chapter has introduced behavioral SystemVerilog and focused on describing registers and register files using it. The key points with regard to behavioral SystemVerilog design include:

1. The synchronous *always_ff* blocks described in this chapter trigger on the rising edge of the clock, forming registers and associated input forming logic.

2. The signal names appearing on the left sides of synchronous block assignment statements refer to the input values (next state values) of flip flops.

3. The signal names appearing on the right sides of synchronous block assignment statements refer to the output values (current state values) of flip flops.

4. Due to these semantics, the ordering of assignment statements in *always_ff* blocks does not affect the circuit produced.

5. If a signal is assigned to more than once in the execution of an *always_ff* block body, the last assignment statement takes precedence.

6. The logic of *if-then* statements usually implies a precedence between control signals such as *clr* and *inc*.

7. A variety of statements such as *if-then-else* and *case* statements can be used in the body of always blocks (including *always_ff* blocks - the use of *case* statements was not seen in the body of this chapter but is perfectly allowable).

8. When coding SystemVerilog, you should consult the documentation for the synthesis tool and target technology you are using to understand how to write your SystemVerilog code to ensure that your design will be mapped most efficiently to silicon.

9. You should make it a practice to regularly look at the synthesis reports produced by the synthesizer to understand how it mapped your design onto the target technology.

10. You should ensure that all register structures in your circuit include signals to either reset or load those registers with known binary values. Otherwise, they will never take on values other than 'X' values.

The skills that should result from a study of this chapter include the following:

1. The ability to write both register and register file circuit descriptions using behavioral SystemVerilog.

2. The ability to create circuit schematics which correspond to behavioral SystemVerilog descriptions.

3. The ability to describe the differences between *always_ff* and *assign* statements and when to use each.

17.7 Exercises

For all of the problems below, enter the designs using SystemVerilog. Enter the code and do enough of a compilation to complete a syntax check of your code to ensure that it is syntactically correct (you need not fully simulate it, however). How you do that will depend on the particular CAD tools you are using. If you are running the SystemVerilog from the command line, a simple *vlog filename.sv* will be sufficient.[2]

17.1. Write the behavioral SystemVerilog code for a shift register that either shifts left or right, depending on the value of a *shift* signal ($shift = 0$ means shift left, $shift = 1$ means shift right). The shift register should be parameterized to be of any length.

17.2. Write the SystemVerilog for any of the circuits in the previous chapter as assigned by your instructor.

17.3. Write the SystemVerilog code for any of the problems from Chapter 16 as assigned by your instructor.

---

[2]However, when running from the command line you must always first create a work library for the compiler to operate with. This is done by first executing *vlib work* once from the command line in the directory where you intend to work. The *vlog* command will then put its compiled files in intermediate form into that work library.

Chapter 18

Modeling Combinational Logic Using Behavioral SystemVerilog

SystemVerilog introduces a new coding structure, called an *always_comb* block, which can be used to describe combinational logic at higher levels of abstraction than either structural gates or dataflow's *assign* statements. The *always_comb* is considered to be part of behavioral SystemVerilog, just as the *always_ff* block is. But, as we will see in this chapter, it is very different from *always_ff* in a number of key ways.

18.1   Combinational *always* Blocks

The benefit of using *always_comb* blocks over structural and dataflow design is that these blocks can contain, *case* statements, *if-then-else* statements, etc. They thus provide a rich set of alternative constructs for describing combinational logic compared to the fairly limited dataflow assignments of the previous chapters.

A second benefit of using SystemVerilog's *always_comb* blocks over the original *always* blocks of Verilog is that your use of an *always_comb* block announces to the synthesizer that your intent is to describe a combinational circuit. The SystemVerilog synthesis tools are thus able to throw warnings if you code something other than pure combinational logic.

Going back to our 2:1 MUX example, Program 18.1.1 shows how this can be described using an *always_comb* block.

Program 18.1.1 Combinational Always Block for a MUX

```
module combAlwaysMUX(
      output logic q,
      input logic sel, a, b);

  always_comb
    if (sel)
      q = b;
    else
      q = a;

endmodule
```

Note that assignments inside an *always_comb* block use the '=' assignment operator rather than the '<=' operator of the *always_ff*. This is similar to the '=' operator used in *assign* statements.

The *always_comb* construct can contain exactly one statement inside it. In this example, that statement is the *if-then-else* statement shown. If you want more complex code inside an *always_comb* block, you can surround the body with a *begin . . . end* pair as shown in this example:

Program 18.1.2 Combinational Always Block for a 2:4 Decoder

```
module combAlwaysDecoder(
        output logic[3:0] q,
        input logic[1:0] a);

    always_comb
    begin
      q[3] = (a == 3);
      q[2] = (a == 2);
      q[1] = (a == 1);
      q[0] = (a == 0);
    end

endmodule
```

In the example above, the resulting circuit will behave *as if the code executes sequentially, one line at a time* and consists of four separate statements.

   VERY IMPORTANT: this is different from the structural gate instantiations of Chapter 8, is different from the dataflow *assign* statements from Chapter 14, and is different from the '$<=$' statements found in the *always_ff* blocks of Chapter 17. All of those SystemVerilog statements have parallel semantics. That is, the circuit behaves as if all those statements are executing in parallel all the time). [1] But, within an *always_comb* block, the individual statement semantics are sequential – the gates driven by inputs to the block should be described first, followed by downstream gates later in the code.

---

[1] In reality, there is much more to it than this. In fact, you can actually use '$=$' assignments in *always_ff* blocks. But, that use if beyond the scope of this text. For now, just always use '$=$' in *always_comb* and use '$<=$' in *always_ff*.

As an example of this, consider the circuit of Figure 18.1. A SystemVerilog representation of that circuit is shown in Program 18.1.3, where the gate level assignment statements have been done in order of logic flow, and which represents how you should code *always_comb* blocks:

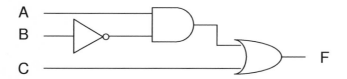

Figure 18.1: A Schematic for: $F = AB' + C$

Program 18.1.3 Multilevel Circuit Designed Using an *always_comb*

```
module multilevelCircuit(
        output logic f,
        input logic a, b, c);

   logic bnot, andout;

   always_comb
   begin

      // List the assignment statements in order of logic flow
      bnot = ~b;
      andout = a & bnot;
      f = andout | c;
   end

endmodule
```

In this case, multiple assignment statements have been used to mimic the flow of logic values through the combinational logic block. [2]

At this point a bit of thinking about coding style is in order. It would be considered overkill to use an *always_comb* block for something which is essentially equivalent to the *assign* statement seen in a previous chapter. Further, it might be considered silly to create a module definition containing seven lines of code to describe three gates when a single *assign* statement will suffice. Also, the use of full module definitions in the SystemVerilog examples seen thus far has been done to get you used to seeing full module definitions. However, if you really needed the logic of Figure 5.2 in your design, you would not go to the trouble of (1) defining a new module to hold it and then (2) structurally instancing that module to create the three new gates. That would be something like 10 or more lines of code to describe three gates! Rather, you would add a single *assign* statement describing the three gates right where they were needed in your larger design.

So, why would you ever use an *always_comb* block then? Remember that an *assign* statement can be exactly one line and can consist only of basic logic and comparison operators. In contrast, *always_comb* blocks can contain large amounts of code surrounded by a *begin . . . end* pair, and can therefore describe a fairly complex piece of logic. Further, *always_comb* blocks can contain complex *if-then-else* statements, *case* statements, function calls, etc. In other words, they contain much of the richness of conventional programming languages. Finally, remember that the semantics of statements of an *always_comb* block are sequential. This means that very complex calculations can be done using multiple statements if necessary to simplify your thinking.

---

[2]That said, this example is overly complex for such a simple block of circuitry but it does illustrate the point being made about the order of statement execution in an *always_comb* block. In real life, a more reasonable approach might be to use a single assign statement for this logic.

As an example of this last point, consider the need to compute a large function as shown here:

Program 18.1.4 Breaking Up a Computation Into Multiple Steps Using *always_comb*

```
always_comb
begin
  t1 = (some large amount of logic);
  t2 = (another large amount of logic);
  if (t1 < t2)
    f = t1*t2;
  else
    f = t2-t1;
end
```

Here, a pair of temporary variables have been used to represent portions of the computation just as one might do in C when a single expression is too complex to write in a single line of code. This can greatly simplify certain circuit structures you might want to create. Just remember, the code doesn't really execute sequentially so the various signal outputs change at different times. Rather, later statements can use the values produced by earlier statements to create complicated sets of logic gates.

18.1.1 The Use of *case* Statements in *always_comb* Blocks

SystemVerilog provides a *case* statement, similar to those found in other languages. As a simple example, consider the following:

Program 18.1.5 A Simple Case Statement for a MUX

```
always_comb
  case (sel)
    0: q = a;
    1: q = b;
  endcase
```

This is simply the design of a 2:1 MUX using a case statement. However, this design has a problem: what happens when the value of sel is X? Remember that the logic type contains four values: 0, 1, X, and Z. The problem with the program above is that it does not specify what should happen when sel is either X or Z. These cases can be covered using a default clause:

Program 18.1.6 Adding a *default* Clause to Cover All Cases (including 'X' and 'Z')

```
always_comb
  case (sel)
    0: q = a;
    1: q = b;
    default: q = 'X;
  endcase
```

In real circuit operation the sel signal will never actually take on the values X or Z but in simulation it may. The default clause ensures that an X will be output by the MUX in this case, alerting you to the fact that the sel signal did not a normal logic value. Another option is to provide a default value for q before the case statement as shown here:

Program 18.1.7 Adding a *default* Assignment Before the *case* Statement

```
always_comb
  q = 'X;
  case (sel)
    0: q = a;
    1: q = b;
  endcase
```

This acts the same way as the default clause above, ensuring that no matter the value of sel, that the q signal will get assigned a valid value. Another example of a case statement is the following (which describes a 2:4 decoder):

Program 18.1.8 Using a *case* Statement for a Decoder Design

```
always_comb
begin
  q = 'X;
  case (x)
    0: q = 4b'0001;
    1: q = 4b'0010;
    2: q = 4b'0100;
    3: q = 4b'1000;
  endcase
end
```

18.2 The Problem With Latches in *always_comb* Blocks

Consider the code of Program 18.2.1 and answer the following question: "what should the circuit do when *ena* is false?"

Program 18.2.1 An Incompletely Specified *always_comb* Block

```
always_comb
  if (ena)
    x = d | e;
```

This is supposed to be combinational logic, with an output which is a function of its current inputs and with no state storage involved at all. But, the code seems to suggest that when *ena* is false that signal *x* should not get a new value. That really does sound like storage.

And, it actually results in storage. This code will cause the synthesizer to create a latch (see Chapter 15 for an example of a D-type latch) to allow signal *x* to hold its old value when *ena==0*. It should go without saying that if you are trying to create combinatonal logic, then having the synthesizer infer a latch from your code is not what you intended but rather is an error.

But, we have told the tools that we want combinational logic through our use of the *always_comb* keyword — doesn't that count for something? Yes, it does. The synthesizer tool will see that we have specified a circuit containing a latch in a combinational logic block and will output a warning.

If this were an *always_ff* block this would not be a problem — if a register is not loaded with a new value in an *always_ff* block then we know the register will hold its old value. That is what we want.

But, when using *always_comb* blocks, you must check the output of the synthesizer for warnings to determine whether any of your *always_comb* blocks have been designed improperly and actually imply latches. What would be really helpful is if the simulation tools also provided warnings regarding this. They do not (and are not required to by the SystemVerilog standard). Simulation tools will simulate the latching behavior as written, but they will not tell you that your *always_comb* block actually does not represent pure combinational logic. So, during your edit-compile-test-edit development cycles you will not receive any feedback that your code is erroneously describing latches. Rather, you will only learn this once you synthesize the code (something you don't do after every single code change due to the time it requires).

As a result of this, *always_comb* blocks must be used with care. First of all, you MUST check the synthesis reports from your tools. It will seem like wasted effort until you spend hours trying to understand why your synthesis results do not match your simulation results.

The author's suggestion is to code them in such a way so as to avoid latches as much as possible rather than rely on the synthesizer to warn you. This will save you much time in the long run.

The first recommendation to avoid latches in *always_comb* blocks is to ensure that all paths through the logic of the statements in an *always_comb* block will assign a value to each and every signal that any of them assign a value to. C

A possible way to accomplish this is to ensure that *if-then* statements always terminate with an *else* clause. The design of Program 18.2.1 does not follow this rule and that should be an indication that a latch will result. In that program, adding an *else* clause such as:

```
else x = d;
```

will suffice. However, even this is insufficient, in general, to prevent latches. Consider the code of Program 18.2.2:

Program 18.2.2 A Tricky Latch Problem in an *always_comb* Block

---

```
always_comb
  if (ena)
  begin
    x = d | e;
    y = d & e;
  end
  else
  begin
    x = d;
  end
```

The *if-then* statement does have a final *else* clause. The problem is that *y* does not get assigned a value through all paths through the code (but *x* does). So, a latch will be generated for signal *y*.

There are two solutions to employ here. One is to be really, really careful. This is a suitable approach for simple logic such as is in the examples in this book. The second solution (preferable when your *always_comb* block is quite complex) is to assign default values to all your signals at the top of the block. If they are then not included in all paths through the remaining statements they will have received a value and no latch will be generated.

This is shown in Program 18.2.3. This may seem to be a bit verbose but after chasing bugs for a time you may develop a different viewpoint.

Program 18.2.3 Solving the Tricky Latch Problem of Program 18.2.2

```
always_comb
begin

  // Assign default values for x and y
  x = d;
  y = 1;

  // Now, do the logic
  if (ena)
  begin
    x = d | e;
    y = d & e;
  end
  else
  begin
    x = d;
  end
end
```

Importantly, this coding style has the advantage that your *if-then* logic could be simplified. That is because since the signals now get default values, you only have to include logic to set them to their non-default values. These non-default values are less likely, resulting in less code. In the code above, that means that you could eliminate the final *else* clause since it is simply re-assigning the same value to signal *x*. This is shown here:

Program 18.2.4 Solving the Tricky Latch Problem of Program 18.2.2 Using Default Value Assignments

```
always_comb
begin

  // Assign default values for x and y
  x = d;
  y = 1;

  // Now, do the logic
  if (ena)
  begin
    x = d | e;
    y = d & e;
  end
end
```

We will rely on this technique heavily in a later chapter on finite state machine design.

18.3 Avoiding Latches When Using *case* Statements

The following program shows the use of a *case* statement. Here we have the same problem — not all cases are covered and thus a latch will be inferred on signal *q*.

Program 18.3.1 A Simple *case* Statement in an *always_comb* Block Which Infers a Latch

```
always_comb
  case (sel)
    2'b01: q = d | e;
    2'b10: q = d & e;
    2'b11:  q = ~d & e;
  endcase
```

To cover all these other cases we can add a *default* case:

Program 18.3.2 A Fix to the *case* Statement

```
always_comb
  case (sel)
    2'b01: q = d | e;
    2'b10: q = d & e;
    2'b11: q = ~d & e;
    default: q = 'X;
  endcase
```

In this example, all cases are now covered and so this circuit is correct (this is similar to adding the final *else* in the previous example). And, it has the advantage that when the *sel* input is not one of the expected values an 'X' value will be output by the *case* statement, hopefully alerting you to a problem in your circuit. In general, it is good practice to propagate 'X' values in this way any time your circuit encounters 'X' values on its inputs — this will minimize the chance you do not see that you have 'X' values in your circuit (which is a sure sign of a problem in your design).

Continuing on, Program 18.2.2 assigned values to multiple signals in its *if-then-else* clauses and adding a final *else* was insufficient. A similar situation occurs here:

Program 18.3.3 A Tricky Latch Problem In a *case* Statement

```
always_comb
  case (ena)
  1:
    begin
      x = d | e;
      y = d & e;
    end
  0:
    x = d;
  default:
    begin
      x = 1;
      y = 1;
    end
  endcase
```

Even with a *default* case, there is a path through the logic which doesn't assign a value to signal *y*. The fix is the same as above — do default assignments at the top of the block:

Program 18.3.4 Solution to the Tricky Latch Problem in a *case* Statement

```
always_comb
begin

  // Default assignments
  x = d;
  y = 0;

  // Now for the real logic
  case (ena)
  1:
    begin
      x = d | e;
      y = d & e;
    end
  0:
    x = d;
  endcase
end
```

The result is that the 0 case can now be eliminated. Also, note that with the default assignments at the top, the *default* clause in the *case* statement is no longer required.

18.3.1 Summary: Avoiding Latches in *always_comb* Blocks

For *if-then* and *case* statements, if the logic is simple enough and/or you are only assigning to a single signal, then making sure you cover all the cases is sufficient (but be careful - it is easy to do it wrong). For *if-then* statements that means making sure there is always an *else* clause. For *case* statements that means making sure you have a *default* case. But, if multiple signals are assigned to in either kind of statement, you should add default signal assignments before the *if-then* or *case* statement to be sure that all signals get a value. Finally, don't forget to always check for synthesis warnings to be doubly sure.

18.4 Mapping SystemVerilog Programs to a Specific Technology

It is important that, as a designer, you develop an understanding of how a given SystemVerilog module will be mapped to silicon. Without such an understanding of this, you will likely create circuit designs which are too large and too slow to meet your design requirements. Remember, a Verlog design *is not a computer program which executes sequentially*. Rather, it is a description of hardware. *If you do not develop a feel for pretty much exactly what circuitry your SystemVerilog code is generating you may ultimately not be very successful as a designer.* Everything you enter in your code has resource and performance impacts. As an example of this, consider the following design:

Program 18.4.1 A Very Large Design

```
module quadratic(
        output logic[31:0] q,
        input logic[31:0] a, b, c, x);

    assign q = a*x*x + b*x + c;

endmodule
```

This seemingly simple design is, in all actuality, very large. It contains three 32-bit multipliers and two 32-bit adders, totalling many 1,000's of logic gates. If this really is the function you need to compute and your design's requirements prevent the use of some smaller iterative computational method, then you may be forced to code it this way. However, you should not simply assume that anything you can type will be implementable — all designs have both resource and performance constraints. If your design uses too many logic gates to implement, it will not be able to fit it onto a silicon chip. Additionally, large designs tend to be slow designs and thus you will likely not be able to hit your performance target.

18.5 Chapter Summary

This chapter has discussed behavioral SystemVerilog, specifically *always_comb* blocks. The key points with regard to these include:

1. *always_comb* blocks can be used to quickly specify complex combinational logic.

2. A variety of statements such as *if-then-else* and *case* statements can be used in the body of these blocks.

3. Latches are undesirable when you know you are trying to describe combinational logic. But, they are easy to mistakenly create in SystemVerilog.

4. You should make it a practice to regularly look at the synthesis reports produced by the synthesizer to understand how it mapped your design onto the target technology, specifically to see if it inferred any latches, which would be an error for *always_comb* blocks.[3]

5. By coding carefully and by using *else* clauses, *default cases* and default value assignments, you can avoid inferring latches in your designs.

The skills that should result from a study of this chapter include the following:

1. The ability to write combinational circuit descriptions using behavioral SystemVerilog.

2. The ability to create circuit schematics which correspond to behavioral SystemVerilog descriptions.

18.6 Exercises

18.1. Write the SystemVerilog for any of the circuits from previous chapters as selected by your instructor. Ensure that your code will not result in latches using the methods outlined in this chapter.

---

[3] SystemVerilog actually has an *always_latch* construct for when you really want a latch. We will not use of cover those in this text.

Chapter 19

Memories

19.1 Introduction

Almost all digital systems consists of more than simply combinational logic and flip flops. An important additional component that is frequently encountered is *memory*. A memory is a storage circuit (and therefore shares some characteristics with flip flops) but which typically holds many values. In many ways, a memory is a direct hardware realization of an array from programming languages — it is viewed as holding a large collection of data items which are accessed using *address* signals. Controlling the reading or writing of those memory locations is done using additional control inputs.

Conceptually, a memory can thought of as an array of registers combined with combinational logic to select which register is being accessed. And, for smaller memories, you might choose to implement a memory that way (as will be shown shortly). However, large memories are usually designed at the transistor level and are optimized to hold many thousands or millions of pieces of data in a small, high performance circuit module.

Memories are typically used in HDL-based designs in one of two ways. First, predefined memory modules or building blocks may be provided to you as a designer in the form of library elements which you can structurally instance in SystemVerilog to include in your designs. To use these blocks, you would need to consult the library documentation and choose a memory block which meets your needs and then structurally instantiate that block into your design.

The second way that you use memory building blocks is that many synthesis tools can *infer* from how you write your SystemVerilog code using arrays that the use of a memory block is needed. For very small memories the synthesis tools may choose to build it out of flip flops and gates. For larger memories, the synthesis tool may consult a technology-specific building block library and determine which, if any of the memory blocks in that library meet your needs and insert it into your design. Thus, with this second method, you can still take advantage of optimized memory blocks from a library. In this case, however, it is the synthesis tool that does the tradeoff analysis and selection of a memory block to use for your design, reducing your design effort. This second method, writing SystemVerilog behaviorally in a way that the synthesis tool can *infer* the needed circuitry for a memory, is the focus of this chapter.

19.2 Register Files

All microprocessors have *registers*, which they use for temporary storage. Microprocessor instructions operate on the values stored in these registers. A typical micorprocessor machine code instruction might be "ADD R3, R0, R2" which would be an ADD instruction which adds the contents of register 0 to the contents and register 2 and writes the result into register 3.

Most microprocessors have many registers and so they are typically organized into what is called a *register file*, an example of which is shown in Figure 19.1(a). As can be seen, it is simply a small memory with an address bus, input and output data busses, and a write enable signal. The presence of a 3-bit address bus indicates it contains eight locations (registers). The 16-bit width on both *DataIn* and *DataOut* indicates that each register is 16-bits wide.

The value on the *Addr* bus specifies which register is the target of a read or write. The value on *DataOut* is always the contents of the register addressed by *Addr*. Raising *regWE* will cause the register file to write to the location specified by *Addr* on the next rising clock clock edge. Conceptually (but not necessarily physically depending on the technology being used), a register file is simply a bank of registers surrounded by decoding and multiplexing logic as shown in Figure 19.1(b).

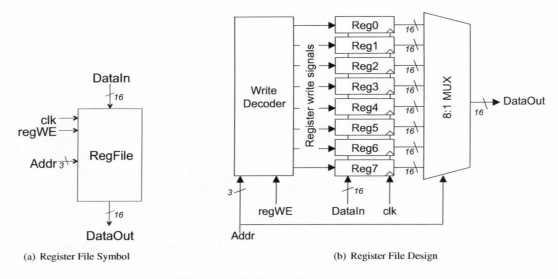

(a) Register File Symbol   (b) Register File Design

Figure 19.1: Transition Table and State Graph For a 2-Bit Counter

As can be seen, the core of the register file is a set of eight 16-bit registers (in this case made from flip flops). On the right is the read logic. It consists simply of an 8:1 MUX which uses the *Addr* value to select which register value should be passed to the *DataOut* wires. On the left is the write logic. It consists of a 3:8 decoder module whose outputs are AND-ed with the *regWE* signal to form the write enable signals for the individual registers. A detailed view of the contents of the write logic are shown in Figure 19.2.

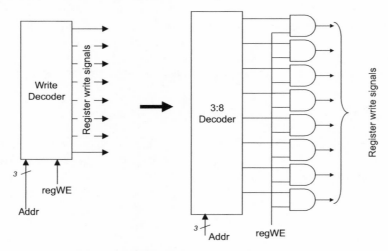

Figure 19.2: Write Logic For A Register File

Because this register file writes into the registers only on a clock edge we say it has a *synchronous write* port. However, note that there is no clocking involved in reading — any time the *Addr* values change, the MUX will immediately select a different register value to gate to the output. We thus say that it has an *asynchronous read* port, meaning that the read operation is independent of the clock signal.

19.3 Register File Design Using Behavioral SystemVerilog

The SystemVerilog design of the circuit from Figure 19.1 is almost trivially simple and is shown in Program 19.3.1.

Program 19.3.1 SystemVerilog Code for a Register File

```
module regFile (
        input logic clk, regWE,
        input logic[2:0] Addr,
        input logic[15:0] DataIn,
        output logic[15:0]  DataOut);

   // An 8-element array, each location holding 16 bits
   logic [15:0] registers [8];

   // The asynchronous read logic is a stand-alone dataflow statement
   assign DataOut = registers[Addr];

   // The synchronous write logic is an always_ff block
   always_ff @(posedge clk)
     if (regWE)
       registers[Addr] <= DataIn;

endmodule
```

This could have been written using eight independent register declarations and many independent assignment statements. However, Program 19.3.1 introduces the use of a SystemVerilog *array* to hold the eight register values, greatly simplifying the design. The synchronous write behavior is accomplished by placing the register write statement inside a clocked *always_ff* block — on a clock edge one element of the array will be assigned to. The asynchronous read behavior is accomplished with a simple dataflow *assign* statement which indexes into the array of register values.

The array declaration is of interest. It states that variable *registers* is an array of 8 words of data. It further states that each word is a 16-bit vector of *logic* values. For beginners, it can be difficult to remember which of the numbers in the declaration represent how many entries there are in the array vs. how many bits wide each entry is. One way to remember this is to note that the bit width is specified as a range (*[15:0]*) and like all width specifiers comes directly after the type (*logic* in this case).

19.4 Multi-Ported Register Files

Often, register files are designed so that multiple locations can be read from in a given clock cycle. A register file with a *triple ported* capability is shown in Figure 19.3. The major differences between this register file and the one of Figure 19.1 include the following:

1. Three different address signals are inputs to this register file. One (the *WAddr* input) specifies the register to be written to if *regWE* is true. Two others specify different registers to be read from. These are the *RAddr1* and *RAddr2* inputs.

2. An additional MUX has been placed in the read logic so that the two different registers can be read from on a given cycle.

For this design, consider what would happen if all three address inputs contained the same address (value 3 for example) and the register file was being written to? What register value would be read - would it be the value already stored in register 3 or would it be the data currently being written to register 3? It should be clear that there is actually no conflict between reading register 3 and writing to register 3. The read operations, being asynchronous, will return the current contents of register 3 during the entire clock cycle. The write of a new value into register 3, however, will not take place until the clock edge at the *end* of the clock cycle. Thus, it is perfectly acceptable to read two copies of the contents of register 3, add them together, and write the result back into register 3, all in the same clock cycle.

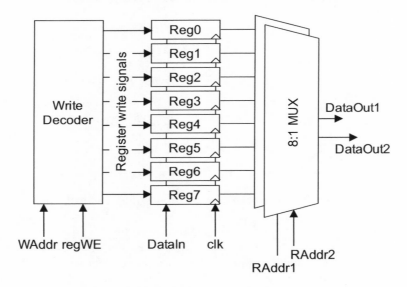

Figure 19.3: A Triple-Ported Register File

19.5 Multi-Ported Register File Design using SystemVerilog

SystemVerilog code for the circuit of Figure 19.3 is shown in Program 19.5.1. As can be seen, adding additional ports is fairly straightforward.

Program 19.5.1 SystemVerilog Code for Triple-Ported Register File of Figure 19.3

```
module regFile3 (
      input logic clk, regWE,
      input logic[2:0] WAddr, RAddr1 RAddr2,
      input logic[15:0] DataIn,
      output logic[15:0]  DataOut1, DataOut2);

  // An 8-element array, each location holding 16 bits
  logic [15:0] registers [8];

  assign DataOut1 = registers[RAddr1];
  assign DataOut2 = registers[RAddr2];

  // The synchronous write logic is an always block
  always_ff @(posedge clk)
    if (regWE)
      registers[WAddr] <= DataIn;

endmodule
```

19.6   Multi-Ported Register Files With Bypass

The code sample above will always read the *current* value of a register. Consider again, however, what if location 3 is both being written to and read on the same clock cycle? You might be happy with the behavior in the example above (called *write-after-read*) where the value already in the register is returned. Or, you may prefer that the data returned on the read lines is the new data being written to that location. This second behavior is called *bypass* or *write-before-read*. Neither behavior is correct or incorrect — which one you implement depends on your system requirements.

The triple ported memory of Figure 19.3 but with bypass capability is shown in Program 19.6.1. Here, a conditional *assign* is used to *forward* or *bypass* the data being written to the read ports when a write is being done to the same address as the read.

Program 19.6.1 SystemVerilog Code for Triple-Ported Register File With Bypass Capability

---

```
module regFile3WithBypass (
      input logic clk, regWE,
      input logic[2:0] WAddr, RAddr1, RAddr2,
      input logic[15:0] DataIn,
      output logic[15:0]  DataOut1, DataOut2);

   // An 8-element array, each location holding 16 bits
   logic [15:0] registers [8];

   // Don't blindly read the register file.  Rather, check to see if
   //   the address being written is the same as being read and, if so,
   //   return the corresponding data value on DataOut1 or DataOut2.
   // Otherwise, do a regular register file read.
   assign DataOut1 = (regWE==1 && WAddr==RAddr1) ? DataIn : registers[RAddr1];
   assign DataOut2 = (regWE==1 && WAddr==RAddr2) ? DataIn : registers[RAddr2];

   // The synchronous write logic is an always block
   always_ff @(posedge clk)
     if (regWE)
       registers[WAddr] <= DataIn;

endmodule
```

A whole range of other options are possible with register files. Using the techniques shown above, you can add as many write and read ports to your register as you want. If you do so, just be sure to think through what you want your design to do in cases like: "write port 1 and write port 2 are both writing to location 3". You may choose to (1) not do a write operation in this case, (2) to give one write port higher precedence than the other, (3) to OR the bits of the written data together. Once again, there are no right or wrong answers — what you do depends on what you want or need the system to do.

In addition to adding additional ports, you might want to register the output of the read logic. Doing so would convert the register file's *asynchronous* read port to a *synchronous* read port. Or, you may choose to add a reset signal to your register file. Because register files are often constructed from flip flops and gates, there are really no rules on what you can and cannot include.

19.7 Larger Memories

Large memories (or even register files beyond just a few registers) are typically not constructed from flip flops and gates as shown above. Rather, they are hand-crafted transistor-level silicon blocks. These are typically provided to logic designers (designers writing SystemVerilog) as part of a technology-specific library. You as a designer then choose the pre-defined building block that meets your needs and structurally instantiate it into your design.

The memories provided in the library may be single-ported, they may be multi-ported. They may have either synchronous or asynchronous write behavior. They may have either synchronous or asynchronous read behavior. It is thus important that you carefully read the documentation associated with the memory blocks in the library and understand precisely how a given memory block behaves before using it in a design.

In addition to using pre-defined memory building blocks from a library, you could choose to code your memory design similar to how the register file designs from above were coded — using an array to hold the memory contents and a combination of *assign* statements and *always_ff* blocks to describe its operation. Many synthesis tools will be able to infer that a memory is desired from the code you write and then select a suitable memory block for insertion into the circuit. As example, Program 19.7.1 shows an example of a RAM containing 1024 words of 4 bits each. It is a fully synchronous RAM, meaning both writes and reads are controlled by a clock. It writes into the RAM on clock edges only when $regWE == 1$ but reads every clock cycle from the RAM into an output register.

Program 19.7.1 Verilog Code for Synchronous RAM

```
module SynchRAM (
        input logic clk, regWE,
        input logic[9:0] Addr,
        input logic[3:0] DIn,
        output logic[3:0]  DOut);

   logic [3:0] registers [1024];

   always_ff @ (posedge clk)
   begin
     if (regWE)
       registers[Addr] <= DIn;
     DOut <= registers[Addr];
   end

   endmodule
```

Most vendors' tools have the ability to map descriptions such as shown in Program 19.7.1 to the built-in memories of that vendor's devices. But, if you were to want to use such a larger memory (which may rely on a predefined library of building blocks to implement), you are moving out of the realm of generic SystemVerilog coding and into the area of technology-specific and CAD tool-specific knowledge. You would need to consult the documentation for those (the available libraries for your technology and your CAD tools) to understand how to proceed.

19.8 Read-Only Memories (ROM)

The memories discussed thus far in this chapter have all been Random Access Memories (RAM), meaning they can be both read and written. It is, however, not uncommon to have a need to include memories in a design which can only be read from.

Why might you want to use a ROM in a design? Imagine you are designing a circuit which needs to use $sin(x)$ values as a part of its computation. You have two options for producing $sin(x)$ where x is a multi-bit binary value.

The first option would be to (1) study up on how to compute $sin(x)$ values from some mathematical formulation such as a Taylor Series and then (2) design a circuit to implement that Taylor Series computation. The resulting circuit likely would be very large (require a large silicon area) and/or run slowly (possibly requiring many clock cycles to compute the result).

The second option would be to create a lookup table of $sin(x)$ values using a ROM and, when needed, simply look up $sin(x)$ by providing x to the address lines of the ROM. Along the way you might perform a variety of enhancements to how you organize your table so that it could be used for both $sin(x)$ and $cos(x)$. Many other uses for ROM blocks exist — think of essentially anywhere you might use a table of read-only values (a lookup table) in a software computation.

In reality, a ROM is not a memory at all and there is no *storage* involved. Rather, it is a collection of wires and gates (or simply transistors) which return an output value in response to an input address value. Since the ROM contents will never be changed, there is no reason to waste silicon creating flip flops to hold the memory contents!

Section 10.7 discussed the use of lookup tables (LUTs) for logic. In that context it used the term ROM to describe those lookup tables. That is precisely what a ROM is — it is a hardware implementation of a lookup table. You provide an address and it returns the value associated with that address in the table.

Program 19.8.2 shows the SystemVerilog code for a ROM design. It consists of a single *assign* statement that outputs data values in response to address values. The synthesis tools know how to convert that description into the circuitry needed to implement the lookup table. Note that the final value in the chain (a '0') covers a number of the addresses, eliminating the need for all addresses to be specified.

Program 19.8.1 SystemVerilog Code for a ROM

```
module myROM(
        input logic[2:0] Addr,
        output logic[3:0]  DataOut);

   assign DataOut = (Addr==0)?5:
                    (Addr==2)?9:
                    (Addr==3)?10:
                    (Addr==4)?2:
                    (Addr==5)?11:
                    0;

   endmodule
```

You may be thinking "this is all fine and good for tiny lookup tables, but for larger ones this is horribly verbose." Yes, it is. And also, it may not generate the most optimal circuit design.

Many vendors' tools have mechanisms which allow you to specify ROM contents as the contents of a text file which can then be read using the functions *$readmemh()* or *$readmemb()* during simulation and synthesis. For example, here is one such example:

Program 19.8.2 SystemVerilog Code for a ROM

```
module dual_port_rom (
        input logic clk,
        input logic[7:0] addr,
        output logic[15:0] q);

    // Declare the ROM as an array
    logic [15:0] rom[256];

    initial // Read the ROM contents from a file
    begin
        $readmemb("rom_init.txt", rom);
    end

    // Access the ROM
    assign q = rom[addr];
endmodule
```

Further, here is a sample memory initialization file for use with the above program. Consult the web for examples using hex values for the data values.

Program 19.8.3 Contents of File "rom_init.txt"

```
// This is a memory initialization file
//    for use in Verilog.
// Addresses of entries must be specified in HEX
//    and are prefixed with the @ symbol.
// Data values are either in binary (for readmemb)
//    or in hex (for readmemh)
// Unitialized locations will contain 'X'
// You can place underscore symbols in the middle of
//    data values to enhance readability if desired.
// Blank lines are ignored.
// C-style comments are allowed.

// This memory has 16 locations of 8 words each
//    and this file is in binary.

    0101_1111  // Location 0
@2  0010_1001  // Location 2
    0100_1001  // Location 3
    0111_1111  // Location 4
    0011_0011  // Location 5
    0101_1100  // Location 6
@A  1111_1111  // Location 10
    0000_1111  // Location 11
```

Consult your tools documentation for details on whether these are supported and, if so, how to use them to specify ROM and RAM initialization values.

19.9   Consulting Tool Documentation

It has been recommended at multiple places in this text for you to consult your tools documentation. Just what are these documents and how to find them?

Here is one example. Xilinx (an FPGA vendor) has always provided a synthesis guide for its most recent CAD tools. This guide describes precisely how to code various HDL constructs so that their CAD tools will most efficiently map HDL constructs to their FPGA devices.

At the time of the writing of this text, the latest such guide from Xilinx is titled "Vivado Design Suite User Guide" (they seem to be updated every few years). Search for it on the web ("Xilinx vivado synthesis guide"). Chapter 4 of the current version of this guide is devoted to providing both Verilog and VHDL code examples to show how to create many different circuit elements such as shift registers, arithmetic circuits, memories (RAM, ROM), etc. In the case of RAM and ROM, it gives detailed examples on how to initialize the contents of those memories in a way that both their simulation and synthesis tools will understand. Altera (now Intel) has similar coding guidelines for their tools and FPGA devices.

As you move beyond simple combinational and registered logic and into designs involving circuitry such as memories and complex arithmetic modules, these coding guides will form an indispensable reference for you and will ensure that you are writing SystemVerilog code which will map efficiently onto the devices you are targeting. Make it a point to locate, on the web, the guide for the devices you are targeting and refer to it regularly. It will save you much time and effort.

19.10 Chapter Summary

This chapter has introduced register files and their implementation using SystemVerilog. It has also discussed using larger memories as well as the design and use of read-only memories (ROMs) Concepts that should be clear before moving on to the next chapter include the following:

1. A memory which can be both read and written to is called a random access memory or RAM.

2. A memory which only be read from is called a read-only memory or ROM.

3. Register files are often used in microprocessor designs and typically support one write port and one or more read ports.

4. Conceptually, a register file can be viewed as an array of registers surrounded by read and write control logic.

5. Small register files may even be implemented that way. Larger register files will often be custom hand-crafted silicon structures.

6. Specialized memory blocks are often provided to you as the designer as part of a technology-specific library of building blocks which you may structurally instantiate into your design.

7. Register files (and multi-ported memories) may be *write-after-read* or *write-before-read* (*bypass*) memories.

8. The array structure provides a convenient and compact way of modelling both register files and memories in SystemVerilog.

The skills that should result from a study of this chapter include the following:

1. The ability to design a variety of memory structures using the SystemVerilog language.

19.11 Exercises

1. Do the design of a register file with both synchronous write ports and synchronous read ports. Have it have one write port and one read port (two different address busses). Have it do read-before-write on address collisions.

2. Do the design of a register file with synchronous write ports and asynchronous read ports. Have it have two write ports and two read ports (four total address busses). If there are write address collisions have it write the OR of the two data values into the single location. For read port A, if the location it is reading from is also being written to by either write port, have it do read-before-write. For read port B, in the case of collisions, have it do bypass.

3. Design a 4-bit gray code counter using a ROM for the next state logic.

4. Consult the documentation for your design and simulation CAD tools and learn how to initialize a ROM's contents using an external text file. Design and simulate a ROM implementing a lookup table of your choice using what you have learned.

Chapter 20

Simple Sequential Circuits: Counters

In previous chapters you learned about the operation of flip flops and how they may be combined to form registers. You then learned in Chapter 16 how to place input forming logic (IFL) in front of those registers to create simple circuits such as loadable registers. In many instances, the somewhat *ad hoc* techniques presented in Chapter 16 will be sufficient for you to design a variety of RTL modules. However, those techniques will be insufficient for the design of circuits with complex sequential behavior. For example, recall that in Chapter 15 we motivated the need for storage circuits using a copy machine. The copy machine controller described there needs the ability to perform operations consisting of mutiple steps such as waiting for the lamp to warm up, driving motors to rotate rollers, updating the display, and so on. What is needed (and what is covered in the next three chapters) is a *design methodology* which will (1) enable us to precisely specify such sequential behavior and (2) provide a series of steps to reduce that specification to a digital circuit.

In this chapter, the basic concepts required are presented using binary counters as examples to help motivate and explain the use of *transition tables* to define and implement sequential circuits. In the next chapter, *state graphs* are then presented which is a powerful mechanism, used in both hardware and software design, to both visualize and specify general sequential behavior. Finally, *finite state machines* are presented in Chapter 22 as the general embodiment of this and then examples are given of their use.

20.1 A Two-Bit Binary Counter

Consider a two-bit binary counter which counts in the sequence: $00 \rightarrow 01 \rightarrow 10 \rightarrow 11 \rightarrow 00 \rightarrow 01 \rightarrow \dots$. By way of review, a block diagram of a general sequential circuit is shown in Figure 20.1. The major blocks include a register (made of flip flops) to hold the current state (count), input forming logic (IFL) to compute what the next state should be, and output forming logic (OFL) to generate any needed outputs in addition to the raw counter output bits. Note that for the counter here, there are no external inputs and there is no output forming logic.

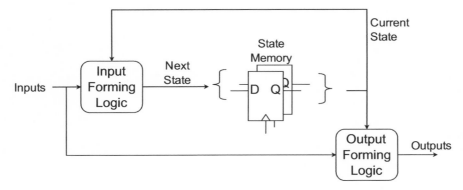

Figure 20.1: RTL Circuit Structure

Figure 20.2 shows the timing diagram associated with this counter. On each rising clock edge, the flip flops load the next state value, making it the new current state value. Heavy arrows in the figure are used to show this. The next state value then updates (after the delay of the IFL) to reflect the new current state plus one. The counter will cycle through this count sequence indefinitely, incrementing its current state value on each clock edge.

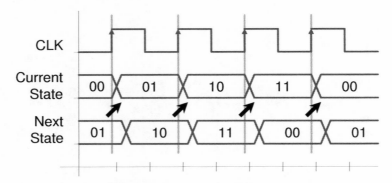

Figure 20.2: 2-Bit Counter Timing Diagram

Because the IFL is a block of combinational logic, a truth table for its function can be created - this is shown in Figure 20.3. This truth table is also called the *transition table* or *next state table* for the counter. The only input to this transition table is the current state because that is the only input to the input forming logic. The convention chosen is to call the next state bits Nn, where the 'n' is the bit number. The convention for the current state bits is Qn, where 'n' is the bit number.

Q1	Q0	N1	N0
0	0	0	1
0	1	1	0
1	0	1	1
1	1	0	0

Figure 20.3: Transition Table for a 2-Bit Counter With Variable Names

The next step is to design the input forming logic. This is done by reducing each output of the truth table (the bits of the next state variable) to a boolean equation, and implementing that with gates. KMaps for both bits of the next state bits are given in Figure 20.4.

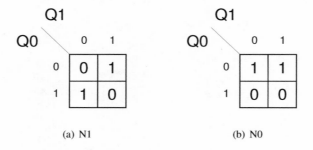

Figure 20.4: KMaps For 2-Bit Counter Next State Bits

Reducing these to Boolean equations results in:

$$N1 = Q1 \oplus Q0$$
$$N0 = Q0'$$

and the final circuit diagram for this counter is given in Figure 20.5. Tracing out the values on the wires on a clock-by-clock cycle basis will verify that it indeed counts in binary, one new value per clock edge.

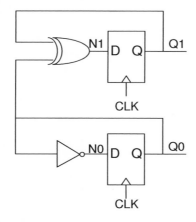

Figure 20.5: Final 2-Bit Counter Design

At this point you may be thinking "that is a lot of work to specify and implement a circuit that simply adds 1 to a 2-bit value — I could do that with a 2-bit adder circuit". While that is true in this trivial case, it is not true in general as will be shown in the next two examples.

20.2 A Two-Bit Gray Code Counter

Consider now the design of a counter which cycles through a different pattern: $00 \rightarrow 01 \rightarrow 11 \rightarrow 10 \rightarrow 00 \rightarrow \ldots$. This is called a *gray code* counter since on each transition only one state bit changes its value. You may encounter gray codes in a variety of application areas and so the following circuit is not simply an artificially created example.

Figure 20.6 is a transition table for the counter. The rows in this transition table have been written in an order to correspond to the count sequence rather than in regular binary order - this was done only to make it easier to write and doesn't change the result (just be sure to re-order them appropriately before creating a KMap for this logic).

Q1	Q0	N1	N0
0	0	0	1
0	1	1	1
1	1	1	0
1	0	0	0

Figure 20.6: Transition Table for a 2-Bit Gray Code Counter

Once KMaps have been solved for this transition table, the resulting schematic is shown in Figure 20.7.

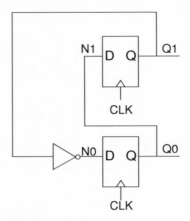

Figure 20.7: The 2-Bit Gray Code Counter Design

From this we see that different count sequences result in different amounts of input forming logic. That is, the binary counter requires more input forming logic than the gray code counter when implemented using D flip flops. Because of this a variety of counter types have been created in the past, each with its own logic gate and flip flop requirements.

20.3   A Counter Example With An Incomplete Transition Table

As a third example, consider the design of a counter where the desired count sequence is: $000 \rightarrow 001 \rightarrow 100 \rightarrow 110 \rightarrow 011 \rightarrow 000 \rightarrow \ldots$. A transition table for a counter with this count sequence is shown in Figure 20.8.

Q2	Q1	Q0	N2	N1	N0
0	0	0	0	0	1
0	0	1	1	0	0
1	0	0	1	1	0
1	1	0	0	1	1
0	1	1	0	0	0
0	1	0	X	X	X
1	0	1	X	X	X
1	1	1	X	X	X

Figure 20.8: Transition Table for a Counter With Don't Cares

Note that three of the possible count values are not used. As a result, those rows of the transition table have don't cares marked. These don't cares can be used when doing KMaps to reduce the amount of logic required.

Minimizing the transition table's function results in the final design shown in Figure 20.9.

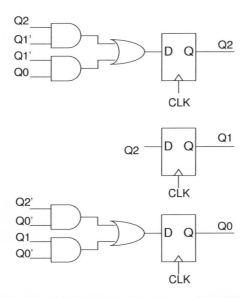

Figure 20.9: The Final Design of the Counter With Don't Cares

At this point you should realize that you could design a counter to use essentially any count sequence desired. We next turn to generating outputs from these counters which are in addition to the raw counter bits.

20.4   Counters With Static Output Signals

The counters derived above have no outputs other than the current state bits. It is often desirable for the counter to generate outputs in addition to these.

Consider a 3-bit binary counter with a single output, where it is desired that this output (Z) is asserted *any time the current count is divisible by three.* A truth table for Z is shown in Figure 20.10. This truth table simply indicates that whenever the value of the counter is 0, 3, or 6 the Z output is asserted. For all other counts it is not asserted.

Q2	Q1	Q0	Z
0	0	0	1
0	0	1	0
0	1	0	0
0	1	1	1
1	0	0	0
1	0	1	0
1	1	0	1
1	1	1	0

Figure 20.10: Truth Table For Counter Output Z

The general circuit structure to implement this counter, as we have already seen, is shown in Figure 20.11. The output forming logic computes the value of Z as a function of the current state, and is the logic implementation of the truth table of Figure 20.10.

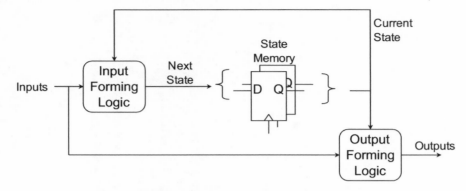

Figure 20.11: Block Diagram of a Counter With an Output

The equation for Z (computed from Figure 20.10) is:

$$Z = Q2' \bullet Q1' \bullet Q0' + Q2' \bullet Q1 \bullet Q0 + Q2 \bullet Q1 \bullet Q0'$$

The output forming logic section of Figure 20.11 is simply the gates required to implement this equation. The Z output in this case is called a *Moore* output for historical reasons. Another name which will be used in the remainder of this text is *static output*. It is called this because the Moore output's value is a function of only the current state.

It is possible to add the Z output to the original transition table for the counter, as shown in Figure 20.12. KMaps can be used to reduce the logic for each output column in the table. In the case of the Nn variables, this logic is the IFL. In the case of the Z output, this logic is the OFL.

Q2	Q1	Q0	N2	N1	N0	Z
0	0	0	0	0	1	1
0	0	1	0	1	0	0
0	1	0	0	1	1	0
0	1	1	1	0	0	1
1	0	0	1	0	1	0
1	0	1	1	1	0	0
1	1	0	1	1	1	1
1	1	1	0	0	0	0

Figure 20.12: Combined Transition/Truth Table For Counter With Output

The combined table shown in Figure 20.12 is a convenient way to represent both the next-state and output behavior of the counter in a single table. It is still called a *transition table*, even though its output section contains output signals (like Z) in addition to next state variables.

Finally, note that a counter can have multiple outputs, each with a different function. For example, a counter could have one output asserted when the current count was a multiple of three and another output asserted when the current count was all 1's. This would simply require an additional output column be added to the transition table of Figure 20.12.

20.5 Delay Characteristics of Counters

A common question about a counter is "how fast will it run"? Another way to ask this is "How often may a clock edge arrive and have the counter still function properly?" Consider the schematic of Figure 20.13. This is a copy of the 2-bit counter design of Figure 20.5, reproduced here for convenience.

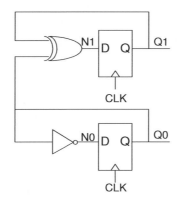

Figure 20.13: A 2-Bit Binary Counter Design

Figure 20.14 is a timing diagram for it with a number of delays shown.

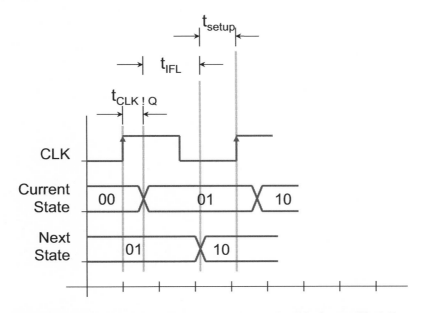

Figure 20.14: Counter Timing Diagram To Determine Maximum Clock Rate

Once the clock edge arrives, the *Q1* and *Q0* values will change after a delay of t_{CLK-Q}. These values then propagate through the input forming logic (the inverter and XOR gates) to create new values for *N1* and *N0*. These next state values must have enough time to load the master latch of the D flip flops before the next clock edge arrives. This is a delay of t_{setup}.

The minimum time between clock edges is called T_{cycle} and is thus $T_{cycle} \geq t_{CLK-Q} + t_{IFL} + t_{setup}$. In the case of this counter, there are two outputs from the IFL (*N1* and *N0*). The value used for t_{IFL} must be the slowest of the two since the clock must wait for the slowest one. In this case, it will be t_{XOR} since XOR gates are slower than inverters.

To put real values on the delays to get a speed value for this counter, assume the following: $t_{CLK-Q} = 2ns$, $t_{XOR} = 5ns$, $t_{setup} = 1ns$. The minimum time between clock edges would be $2ns + 5ns + 1ns = 8ns$. We would say that the *minimum clock period* for the counter is $8ns$ and that the *maximum clock rate* for the counter is 125×10^6 clock edges per second ($125 \times 10^6 hertz$ or $125MHz$). This was computed by noting that clock rate is simply the reciprocal of clock period.

This counter will count properly, provided a rising clock edge never appears earlier than $8ns$ after the previous rising clock edge. If a clock edge ever did appear sooner than $8ns$, the setup time of at least one of the flip flops would be violated, leading to undefined behavior. We thus say that the maximum clock rate of this counter is $125MHz$.

Counter Clock Rate Review

The minimum clock period of a counter can be determined from the equation: $T_{cycle} \geq t_{CLK-Q} + t_{IFL} + t_{setup}$. It is important to use the slowest path through the input forming logic for t_{IFL}, since the worst case delay is desired. A similar timing analysis can be applied to any of the counters in this chapter.

20.5.1 Moore Output Delay Characteristics of Counters

The above discussion has focused on determining the maximum clock rate a counter can be clocked at. The timing of any output signals are described in this section.

The timing diagram of Figure 20.15 shows the timing of the Z output signal of Figure 20.11. The *Qn* outputs (the counter current state) change t_{CLK-Q} after the clock edge. The Z output then changes t_{OFL} later, where t_{OFL} is the delay through the output forming logic. Given values for t_{CLK-Q} and t_{OFL}, the timing response of any output signals from a counter can be determined.

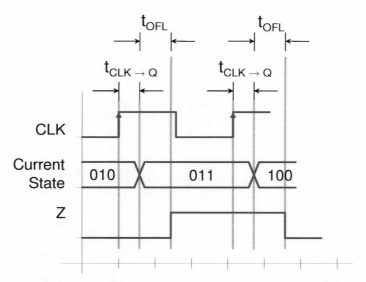

Figure 20.15: Timing Diagram To Illustrate Counter Output Timing

20.6 Counters With Additional Inputs

Consider the design of a counter which doesn't increment every clock cycle but, rather, has an input called *INC* which controls which clock cycles it will increment on. A transition table for this counter is shown in Figure 20.16. The top half of the transition table covers the case where *INC*='0', indicating that the counter should not increment (the current and next state values are the same). The bottom half of the transition table corresponds to *INC*='1', indicating that the counter should increment. The next state value is the current state value plus one in this case.

INC	Q1	Q0	N1	N0
0	0	0	0	0
0	0	1	0	1
0	1	0	1	0
0	1	1	1	1
1	0	0	0	1
1	0	1	1	0
1	1	0	1	1
1	1	1	0	0

Figure 20.16: Transition Table for a 2-Bit Counter With *INC* Input

Completing the design for such a counter is straightforward. The only difference from the examples seen previously in this chapter is that the input forming logic has external inputs (*INC* in this example), in addition to the current state bits.

A timing diagram for this counter is given in Figure 20.17. The counter increments only on clock edges when *INC*='1', and holds its previous value at all other times. The gate-level design of the counter is derived as above by creating input forming logic which implements the *Nn* equations, and drawing the resulting schematic.

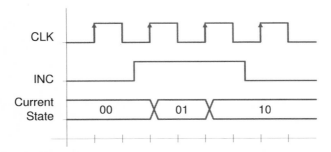

Figure 20.17: Timing Diagram for 2-Bit Counter With *INC* Input

20.7 Mealy (Dynamic) Outputs

As we saw, a Moore output is an output which is only a function of the current state (we called them *static* outputs). A further refinement to the sequential systems of this chapter is to add outputs which depend *both* on the current state as well as the external inputs. These are called Mealy or *dynamic* outputs.

Consider again the counter example of Figure 20.16. A possible Moore output for this circuit would be an output which is equal to '1' when the counter is at its most positive count value ('11'). This would be implemented as:

$$Z = Q1 \bullet Q0$$

However, it might be desired instead to generate an output which signified that not only did the counter contain the value '11', but that it was also being incremented. The above Moore output *Z* can only signify when the counter state is '11' — it depends only on the current state and so cannot determine when the counter is also being incremented from '11' to '00'.

An output which can do this is called a *Mealy* output (for historical reasons). It depends on both the current state as well as the inputs, in this case the *INC* signal. We will call such an output a *dynamic* output in this text.

A transition table showing both a Moore output and a Mealy output for the counter of Figure 20.16 is given in Figure 20.18. The Moore (static) output is called Z, and the Mealy (dynamic) output is called Y.

INC	Q1	Q0	N1	N0	Z	Y
0	0	0	0	0	0	0
0	0	1	0	1	0	0
0	1	0	1	0	0	0
0	1	1	1	1	1	0
1	0	0	0	1	0	0
1	0	1	1	0	0	0
1	1	0	1	1	0	0
1	1	1	0	0	1	1

Figure 20.18: Transition Table for a 2-Bit Counter With *INC* Input and Both Moore and Mealy Outputs

The Moore output Z will be TRUE *any time* the current state is '11' and thus is is given as:

$$Z = Q1 \bullet Q0$$

In contrast, the Mealy (dynamic) output Y is TRUE only when the counter is being incremented to roll it over from '11' to '00'. This is shown in the table by the condition: *INC*='1' and the current state is '11'. The equation for Y from the transition table is given as:

$$Y = INC \bullet Q1 \bullet Q0$$

A timing diagram of the operation of this counter, along with its two outputs is given in Figure 20.19. Any time the counter current state is '11', Z='1'. This is true regardless of whether the counter is being incremented or not. This also shows why Moore outputs are also called static outputs since they can only change when the current state changes — they are *static* for the duration of each state.

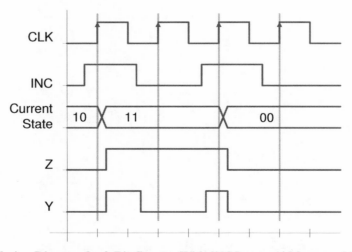

Figure 20.19: Timing Diagram for 2-Bit Counter With *INC* Input and Moore and Mealy Outputs

In contrast, note the waveform for the Y output. It is TRUE any time the current state is '11' and *INC*='1'. Thus, there are times when Z='1' but Y='0'. Note in particular the cycles where the *INC* signal changes. Because Y is a function of *INC* as well as the current state, it reacts immediately (provided the current state is '11') to each change on the *INC* input. This is the reason a Mealy output is called a dynamic output — it will dynamically react to changes on the input values.

20.7.1 Mealy vs. Moore Outputs

The differences between Mealy and Moore outputs are a common source of confusion to new digital designers. Part of the problem likely stems from the similarity of their names! This text has chosen to call Moore outputs *static outputs* and Mealy outputs *dynamic outputs* for the reasons discussed above.

Is one type of output preferable to the other? No. Rather, each will find use depending on the requirements of your design. What is important for now is to understand their differences and the timing behavior of each. Later, as they are used in real designs you will begin to learn when to use each.

At this point you have seen how to (a) specify the behavior of a sequential circuit using transition tables, (b) how to include inputs in the transition table to control the counter's behavior, (c) how to include both Moore (static) and Mealy (dynamic) outputs in those transition tables, and (d) how to reduce those transition tables to IFL and OFL and draw the final circuit schematic.

20.8   Counter Design Using Behavioral SystemVerilog

If you have SystemVerilog tools available, the design of counters using SystemVerilog is straightforward (actually, quite simple) and closely follows that for designing registers as shown in Chapter 16. The steps are (1) use an *always_ff* block to describe your register to hold the current count and (2) describe the input forming logic for the counter in the body of the *always_ff*. Here is a simple up counter with clear and enable:

Program 20.8.1 A Simple Up Counter

```
always_ff @(posedge clk)
  if (clr)
    q <= 0;
  else if (ena)
    q <= q+1;
```

It is a simple matter to additional control inputs to load the counter, cause it to decrement in addition to (or instead of) incrementing, etc.

Below is the SystemVerilog code for a modulo-10 counter (a counter that counts from 0-9 and then repeats):

Program 20.8.2 A Modulo-10 Counter

```
always_ff @(posedge clk)
  if (clr)
    q <= 0;
  else if (ena)
  begin
    if (q == 9)
      q <= 0;
    else
      q <= q+1;
  end
```

Here, an additional *begin . . . end* pair has been added to the *ena* clause to make very clear the grouping of the inner *if-then-else* statements.[1]

Note that, when designing counters this way with SystemVerilog, no truth tables are required nor is any attention to don't care values required. The SystemVerilog compiler is able to manage all those details for you based on the code you write and automatically perform the proper optimizations.

How would you design a gray code counter? The use of the $+$ operator will no longer work since the count sequence does not follow a simple pattern. One approach would be as shown here:

Program 20.8.3 A 2-Bit Gray Code Counter

```
always_ff @(posedge clk)
  case (Q)
    2'b00: Q <= 2'b01;
    2'b01: Q <= 2'b11;
    2'b11: Q <= 2'b10;
    2'b10: Q <= 2'b00;
  endcase
```

This simply uses a case statement to enumerate what the next state should be for every current state. To use this approach with an 8-bit counter, however, would be very time consuming (but conceptually possible - maybe you write a Python program to automagically generate the needed SystemVerilog code?). But, for small widths it works nicely. Another approach might be to implement a conventional counter as above and then design a block of combinational logic (possibly implemented with a ROM) to convert the counter's binary output to a gray code. Finally, there are published equations which can convert a conventional binary value to a gray code value — you could design Verilog code to implement such an equation to convert the output of a conventional counter to gray code.

Designing counters with outputs is trivial — you simply design the counter using an *always_ff* block and then describe the output forming logic using either dataflow *assign* statements or an *always_comb* block. The former is shown below for the counter of Figure 20.11. Similar approaches can be used for both Mealy and Moore outputs.

Program 20.8.4 SystemVerilog Code Fragment for the Counter of Figure 20.11

```
always_ff @(posedge clk)
  Q <= Q + 1;

assign Z = (Q==0 || Q==3 || Q==6)?1:0;
```

A reality check is in order at this point. Deep down, there is no fundamental difference between designing a counter using transition tables and KMaps vs. designing that counter using behavioral SystemVerilog. In both cases you are specifying the IFL and OFL functionality and then reducing that to logic gates and combining that with a register to form the final counter. In both cases the equivalent of a transition table exists.

However, there are two differences. First, in one case the specification was via a transition table and in the other it was SystemVerilog based *if-then-else* or *case* statements. Second, in one case you did all the optimization by hand and in the other case a SystemVerilog compiler performed the optimization. But, the same essential steps were performed in both cases with the same results.

---

[1]Due to the grammar specificaton for SystemVerilog, this additional *begin . . . end* pair is not strictly necessary. However, including it will likely make your code more clear so that other engineers will be able to easily maintain it after you have been promoted.

20.9 Chapter Summary

This chapter has introduced the design of counters, simple sequential systems consisting of flip flops, IFL, and OFL. The key high-level points to master from this chapter include the following:

1. The terminology of sequential systems including: current state, next state, state register, state vector, and input forming logic.

2. A counter is designed by first creating a transition table which shows the next state of the counter as a function of the current state. A transition table can be created for any desired count sequence.

3. If there are unreachable states in the counter's state vector space, they result in don't cares in the transition table. These don't cares help to reduce the size of the input forming logic.

4. A counter may have outputs which are a function of the current state. These are created using output forming logic and are called Moore or static outputs.

5. The minimum clock period for a counter is $T_{cycle} \geq t_{CLK-Q} + t_{IFL} + t_{setup}$. The value for t_{IFL} should be the worst case delay through the input forming logic.

6. The maximum clock rate for a counter is the reciprocal of the minimum clock period. A clock period of $20ns$ implies a clock rate of $50MHz$.

7. Counters can be readily design using SystemVerilog *always_ff* blocks and *if-then-else* or *case* statements.

The skills that should result from study of this chapter include the following:

1. The ability to write a transition table for any count sequence desired. This includes the use of don't cares as appropriate.

2. The ability to determine the minimum clock period for any given counter.

3. The ability to incorporate inputs and outputs into a counter design.

4. The ability to design counters using SystemVerilog.

20.10   Exercises

For all problems, use rising-edge triggered flip flops. If the problem requests that you *design* a counter this implies (a) writing the transition table (using don't cares where appropriate), (b) creating minimized equations for the *Nn*, *Tn*, *Jn*, or *Kn* variables as appropriate, and (c) drawing a schematic of the resulting counter. If the problem requests that you *implement* a counter this implies writing the SystemVerilog code for it.

20.1. If one desires to count to M, what is the minimum number of bits required in the resulting counter?

20.2. Design a 3-bit counter that counts in multiples of 3. That is, the count sequence is: $000 - 011 - 110 - 000 - \ldots$.

20.3. Implement the counter from the previous problem using SystemVerilog.

20.4. Design a 3-bit binary counter which counts down rather than up.

20.5. Implement the counter from the previous problem using SystemVerilog.

20.6. Design a counter which counts in the sequence: $000 \rightarrow 010 \rightarrow 000 \rightarrow 111 \rightarrow 000 \rightarrow \ldots$. Use D type flip flops. HINT: a 3-bit counter will not suffice. You should design a 4-bit counter, 3 bits of which contain the desired sequence. Those 3 bits will be the output you use.

20.7. Implement the counter from the previous problem using SystemVerilog.

20.8. Determine the minimum clock period for the counter of Figure 20.9. Use the following delays: $t_{NOT} = 1ns, t_{AND} = 2ns, t_{OR} = 3ns, t_{CLK-Q} = 2ns, t_{setup} = 3ns, t_{hold} = 1ns$. Note that the flip flops are shown without a Q' output. Thus, you *must* use inverters as a part of the input forming logic as necessary.

Chapter 21

State Graphs

The previous chapters introduced sequential systems through the design of counters — circuits which sequence through a predetermined pattern of states. Additional inputs such as *CLEAR* or *ENABLE* signals were also added to control the counter's functionality. Transition tables or SystemVerilog were used to summarize the behavior of the desired circuit in these examples. However, graphical methods are often used to specify sequential behavior since they can provide more insight into the operation of the circuit and more importantly, can be an important design entry aid in the creation of sequential systems. *State graphs* are such a graphical method for representing the current state/next state behavior of a sequential system.

An important point needs to be made at the outset of this discussion, however. There is a direct correspondence, in all cases, between the features of a given state graph and the circuit's corresponding transition table. State graphs provide no additional features or power for expressing the functionality of sequential systems beyond that provided by transition tables. *They merely provide a graphical alternative to the tabular representation of transition tables.* If you can represent a design using a transition table, there is always a corresponding state graph. The converse is also true.

21.1 An Example State Graph

Consider a simple binary counter which counts through the sequence $00 \rightarrow 01 \rightarrow 10 \rightarrow 11 \rightarrow 00 \cdots$. The transition table and state graph for this counter are shown in Figure 21.1.

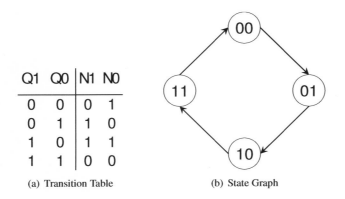

Q1	Q0	N1	N0
0	0	0	1
0	1	1	0
1	0	1	1
1	1	0	0

(a) Transition Table   (b) State Graph

Figure 21.1: Transition Table and State Graph For a 2-Bit Counter

Each counter state (current state value) is shown as a solid circle with the current state value written inside it. The arcs correspond to transitions between states. These transitions further correspond to rows in the transition table. The arc between states '00' and '01' in the graph corresponds to the first row of the transition table. The arc between states '01' and '10' corresponds to the second row, and so on.

21.2 State Graphs For Counters With Inputs

Consider now an incrementable counter where an *INC* signal controls whether the counter increments or not. The corresponding state graph is shown Figure 21.2. There is a one-to-one correspondence between the rows of the transition table and the arcs in the graph (eight rows, eight arcs). Each arc is labeled with the input condition for which the state transition occurs. The arc between states '00' and '01' is labeled with *INC* — when *INC*='1' and the current state is '00', the next state is state '01'. Similarly, the arc that loops state '00' back onto itself is labeled with *INC'* — when *INC*='0' and the current state is '00', the next state is '00'.

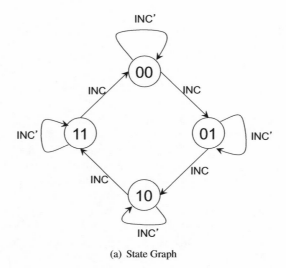

(a) State Graph

Figure 21.2: State Graph For a 2-Bit Counter With *INC* Input

The state graph back in Figure 21.1 has no labels on the arcs, implying that those arcs are *always* taken when in the specified current state. In contrast, decision making is shown in the transitions of Figure 21.2 — a given arc is *only* taken when the expression on its label is true and the circuit is in the specified state.

21.3 State Graphs For Counters With Multiple Inputs

Now consider the design of a counter with both *CLR* and *INC* inputs as shown in in Figure 21.3. When *CLR*='0' and *INC*='1', the counter increments. These are the arcs labeled *CLR'* • *INC*. When *CLR*='0' and *INC*='0', the counter stays in the current state. These are the arcs labeled *CLR'* • *INC'*. Whenever *CLR*='1', the counter resets to state '00'.

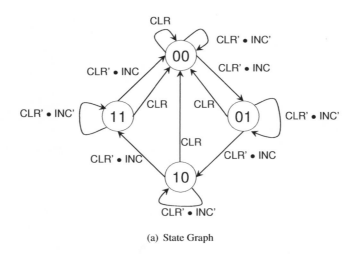

(a) State Graph

Figure 21.3: Transition Table and State Graph For a 2-Bit Counter With *INC* and *CLR* Input

The above graph is fairly messy in that for every state it has to be specified what happens when $CLR = 1$ and what happens when $CLR = 0$. A simplified version of the state graph is shown in Figure21.4.

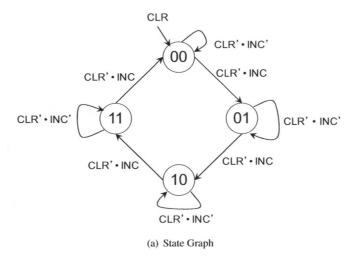

(a) State Graph

Figure 21.4: Simplified State Graph Showing Single Reset Arc

At the top of the graph is an arc which comes *from nowhere* and is labeled with *CLR*. It signifies that - when *CLR*='1', the counter will reset *independent* of the *INC* input <u>and</u> independent of the current state. Thus, that transition takes precedence over the rest of the behavior. Does this state graph contain different information than the state graph of Figure 21.3? No. It is merely a shorthand version of the original state graph.

21.4 Design Procedure Using State Graphs

The above examples suggest a design methodology based on state graph and transition table techniques:

1. Draw a state graph which represents the design of interest.

2. Create a transition table from the state graph.

3. Complete the design as outlined in previous chapters using KMaps or other techniques

4. Implement the resulting IFL, register, and OFL.

21.5 Representing Counter Outputs in State Graphs

21.5.1 Moore (Static) Outputs

Circuit outputs such as those described in previous chapters can also be represented in state graphs. Consider the incrementable counter of Figure 21.5. The Z output is asserted in states '00' and '11'. and so the name of the output signal (Z) has been written in the state graph next to each state where it should be asserted. It is assumed that the signal Z is not asserted in states where it is not listed. It is underlined where asserted to improve the readability of the graph.

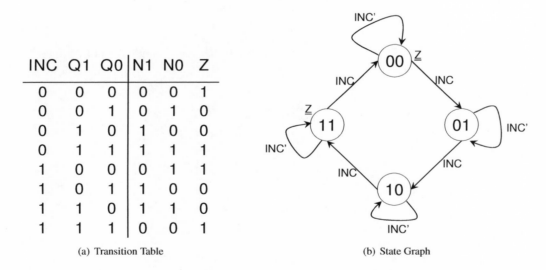

INC	Q1	Q0	N1	N0	Z
0	0	0	0	0	1
0	0	1	0	1	0
0	1	0	1	0	0
0	1	1	1	1	1
1	0	0	0	1	1
1	0	1	1	0	0
1	1	0	1	1	0
1	1	1	0	0	1

(a) Transition Table   (b) State Graph

Figure 21.5: An Incrementable Counter With A Moore (Static) Output

A Note About Assertion Levels and State Graphs

The discussion above assumes that when a signal is asserted it is to be driven to a '1'. While this is often true, it is not universally true. Some signals are *active low* or *low asserted*. That means that they are usually '1' and, when asserted, go to a '0'. The write enable signal on many memory chips is low asserted meaning that the memory is written to when the write enable signal is '0'. This signal is usually named something like *WE#* to indicate that it is active low. The user has a number of options when entering such signals into a state graph:

1. List the signal by name any time it is asserted in a state. In this case, the signal name (*WE#* for example) would imply the low assertion.

2. Explicitly state *WE#* ← 0 in the state graph to emphasize the fact that the signal was being asserted low.

3. List the value of *WE#* with its value in every state in the state graph to avoid any confusion.

The choice of which to use is up to you. The most important consideration is that you understand exactly what is implied by any notation used in a state graph, and can draw the transition table and write the corresponding SystemVerilog code.

21.5.2 Mealy (Dynamic) Outputs

Mealy or dynamic outputs can also be represented in a state graph. Consider a counter which has an asserted output any time the current state is '11' *and* the counter is being incremented. This is often called the *rollover* condition for the counter, since it represents the transition when the counter *rolls back over to zero*. It is a Mealy output because the output depends on both the current state and the *INC* input.

The design for this counter is shown in Figure 21.6. The state graph contains a new feature not previously seen — the *Y* output is *associated with the arc from '11' to '00'*. The interpretation of this is that output *Y* will be asserted any time the current state is '11' <u>and</u> *INC*='1'.

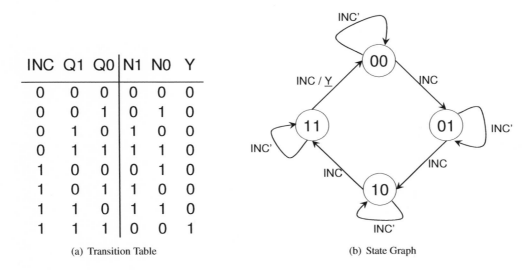

INC	Q1	Q0	N1	N0	Y
0	0	0	0	0	0
0	0	1	0	1	0
0	1	0	1	0	0
0	1	1	1	1	0
1	0	0	0	1	0
1	0	1	1	0	0
1	1	0	1	1	0
1	1	1	0	0	1

(a) Transition Table   (b) State Graph

Figure 21.6: An Incrementable Counter With A Mealy (Dynamic) Output

21.6 Properly Formed State Graphs

Care must be taken when creating a state graph to ensure *that it specifies exactly one next state transition for each and every possible input condition*. The machine will not perform as desired otherwise. To determine whether a state graph is properly formed, one must determine whether it is *complete* and whether it is *conflict-free*.

A state is said to be *incomplete* if the graph does not specify what should happen for some combination of inputs. Just as it is easy to forget to cover some cases when writing complex *if-then-else* statements in a software program, it is easy to overlook some conditions when designing a state graph. To determine whether the arcs leaving a state are complete, you should OR together all the conditions on those arcs. If the result is 1 (true) then you have covered all the cases. If it is not 1, then you have forgotten to cover at least one input combination.

A second problem that arises in the creation of state graphs is *conflicts*. As an example of a state graph which has a conflict, consider the state graph of Figure 21.7 and carefully look at state '10'. To see the conflict, consider what the state graph specifies when in state '10' and *CLR=INC*='1'. One transition arc indicates the next state should be '00', another indicates it should be '11'. There is clearly a conflict between these two arcs.

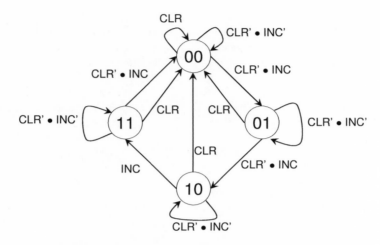

Figure 21.7: State Graph With A Transition Conflict

To determine whether a state has any conflicts, you can AND together the transition conditions on *pairs* of arcs leaving a given state. If the result is '0' for all such pairs, then there are no conflicts for that state, and the state is said to be conflict-free. If the result is not '0' for any such pair, then a conflict exists (they overlap). In the case of state '10' from Figure 21.7, there are three different pairings which must be considered:

$$CLR \bullet (CLR' \bullet INC') = 0 \quad (10 \to 00 \bullet 10 \to 10)$$
$$INC \bullet (CLR' \bullet INC') = 0 \quad (10 \to 11 \bullet 10 \to 10)$$
$$INC \bullet CLR \neq 0 \quad (10 \to 11 \bullet 10 \to 00)$$

The last pairing shows that there is a conflict between two arcs leaving state '10' (this is the conflict we saw above). This can be repaired by changing the arc labeled *INC* to have a label of *CLR'* • *INC* as was shown originally in Figure 21.3.

There is an importance difference between this analysis and that for completeness. All the arcs leaving a state are simply OR-ed together in the completeness test. *All pairs* of arcs leaving a given state must be tested for the conflict test. In the case of a state with three exit transitions, a total of three tests must be made, for four exit transitions a total of six tests must be made, for five exit transitions a total of ten are required, and so on.

Exceptions to both the completeness and conflict tests may be acceptable when certain input conditions are *known* to never occur. In these cases, it is acceptable for these two tests to fail. However, if the assumption that certain input conditions turns to be false, then the circuit's behavior may not be what you intend. The safer course would be to define what should happen even if those input conditions were to occur - this would result in predictable (and known) behavior in all cases.[1]

---

[1] In cases involving safety critical systems such as health care devices or vehicle controls, it would undoubtedly be required that you specify all cases, even if you believe they can never happen.

21.7 Chapter Summary

The key high-level points to master from this chapter include the following:

1. State graphs are a graphical method for representing digital designs which are often more readable than transition tables.

2. Every state graph has a corresponding transition table which it represents. State graphs present no new capabilities with respect to digital systems design — they are merely another way of representing the same information contained in transition tables.

3. State graphs consist of states and transitions. The conditions which cause the various transitions to occur in the design are written as Boolean expressions next to the arcs for the transitions. Arcs without labels will always be taken when in the specified current state.

4. Design using state graphs consists of three steps: (1) draw a state graph representing the design to be constructed, (2) convert it to a transition table, and (3) implement the transition table design using techniques presented in previous chapters.

5. Moore (static) outputs can be represented in state graphs. This is done by simply listing the signal to be asserted in a given state next to that state. It is understood that all signals not listed next to a state will not be asserted in that state. This applies for both high-asserted signals and low-asserted signals.

6. Mealy (dynamic) outputs can also be represented in state graphs. They are associated with transitions (arcs). The nomenclature for such transitions and outputs is "transitionCondition / output". If more than one output is listed on a transition they are simply separated by commas.

The skills that should result from study of this chapter include the following:

1. The ability to draw a state graph representing the behavior of any kind of counter circuit, with or without inputs, with or without outputs.

2. The ability to determine whether a state graph is properly formed. That is, to determine whether it is complete and conflict free.

21.8 Exercises

For each exercise below, be sure that the state graphs created are both complete and conflict-free.

21.1. Draw the state graph and corresponding transition table for a 3-bit counter with no control inputs that counts in multiples of 3. That is, the count sequence is: $000 - 011 - 110 - 000 - \cdots$. Use don't cares in the transition table as appropriate.

21.2. Draw the state graph and corresponding transition table for a 3-bit binary counter with no control inputs which counts down rather than up. Include a Z output which signifies when the "count value modulo 3 is equal to 0".

21.3. Draw the state graph for a 3-bit counter which counts in a gray code (you choose the code). Include a Z output which signifies when the even/odd characteristic of the current state and of the next state values (when interpreted as unsigned integers) are the same. That is, if the transition is '000' $\rightarrow$ '010' ($0 \rightarrow 2$) the output should be asserted. However, if the transition is '101' $\rightarrow$ '100' ($5 \rightarrow 4$) the output should not be asserted.

21.4. Draw the state graph for a 3-bit up/down counter which has the following inputs: *CLR, INC, DEC*. Make it so the inputs have priority in that order. Add a Z output which signifies whenever the current state of the counter is either '010' or '110'.

21.5. Perform the completeness and conflict tests on the state graph created for the previous problem. For each state, show the OR of all the conditions on arcs leaving that state and verify that it is indeed '1'. For each state, list all the pairs of arc conditions that must be ANDed for conflict testing. Then, do all the ANDs and verify that they indeed all result in 0's.

21.6. Draw the state graph and transition table for a 2-bit counter which has the following inputs: *CLR, ONE/TWO#, UP/DOWN#*, where *CLR* has the highest priority. When *ONE/TWO#*='1', have it count by 1. When it is '0', have the counter count by 2.

Chapter 22

Finite State Machines

The operation of a copy machine was described in an earlier chapter as a 6-step process. The following was then stated:

> The key component of a sequential circuit which could perform the above 6-step process is its ability to remember where it is in the process so that as signals arrive from the parts of the copier it can react appropriately. During certain steps user input from the console might be ignored. This *remembering* of the current state of the copy operation is implemented by sequential circuits using storage (memory).

It should now be obvious that this ability to *remember* is embodied in the concept known as *state*. The previous chapters have introduced a number of other important concepts, all of which can now be used in the creation of general purpose sequential circuits. Although these concepts were all presented in the context of registers and counters, they apply equally as well to the design of general state-based sequential circuits. These include the following:

- The concepts of *state*, *current state*, *next state*, and *state registers*.

- The concepts of *input forming logic*, *output forming logic*, Moore (static) outputs, and Mealy (dynamic) outputs.

- The use of transition tables in the specification of the current state/next state/output behavior of sequential systems.

- The use of state graphs as an alternative to transition tables for the representation of sequential system designs.

We now turn to one of the most important design concepts in all of digital systems design — the design of *finite state machines*. The counters of the previous chapters are all examples of state machines, albeit with fairly limited next state functions. With counters one is usually interested in the actual state encodings used (binary vs. gray code for example). The current state bits of a counter are often directly used as outputs. A digital clock circuit (where the current state bits drive a display) is an example of this.

In contrast, the state encoding of a state machine is often not of concern. Rather, the important outputs of a copy machine controller are not its current state values but rather the output signals it generates to control the copy machine's lights, motors, and rollers. In this case, the current state bits may not even be used outside the state machine as outputs — they may only be used internally by the machine to help it sequence properly.

22.1 A Simple State Machine - A Sequence Recognizer

Consider the state graph of Figure 22.1. This is a finite state machine (FSM) with a single input (Xin) and a single output (Z). This FSM will detect an occurrence of the serial pattern '011' on the input stream. That is, it looks at the input, and if the values '0'-'1'-'1' appear on three successive clock cycles, it will signal that it found the pattern by asserting its output signal.

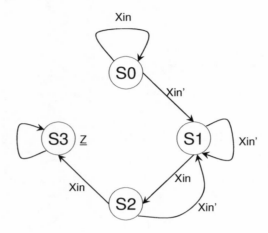

Figure 22.1: A Finite State Machine Recognizing the Input Pattern '011'

Symbolic names have been used for the states (**S0, S1, S2, S3**) in the state graph. This is because the actual binary encodings of the state values are unimportant at this stage of the design. The behavior of the machine in each state can be summarized as follows:

- The machine waits in state **S0** as long as '1' values appear on Xin. This is the loop back arc for **S0**. The *meaning* of state **S0** can be stated as: **S0** *represents the fact that the first value in the desired sequence (a '0') has not occurred.* When a '0' on Xin does occur the machine transitions to state **S1**.

- State **S1** represents the condition *that the first value in the desired sequence (a '0') has occurred.* Two things can happen in state **S1**: (1) If a '1' appears on the input, the machine will move on to state **S2**, or (2) if another '0' appears on the input, the machine will remain in state **S1**.

- State **S2** represents the condition *that the first two values in the desired sequence ('01') have occurred.* This state also has two different arcs leaving it. A '0' on the input sends it back to state **S1** (the first value in the sequence may have just occurred). A '1' on the input sends the machine on to state **S3**.

- State **S3** represents the condition *that the whole desired sequence ('011') has occurred.* The output signal Z is generated as a Moore (static) output in state **S3** to indicate this. Once the machine reaches state **S3**, it is designed to stay there indefinitely while asserting signal Z.

A timing diagram representing the operation of the machine in response to a sequence of values on the *Xin* input is shown in Figure 22.2. The values of *Xin* at each rising edge of the clock have been added as text to help show the circuit's operation.

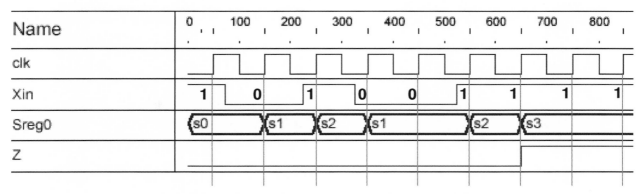

Figure 22.2: Timing Diagram for the '011' Sequence Detector

22.1.1 A Continuous '011' Detector - Moore Version

The above machine was designed to detect and signal the presence of only the first '011' pattern in the input stream. Once that is detected, the machine ceases useful operation and loops in state **S3** while holding its output at a '1' value.

The machine of Figure 22.3 is a modified version which will detect and signal *all* occurrences of the pattern '011' on the input. The difference is that it remains in **S3** for only one clock cycle and immediately begins attempting to recognize another occurrence of '011' beginning with the very next input value. From state **S3**, a '0' sends it to state **S1** while a '1' sends it to state **S0**;

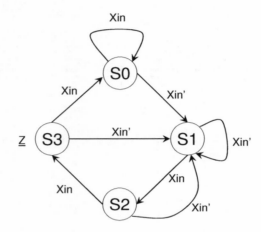

Figure 22.3: A Moore FSM Recognizing All Occurrences of the Input Pattern '011'

A timing diagram of the operation of this machine in response to a stream of *Xin* values is shown in Figure 22.4. At first glance, this timing diagram may seem to be incorrect because the Z output always goes high one cycle *after* the occurrence of '011' on the input stream. A careful analysis will reveal that the timing diagram accurately reflects the circuit's behavior — the output is asserted any time the machine is in state **S3**. And remember, the machine will enter state **S3** on the clock edge when the second 1 has appeared on the input.

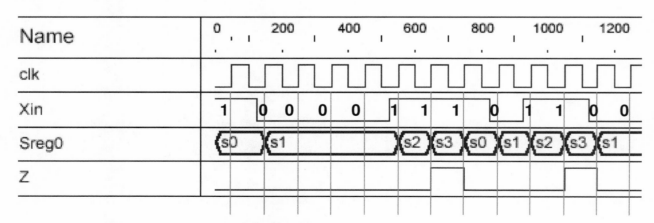

Figure 22.4: Timing Diagram for the Continuous '011' Sequence Detector (Moore version)

This brings up an important point about design specification vs. design behavior — English descriptions are sometimes (usually) ambiguous. The state graph (and associated transition table) precisely defines the machine's operation. Learn to understand exactly how state graphs are mapped to hardware so they can serve as your formal specification of the machine's operation. Doing so will result in fewer surprises when the behavior and timing of the final machine doesn't quite match what you thought your original English problem statement implied.

22.1.2 A Continuous '011' Detector - Mealy Version

The use of a Mealy output makes it possible to signal the successful recognition of the '011' sequence concurrently with the appearance of the third bit of the '011' pattern. A state graph for this design is shown in Figure 22.5, and the timing diagram of Figure 22.6 shows the resulting circuit behavior. The only difference from the Moore version is the timing of the Y output — it appears *concurrently* with the second '1' bit on the input, and thus appears a cycle earlier than in the Moore machine. Output Y is asserted any time the machine is in state **S2** and Xin='1' according to the state graph. This is reflected in the timing diagram.

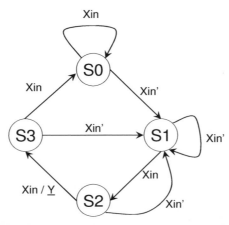

Figure 22.5: A Mealy FSM Recognizing All Occurrences of the Input Pattern '011'

Name	0	100	200	300	400	500	600	700	800
clk									
Xin	0	1	1	1	0	1	1	1	
Sreg0	s0	s1	s2	s3	s0	s1	s2	s3	s0
Y									

Figure 22.6: Timing Diagram for the Continuous '011' Sequence Detector (Mealy version)

The figure also shows a characteristic of Mealy outputs - note that at about 230ns in the timing diagram Xin transitions up and down multiple times. Because the machine is currently in state **S2**, the output Y responds accordingly. Whether this represents a concern depends on what signal Y is being used for elsewhere in the system.

All input and output forming logic is simply combinational logic, and so false outputs (discussed in Chapter 13) can occur at any time. The output signal transitions at 230ns in the timing diagram are due to an entirely different phenomenon, however. They are not a function of how the KMap was covered. They are a Mealy output which is asynchronously changing in response to an input change. *This is a key characteristic of Mealy outputs.*

Another advantage of Mealy outputs is that they often allow a reduction in the number of states in the FSM. A simplified version of the Mealy machine is shown in Figure 22.7. State **S3** has been removed since it was determined that correct operation with just three states is possible. Such a reduction is only possible for the Mealy version of the machine — the Moore machine always requires four states for proper operation. A careful analysis of the operation of this machine will reveal that its input/output behavior is the same as that of Figure 22.6, except that it goes directly from state **S2** to state **S0** without passing through state **S3**. The timing of the Y output will be the same, however.

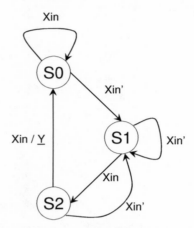

Figure 22.7: An Improved FSM Compared to Figure 22.5

22.2 Finite State Machine Example - Car Wash Controller

As another example, consider the design of a controller for a simple car wash. Its behavior can be summarized as follows:

1. Wait for a token to be deposited into the coin box. Move on to the next step when a token is deposited.

2. Reset a free-running timer which will be used to time the duration of the car wash and move on to the next step.

3. While waiting for the timer to expire (indicating that the car wash has completed), assert a signal which will turn on a water pump (to spray the car with water). When the timer expires, return to the first step to await the deposit of another token so the process can start over again.

A state graph for this simple car wash controller is shown in Figure 22.8(a). This machine has two inputs: *TOKEN* and *TDONE* and two outputs: *CLRT* and *SPRAY*. Each step in the English description above translates to a single state in the graph. The machine awaits the deposit of a token in state **S_IDLE** and transitions to state **S_TOKEN** when a token is deposited. The machine clears the timer in state **S_TOKEN** and then transitions immediately to state **S_SPRAY** on the very next clock cycle. The machine sprays the car in state **S_SPRAY** while awaiting the receipt of a *TDONE* signal. The machine returns to state **S_IDLE** when *TDONE* indicates that the car wash is complete.

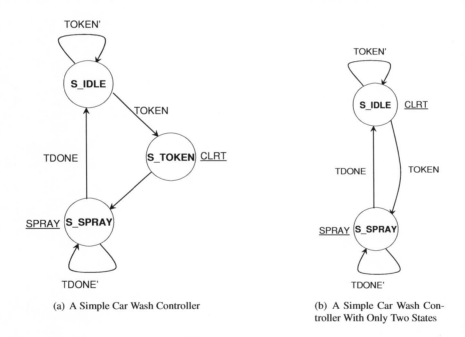

(a) A Simple Car Wash Controller

(b) A Simple Car Wash Controller With Only Two States

Figure 22.8: Simple Car Wash Controller

A simplification to this state machine can be made. Specifically, state **S_TOKEN** can be eliminated as shown in Figure 22.8(b). The timer is continuously being reset in this design while the machine is in state **S_IDLE**. When a token is received, the timer will already be reset, and the machine can proceed directly to state **S_SPRAY**. The result is a simpler machine.

22.2.1 Implementation Details

A number of assumptions were made in the design of the car wash controller above. The first was that a spray mechanism exists which will turn on the sprayer in response to a simple one-bit signal output from the state machine. Clearly, the inclusion of such circuitry must be included in the overall car wash system. Our concern here was the design of just the digital control for the car wash, and so it was adequate to *assume* that such a mechanism exists elsewhere in the system.

The same was true of the timer — no detail was provided with respect to its design. It should be obvious from the description of the above controller, that the timer runs continuously, but can be reset. It asserts the *TDONE* signal to indicate that time has expired. A time duration of 60-120 seconds might be adequate for a car wash. This is easily designed using the counter design techniques of the previous chapters.

Finally, the token input mechanism was also abstracted away in the design above. We understood that a physical mechanism for accepting tokens would be present in the final car wash system, and that it asserts the signal *TOKEN* when a token has been inserted.

This is a common approach in the design of digital state machine controllers — the behavior of the remainder of the system is abstracted away to a collection of devices which accept digital control signals, and which generate digital signals in return. This simplifies the design of the controller by allowing the design process to focus on the creation of a state graph which represents the desired input/output behavior, and its subsequent conversion to a digital logic circuit. Ultimately, the entire system must be assembled and so the other modules must be designed. That is the topic of a later chapter.

22.2.2 A Car Wash With Two Different Wash Settings

A more interesting car wash is one with two kinds of washes — an inexpensive one and an expensive one. The inexpensive wash is as above - simply spray the vehicle for a set period of time. This costs the customer a single token. The deluxe wash consists of three steps: (1) rinse the vehicle with water, (2) apply soap, and (3) rinse the vehicle again. This costs the customer two tokens.

A question is how to determine which wash the customer desires? A simple solution is to add a *START* signal to the controller — the customer inserts a single token and then presses the *START* button for the simple wash OR the customer inserts a second token, indicating a desire for the deluxe wash. The state machine determines which wash is desired by which of these two actions the user performs. A state graph for this state machine is shown in Figure 22.9.

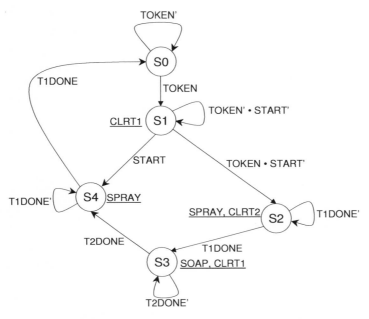

Figure 22.9: A Deluxe Car Wash Controller

This is a machine with all Moore outputs. It has four inputs: *TOKEN, START, T1DONE, T2DONE* and four outputs: *CLRT1, CLRT2, SPRAY,* and *SOAP*. Its operation is as follows:

1. The machine awaits the insertion of a token in state **S0**.

2. One of two things can happen in state **S1**: (1) a second token is inserted and the machine transitions to state **S2** to begin the deluxe wash, or (2) the start button is pressed and the machine transitions to state **S4** to do the simple wash.

3. The *SPRAY* signal is asserted for a pre-rinse step in state **S2**. This continues until the timer expires (*T1DONE*), indicating it is time to move on to the soap step.

4. Soap is applied to the car in state **S3** until the second timer expires (*T2DONE*).

5. The final rinse is done in state **S4**. The rinse timer done signal (*T1DONE*) indicates when the car wash is complete, and the machine then transitions back to state **S0** to await the input of another token.

The last step of the deluxe wash is the same as the entire simple wash (state **S4**). Two timers are used — one is used for timing both rinse steps, and a different one used for timing the soap step. As a result the duration of the rinse steps may be different than the duration of the soap step — it depends of the design of the timers. Note in the state graph where the various timers are reset to ensure they are ready for use when needed.

Many system-level decisions must be made in the design of a controller like this. It is sometimes difficult to ensure that the design covers all possible scenarios. A list of issues for this design includes:

- It was determined that the *START* button would only be used to start the simple wash. A second *TOKEN* input would be taken as an indication that the customer desired a deluxe wash.

- If the customer happens to accidentally insert a second token and press the *START* button at *precisely* the same instant, the machine will only provide the simple wash and steal the customer's token[1]. This can be seen by examining the transition from state **S1** to state **S4**, and could be easily changed by modifying the transition conditions leaving state **S1** to give the *TOKEN* signal precedence over the *START* signal.

- There is no provision in this design to return extra tokens inserted by the customer. If tokens are inserted when the machine is in any states other than **S0** and **S1**, it will ignore them (and presumably keep them). This could be changed if the coinbox would accept a signal instructing it to refuse tokens. An output driving that signal could then be added to the state machine so that tokens inserted in states other than **S0** and **S1** would be refused (and returned to the customer).

- The design of the machine assumes two different timers — one for timing the spray step, and a different one for timing the soap step. A timer which could time both periods could be used. A common approach to this might be a timer which counts down to 0. When one CLR signal is asserted it loads with one value and it loads a different value when the other CLR signal is asserted. Then, it counts down, asserting a $DONE$ signal when it reaches zero. The advantage of this is that a single counter can be used to perform both functions and only a single $DONE$ signal is required.

- Pushing the *START* button in any state other than state **S1** is ignored. This is acceptable.

- The timer done signals are ignored in all but a few states. This is also acceptable.

22.3 Resetting State Machines

An important consideration in the creation of any digital system is the inclusion of circuitry to ensure that the machine can be easily reset to a known state. There may be instances where this is not necessary for normal operation, but the ability to reset the system is essential for testing.

A good practice to follow is to *always* include a reset capability in any state machine. This can be done two ways. The first was shown back in Figure 21.4 where CLR is a part of the state graph (and therefore the transition table and the input forming logic). That figure is reproduced below for reference.

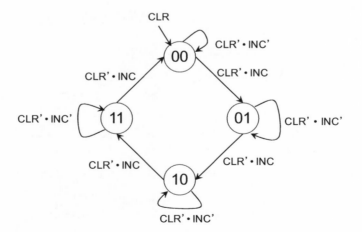

Figure 22.10: State Graph Showing *CLR* Signal

---

[1]This may be an unlikely possibility but could conceivably happen. For example if the state machine were running at 50MHz, the *TOKEN* signal would be sampled every 20ns. For this case to occur, the token would have to trigger the coin box mechanism during precisely the same 20ns time window as the user pressed the button — highly unlikely but theoretically possible.

The second way to provide a reset capability is to take advantage of the reset capability built into many flip flops. Section 15.5 showed both synchronous and asynchronous clear signals for flip flops. A flip flop symbol with a synchronous clear signal is shown below in Figure 22.11.

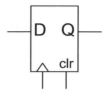

Figure 22.11: A Flip Flop Symbol With A Synchronous Clear Input

These can be used to reset the state machine when they are available. This results in less complex state graphs, transition tables with one less input, and smaller input forming logic. It is well worth the cost, using either method discussed in this section, to provide a reset capability for any digital system design.

22.4 Completeness and Conflicts in State Graphs Revisited

One of the most common errors in the creation of real finite state machine designs is to create an incomplete or conflicting state graph. The transitions leaving state **S1** in Figure 22.9 represent a typical problem area — multiple transitions leaving a state with somewhat complex conditions. This is similar to the problem encountered when writing computer programs with complex if-then-else structures — it is easy to miss a condition and end up with a state graph which will not work for all input combinations. Be sure to apply the tests for completeness and conflict given in the previous chapter as you do state machine design to avoid these problems.

22.5 Chapter Summary

This chapter has introduced finite state machines via an example of a '011' sequence detector and a collection of car wash controllers. Key concepts from this chapter include the following:

1. As with counters, finite state machines sequence through a set of states in response to inputs.

2. As with counters, finite state machines can have either Moore or Mealy outputs.

3. As with counters, the behavior of a finite state machine can be described by a state graph or transition table.

4. A common characteristic of finite state machines used for control is the existence of many don't cares in the transition table.

5. A finite state machine with Mealy outputs will often have fewer states than the corresponding finite state machine with Moore outputs.

6. You can mix Mealy and Moore outputs in the same state machine.

7. All of the considerations regarding complete and conflict-free state graphs for counters apply to the creation of finite state machine state graphs.

8. When designing the state graph for a finite state machine, many assumptions must be made regarding the existence of other circuitry such as counters and timers which are required to fully implement the system functionality.

9. English descriptions of state machine behavior are often (actually, almost always) ambiguous. State graphs provide a less ambiguous way to describe machine behavior.

The skills that should result from your study of this chapter include the following:

1. The ability to convert a word description of a desired state machine into a state graph.

2. The ability to draw a timing diagram reflecting the operation of a state machine from a state graph.

3. The ability to create either a Mealy or a Moore machine to implement desired functionality.

22.6 Exercises

22.1. Draw the state graph for a car wash controller which has 3 different kinds of washes - a simple rinse-only wash, a rinse-soap-rinse wash, and a rinse-soap-rinse-blow dry wash. The first two of these wash types are the same as those in this chapter. State any assumptions you make as you create the state graph.

22.2. Draw the state graph for a machine which has a single input. Have it output a signal which indicates whether an even number of 1's has been seen this far in the input stream (no 1's seen so far counts as even). Use a Moore output. Use a minimum number of states.

22.3. Repeat the previous problem, but with a Mealy output. Use a minimum number of states.

22.4. Draw a timing diagram showing how the previous two state machines behave differently in response to a sequence of inputs.

22.5. Design the coin counting and change mechanism for a vending machine. NOTE: you are to design only the FSM state graph, assuming that circuitry elsewhere generates inputs for it and that it generates outputs to control the rest of the machine. Here are the parameters for the machine:

- Everything in the machine costs $0.30.

- The only inputs to your machine include: *n*, *d*, *q*, and *v*. One of the *n*, *d*, *q* signals will go high for a single cycle whenever a nickel, dime, or quarter is inserted. Only one of them will go high at a time.

- The *v* signal goes high when the user has selected an item (it is the *vend* input). You may assume the user won't push the vend button until enough money has been inserted.

- Your state machine should generate an output called *enough*. This signifies when the user has put in at least $0.30. Your machine may assume that after that point, no additional coins can be input (maybe the coin box mechanism will use *enough* to refuse additional coins).

- Your machine doesn't control actually dispensing the item. It simply counts the money that is input. When enough money has been input, it asserts *enough* and waits for the *v* vend signal to go high. When that happens, your machine is to dispense change using nickels only. To dispense change, your machine should assert the output signal *ejN* one or more times to output the change (one per cycle). Thus, it may take a few cycles to output the correct change.

- Once your machine outputs the correct change, it should transition back to the start state to await the input of more money.

- Your FSM should be a Moore machine.

Draw the state graph for an FSM which will implement this controller without any external circuitry. That is, the states themselves represent how much money has been input and also how much needs to be returned as change. This may require many states. Turn in a drawing of your state graph with symbolic state names in the circles. Also turn in a written description of any assumptions you made, along with evidence that your machine is both complete and conflict-free. If certain input conditions cannot occur and your machine takes advantage of those (which it should), then discuss how you took advantage of those.

22.6. Do the design above but with some changes:

- The machine only accepts dimes and returns change using only dimes.

- The machine uses a state machine plus an external accumulator. An accumulator is nothing more than an up/down counter in this case.

- The accumulator has two inputs. The *inc* input tells it to add ten cents to its accumulated total. The *dec* input tells it to subtract ten cents from its accumulated total. Thus, the only way to clear the accumulator once something has been ordered from the vending machine is to repeatedly decrement the accumulator to get its total back to zero.

- The accumulator has two outputs. Its *enough* output signifies that the accumulator contains $0.30. Its *zero* output signifies that it contains $0.00.

- You may also assume that once $0.30 has been input, the machine will refuse additional coins (your FSM doesn't need to accomodate additional coins beyond $0.30).

- Your FSM should monitor the *d*, *enough*, and *zero* signals and output whatever signals are required for the machine's proper operation.

- Your FSM should be a Moore machine.

As with the problem above, turn in your state graph and a written description of any assumptions you have made.

22.7. Design a Mealy machine for the problem above. It should take fewer states. You may assume the inputs to the FSM are synchronous.

22.8. In Problem 22.6, it was stated that the *d* signal would only be asserted for a single cycle. Imagine now that your design is to work with a *d* signal that is asserted for many cycles for each dime insertion. Modify your FSM state graph to accommodate this different behavior.

Chapter 23

State Machine Design Using SystemVerilog

The coding of state machines using SystemVerilog is very similar to the coding of counters. However, a few new features of SystemVerilog are used in the process as will be seen in this chapter.

23.1 SystemVerilog Features for Coding State Machines

The finite state machine of Figure 22.1 can be coded as in Program 23.1.1. In this code, a *reset* signal not present in Figure 22.1 has been added.

State machines could be coded similarly to counters from previous chapters, with a clocked *always_ff* block used for the IFL and registers, and with one or more dataflow $assign$ statements (or *always_comb*) blocks being used for the OFL. But, all of the examples in this chapter show a slightly different coding style. While using this style is not a strict requirement, many (the author included) believe it makes the design of state machines simpler and less error-prone.

In this style, a single *always_comb* block is used for the combined IFL/OFL. Then, a single *always_ff* block is used for the state register. Thus, in the code of Program 23.1.1 you will see these two *always* blocks.

This example introduces a number of other new features in SystemVerilog coding. The first new feature is the SystemVerilog enumerated type capability (used to define the state names). Note that you first create a new type using a *typedef* statement and then you declare the state variable to be of that type.

In this case, the compiler will (by default) enumerate the states to be $s0 = 00, s1 = 01, s2 = 10, s3 = 11$. The type will be of type *int* and is 32-bits wide. It will use as many bits wide a representation as is required and assign the enumerated names to successive binary values, starting with 0.

If you use enumerated types, you may never really even care about the actual state encoding chosen nor its bit-level representation — another case of higher level abstraction simplifying your job as the designer. But, an interesting question to consider is: can you achieve a higher performance circuit or a circuit that requires less silicon area by choosing a specific state encoding yourself? Does allowing the compiler to choose the binary values for $s0 - s3$ result in a less than optimal solution? The answer to both questions is *absolutely*, yes, you can often do better by choosing your own encoding. There has been significant research in the past on algorithms to choose optimal state encodings to achieve minimum circuit area and/or maximum performance. Some CAD tools which compile and process HDL code have such optimization algorithms built into them. If your tools do not, should you expend energy and time to optimize your circuit to use such an optimal encoding? The author's thoughts are no, you should not do so except only under very specialized circumstances (where circuit area and/or performance are at a premium).

Why? Modern integrated circuits contain billions of logic elements and flip flops and saving a few gates or flip flops in a state machine design may not be worth the effort in light of the other challenges inherent in the design process. That said, you should be aware that there may be times when this is desired and that a host of techniques have been developed to help you do so. Consult the research literature for more details.

Also, note that a *case* statement has been used in the body of the *always_comb* block. This is a natural way to code a finite state machine where each state gets its own clause in the *case* statement. Just remember, all the inferred latch considerations of Section 18.2 apply here since it is an *always_comb* block.

Program 23.1.1 SystemVerilog Code for State Machine of Figure 22.1

```
// Define a 'states' type and next and current state variables of that type
typedef enum {s0, s1, s2, s3} StateType;
StateType ns, cs;

// The IFL and OFL is in one always_comb block
always_comb
begin
  // Assign default values to the next state and output signals
  ns = cs;
  Z = 0;

  // Here is the IFL/OFL
  if (reset)
    ns = s0;
  else
    case (cs)
      s0: if (!Xin)
             ns = s1;
      s1: if (Xin)
             ns = s2;
      s2: if (Xin)
             ns = s1;
          else
             ns = s3;
      s3: Z = 1'b1;
    endcase
end

// Here is the state register
always_ff @(posedge clk)
  cs <= ns;
```

This example illustrates a feature of SystemVerilog described previously. Note how multiple assignments have been made to the *ns*, *clrt*, and *spray* signals in the *always_comb* block. The initial assignments at the top of the block essentially provide *default* values for the signals. However, when in certain states, those default values are over-ridden and the signals given new values. This goes for both the next state variable as well as any outputs from the state machine. This style of coding simplifies the IFL and OFL by only requiring *differences* from the default values be indicated in the *case* statement clauses. This can be a great aid to your productivity since most output signals are only asserted in a few states. It also helps avoid latches as in the discussion of Section 18.2.[1]

---

[1]What does assigning two values to a signal in succession in an *always_comb* block really do? Does the signal take on the default value for some time period and then switch to the final value? No. The way an *always* block is modelled is that once the block is activated, the code inside it is executed and, at the end of that, the final signal values thus computed are actually assigned to the signals. So, no, there will not be any signal glitching when multiple assignments are done in this way.

As another example, the SystemVerilog design of the state machine of Figure 22.8 is shown in Program 23.1.2.

Program 23.1.2 SystemVerilog Code for Car Wash State Machine of Figure 22.8

```
// Define the state register
typedef enum {sIdle, sToken, sSpray}  StateType;
StateType ns, cs;

// The IFL and OFL
always_comb
begin
  // Default values
  ns = cs;
  clrt = 0;
  spray = 0;

  // The actual logic
  if (reset)
    ns = sIdle;
  else
    case (cs)
      sIdle:   if (token)
                  ns = sToken;
      sToken:  begin
                  clrt = 1;
                  ns = sSpray;
               end
      sSpray:  begin
                  spray = 1;
                  if (tdone)
                     ns = sIdle;
               end
      default: ns = sIdle;
    endcase
end

// The state register
always_ff @(posedge clk)
  cs <= ns;
```

Mealy machines can be coded in a similar style to those from above. The major difference is that their outputs are dependent on both the current state value as well as the inputs. The design of the state machine of Figure 22.7 (which does have a Mealy output) using SystemVerilog is shown in Program 23.1.3.

Program 23.1.3 SystemVerilog Code for State Machine of Figure 22.7

```
// Define the state register
typedef enum {s0, s1, s2} stateType
stateType ns, cs;

// The input forming logic and the state register circuitry
always_comb
begin
  ns = cs;
  Z = 0;
  if (reset)
    ns = s0;
  else
    case (state)
      s0: if (!Xin)
            ns = s1;
      s1: if (Xin)
            ns = s2;
      s2: if (Xin)
          begin
            ns = s0;
            Z = 1;   // This is the Mealy output
          end
          else ns = s1;
    endcase
end

// The state register
always_ff @(posedge clk)
  cs <= ns;
```

23.2   State Machine Coding Styles

The above coding style contains two *always* blocks, one of which is combinational and describes the IFL and OFL. The other one is clocked and describes just the state register.

However, other styles are often used. For example, the style used for counters as shown in Chapter 20 could be employed. There, the state register and IFL were described by one *always_ff* block and the OFL done using either dataflow *assign* statements or an *always_comb* block. In fact, there is even be a third style (rarely used) where three different *always* blocks are used for the state register, the IFL, and the OFL.

As mentioned, the author prefers the style of Program 23.1.1. The reason is that a single *case* statement inside the *always_comb* block describes both the IFL and OFL. This keeps all the state graph information for a single state together in one place and makes it easy to compare the state graph contents to the SystemVerilog code. However, which style you ultimately use is a matter of personal preference.

23.2.1 A Defensive Coding Style for Finite State Machines

This preferred state machine coding style from above requires the minimal amount of code to describe a given state machine. This is because the default value for the next state is the current state value. This means that any loopback arcs in the state graph where the state doesn't change (and where no outputs are asserted) do not need to be included in the code since that is the default.

But, this could be improved upon. The problem with it is if the state machine is incomplete there will be cases where errors will be hidden.

Consider a state with two exit branches, one on *inputA* and one on *inputB*. Further, assume you forgot to code the transition arc corresponding to *inputA* into your SystemVerilog. During simulation when *inputA* arrives the machine will ignore it, but if *inputB* were to arrive a cycle or two later the state machine would then make that transition. And, you may have never noticed that the machine idled extra cycles in the original state due to it missing the arrival of *inputB*. This is a classical error that would be really nice to catch easily.

A more defensive approach could be adopted which would immediately catch such an error and signal to you during simulation that your state machine design was incomplete. Instead of making the default value for the next state be the current state value, make the default value for the next state an error state. If the state machine ever enters that error state you will know that it was due to a coding error consisting of missing conditions and arcs. To accomplish this, you would do the following to your state machine design:

1. You would add an error state to the *typedef* for the state variables. This error state would consist of an 'X' value,

2. You would then change the default assignment to *ns* to be to that error state.

3. This would then require that all state transition arcs (even loopback arcs) be coded into the state machine's *case* statement. While this will take a bit more code, the advantages are worth it.

This will accomplish two things. First, if the case statement doesn't cover all situations then the state machine will enter the error state during simulation to tell you this has happened. You can then track down what you forgot to include in the *case* statement code. And, by explicitly setting the state encoding for that error state to be 'X' you will ensure that it results in 'X' values propagating throughout the rest of your design which will make it easy to spot.

The second thing this will accomplish is that it will make it trivial to compare your SystemVerilog code to your state graph to make sure you coded it just as you drew it. That is, there will be a one-to-one correpsondence between arcs in the state graph and assignments to the next state variable. If there are 13 arcs in the state graph, there should be 13 assignments to the next state variable in the SystemVerilog code, one for each arc in the graph (no exceptions).

To accomplish this change, you define a new state called ERR and specify that you want it encoding to be 'X'. To do so you must modify the *typedef* statement to specify that the enumerated type should be of type *logic* instead of the default *int* type that is usually used for enumerated types. This then allows you to specify that one of the states has an encoding of 'X' values. [2]

---

[2] Above, it was discussed that you normally do not care what the state encoding is. This is an exception to that. Also, it shows you how you can specify your own encodings if you want to.

Now, during simulation if the state machine *case* statement doesn't explicitly specify what the state transition should be for some set of conditions, the state machine will transition to the ERR state, the current state will become an 'X' value, and your simulation will immediately show that you have a problem in your design. The code is shown here:

Program 23.2.1 Defensive Coding Style for State Machine of Figure 22.7

```
// Define the state register and the next state variable
typedef enum logic[1:0] {s0, s1, s2, ERR='X} stateType;
stateType cs, ns;


// The IFL and OFL
always_comb
begin
  // Default assignments
  ns = ERR;
  Z = 1'b0;

  // Actual state machine logic
  if (reset)
    ns = s0;
  else
    case (cs)
      s0: if (!Xin)
            ns = s1;
          else
            ns = s0;
      s1: if (Xin)
            ns = s2;
          else
            ns = s1;
      s2: if (Xin)
          begin
            Z = 1'b1;
            ns = s0;
          end
          else
            ns = s1;
    endcase
end

// The state register
always_ff @(posedge clk)
  cs <= ns;
```

Note that the loopback arcs are trivially added — they consist of *else* statements at the end of every one of the *if-then* statements. This is a small price to pay for the error detection capabilities it provides.

23.3 Chapter Summary

This chapter has discussed behavioral SystemVerilog for designing finite state machines. The key points include:

1. State machines are coded slightly differently from counters as we showed in Chapter 20. They use a single combinational *always_comb* block for the combined IFL and OFL and a single *always_ff* block for the actual state register. The rules for avoiding latches from Section 18.2 fully apply here.

2. An alternative to this is similar to coding registers and counters in SystemVerilog — you use *always_ff* blocks for the state register and IFL and then separate *assign* or *case* statements for the OFL.

3. Enumerated types and *typedef* statements are typically used to define the states in a state machine. This allows you to not worry about the actual bit-level encodings and create very readable state machine descriptions.

4. Assigning default values for all outputs at the top of a *always_comb* block simplifies the SystemVerilog since only differences from those default output values need to be specified for each state in the state machine. It also helps avoid latches.

5. By setting the default next state value to an error state as in the defensive coding style, you will discover very quickly during simulation if your state machine description is incomplete.

The skills that should result from a study of this chapter include the following:

1. The ability to express finite state machine designs in SystemVerilog.

2. The ability to use enumerations to define state values.

3. The ability to use *typedef* statements to create new types which can be used for state variables.

4. The ability to code state machine descriptions either using a variety of styles.

23.4 Exercises

For all of the problems below, enter the designs using SystemVerilog. Enter the code and do enough of a compilation to complete a syntax check of your code to ensure that it is syntactically correct (you need not fully simulate it, however). How you do that will depend on the particular CAD tools you are using. If you are running the SystemVerilog from the command line, a simple *vlog filename.sv* will be sufficient.[3]

23.1. Write the behavioral SystemVerilog code for the state machine of Figure 22.1.

23.2. Write the behavioral SystemVerilog code for the state machine of Figure 22.3.

23.3. Write the behavioral SystemVerilog code for the state machine of Figure 22.5.

23.4. Write the behavioral SystemVerilog code for the state machine of Figure 22.9.

23.5. Write the behavioral SystemVerilog code for the state machine of Figure 22.10.

23.6. Write the behavioral SystemVerilog code for the state machine of Figure 22.1. Use the defensive coding style described in this chapter.

23.7. Write the behavioral SystemVerilog code for the state machine of Figure 22.3. Use the defensive coding style described in this chapter.

23.8. Write the behavioral SystemVerilog code for the state machine of Figure 22.5. Use the defensive coding style described in this chapter.

---

[3]However, when running from the command line you must always first create a work library for the compiler to operate with. This is done by first executing *vlib work* once from the command line in the directory where you intend to work. The *vlog* command will then put its compiled files in intermediate form into that work library.

23.9. Write the behavioral SystemVerilog code for the state machine of Figure 22.9. Use the defensive coding style described in this chapter.

23.10. Write the behavioral SystemVerilog code for the state machine of Figure 22.10. Use the defensive coding style described in this chapter.

Chapter 24

Asynchronous Input Handling

A careful reading of the previous chapters will reveal that all of our examples have assumed that, once the inputs to a system arrive, the input forming logic has time to stabilize before the clock edge occurs. This is equivalent to saying that in all of the previous examples, the inputs were synchronous (their arrival times were constrained so that the IFL outputs would be stable prior the clock edge).

In many systems this may be a reasonable assumption, especially when the inputs to a state machine are generated elsewhere in the same digital design (where all parts share a common clock). Many systems, however, must react to truly asynchronous inputs — inputs whose value can change at any time with respect to the clock edge. A source of such signals is the physical world (buttons being pushed, etc). Dealing with truly asynchronous inputs presents a number of problems to digital systems designers. These problems are illustrated in this chapter using an example circuit. A series of solutions are then proposed which lead to proper operation of that circuit.

24.1   Asynchronous Inputs and Metastability

The problem of metastability was discussed briefly in Chapter 15. Metastability means that the behavior of a flip flop (and thus its output) is undefined, un-knowable actually, when its setup or hold times are violated by a change on its D input too close to the clock edge. By definition we do not know the arrival time of asynchronous inputs and so there is always the possibility of incorrect circuit behavior caused by an asynchronous input arriving at the wrong time and putting a flip flop into a metastable state. See the discussion of Chapter 15 for more details on this. For the remainder of this chapter we will ignore metastability and worry about the other problems that asynchronous inputs cause.

24.2 An Example Asynchronous Input Problem

Consider the state graph fragment and associated circuit structure shown in Figure 24.1. Signal *A* causes a state transition from state '00' to '11'. There are two combinational logic paths through the input forming logic shown: one from signal *A* to signal *N1* and one from signal *A* to signal *N0*. One path is shown in the figure as having a 5ns delay, and the other a 10ns delay.

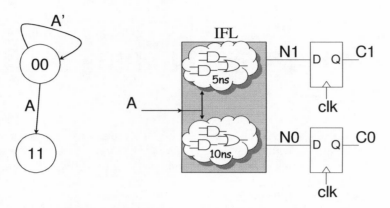

Figure 24.1: A State Machine With an Asynchronous Input

Now refer to Figure 24.2. Once signal *A* changes, both signals *N1* and *N0* change. Signal *N1* changes after 5ns, and *N2* after 10ns. The problem arises when the clock edge arrives <u>between</u> the two transitions (between 5ns and 10ns after *A* changes). This is shown in the figure. Because *N1* has already made its transition for the change from state '00' to '11', but *N0* has not yet made its transition, the clock edge loads '10' into the state register. The result is an erroneous transition from '00' to '10' (which doesn't even exist in the state graph and therefore shouldn't be possible).

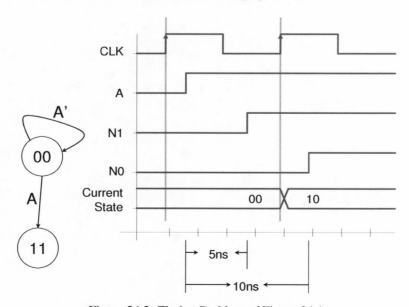

Figure 24.2: Timing Problem of Figure 24.1

The key considerations are these:

1. Asynchronous inputs can appear at any time with respect to the clock edge. Put another way, a clock edge can occur *at any time* with respect to an asynchronous input.

2. Combinational logic blocks often affect multiple output signals (*N1* and *N0* in the example above).

3. The various gate delays making up a particular combinational logic block will result in each of its multiple outputs stabilizing at a different time.

4. If a clock edge occurs after some of these outputs have settled, but before the rest have, an inconsistent next state will be loaded into the state register, as in this example.

A number of mechanisms have been developed to solve this problem. Each has advantages and disadvantages, and it requires thought on the part of the designer to choose a solution that meets the constraints of the design at hand. Two commonly used approaches will be described in the remainder of this chapter.

24.3 Synchronizing Asynchronous Inputs - The Easiest and Preferred Approach

The simplest solution (from a design viewpoint) is to constrain when the asynchronous input is allowed to reach the IFL. This is done by running the asynchronous input into a D-type flip flop before it enters the rest of the circuit, and is shown in Figure 24.3. The arrival time of signal *S* (the synchronized version of signal *A*) is now known — it is $t_{CLK \to Q}$ after a clock edge. There is now no possibility of the failure shown above — as long as the clock period is long enough for the entire IFL to settle, the machine will operate according to the state graph.

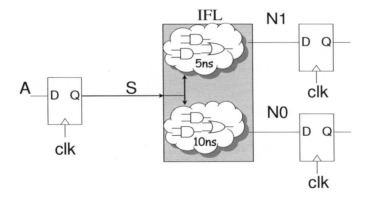

Figure 24.3: Synchronizing an Asynchronous Input

Another way to state this is we now have control over when the clock edge occurs with respect to changes on signal *S*. This solution is simple, but comes with a performance cost. Signal *S* arrives at the input forming logic later than *A* would have — by almost a full clock cycle in the worst case. This may or may not be acceptable for a particular design, and so a solution not requiring this delay would be useful in certain cases.

24.4   Hazard Free Design Combined With Adjacent State Encodings - Another Approach (Advanced Topic)

There may be times when you really need to use the input as-is without first running it through a synchronizing flip flop (which delays the arrival of the input). This section describes a method to achieve this.

24.4.1   Adjacent State Encodings - A Partial Solution

A solution which does not suffer from the delay problems above is to limit the kinds of state transitions that are allowed. Figure 24.4 shows this. The original state transition has been replaced with a *gray code* transition (the current state values spanning the transition arc differ by exactly one bit). The transition from $00 \rightarrow 11$ has been replaced by a transition from $00 \rightarrow 01$. The next state will be '01' if signal A arrives early enough; the next state will be '00' it it doesn't. There is no chance that one of the next state variables will change value while the other (slower) next state variable will not. The erroneous transition shown above in Figure 24.2 cannot now occur.

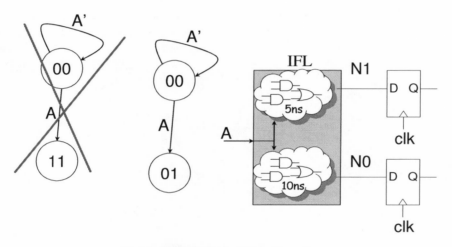

Figure 24.4: Adjacent State Encodings

Follow these steps to apply this approach:

1. Identify an asynchronous input to the circuit.

2. For each transition dependent on this asynchronous input, look at the state values the arc is bridging (00 and 01 in the example above). Ensure that these two states are adjacent in terms of gray code.

3. Repeat the above two steps for all additional asynchronous inputs.

It is not necessary for *all* state transitions in the machine to be *adjacent* in this way. Only transitions which depend on an asynchronous input value need to be adjacent transitions. If a transition depends on more than one asynchronous input's value, the problem is more difficult, and will not be covered here in detail. One solution, however, is this case is to break up such a transition into a series of transitions and states, each such transition depending on only one asynchronous input.

It would thus seem that using adjacent state encodings for all arcs dependent on asynchronous inputs solves the problem of this chapter (handling asynchronous inputs). This is not quite so, as the next section explains.

24.4.2 False Outputs and Hazards

This adjacent state encoding solution is incomplete, unfortunately, and may still result in erroneous transitions. To understand why, we need to review false outputs and hazards as described in Chapter 13.

Recall that in the circuit of Figure 24.5, a false output can occur when when A goes from '1' to '0'. The reason is that gate $g2$ may turn off before gate $g1$ turns on. The false output is shown in the timing diagram on signal F. If such a false output were to occur on a next state variable, and the clock edge were to occur during that false output, an erroneous state transition would occur.

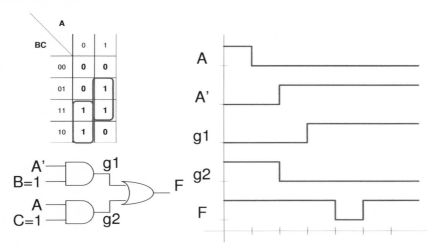

Figure 24.5: A Simple Logic Circuit Exhibiting a Hazard

False outputs are only a problem with respect to asynchronous inputs (but not synchronous inputs). The reason is that we know the arrival times of synchronous inputs and can therefore guarantee that any false output will be resolved before the clock edge. For an asynchronous input, however, we don't know when it will arrive, and therefore cannot determine when any false output might occur.

The avoidance of false outputs could conceivably be achieved by doing careful timing analyses of all the delays in a circuit, and ensuring that the circuit is glitch free. This is impossible in practice. First, such an analysis would need to take into account all possible signal arrival times for all possible signals (and in all signal combinations). Second, gate delays in real circuits cannot be precisely specified and vary with temperature, power supply voltage, etc.

A superior method is to modify the KMap logic minimization procedure to eliminate hazards. This was discussed in Chapter 13, and is called hazard-free minimization. Redundant prime implicants are added to the solution during the KMap logic minimization process, eliminating false outputs due to single-input changes. Importantly, only next state variables dependent on asynchronous inputs need to be minimized using this technique. You should review the discussion in Chapter 13 before proceeding.

24.4.3 The Complete Solution

A complete solution to the problem of handling asynchronous inputs combines adjacent (gray code) state encodings <u>with</u> hazard-free logic minimization[1]. A final (and correct) solution to the example of this chapter is shown in Figure 24.6. The adjacent state encoding ensures that only a single next state variable will change in response to the asynchronous input; the hazard free logic design for the input forming logic ensures that that single next state variable will not have any false outputs.

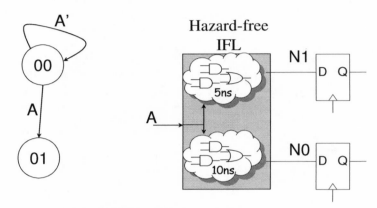

Figure 24.6: Combining Gray State Encodings with Hazard-Free Logic

Remember that this technique will only function correctly in the presence of a single input change. If multiple inputs change at once, the hazard free logic design approach described here cannot prevent false outputs.

In light of the level of work required for this second method of handling asynchronous inputs it should be obvious that you would only use it if you *absolutely* could not tolerate the extra delay introduced by the first and simpler method (the insertion of a synchronizing flip flop on the input). Note — if you were to use this second method you would not be able to rely on a Verilog compiler to handle it for you — you would have to manually do the low level design of the state machine. For this reason, it is suggested that you always use the first technique unless it is absolutely necessary to consider the second.

---

[1]It is important to note that both parts of the solution are required. Scores of students have completed logic design courses erroneously believing that adjacent state encodings will solve the asynchronous input problem. This is simply not true.

24.5 Chapter Summary

This chapter introduced a number of the problems associated with handling asynchronous inputs to a digital system. It also presented a series of solutions to some of these problems. Key concepts from this chapter include the following:

1. Asynchronous inputs can cause illegal state transitions when the transition is between two states which are not adjacent (in gray code). Unequal delays through the input forming logic are the cause.

2. Synchronizing an asynchronous input by passing it through a flip flop is a solution to the asynchronous input problem.

3. The use of adjacent state encodings provides part of the solution by ensuring that, for a given transition, only one state bit will change.

4. Adjacent state encodings only provide part of the solution.

5. Hazard-free logic minimization, when combined with adjacent encodings are a complete solution.

6. Metastable flip flop behavior is always a possibility in the presence of asynchronous inputs.

7. No techniques are known which are able to completely eliminate metastable behavior. Techniques are known which can greatly reduce it, however.

The skills that should result from your study of this chapter include the following:

1. The ability to identify asynchronous inputs to a state machine.

2. The ability to assign adjacent state encodings for transitions dependent on asynchronous inputs.

3. The ability to do hazard-free logic minimization.

24.6 Exercises

24.1. Plot the following function in a KMap and find a minimum solution for it. Then, solve it a second time using hazard-free minimization. Show your work.

$$F(A, B, C, D) = m0 + m1 + m2 + m4 + m5 + m6 + m9 + m11 + m13 + m15$$

24.2. Make a copy of the state graph of Figure 22.9. On it, list the asynchronous inputs. Circle the transitions dependent on those asynchronous inputs. Do any of these transitions depend on more than one asynchronous input? If so, redraw the state graph by adding additional states and transitions so that no transition is dependent on more than one asynchronous input.

24.3. Plot the following function in a KMap:
$$F = m1 + m3 + m7$$

Use variables A, B, and C and solve it and draw the resulting circuit.

Imagine that prior to time $t = 0ns$ that $A = B = C = TRUE$, and at time $t = 0ns$ $A \to FALSE$ and $B \to FALSE$. Due to unequal delays through the gates the circuit may react as if $A \to FALSE$ before $B \to FALSE$. Or, the circuit may react as is B changed before A. There is thus the possibility that the resulting function will temporarily *pass through* a number of different squares in the KMap as it makes the transition. Draw the path the circuit would take on the KMap if it were to react as if A changed first. Using a second copy of the KMap, draw the path the circuit would take if it were to react as if B changed first.

How does this relate to false outputs? Is it another instance of a problem which can be solved using redundant prime implicants or is the problem due to another phenomenon? If so, what is that phenomenon? Has that been mentioned in this text? HINT: it has. Find it, discuss it, compare it to hazard-free minimization.

24.4. Consider the FSM state graph shown below. No expressions have been shown for the transition conditions since they are not material to this problem. What is important is the set of state transitions and the Z output.

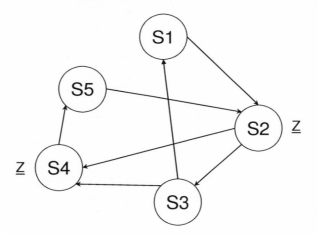

As can be seen, the Z output is asserted in both state **S2** and state **S4**. Further, it is desired that signal Z contain no false outputs on state transitions. Plot how you would assign state encodings using a KMap and explain the conditions required to avoid false outputs on signal Z. Then, list the state encoding chosen.

Chapter 25

Field Programmable Gate Arrays (FPGAs) - An Introduction

This text has repeatedly hinted at the fact that there are many different technologies available for implementing digital circuits, but has provided little concrete detail on any of these technologies. Today, the main choices for implementing a digital circuit include CMOS custom integrated circuits (designed using n-type and p-type transistors), and Field Programmable Gate Arrays (FPGAs). Both of these technologies provide a way to implement combinational logic and storage to support the creation of sequential digital systems, but with each having different advantages and disadvantages in terms of cost, performance, power consumption, and development time.

Field Programmable Gate Arrays (FPGAs) are introduced in this chapter. They are covered here not only because they are used as the target technology in many laboratory courses on digital design, but also because they find widespread use in the commercial world. A particular simplified FPGA architecture is introduced in this chapter, the goal being to provide an overview of the concepts behind FPGAs and to show how user designs are mapped to FPGAs. Advanced features of some currently-available commercial FPGAs are also described.

25.1 Lookup Tables - Universal Function Generators

Read only memories (ROMs) were covered in Chapter 10. It was described there how a ROM can be used as a lookup table (LUT). It was further described how a LUT with n inputs can implement any function of n inputs. Consider the truth table and corresponding schematic of Figure 25.1 as an example of this.

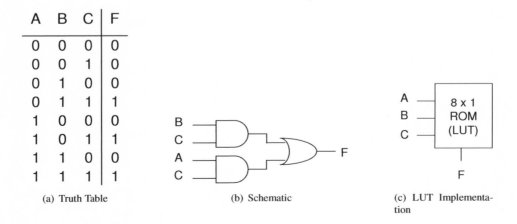

A	B	C	F
0	0	0	0
0	0	1	0
0	1	0	0
0	1	1	1
1	0	0	0
1	0	1	1
1	1	0	0
1	1	1	1

(a) Truth Table

(b) Schematic

(c) LUT Implementation

Figure 25.1: Truth Table, Schematic, and LUT Implementation of F = BC + AC

271

An alternative to the gate-level schematic is to use a ROM or lookup table to implement the truth table logic. This is shown in part (c) of the figure where an 8-by-1 ROM is used. If the ROM contents are initialized with the contents of the truth table, then wiring A, B, and C to the inputs of the ROM will result in F reflecting the function of the truth table. There is no need to do logic minimization, KMaps, or the like when using a ROM for logic in this manner. Lookup tables or LUTs can be designed to be of any size desired. Common LUTs in commercial FPGAs might have four or even six inputs. These would be called *4LUTs* and *6LUTs* respectively.

25.1.1 Mapping Larger Combinational Circuits to LUTs

The example above showed how a simple truth table could be mapped to a LUT. Now consider mapping a 4-input function, such as is shown in Figure 25.2, to 3LUTs. The truth table must somehow be *partitioned* into sections of logic that can be implemented by a collection of 3LUTs.

A	B	C	D	F
0	0	0	0	0
0	0	0	1	0
0	0	1	0	0
0	0	1	1	1
0	1	0	0	0
0	1	0	1	0
0	1	1	0	0
0	1	1	1	1
1	0	0	0	0
1	0	0	1	0
1	0	1	0	1
1	0	1	1	1
1	1	0	0	1
1	1	0	1	1
1	1	1	0	1
1	1	1	1	1

Figure 25.2: A Four-Input Truth Table for F = A'CD + A(B+C)

One way to do this is:

1. Implement the top half of the truth table using a single 3LUT (with inputs B, C, and D). The function implemented would be CD. Call this LUT's output $f1$. An examination of the top half of Figure 25.2 shows that it represents this function (given that $A = 0$).

2. Implement the bottom half with another 3LUT. The function implemented would be $B + C$. Call this LUT's output $f2$. The bottom half of Figure 25.2 represents this function (given that $A = 1$).

3. Use a third 3LUT to build a 2:1 MUX to select between $f1$ and $f2$. The final function implemented will be: $F = A'f1 + Af2 = A'CD + A(B + C)$.

The resulting design is shown in Figure 25.3. A little thought will show that this is exactly the same procedure used previously in Figure 10.7 to use MUXes to implement logic.

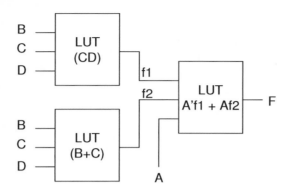

Figure 25.3: LUT Implementation of Figure 25.2

25.1.2 Mapping Gate-Level Circuits to LUTs

The above techniques work if the logic to be implemented is specified as a set of truth tables. Many (most) designs, however, are specified at the level of logic gates. It is important to be able to partition a gate-level design across a set of LUTs.

Consider the gate-level circuit of Figure 25.4, and the problem of mapping it to 4LUTs. Since this circuit has a total of seven inputs, it will require at least two 4LUTs to implement. One solution is shown in Figure 25.5. The gate-level schematic is partitioned by searching for regions of gates with four or fewer inputs, and one output. Each region is implemented using a single LUT, and then all the LUTs are wired together.

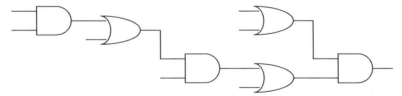

Figure 25.4: A Sample Gate-Level Circuit

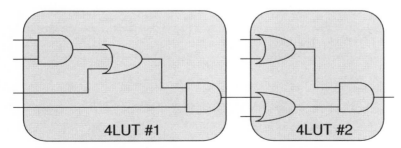

Figure 25.5: One Solution to the Circuit of Figure 25.4

When designing for FPGAs using HDL code such as SystemVerilog, a synthesizer program is first used to convert the HDL code into some form of gate-level netlist corresponding to the desired circuit. A CAD tool specific to the particular FPGA being targeted is then used to do this LUT partitioning. This step is called *mapping*, and consists of mapping whatever logic is required for the design onto the primitive elements of the FPGA (LUTs and flip flops).

25.2 FPGA Logic Elements

The basic building block of a typical FPGA architecture is a LUT combined with a flip flop. We will call this a logic element (LE). Many different LEs could be used (and have been used in commercial FPGAs). A simple LE is shown in Figure 25.6. Its 4LUT can be configured to perform any function of the four inputs $inA - inD$. Its output MUX can be configured to select between the LUT output or the flip flop output.

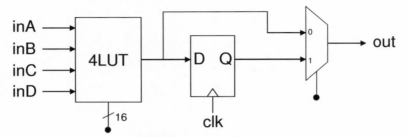

Figure 25.6: A Representative LE

The heavy black dots in the figure indicate configuration bits. The LUT requires 16 configuration bits to specify its function, and the output MUX requires a single configuration bit to specify its function. This requires a total of 17 configuration bits for this LE. It should be noted that these bits are specified when the FPGA is configured to perform a particular function, and are not changed during the operation of the FPGA. They are not accessible to the user's design either, but are specified by the CAD tool that configures the FPGA for use.

Another LE structure is shown in Figure 25.7. This LE has five inputs, two outputs, and has three configurable components. Due to its structure, this LE can be used for *both* combinational and sequential functions at the same time.

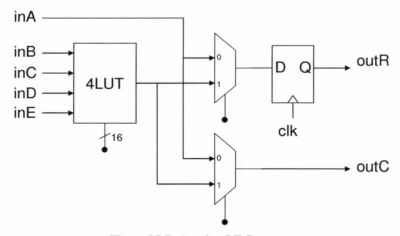

Figure 25.7: Another LE Structure

Examples of the use of this LE are shown in Figure 25.8. In part (a) of the figure, the LE has been configured to compute the combinational function $outC = inB(inC + inD)$. This is routed through the flip flop to give a registered version of that on the output. In part (b) of the figure, the LE has been configured to register inA using the flip flop and to also generate $outC = inC'$. Other configurations are possible given the existence of the two MUX blocks in the figure.

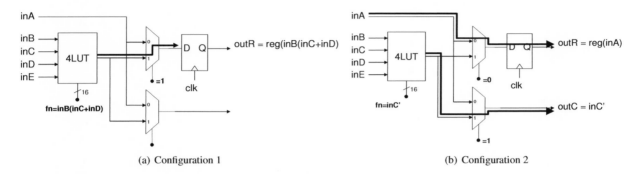

(a) Configuration 1   (b) Configuration 2

Figure 25.8: LE Configurations

An additional feature found in many FPGA LEs is the inclusion of special-purpose carry/cascade logic as shown in Figure 25.9. Here, additional logic has been included in the 4LUT block for computing carry and cascade logic values. This LE can accomplish a full 1-bit addition — the normal output of the LUT/carry/cascade block contains the sum output, and the $Cout$ signal exiting the top is the carry out signal.

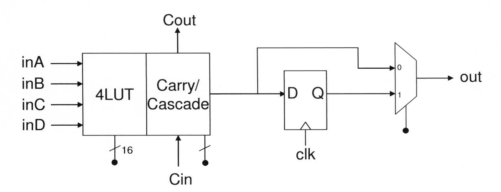

Figure 25.9: An LE With Carry/Cascade Logic

Most importantly, the Cin and $Cout$ signals are directly wired to adjacent LEs, making the carry path for the addition significantly faster than if it were connected between LEs using the normal out signals. The carry chain is always the critical path in the delay of an adder; an adder which takes advantage of carry/cascade logic will be significantly faster than one that does not.

25.3 Global FPGA Architecture

A complete FPGA is made by replicating LEs and providing a programmable or configurable set of routing wires to interconnect them. Figure 25.10 shows an example architecture. This is called an *island* style FPGA architecture in that the LEs are surrounded by routing wires. The LE used in this particular architecture is shown in Figure 25.11 along with its symbol. As can be seen, the LE inputs come into its left side and the LE output goes out the bottom.

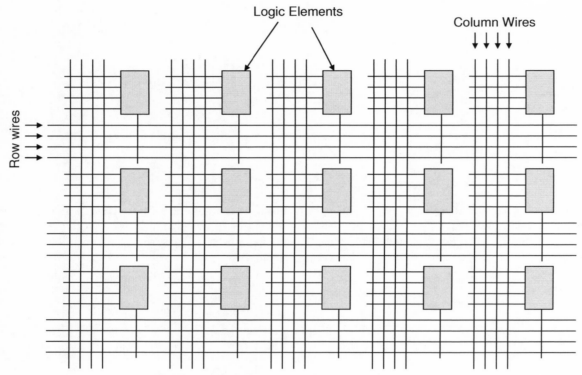

Figure 25.10: A Representative FPGA Architecture

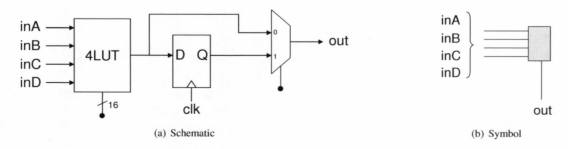

Figure 25.11: The LE Used in the Representative FPGA Architecture in Figure 25.10

Many details are omitted from this figure. For example, the LE used requires a CLK signal for its flip flop. The routing of this CLK signal throughout the array is not shown — only configurable routing is shown in the figure. Circuitry required to support configuring the device is similarly not shown.

The possibility of making a connection exists at each junction between a vertical and horizontal wire in the figure. Making this connection can be accomplished by turning an n-type transistor on or off, to connect or disconnect the two wires. Figure 25.12 shows one such programmable interconnect point. As with the LE diagrams above, the heavy black dot indicates a configuration bit. Setting it to TRUE turns on the connection, setting it to FALSE turns it off.

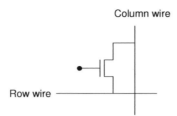

Figure 25.12: A Programmable Interconnect Junction

25.3.1 A Mapping Example

An example of a design to be mapped to this FPGA is shown in Figure 25.13. Given a six-bit input, this circuit computes Z, N, and P outputs from it. The Z output signifies whether all six inputs are zero. The N output signifies whether the six input bits represent a negative number. The P output signifies whether the six input bits represent a positive number by computing $P = Z' \bullet N'$.

Figure 25.13: Logic Function of Figure 25.14

Figure 25.14 shows the implementation of this logic.

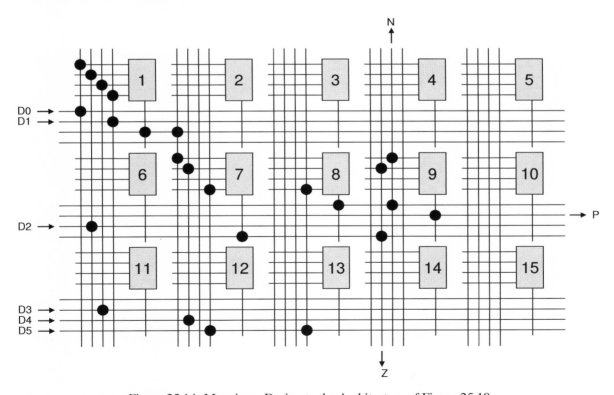

Figure 25.14: Mapping a Design to the Architecture of Figure 25.10

The six bits of input are brought in on row wires on the left of the diagram. The heavy black dots indicate programmable connection points that are turned ON. Follow the heavy black circles to see how the routing between inputs, LEs, and outputs is done. LEs #1 and #7 are used to compute the six-input AND function (Z). That output (Z), is then routed out of the bottom of the circuit. LE #8 is used to generate the N output, where $N = D5$. The resulting N output is then routed out the top of the array. In addition, both N, and Z are routed into logic element #9 where $P = Z' \bullet N'$ is computed. The resulting P signal is routed out the right side of the array. If you carefully follow the wire connections as indicated by the heavy black dots, you will see that the circuit is wired correctly to perform these functions.

25.4 Configuring an FPGA Device

When an FPGA device is *configured*, its configuration bitstream is used to configure it to perform the desired function. This configuration can be done a number of ways. A popular form of FPGA is called an SRAM-programmable FPGA. In this type of FPGA, memory storage elements are distributed throughout the FPGA to hold the configuration bits. 16 bits of storage are required, for example, to configure a LUT. The configuration storage for a LUT would be included in the logic element itself in most cases. Each LE would thus contain these 16 bits of configuration storage, plus whatever configuration bits were needed for other configurable LE elements.

25.4.1 Configuring a LUT

Figure 25.15 shows a typical 3LUT implementation. This 3LUT is nothing more than a 8:1 MUX where the select lines are the LUT inputs, and the configuration bits are the contents of the truth table that the 3LUT is implementing. When the inputs are '000', the top configuration bit is output. When the inputs are '001', the next configuration bit is output, and so forth.

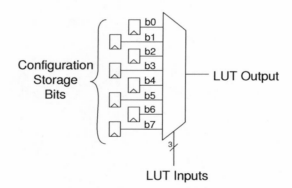

Figure 25.15: One Implementation of a LUT

Figure 25.15 does not show how the configuration bits are initialized. One method is shown in Figure 25.16, where just a few configuration bits are depicted. The configuration bits in this figure are organized into a serial-in, parallel-out (SIPO) shift register. The LUT contents are shifted in serially, one per clock cycle during configuration. Once configuration is complete, the $CONFIG$ signal is lowered, and the configuration elements retain their old values.

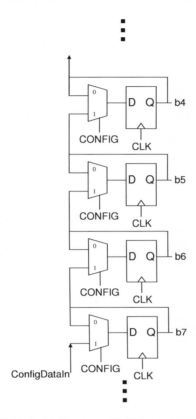

Figure 25.16: Initialization of LUT Configuration Bits

25.4.2 Configuring the Fabric

Now consider the case of the wire junctions in the programmable routing fabric. One bit of storage is required for each junction between a horizontal wire and a vertical wire as shown in Figure 25.17. If a '1' is stored in the storage element, the wires are connected to one another; if a '0' is stored, they are not.

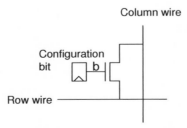

Figure 25.17: Configurable Wire Junction Implementation

This figure does not show how these particular configuration storage elements are initialized. As above, one method is to string them together into a serial-in, parallel-out shift register, and load them serially during configuration.

A complete configuration *bitstream* for an SRAM-programmable FPGA is thus a serial stream of 1's and 0's. When these bits are loaded (shifted) into the configuration storage elements, they configure all the LEs in the circuit and the routing network. Both combinational and sequential designs can be implemented on an FPGA in this manner.

25.5 More Advanced FPGA Architectures

The above discussion is sufficient to provide an overview of how simple FPGAs are organized, designed, and configured. A number of more advanced features are usually provided by commercial FPGAs, however. This section is provided to illustrate the variety of architectural features commercial FPGAs include.

25.5.1 Configurable Input/Output

The examples above neglected to discuss how signals get into and out of the FPGA chip. Like any integrated circuit, an FPGA has input/output sites around its perimeter. Each site in an integrated circuit is either an input site or an output site. An input site has circuitry to protect the input against electrostatic discharge damage when handling the finished IC package, as well as an input buffer to drive the external signal into the chip. An output site has circuitry (an output buffer) to provide sufficient strength to drive a signal from within the chip out to the outside world. In either case, the external signal is connected to the input or output site via a *pin*. This is the physical connection on the IC package that is soldered onto the printed circuit board.

It is not known up front which sites will be input sites and which will be output sites when FPGAs are manufactured. This will depend on the function the end-user has in mind for the FPGA. Thus, the perimeter of an FPGA contains *configurable* input/output sites. Configuring the FPGA entails configuring which sites are used for input and which are used for output. Typical configurable input/output cells also contain flip flops which can be used to register signals entering or leaving the chip. Numerous electrical standards exist in the world of digital systems (3.3V CMOS signals, 2.5V CMOS signals, differential low-voltage swing signals, etc). Most input/output cells are also configurable to operate according to any one of a variety of these electrical standards. All of these features combine to make FPGAs extremely flexible for interfacing with other digital circuitry on a printed circuit board.

25.5.2 Configuration Technology

The configuration storage in commercial FPGAs does not usually consist of master-slave D-type flip flops as shown earlier. Commonly used configuration storage circuits are smaller than flip flops (a 5-transistor SRAM cell is common). The entire configuration store in a commercial FPGA is also not usually linked together into one large shift register. The specific methods used are selected for their area and speed characteristics, and are smaller than the general approaches shown above (they are functionally equivalent, however).

However, a number of FPGA families are based on technologies other than SRAM for their configuration. Some FPGAs are manufactured with all possible circuit wire connections built-in. They contain fuses which are *blown* during configuration to remove the unwanted connections. Other FPGAs contain anti-fuses. These are connection points which are initially *not connected*, but which can be connected by applying a voltage or current to them during configuration.

A number of comparisons can be made between SRAM-programmable FPGAs and fuse/anti-fuse FPGAs. First, fuse and anti-fuse FPGAs can be programmed (configured) only a single time while SRAM-programmable FPGAs can be repeatedly programmed. A printed circuit board can be designed containing an SRAM-programmable FPGA and then used for a number of different applications by re-configuring it. In fact, if the board is designed correctly the FPGA can even be reprogrammed from a remote location such as over a network or radio link. In contrast, if the design you configure into a fuse or anti-fuse FPGA turns out to not work as expected and you want to change the design, you must throw away that fuse or anti-fuse FPGA and program another.

Not only *can* SRAM FPGAs be repeatedly programmed, they *must* be programmed every time they are powered on. Thus, the flexibility that an SRAM FPGA provides requires that additional circuitry be added to the printed circuit board when an SRAM-FPGA is used, the function of the circuitry being to hold the SRAM-FPGA's configuration bits and help load them into the FPGA every time the board is powered up. This is an added cost that must be accounted for.

As another point of comparison, SRAM-programmable FPGAs pack more circuitry into a chip than fuse and anti-fuse FPGAs do. The largest parts from Xilinx Corporation and Altera Corporation contain the equivalent of millions of gates of logic. The largest fuse and anti-fuse parts are much, much smaller than these in terms of equivalent gates of logic.

Finally, fuse and anti-fuse FPGAs are more tolerant of high radiation doses than SRAM-based FPGAs are, and thus can be more easily used for satellite electronics and other space-based applications. An explanation of radiation and electronics may help you understand why this is so. When a high-energy particle such as an alpha particle strikes a storage element in a circuit (such as the cross-coupled NOR gates of a flip flop), it can transfer enough energy to the storage element to flip its stored value from a '1' to a '0' or from a '0' to a '1'.

In an SRAM-programmable FPGA, the configuration bits which configure the chip are stored inside the FPGA in SRAM memory cells and thus high energy particles can *upset* the configuration of the chip. Such an upset may change the contents of a LUT or may change how wires are routed through the circuit — it may actually change the circuit's programmed function! However, fuse and anti-fuse FPGAs do not have configuration bits that are stored inside the chip during operation — their configuration bits are used only when the chip is programmed to control which fusible links are blown or connected. For this reason, fuse and anti-fuse FPGAs have found much more use in high-radiation applications (such as in satellites in space) than SRAM FPGAs have. However, the problem is no longer limited to space. Ground-based electronics have traditionally not suffered significant numbers of circuit upsets due to the shielding effects the earth's atmosphere provides against high energy particles from space. However, as circuit geometries continue to shrink, such upsets are becoming more of a concern for ground-based electronics and in the future will have to be mitigated, something that has been done for space-based electronics for many years.

25.5.3 Carry/Cascade Chains

The use of a carry/cascade chain was illustrated above only in the context of designing an adder circuit. Some FPGAs have a more general carry/cascade chain which makes it easy to perform wide AND or OR operations by cascading the results of smaller AND or OR operations together. The advantage of using this over conventional LUT logic is that the carry/cascade chain is optimized for high speed.

25.5.4 Programmable Interconnections

Programmable junctions were shown at every intersection of a horizontal wire with a vertical wire in the FPGA architecture of Figure 25.10. In reality, only a fraction of the junctions need to be programmable without any loss of flexibility in the use of the FPGA. This is because the inputs to any given LUT are interchangeable and all the LUTs in an FPGA are also interchangeable. A significant reduction in circuit area can be achieved by populating only a subset of all the possible row and column wire intersections with programmable interconnections. The choice of which intersections to populate has been the subject of much research, and each FPGA vendor does it differently.

25.5.5 Segmented and Hierarchical Routing

The design of Figure 25.14 had much wasted wire. Once a signal was routed onto a row wire, that signal occupied the entire row wire across the width of the FPGA. Look back at that figure and note the row wire carrying signal $D1$. If there were a way to cut the wire just to the right of the connected junction on that row wire, the right-hand portion of that row wire could be used for some other purpose. One way to do this is to put programmable connections between horizontal sections of a given row wire. By turning these programmable connections on and off (using configuration bits), the CAD tool can control how much of a row wire a signal occupies. The same could be done for column wires. This requires fewer total horizontal and vertical wires in the FPGA since two different signals can now be carried on two different sections of the same wire (with a turned-off programmable connection separating them).

The inclusion of these programmable connections along a row or column wire, however, significantly slows down a signal which uses the entire wire. This is because the signal has to pass through multiple n-type transistors to get from one point to another. A solution to this is known as hierarchical routing.

With hierarchical routing, row and column wires of different lengths are mixed together in the FPGA fabric. Some row wires traverse the entire width of the chip, others traverse only a few columns' distance. A signal that needs to travel only one column to the right can use a short wire (the CAD tool would make that decision when it generates the bitstream). A signal needing to go farther can use a longer wire. A modern FPGA contains a combination of segmented and hierarchical routing.

25.5.6 Clustered LEs

The use of clustered LEs is closely related to the use of hierarchical routing. A cluster of LEs is some number of logic elements interconnected to one another using short (and therefore high-speed) configurable wires. Only signals which leave the cluster need be routed onto the general interconnect fabric. This has the advantage of providing for higher performance designs. It also reduces the amount of general interconnect that must be provided.

25.5.7 Embedded Functional Units

FPGAs are even more useful for the creation of complete digital systems when they contain additional computational capabilities beyond those provided by simple LUTs and flip flops. The FPGA devices from the major manufacturers include a range of the following embedded special-function units.

Embedded Memories

Many FPGAs provide the ability to convert LUTs to small 16-by-1 bit RAM memories, thereby providing more efficient storage of data than with flip flops. Larger blocks of memory are also provided in most FPGAs. A typical large memory in an FPGA might contain 16K bits of storage and can be configured to be of various sizes: 16K-by-1, 8K-by-2, 1K-by-16, and so on. Physically, the RAM inputs and outputs are wired into the general interconnect fabric on the FPGA and so they can interact with the rest of the FPGA circuit. A large FPGA might contain 100's of such memories. Further, some vendors' chips provide only one size of memory while others may provide a range of memory block sizes (512 bits, 1K bits, 16K bits, ...) within a given chip.

Embedded Arithmetic Units

Most FPGAs now contain specialized arithmetic circuits which, like the above embedded memories, are built as custom silicon circuits on the FPGA and interconnected to its interconnect fabric. A common arithmetic unit provided might be a 16-by-16 bit multiplier, configurable to do signed or unsigned arithmetic and configurable to include registers on its inputs and/or outputs. Such built-in arithmetic units are able to perform computations far faster than could be performed if built out of LUTs and programmable routing.

Embedded CPUs

FPGA vendors have also integrated 32-bit processors into their FPGA fabrics. As with the arithmetic units just mentioned, these are much higher performance and require much less circuit area than the corresponding CPU would take if created out of LUTs and routing. This makes it possible to create systems consisting of programs running on the embedded CPU's and communicating with custom gate-level hardware circuitry in the FPGA fabric — a complete electronics system on a chip.

Embedded Functional Units Summary

Additional features are continually being added to FPGAs by the vendors, further blurring the lines between custom hardware chips and programmable processor-based embedded systems. The result of this, over time, will be to increase the set of applications for which FPGAs can be used.

25.6   FPGA vs. ASIC Technology

It is easy to forget that the cost for programmability (configurability) is high. An example can help illustrate this. Imagine that you are interested in creating a circuit to perform high-speed video encoding. You have available to you essentially three choices to create your circuit. The first is to program an embedded CPU (a CPU on a printed circuit board) to do the encoding. Let us assume, for purposes of this discussion, that no available embedded CPU is fast enough to meet your needs. Your only alternative is thus to do a custom hardware design using an HDL like SystemVerilog. Once your design is complete, you now have two choices for implementing it.

Your first choice is to use an FPGA, as discussed in this chapter. You would select one which was large enough (had enough LEs and I/O pins) for the design. You would then synthesize the design and run the FPGA-specific CAD tools required to map it to the desired FPGA. The resulting configuration bitstream could then be loaded into the FPGA to configure it for your purpose. Let us further assume that the final design runs at 150MHz on an FPGA which costs $10 to purchase.

The alternative is a custom integrated circuit, also called an ASIC (application-specific integrated circuit). This is a custom silicon VLSI chip which is not configurable, but which will perform only the video encoding of your design. Because the chip is specific to your needs (is non-configurable), it can perform the computation much more quickly, and at a lower cost. The resulting chip may run at 1.5GHz and cost $1 to produce. This is 10 times the performance for 1/10th the cost, compared to the FPGA solution. In light of this disparity in cost and performance, why would you ever choose to use an FPGA? Keep reading...

Once you have chosen to do an ASIC, the next step in the development process is to go through synthesis and place-and-route, just as with the FPGA, to implement the design. The outcome of this process is not a configuration bitstream, but rather the mask data required to manufacture your custom integrated circuit at a semiconductor foundry (factory). This manufacturing process is very expensive and time-consuming. A leading-edge manufacturing line may require initial up-front costs of $1,000,000 or more for a large integrated circuit. These are called non-recurring expenses (NRE), and are the costs to set up the manufacturing line to make your chip.

There is also high risk with the ASIC approach. If the final chips turn out to not function just as intended due to a design error, many (if not most) of those up-front costs must be paid a second time for a second manufacturing run. Many ASIC designs require a second manufacturing run before the chip is ready for market, and a manufacturing run can take from weeks to a few months to complete.

In contrast, if the FPGA design has a design error it can be fixed by modifying the HDL code, generating a new configuration bitstream, and *immediately* reconfiguring the FPGA.

The choice between FPGA and ASIC can thus be a difficult tradeoff to make:

- The FPGA approach has low initial costs but a high per-part cost. The ASIC approach has high initial costs but a low per-part cost. Thus, the number of video encoders you believe you can sell, as well as their selling price, is an important consideration in your decision.

- The ASIC approach promises much higher rewards for high-volume products, but with significant risks if your product doesn't turn to be as popular as you hoped.

- For many applications, the FPGA may simply be infeasible. You can't put a $10 FPGA into an electronic item that sells for $15 — the economics don't work.

- Some applications may demand the high performance that only an ASIC can provide.

- Some applications may not be able to tolerate a long time-to-market (the product needs to be out sooner rather than later). In these cases, the long manufacturing times of an ASIC may be unacceptable.

- You may simply be unable to pay the NRE costs of an ASIC if you are on a tight budget. Or, your boss may be simply unwilling to bet the company's future on an ASIC.

In the real world the decision of which to use is made based only *in part* on technical considerations. Other consideration such as risk, current market conditions, and a host of other business issues are just as, if not more, important.

25.7   Chapter Summary

The key points to master from this chapter include the following:

1. FPGAs attempt to provide a universal chip on which any digital circuit can be implemented.

2. All FPGAs rely on some form of configuration to customize them to perform the desired digital function.

3. Logic is commonly performed in an FPGA using a lookup table (LUT) which is nothing more than a configurable ROM or MUX circuit.

4. One FPGA architecture is the island style of architecture where LEs are surrounded by programmable routing resources.

5. A typical LE consists of a LUT, a flip flop, and possibly other circuits such as multiplexers.

6. LEs are interconnected via the configurable routing fabric.

7. A complete FPGA configuration bitstream consists of the configuration information for all of the LEs in the FPGA, the configurable routing, and the configurable input/output blocks.

8. A designer creates a design for an FPGA in the normal fashion by drawing schematics or writing HDL code. In the case of HDL's, a synthesizer is then used to convert the HDL code into a gate-level description of the desired circuitry.

9. Special vendor-specific CAD tools are then used to map the resulting circuitry onto the LUTs and other structures contained in the target FPGA.

10. The result of this process is a bitstream (a file of 1's and 0's) which, when properly applied to the FPGA's configuration inputs allows the FPGA to be configured.

11. Modern FPGAs contain many additional features beyond those outlined in this chapter. The list of available features grows monthly as FPGA manufacturers announce new products. The result is that over time more and more applications become amenable to FPGA implementation.

12. FPGAs have low up-front (NRE) costs but expensive production costs on a per-part basis. ASIC's have high up-front costs but very low production costs on a per-part basis. The choice of which approach to use for a design is a complex decision and involves a number of non-technical issues such as risk assessment and the perceived size of the market for a particular circuit.

The major skills that should result from a study of this chapter includes:

1. The ability to partition a large function across a collection of LUTs.

2. The ability to appreciate FPGAs as used for implementing digital systems design at a conceptual level.

Beyond that, however, you should consult the FPGA vendor's WWW site for a specific FPGA to understand the particular features it provides as well as how to use those features in your designs.

25.8 Exercises

25.1. Show how to implement a 5-input function using 4LUTs. HINT: the decomposition is very similar to that done using MUX blocks previously in this text. Consult that section for ideas on how to accomplish it. Next, show how to implement a 5-input function using 3LUTs.

25.2. Derive a formula showing how many 4LUTs it takes to implement a k-input function where $k \geq 4$. Express this formula in terms of k.

25.3. Consider the problem of using 4LUTs to implement a 9-input function. Show how you would do this.

25.4. Repeat the above problem but use 3LUTs.

25.5. Using Figure 25.10 as a template (print it out and color on it), complete the design of a circuit which will add two numbers. Call the numbers A and B. They are each three bits wide. Have your circuit generate a four-bit result and output it on pins. If your circuit will not fit onto one copy of Figure 25.10, make multiple copies and tape them together to obtain an FPGA fabric large enough for this design.

Chapter 26

Case Study - Debouncing Switches and Detecting Edges

Digital systems design is an art in many respects. Only a portion of what constitutes good design lends itself to formalizing in a textbook. Experience beyond what a a textbook can provide (in terms of step-by-step processes and formulae) is required to become a competent designer. In the course of gaining this experience, a designer learns to identify commonly occurring patterns and design paradigms.

Each of the designs in this and the next two chapters is completed to a certain level of detail, but is not finished. The reason is that, by now, you should be adept at reducing truth tables and state graphs to gates and flip flops and in writing SystemVerilog code. The important thing to learn from these examples is how to decompose a large problem into a set of interacting circuit blocks to accomplish the desired function. Thus, it is the early stages of the design process which are of interest in these chapters.

26.1 Debouncing a Switch

A common problem in digital systems design is interfacing to real-world inputs. A common input is a mechanical push-button or switch which generates a '1' when pushed and a '0' when released. The problem with such switches is that their output doesn't cleanly transition from a '0' to a '1' (and back to a '0'). A (somewhat stylized) example of a noisy switch output transitioning from a '0' to a '1' and back to a '0' is shown in Figure 26.1.

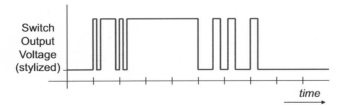

Figure 26.1: A Noisy Switch Waveform

The general problem is called 'bouncing', and is due to the mechanical characteristics of the switch as the contacts mechanically make and break contact with one another when the switch is thrown from one position to the other. Depending on the time duration of the 'bounces', a digital circuit may erroneously act as if the switch had been pushed multiple times. The typical duration of a bouncing switch is on the order of $5ms$ (5×10^{-3} seconds).

Our task here is to design a digital circuit to interpret this noisy waveform as a single transition from '0' to '1', or from '1' to '0'. Our chosen approach is to create a state machine which waits until the switch signal has gone high (or low) and stayed high (or low) for at least $5ms$ before deciding that the button has indeed been pushed (or released). Figure 26.2 is a timing waveform of the desired behavior. It shows that, only after the noisy signal has stabilized for $5ms$ or more, will the debounced signal react.

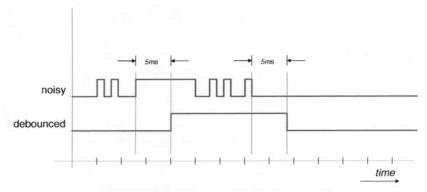

Figure 26.2: Timing Diagram for Switch Debouncer

The first step is to create a high-level block diagram of the system as shown in Figure 26.3. The state machine accepts the noisy signal (*noisy*) as input, and generates a debounced version of it (*debounced*). The state machine requires the services of a timer to help, which timer is nothing more than a counter that will signal after approximately $5ms$ has passed.

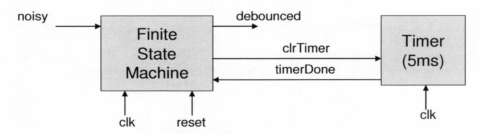

Figure 26.3: Block Diagram for Switch Debouncer

The next step is to design each of the blocks in the system, one at a time.

Debouncer State Machine

This design is simple enough that, at this point, a state graph for the state machine can be drawn. This is shown in Figure 26.4. All signals in this machine are asserted TRUE when listed in the state graph, and are FALSE otherwise.

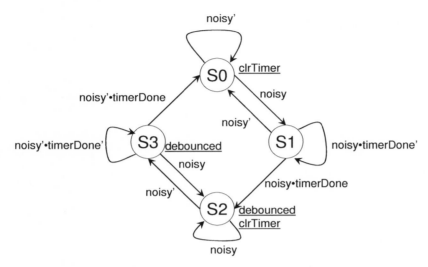

Figure 26.4: State Graph for Switch Debouncer

- In state **S0**, the state machine waits for the *noisy* signal to go high, and clears the timer while waiting. When the *noisy* signal goes high, the state machine transitions to state **S1**.

- In state **S1**, the timer is allowed to run. The state machine waits here for the timer to expire, signifying that $5ms$ has passed. When the timer expires, it transitions to **S2**. If, on the other hand, the *noisy* signal doesn't stay high for the whole $5ms$, the state machine transitions back to state **S0** where the timer is reset, and the process starts over. Only when the *noisy* signal has been high continuously for $5ms$, will state **S2** be entered and *debounced* asserted.

- In state **S2**, the state machine asserts *debounced* and waits for *noisy* to go FALSE. The remainder of the state graph is similar to above except handles the case when *noisy* is going low.

Debouncer Timer

The timer is simply a clearable counter which outputs a done signal after $5ms$. If we assume that the incoming clk signal is a $50MHz$ clock ($20ns$ period), we can compute that the counter needs to be able to count up to $\frac{5ms}{20ns} = 250,000$. An 18-bit counter will be able to count to $256K$, and so we determine that an 18-bit counter will work. On further consideration, we decide that $256K$ is fairly close to $250,000$, so we decide we will allow the counter to count all the way to its maximum value of all 1's ($2^{18} - 1$) before asserting *timerDone*. This will slightly simplify the design of the timer (a precise $5ms$ is not required in this design).

26.1.1 Design of the Debouncer Using SystemVerilog

As has been stated repeatedly in this text, the use of an HDL such as SystemVerilog relieves you as the designer from many of the details considered above and simplifies your design process. For example, in this case worrying about adjacent state encodings in the state machine is not really necessary — rather, running the asynchronous input signal through a synchronizing flip flop will be adequate to solve any timing issues it might have (in this application do we really care if the button push is noted by the state machine one cycle after it is pushed?).

The important portions of a SystemVerilog design for this debouncer is shown in 26.1.1. Note that it consists of 3 *always_ff* blocks - one for each register used in the design. It is important to note these could actually all be collapsed into a single *always_ff* block. The choice of whether to leave them separate or to combine them is a matter of style and should be guided by the readability and maintain-ability of the resulting code.

Program 26.1.1 SystemVerilog Code for Debouncer

```
// The state type and state register
typedef enum logic[2:0] {S0, S1, S2, S3, ERR='X}  StateType;
StateType ns, cs;

// Declare the signal for the synchronized version of the asynchronous input
logic synchNoisy;

// The actual synchronizing register
always_ff @(posedge clk)
  synchNoisy <= noisy;

// The 18-bit timer
always_ff @(posedge clk)
  if (clrTimer) timer <= 0;
  else timer <= timer + 1;

// The timer output
assign timerDone = (timer==18'h3FFFF)?1:0;

// The input forming logic and the state register circuitry
// This uses clrTimer, synchNoisy, and timerDone to control its operation
always_comb
begin
  // Default assignment values
  ns = ERR;
  debounced = 0;
  if (reset)
    ns = S0;
  else
    case (cs)
      // Put the state machine logic here (both IFL and OFL)
    endcase
end

// The state register
always_ff @(posedge clk)
  cs <= ns;
```

Does this design have a problem with false outputs? As we learned in Section 13.7, as combinational logic settles its output may momentarily glitch up or down as gates turn off and on in different orders. But the whole point of this design is to generate a *clean* version of the button push. The way it is coded with combinational OFL, it is possible that *debounced* will glitch (contain false outputs).

But, does that matter? Think carefully about this. Now think again — can you outline the conditions under which this will matter and conditions under which it may not matter?

The *debounced* signal, like all combinational logic outputs, will have false outputs only in the time period right after clock edges. It will have settled in time for the next clock edge. If that signal is being used by another RTL module which is clocked with the same clock as the module which generates it (Program 26.1.1), then the false outputs don't matter and the code is just fine. But, if *debounced* appears as an asynchronous input to another circuit module (a circuit being clocked with a different clock, for example), then it ought to be run through a flip flop to synchronize it so as to avoid the problems of Chapter 24. So, how that signal is used will dictate whether it is a problem or not. You should always evaluate this in all designs you create.

26.2 A One-Shot (Also Known as Pulse Generator)

An enhancement to the above edge detector could be made by adding a synchronous one-shot circuit to it. A one-shot circuit is a circuit that outputs a one-clock-cycle-wide pulse when some other signal changes from low to high.

Back in Section 13.6 you saw a combinational circuit which generated such a pulse (Figure 13.7). Its operation was based on gate delays where the width of the pulse was a function of the number of inverters in series. Such a pulse generator has many limitations for use in general digital systems because it is asynchronous (the timing and width of the pulse have no relation to the system clock).

What we want instead is a circuit which will output a pulse which is one clock cycle wide in response to rising edge on another signal. Since it is a full clock cycle wide we can be guaranteed that other sequential circuit blocks will see it for exactly one clock edge. Such a pulse generator is shown in Figure 26.5 along with a timing diagram showing its operation.

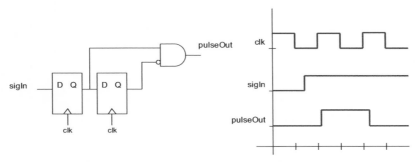

Figure 26.5: A Synchronous Pulse Generator Circuit

This is a shift register where the AND gate is detecting the case that a 1 value has just been clocked into the shift register's left flip flop after one or more 0's have been clocked in on previous cycles. In other words, it is a '01' sequence detector.

By combining this circuit with the debounce circuit of the previous section we can create a circuit which both debounces and synchronizes a noisy input and then outputs a single cycle wide pulse any time the noisy input goes high and stabilizes there. This combined circuit is shown in Figure 26.6.

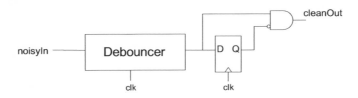

Figure 26.6: A Combined Debouncers/Pulse Generator

Note in the figure that the pulse generator has only a single flip flop rather than two flip flops. Why? The purpose of the first flip flop in the circuit of Figure 26.5 was simply to synchronize the input with the clock (allow it to only change on clock edges). Since the debouncer circuit output is a Moore output from the debouncer finite state machine, we know that it is already synchronized with the system clock. Thus, we only need a single flip flop in the pulse generator circuit. If we did not know this about the input signal to the pulse generator, we would need both flip flops as in Figure 26.5.

Assume that we have already designed the debouncer circuit and that it is contained in a SystemVerilog module called *Debouncer*. A complete debouncer/pulse generator circuit using this module is shown in Program 26.2.1. This circuit instances a copy of the debouncer and then adds the additional logic to it for the pulse generator.

Program 26.2.1 SystemVerilog Code for Debouncer/Pulse Generator Circuit

---

```
module DebounceAndPulseGen(
      input logic clk, noisyIn,
      output logic cleanOut);

   logic debounced, delayedDebounced;

   // Instance the debouncer
   Debouncer debounceInstance (clk, noisyIn, debounced);

   //Add the additional flip flop and logic gate for the pulse generation
   always_ff @(posedge clk)
     delayedDebounced <= debounced;

   assign cleanOut = debounced & ~delayedDebounced;

endmodule
```

26.3 Exercises

26.1. Create a SystemVerilog design of the debouncer described in this chapter. Make it parameterizable (within a reasonable range) so that the length of the delay used by the timer can be specified when the block is instantiated in a design.

26.2. The state machine for the debounce circuit ensures that the input signal is stable for at least $5ms$ before generating its output. An alternative would be for the machine to unconditionally generate its output $5ms$ after the first transition occurred on the input. If you know the upper bound on the time a switch might bounce ($5ms$ for example), is this an acceptable solution? Does this change appreciably affect the size of the final circuit? Quantify that by doing the design in SystemVerilog and then determining (roughly) in terms of gates and flip flops needed.

26.3. If you need to debounce a whole set of buttons (say 10 of them), you could use 10 different debounce circuits as shown in this chapter. There is a much simpler design which uses a 10-bit loadable register, a comparator, a timer, and a state machine. The idea is that all 10 inputs must be stable for $5ms$ before any outputs are allowed to change. The register is used to hold the previous stable 10-bit value. Do this design and compare it to using 10 conventional debouncers as shown in this chapter.

26.4. The debouncer FSM shown earlier in this chapter was a 4-state Moore machine. It can be coded in SystemVerilog as a 2-state Mealy machine. Do that design.

Chapter 27

Case Study: A Soda Machine Controller

A very simple soda machine was used as a homework problem in Chapter 22. A more complete soda machine controller will be designed in this chapter. All drinks in this soda machine cost $0.45. The machine accepts quarters, dimes, and nickels, and dispenses change using a minimum number of coins. It also responds to a coin return button. This is a much more complex design than the switch debouncer of the previous chapter, and so a step-by-step approach will be described as we work through the design.

27.1 Step 1 - Understand the Complete System Requirements and Organization

The controller we are designing is only a small part of the system. The other parts include:

1. A coin acceptance and return mechanism.

2. A mechanism to physically dispense the soda.

3. A user interface mechanism (the buttons on the machine).

The first step of the design process is to understand the functionality of these parts of the system so we can make educated decisions regarding the organization and functionality of the required controller. The best way to ensure that we have enough information about each of these items is to review their functionality in general, and the behavior of each of their input and output signals.

27.1.1 Understanding the Coin Mechanism

The coin acceptance mechanism is provided by a local manufacturer and is intended to interface to electronic systems. Figure 27.1 is a high-level depiction of the coin acceptance mechanism we are considering. It is called the $VCM7$.

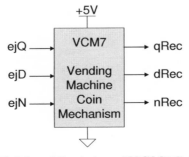

Figure 27.1: High Level Depiction of $VCM7$ Coin Mechanism

The first question to consider is one of electrical interface. The technology we intend on using is a 3.3V FPGA from FPGAs-R-Us Corporation. We note from the documentation for the $VCM7$ that all its signals are $5V$ signals. Consulting the documentation for our chosen FPGA, we see that it can receive and drive $5V$ signals. This is a configuration option for its configurable I/O blocks. It will thus be possible to directly wire the FPGA to the $VCM7$'s inputs and outputs.

The second question to consider is the operation of the $VCM7$'s signals. The documentation for the $VCM7$ states the following:

1. The $VCM7$ will reject all coins other than legal US quarters, dimes, and nickels. When a valid coin is inserted, the corresponding output ($qRec$, $dRec$, or $nRec$) will pulse <u>low</u> (from $5V$ to $0V$) for a time period of between $10ms$ and $12ms$.

2. To instruct the $VCM7$ to eject a coin, one of ejQ, ejD, or ejN should be pulsed high (from $0V$ to $5V$) for at least $45ms$, but no more than $50ms$.

We see that the $VCM7$ has no ability to count money, but is strictly a coin chute that will signal when a coin has fallen through, and which can be instructed to output a coin. Due to the poor documentation provided for the $VCM7$, however, some unanswered questions remain regarding its operation:

- Is it safe to assume that only one "coin received" signal will be pulsed low at a time?

- Is there a guaranteed gap between these pulses so that each coin deposited generates a unique pulse (even if successive coins are the same denomination)?

- Is it safe to assume that the $VCM7$ will reject incoming coins any time it is in the process of ejecting a coin?

- How fast can the $VCM7$ eject coins?

We learn the following additional characteristics of the $VCM7$ after a phone call to the manufacturer:

1. Only one "coin received" signal will pulse at a time.

2. Once one of the "coin received" outputs has pulsed low and then high again, no additional coins will be accepted for at least $2ms$. This guarantees a $2ms$ gap between pulses.

3. Once a request to eject a coin has been made, no additional request to eject a coin should occur for at least $500ms$, measured from the trailing edge of the eject pulse sent to the $VCM7$.

4. The $VCM7$ will reject any coins inserted from the time one of the eject signals has been asserted, through the end of the $500ms$ wait period.

The next step in understanding the operation of the $VCM7$ is to draw a timing diagram diagram. This is shown in Figure 27.2. The critical timing values in the figure include the pulse width of the "coin received" signals ($10 - 12ms$), the timing gap after one of these signals (at least $2ms$), the pulse width of the "eject coin" signals ($45 - 50ms$), and the gap between these signals (at least $500ms$).

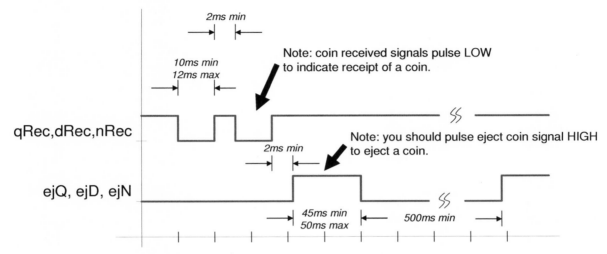

Figure 27.2: Timing Diagram for $VCM7$ Coin Mechanism

We realize at this point that we have additional questions regarding the operation of the $VCM7$:

1. Is there any way to tell if the $VCM7$'s coinbox contains a particular coin (quarter, dime, or nickel)? Without this knowledge, we may design a controller which will attempt to eject coins not present in the $VCM7$'s coinbox.

2. Is there a way to tell the $VCM7$ to refuse coins? We would like to be able to prevent it from accepting coins during certain operations (like when the soda can is being dropped out the discharge chute.

We again contact technical support and learn that if we want these additional features, we will need to use a $VCM8$ instead of a $VCM7$. It has an *acceptCoin* input which controls whether it accepts or refuses coins. It also has three additional outputs: $qPres$, $dPres$, and $nPres$ which signify whether any quarters, dimes, and nickels are present in the coinbox. We know that if the coin mechanism has at least one nickel in its coinbox, it can always successfully make change for a \$0.45 purchase (you can prove this to yourself by looking at finite number of ways that too much money can be inserted and then what will be required to make change).

We also learn that when a coin is inserted, the corresponding "presence" signal ($qPres$, for example) will be asserted *before* the end of the corresponding "coin received" pulse. If the machine currently has no dimes in its coinbox, and a dime is inserted, the $dPres$ signal will be asserted (go high) before the end of the $dRec$ pulse. When an eject coin signal is received by the $VCM8$, the corresponding "coin present" signal will be deasserted (go low) before the end of the eject pulse (if this ejection is for the last such coin in the coinbox).

Besides these few changes, the $VCM8$ is otherwise identical to the $VCM7$. A representation of the $VCM8$ is shown in Figure 27.3.

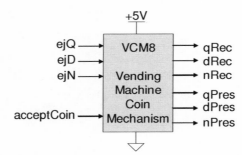

Figure 27.3: High Level Depiction of the $VCM8$ Coin Mechanism

27.1.2 Understanding the Dispense Module

The $SDM3$ dispense module is the mechanism that delivers a soda to the customer. It takes, as input, a 4-bit address to tell it which soda to dispense and a 1-bit *dispense* signal. In response it dispenses the correct soda. The rising edge of the *dispense* signal causes it to latch the 4-bit address and begin a dispense operation. A timing diagram showing this is given in Figure 27.4. This timing diagram shows that there is a $5\mu s$ setup time for the *sodaAddr* signal — it must be stable for at least $5\mu s$ before the rising edge of the *dispense* signal.

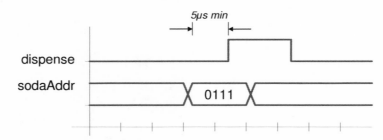

Figure 27.4: Timing Diagram for $SDM3$ Soda Dispensing Mechanism

27.1.3   Understanding the User Interface

There is a keypad on the front of the soda machine which contains ten buttons. Of these, nine are used to select the soda desired, and are arranged in a three-by-three grid as shown in Figure 27.5. In addition, the keypad contains a coin return signal called cr. An individual wire for each button on the keypad comes out of the keypad mechanism. The numbered buttons have names from $b1$ through $b9$.

All keypad wires are asserted high ($5V$) and the documentation states that these buttons are NOT debounced, and will have a maximum bounce time of $10ms$.

Figure 27.5: Soda Machine Keypad

There are a number of other inputs and outputs to the soda machine:

1. A global reset input, $globalReset$, can be used to reset the controller.

2. A light appears on the front of the soda machine to indicate it is ready to accept coins. We will use the previously mentioned $acceptCoin$ signal to drive this light.

3. There is a "select" light on the front of the machine which indicates that enough money has been inserted to purchase a soda. We will produce a signal called $enough$ to drive this light.

27.2 Step 2: Determine a System Architecture

Any sequential design can be implemented, in theory, by a single finite state machine and associated logic. There are some natural ways, however, to partition this system into a set of communicating modules:

1. A central finite state machine will be used to control the activities of the other pieces of the design. This will be called the Central Control Subsystem.

2. Due to the timing requirements of a number of the blocks, a timer will be required (the Timer Subsystem).

3. The keypad interface is complicated enough to be a separate module (the Keypad Interface Subsystem).

The resulting system block diagram is shown in Figure 27.6.

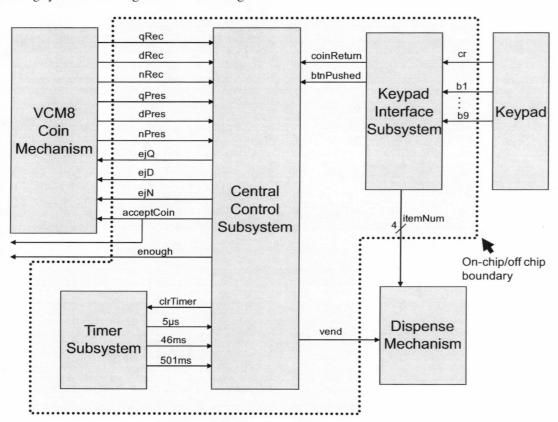

Figure 27.6: Complete Soda Machine Block Diagram

The following considerations and assumptions are associated with this block diagram:

- The $VCM8$ has the same basic timing as the $VCM7$.

- The $VCM8$ will be wired directly to our design.

- The timer subsystem will be used for all operations requiring delays.

- The keypad interface subsystem will perform a number of functions: (1) debounce the signals coming from the keypad, (2) encode the button signals into a 4-bit value to identify what was ordered ($itemNum$), and (3) generate a $btnPushed$ signal to indicate that one of the buttons has been pressed. The $btnPushed$ signal is connected to the central control subsystem. The $itemNum$ signal is wired directly to the dispense mechanism.

- The central control unit will instruct the dispense mechanism when to vend a drink using the $vend$ signal.

27.3 Step 3 - Design the System Parts

We now know enough about the system parts and have completed a block diagram. The next step is to design the individual parts of the system.

27.3.1 Design of the Timer Subsystem

We start with the simplest subsystem — the timer. It is a counter with multiple outputs to indicate when it has reached various values. We note that the entire system will be clocked at a rate of $1MHz$. From this, we can calculate the required delays in terms of clock cycles:

1. The $5\mu s$ delay required for the setup time for the dispense mechanism can be accomplished by comparing the timer value to 5.

2. The eject coin pulses must be $45ms - 50ms$ wide. We will choose $46ms$ for this pulse width. The $46ms$ output will be asserted when the timer reaches $46,000$.

3. There is a requirement to wait at least $500ms$ between eject pulses. A $501ms$ signal will be asserted when the timer reaches $501,000$.

We will use a 19-bit clearable counter for this module. Its design is a fairly simple 19-bit clearable counter, similar to those seen previously in this text. The 3 different outputs can each be generated with an *assign* statement in the SystemVerilog code. The design of this module is so simple that its SystemVerilog code will not be given here.

You may be surprised at this point to see that there are no $10ms$, $12ms$, or $2ms$ delay outputs. The reason is that these are timings that the $VCM8$ manufacturer guarantees to meet on signals that <u>it</u> generates ($qRec, dRec, nRec$) — these are not signals our circuit generates.[1]

---

[1] An experienced designer will always test a part such as the $VCM8$ and take timing and voltage measurements to verify that indeed it functions as promised. This is not solely because the designer distrusts the manufacturer but also because it is very easy to misunderstand the specifications associated with an electronics part. By experimenting with the part before incorporating it into a design the designer verifies that her/his understanding of it is correct, thereby avoiding painful re-design work.

27.3.2 Design of the Keypad Interface Subsystem

The next subsystem is the keypad interface. Its purpose is to simplify the signals coming out of the keypad for the rest of the circuit. It does this in a number of ways:

1. It uses 10 debounce/pulse generator circuits to remove bounces on the inputs received from the keypad.

2. It determines when a button has been pressed by monitoring the $b1 - b9$ signals. When it determines a button has been pressed, it informs the Central Control Subsystem using the $btnPressed$ signal.

3. When a button is pressed, it encodes the button number into a 4-bit quantity called $itemNum$, and sends that to the dispense mechanism.

A block diagram for the the Keypad Interface Subsystem is given in Figure 27.7.

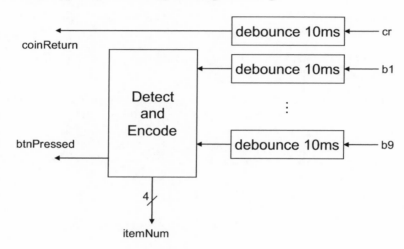

Figure 27.7: The Keypad Interface Subsystem

This subsystem is relatively straightforward to design using SystemVerilog and is shown in Program 27.3.1. After instancing 10 debounce/pulse generator instances (similar to those from the previous chapter), it contains an OR gate to generate the *btnPressed* signal and a *case* statement to generate the *itemNum* value.

The circuit has nine different button inputs but we would like to consider those nine signals to be the bits of a single 9-bit signal. Note how the *case* statement concatenates them all together and then tests that 9-bit collection to generate the *itemNum* signal.

Program 27.3.1 SystemVerilog Code for Keypad Interface

```
module KeypadIF(
        input logic clk, cr, b1, b2, b3, b4, b5, b6, b7, b8, b9,
        output logic coinReturn, btnPressed,
        output logic[3:0] itemNum);

  logic b1x, b2x, b3x, b4x, b5x, b6x, b7x, b8x, b9x;

  DebounceAndPulseGen dpgcr (clk, cr, coinReturn);
  DebounceAndPulseGen dpgb1 (clk, b1, b1x);
  DebounceAndPulseGen dpgb2 (clk, b2, b2x);
  DebounceAndPulseGen dpgb3 (clk, b3, b3x);
  DebounceAndPulseGen dpgb4 (clk, b4, b4x);
  DebounceAndPulseGen dpgb5 (clk, b5, b5x);
  DebounceAndPulseGen dpgb6 (clk, b6, b6x);
  DebounceAndPulseGen dpgb7 (clk, b7, b7x);
  DebounceAndPulseGen dpgb8 (clk, b8, b8x);
  DebounceAndPulseGen dpgb9 (clk, b9, b9x);

  always_comb
  begin
    // Will set bntPressed low here,
    // default clause below will reset it if needed
    btnPressed = 1;
    case ({b1x, b2x, b3x, b4x, b5x, b6x, b7x, b8x, b9x})
      9'b100000000: itemNum = 4'b0001;
      9'b010000000: itemNum = 4'b0010;
      9'b001000000: itemNum = 4'b0011;
      9'b000100000: itemNum = 4'b0100;
      9'b000010000: itemNum = 4'b0101;
      9'b000001000: itemNum = 4'b0110;
      9'b000000100: itemNum = 4'b0111;
      9'b000000010: itemNum = 4'b1000;
      9'b000000001: itemNum = 4'b1001;
      default:      begin
                      itemNum = 4'b0000;
                      btnPressed = 0;
                    end
    endcase
  end
endmodule
```

Also, what happens in this code where two buttons are pressed at exactly the same time (something which is very unlikely)? The *default* clause takes care of that by setting *itemNum* to 0 and setting *btnPressed* to 0 so the state machine will not interpret it as a button push. In this case the user will realize that their pushing the button didn't 'take' (a common occurence with vending machines), and the user will then push the intended button a second time.

What about the case of a multi-button push where one button's pulse appears one or more clock cycles before the other's? The system will accept the first one and ignore the second one. How do we know this? Later you will see that the state machine waits for a single button push and, immediately upon receiving one, moves on and starts dispensing the soda and returning change. If a second button push is received a few cycles after the first, the state machine won't notice because it will not be in a state which is even looking for a button push.

It is left to you as the reader to convince yourself whether these are acceptable design decisions or not. Is there any way this design would enable someone to cheat the machine and get a soda for free? Could the machine cheat someone out of their money? Could the machine dispense the wrong soda?

27.3.3 Design of the Central Control Subsystem

The central control subsystem itself can be decomposed further into multiple subsystems (subsubsystems?). A diagram of this is shown in Figure 27.8.

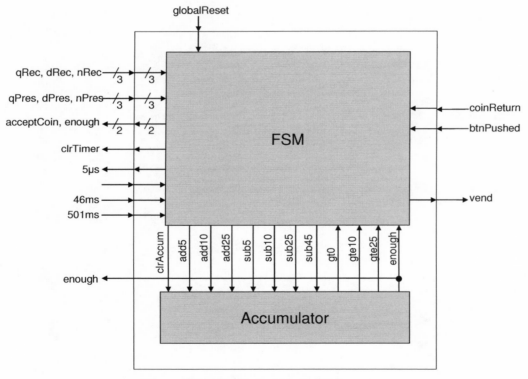

Figure 27.8: The Central Control Subsystem

The heart of the central control is a finite state machine. In addition, an accumulator helps it keep track of the amount of money deposited during a transaction. The accumulator can be instructed to add to or subtract in increments of 5, 10, or 25 cents. It can also be instructed to subtract 45 cents from its total. This last functionality is used when a soda is ordered.

The accumulator has four outputs which provide information on its balance. These are used by the central control state machine to determine what change to eject, when a soda may be ordered, etc. The $gt0$ (greater-than-0) signal indicates that the accumulator does not contain a zero (at least some money has been inserted). The $gte10$ signal indicates that the accumulator contains 10 cents or more. The $gte25$ signal indicates that the accumulator contains 25 cents or more. The *enough* signal indicates that the accumulator contains 45 cents or more (enough to purchase a soda).

27.3.4 Design of the Accumulator

The accumulator is a register and IFL which can select between a number of input values to add or subtract. It is intended to count how much money is in the coin box for the current transaction. Since money can be inserted into the soda machine in 5 cent increments only, there is no reason to accumulate actual cents. Rather, we will design the accumulator to count in 5 cent increments. It will thus take 9 of these increments to accumulate enough money to buy a soda. When a quarter is inserted, the accumulator should increment by 5 and so on.

The central control state machine will instruct the coin mechanism to quit accepting coins once the user has inserted 45 cents or more. As a result, we can determine that 65 cents is the maximum amount of money that will ever accumulate during a transaction (40 cents followed by a quarter). This corresponds to a 13 when counting in 5 cent increments. A 4-bit accumulator is thus wide enough.

A block diagram of the accumulator design is shown in Figure 27.9. The rightmost block is a clearable accumulator which can be commanded to add 1, 2, or 5 or to subtract 1, 2, 5, or 9. The output forming logic (OFL) computes the four outputs which describe the contents of the accumulator as described above.

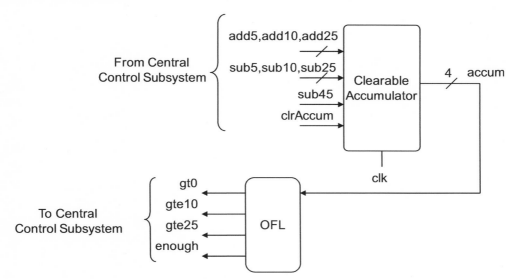

Figure 27.9: Accumulator Block Diagram

If this accumulator subsystem were being designed using gates it would be a fairly complex hand design. However, using *always* blocks in SystemVerilog, the design is quite straightforward as shown in Program 27.3.2. The code takes advantage of an important assumption — that is, that the finite state machine controller will never assert more than one control input to the accumulator block at a time.

Program 27.3.2 SystemVerilog Code for Accumulator Subsystem

```
module Accumulator(
        input logic clk, clrAccum,
        input logic add5, add10, add25, sub5, sub10, sub25, sub45,
        output logic gt0, gte10, gte25, enough);

    logic[3:0] accum;

    //Generate the outputs
    assign gt0 = (accum != 0)?1:0;
    assign gte10 = (accum >= 2)?1:0;
    assign gte25 = (accum >= 5)?1:0;
    assign enough = (accum >= 9)?1:0;

    //The accumulator itself
    always_ff @(posedge clk)
    begin
      if (clrAccum)
        accum <= 0;
      else if (add5)
        accum <= accum + 1;
      else if (add10)
        accum <= accum + 2;
      else if (add25)
        accum <= accum + 5;
      else if (sub5)
        accum <= accum - 1;
      else if (sub10)
        accum <= accum - 2;
      else if (sub25)
        accum <= accum - 5;
      else if (sub45)
        accum <= accum - 9;
    end

    endmodule
```

An alternative which uses a *case* statement instead of *if-then-else* statements is shown in Program 27.3.3.

Program 27.3.3 SystemVerilog Code for Accumulator Subsystem Using A *case* Statement

```
module Accumulator2(
        input logic clk, clrAccum,
        input logic add5, add10, add25, sub5, sub10, sub25, sub45,
        output logic gt0, gte10, gte25, enough);

   logic[3:0] accum;
   logic[6:0] controlInputs;

   //Generate the outputs
   assign gt0 = (accum != 0)?1:0;
   assign gte10 = (accum >= 2)?1:0;
   assign gte25 = (accum >= 5)?1:0;
   assign enough = (accum >= 9)?1:0;

   //The accumulator itself
   //This is implemented with a case statement instead of if-then-else
   //First, concatenate the control signals together:
   assign controlInputs = {add5,add10,add25,sub5,sub10,sub25,sub45};

   always_ff @(posedge clk)
   begin
     if (clrAccum)
       accum <= 0;
     else
       case (controlInputs)
         7'b1000000: accum <= accum + 1;
         7'b0100000: accum <= accum + 2;
         7'b0010000: accum <= accum + 5;
         7'b0001000: accum <= accum - 1;
         7'b0000100: accum <= accum - 2;
         7'b0000010: accum <= accum - 5;
         7'b0000001: accum <= accum - 9;
       endcase
   end

endmodule
```

27.3.5 Design of the Central Control Subsystem State Machine

The last part of this design is the central control state machine controller. It is a complex state machine and so its design will be described in pieces.

The first piece is shown in Figure 27.10, and represents the section of the machine which waits for coins to be inserted. In state **S1**, one of two things can happen. The first is that the *coinReturn* signal can be asserted. A transition occurs to a later state, in this case, which will return any accumulated money. The second possibility is that a coin will be inserted. Since we know the $VCM8$ is guaranteed to assert only one of its "coin received" signals at a time, the conditions on the arcs leaving state **S1** can be simplified beyond that which would be required by the rules for complete and conflict-free state graphs. These conditions are shown in the figure. *Remember that the "coin received" signals are asserted low.*

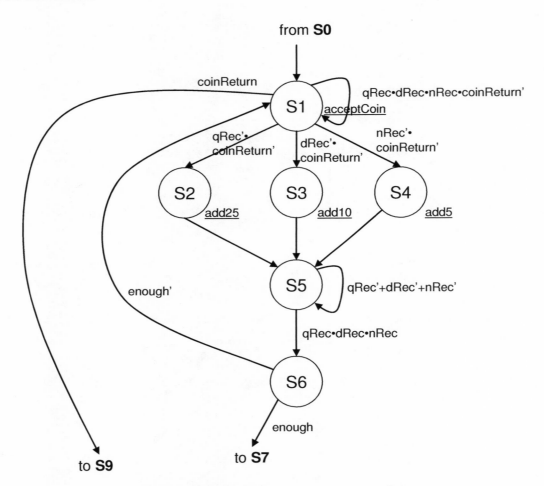

Figure 27.10: State Graph - Part 1 (Accepting Coins)

When a coin is inserted, the appropriate signal is asserted to increment the accumulator's contents (states **S2**, **S3**, and **S4**). State **S5** is then immediately entered (on the next clock cycle), where the machine waits until the end of the "coin received" pulse. At this point, a coin has been received and properly accounted for. The state machine then checks, in state **S6**, whether enough money has been inserted or not. If enough has been inserted, it transitions on to the next part of the state machine. Otherwise, it transitions back to state **S1** to await the insertion of more coins.

The next part of the state machine is shown in Figure 27.11. One of two things can happen while the machine is in state **S7**. The first is that the coin return button can be pressed, and state **S9** is entered to refund any money previously inserted. The second possibility is that a button is pushed to order a soda. The soda is dispensed in state **S8** (the *vend* signal is asserted), the accumulator is decremented by 45 cents (*sub45* is asserted), and the machine transitions to state **S9** to begin returning any change required[2].

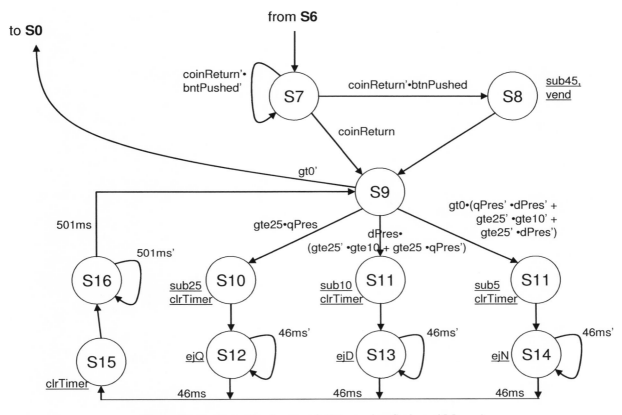

Figure 27.11: State Graph - Part 2 (Dispensing Soda and Money)

State **S9** is entered in two cases: (1) the coin return button is pressed, or (2) a soda is ordered. State **S9**, and the states below it in the figure, return any needed change to the customer. A quarter will be returned if the outstanding change is greater or equal to 25 cents (*gte25*), and if there are quarters in the coin mechanism. The accumulator balance is then adjusted (state **S10**), and state **S12** is used to time the $46ms$ required for the *ejQ* pulse. States **S15** and **S16** combine to time the $501ms$ wait required before another coin can be ejected.

The conditions for when dimes and nickels are returned are fairly complex, and a truth table is created to generate the equations shown in the figure. In each case, the goal is to ensure that the largest possible denomination coin is ejected each time around the loop. This will return the minimum number of coins (which may or may not be a good strategy - but it is the one chosen here). Finally, when the *gt0* signal becomes false in state **S9**, the accumulator is empty, and the machine returns to the top of the state graph.

The complete state graph is shown in Figure 27.12. A reset state, state **S0**, has been included in addition to the two sections previously shown. The machine will only leave state **S0** if the coin return button is not being pushed, if no other buttons are being pushed, and if there is at least one nickel in the coin mechanism. This last condition is to ensure that regardless of what is inserted, the machine can make proper change. The *globalReset* arc shown indicates that, regardless of what state the machine is in, when *globalReset* is asserted state **S0** will be the next state.

---

[2]Since the buttons are being debounced for $10ms$, we can be certain that the $5\mu s$ setup time on the *vend* and *itemNum* signals has been met, and therefore can ignore the $5\mu s$ timer signal we initially anticipated needing.

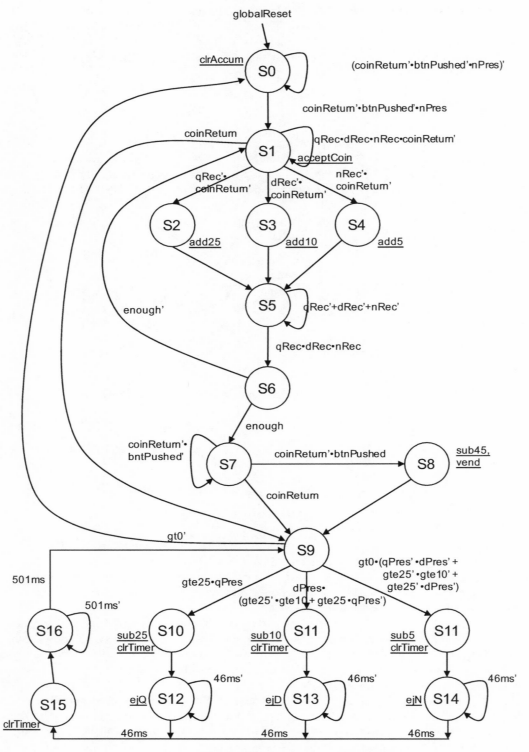

Figure 27.12: State Graph - Complete

27.3.6 A Complete and Conflict-Free State Graph

The test for completeness will fail for state **S9** in the final state graph. Why, then, is the state graph correct? The design of the accumulator ensures that if $gte25=$'1', then $gte10$ and $gt0$ are both also TRUE. Our knowledge of the possible output combinations that the accumulator can generate allows us to simplify the conditions on the arcs leaving state **S9**. Other states may show similar simplifications.

27.3.7 Implementing the State Machine Using SystemVerilog

The creation of the SystemVerilog code for the state machine corresponding to the state graph above is straightforward and follows the approach outlined in the Chapter 23. The decision regarding how many *always* blocks to use to to describe it is left up to the designer. Because this is a complex state machine with many inputs and many outputs, the author's preference is to use a single *always_comb* block to describe the IFL and OFL together and then to use a single *always_ff* block to describe the state register. A fragment of the IFL/OFL logic is shown in Program 27.3.4. As can be seen, it follows directly from the state graph in a straightforward manner.[3]

---

[3]In fact, CAD tools exist which allow you to draw state diagrams such as are shown here and which then automatically convert those drawings to the equivalent Verilog code.

Program 27.3.4 SystemVerilog Code for A Portion of the Soda Controller State Machine

```
module SodaFSM(
        input logic clk, globalReset, qRec, dRec, nRec, qPres, dPres, nPres,
        input logic timer5us, timer46ms, timer501ms, coinReturn, btnPushed,
        output logic ejQ, ejD, ejN, acceptCoin, enough,
        output logic clrTimer, vend, clrAccum,
        output logic add5, add10, add25, sub5, sub10, sub25, sub45);

    typedef enum logic[4:0] {s0, s1, s2, s3, s4, s5, s6, s7, s8,
                  s9, s10, s11, s12, s13,
                  s14, s15, s16, ERR='X} StateType;
    StateType ns, cs;

    // The state register
    always_ff @(posedge clk)
      cs <= ns;

    // The IFL/OFL
    always_comb
    begin
      // Default output values
      ns = ERR;
      ejQ = 0;  ejD = 0;  ejN = 0;
      acceptCoin = 0;
      enough = 0;
      clrTimer = 0;
      vend = 0;
      add5 = 0;  add10 = 0;  add25 = 0;
      sub5 = 0;  sub10 = 0;  sub25 = 0;  sub45 = 0;

      //Now for the actual FSM logic
      if (globalReset)
        ns = s0;
      else case (cs)
        s0: begin
            clrAccum = 1;
            if (~coinReturn & ~btnPushed & dPres & nPres) ns = s1;
            else ns = s0;
          end
        s1: begin
            acceptCoin = 1;
            if (coinReturn) ns = s9;
            else if (~qRec) ns = s2;  // Remember - coin signals active low
            else if (~dRec) ns = s3;
            else if (~nRec) ns = s4;
            else ns = s1;
          end
        s2: begin
            add25 = 1;
            ns = s5;
          end

        // Rest of module definition not included due to
        // space limitations...
```

27.3.8 Asynchronous Inputs, Adjacent State Encodings, and Glitch-Free Outputs

Before we complete our design, the issues of asynchronous input handling and the production of glitch free outputs needs to be addressed.

The input signals from the $VCM8$ are asynchronous with respect to the $1MHz$ clock used for our design and so should be passed through a flip flop before reaching the central control state machine to synchronize them. The debounce circuits in the keypad interface subsystem will synchronize the keypad outputs with the global clock so nothing needs to be done to them.

The production of glitch-free outputs on all output wires is also important. Why? The mechanisms driven by the control circuit (the coinbox and dispense mechanisms) are not synchronous with the soda machine controller. Rather, they are always monitoring their inputs for changes to indicate an action is needed. Thus, any glitches will be interpreted as commands to eject coins, dispense a soda, etc. The signals to address regarding this include: ejQ, ejD, ejN, $acceptCoin$, and $vend$. The simplest way to do this is to pass these signals through flip flops before they leave the design to eliminate any glitches (false outputs) that the combinational logic in the state machine's OFL may introduce.

You may wonder if delaying signals entering the soda controller and delaying signals leaving the soda controller in this way will cause problems. For example, the controller will learn that a coin has been inserted one clock cycle later than it otherwise might. That translates to a delay of at most $1\mu sec$, hardly a problem in this application. The same goes for button pushes on the keypad. The signals generated by the state machine will also reach their destinations one clock cycle later than they otherwise would. Once again, this delay of $1\mu sec$ is not a problem given that we are dealing with physical mechanisms. If our controller were controlling some high speed circuitry such as a memory or CPU pipeline, however, we would want to carefully think about every single cycle on both the input and output paths since additional delays could translate into significant performance degradation for the entire system.

27.4 Summary

The steps of designing a soda machine control system have been shown in this section. Given the skills learned over the previous chapters, you should be able to reduce this design to a complete implementation using SystemVerilog.

27.5 Exercises

27.1. Create a complete soda machine controller design and simulate it to verify its proper operation. To speed up simulation, simulate it with shortened delays on the actual timer values.

27.2. Synthesize the soda machine controller you created in the previous problem but with full delays everywhere. From the synthesis reports for this, determine how much circuitry (and therefore how large an FPGA) your design would require. Find out from the WWW what the cost for such an FPGA would be. How does that compare to the cost of a microcontroller and associated circuitry?

27.3. What can you say about whether the use of a custom hardware design for this task might be warranted? Summarize what you see as the main considerations you woudl take into account when deciding. Could this have been done using a programmable microcontroller? If so, can you estimate how much software might have to be written for the microcontroller?

Chapter 28

Case Study: The Design of a UART

As another example of the design of a multi-part digital system, this chapter introduces the design of a UART. The term UART stands for Universal Asynchronous Receiver Transmitter. In this chapter the basics of serial communication will be described in sufficient detail to understand the design of a UART interface circuit. Actual UART devices have many, many more features than those shown here. But what is shown here is sufficient for the design of a basic UART.

28.1   UART Protocol Design

Consider the problem of transmitting multiple bits of data over a single signal wire. Further, lets assume we are limiting ourselves to just digital data — only high-voltages (1's) and low voltages (0's). A listener (receiver) will then monitor the high and low voltages on the wire and reconstruct the data. A sample waveform which might be received is shown in Figure 28.1 and consists of a high voltage followed by a low voltage.

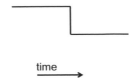

time

Figure 28.1: A Sample Received Waveform

So, what is the received value? An obvious interpretation is that it is the sequence '10'. However, can you be sure? Could it be the sequence '11110000' or '1100'? The first piece of information required, then, is to know the *transmission rate* for the communication. Knowing that, you would then know if the initial high voltage was one bit-period long or multiple bit-periods long. Let's assume that you are told that the bit period corresponds to the length of time in the figure where the signal is high. Now you know it is the bit pattern '10'. Or, do you?

There is no rule that requires that high voltages correspond to '1' values and low voltages correspond to '0' values. The second piece of information you need, then, is to understand how voltages map to logical values. Let's assume that you are told that this is a *positive logic* system and therefore that high voltages map to '1' values. At this point you may assume that this represents the bit pattern '10'.

Consider another received waveform as shown in Figure 28.2. What received bit pattern is it?

time

Figure 28.2: A Second Sample Received Waveform

315

Knowing what the bit period is, you may determine that the received data is the bit pattern '11'. But this illustrates a fundamental problem — what does the transmitter do when it is not actually transmitting data (which can happen)? If the line were to be high when it was idle, you could not distinguish that from the bit pattern '11111 . . .'. If it were to idle low, you could not distinguish that from the bit pattern '00000 . . .'. What is needed, then, is a way to mark when the transmitter is ready to transition from idling to actually sending data.

The way a UART does this is that it defines the idle state for the wire to be a '1' value. Then, when it wants to start sending a pattern of 1's and 0's, it first starts by sending a *start bit* (which is a '0') followed by the data. This shown in Figure 28.3 which is a start bit followed by three '1' bits. The start bit is not a part of the data but marks the beginning of a data transmission.

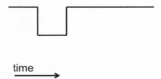

time

Figure 28.3: A Transmitted Waveform Consisting of a Start Bit Followed by Data Bits

Here, the line is initially idling at a '1' (the leftmost '1' value) and then a start bit is sent (the '0') bit (knowing the bit rate helps us to know it is a single start bit rather than a start bit followed by one or more '0' values). But, when does the actual data end? Is the data pattern '111' or is it '11' followed by the line returning to idle?

This can be solved by agreeing on just how much data will be sent in a burst or packet. UART devices were originally invented and used in the days of ASCII terminals — display devices capable of displaying 7-bit characters (see Section A for a table of how ASCII characters correspond to bit patterns). In such cases, the data packet was seven bits. Once those bits were transmitted, the line was required to return to the idle state for some minimum time period before the next character could be transmitted. This is shown in Figure 28.4.

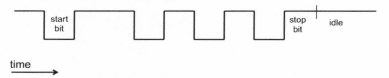

time

Figure 28.4: A Transmitted Waveform Corresponding to '1101010'

In this waveform, the start bit is marked. The *stop bit* on the right, is a required '1' bit before another transmission can begin, and is also marked. The data bits are those between and consist of '1101010', which is the hex value 6A. Or is it?

The final piece of information you need to decipher this waveform is to understand the bit order. Is the first '1' bit received the most significant bit (the MSB) or is it the least significant bit (the LSB)? While it is somewhat arbitrary, the serial standard supported by traditional UART devices (called the RS-232 standard), defines that bits are sent LSB-first. Thus, the bit pattern really corresponds to the ASCII value 2B. Looking that up in Chapter A, we see that this could represent the '+' character (if what was being sent really are ASCII characters - otherwise, it is simply the hex value 2B, which is the number 43 in decimal).

Finally, it is common to include some simple error detection capability into serial communications. The mechanism chosen for RS-232 is known as *parity*. Put simply, a word with even parity will have an even number of '1' bits in it and a word with odd parity will have an odd number of '1' bits in it. If it was agreed upon that the UART was operating in odd parity mode, a character received with an even number of '1' bits in it would be an error (and an error signal could be raised by the UART to let the rest of the system know that).

This is a very simple form of error detection — the occurence of such a parity error tells us that a bit must have gotten inverted during transmission (due to some error in the transmission line) but tells us nothing about which bit it might be. In fact, even that is not quite true. Rather, it tells us that an odd number of bits must have gotten flipped during transmission, thereby converting an odd parity word to an even parity word. Do you see why this is the case?

But, how can we guarantee that all words transmitted have an odd number of '1' bits in them? The answer is to add an extra bit, a *parity bit*, to the end of the word. The transmitter will look at the seven bits of data and count the

'1' bits. If there is an even number, it will append a '1' bit to the end of the word so that the collection now has an odd number of '1' bits. If, however, the there is an odd number of '1' bits in the original 7 bits, the transmitter will append a '0' bit to the end of the word. In either case, a single bit has been appended to the end of the word (changing it from a 7-bit word to an 8-bit word). The bit appended is selected to ensure the overall 8-bit word has an odd number of '1' bits in it. Like the start and stop bits, this bit is overhead. The receiver will remove it from the received data but then use it to check if a parity error has occurred by counting the '1' bits in the word.

The above discussion assumed that the transmission is using odd parity. Hopefully you can figure out how this would be done for even parity. In the remainder of this chapter we will use odd parity.

This is all summarized in Figure 28.5, which shows a start bit, seven bits of data, a parity bit (odd parity in this case), and a stop bit.

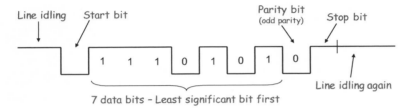

Figure 28.5: A Full Transmission Waveform

It should be obvious to you that the efficiency of this scheme is 70%. It takes the transmission of ten bits to actually send seven bits of data.

Typical UART circuits have a number of additional features or parameters assoiciated with them which both transmitter and receiver must agree upon for successful communication to occur. However, we will not include any of these in our design. They include the following:

- The number of data bits may be selectable to be either 7-bits or 8-bits.

- Parity can be even, odd, or none. For 'none', no parity bit is included.

- The speed can be specified. This is usually specified in number of bits per second, also known as *BAUD rate*. Typical values range from 110 BAUD (ancient and slow) up to about 256K BAUD.

- UART devices also usually allow for the specification of the number of stop bits which will be used, typically 1 or 2.

Putting all of this together, a UART operating in 9600-7-o-1 mode is a UART operating at 9600 BAUD, seven data bits, odd parity, and one stop bit.

A common mistake is to confuse BAUD rate with transmission rate. As we saw above, only 70% of the bits transmitted in the scheme of Figure 28.5 are data and the other 30% are overhead. Thus, at 256K BAUD while you are transferring 256K bits-per-second, you are only transferring user data at the rate of just under 205Kbps.

28.1.1   Protocol Summary

The above discussion has described how chunks of data are transmitted on a serial wire. This provides a sufficient discussion for the remainder of this chapter, which is devoted to the design and SystemVerilog coding of a UART design.

28.2 Designing the UART

In the balance of this chapter a simple UART will be designed. It will run at a BAUD rate of 256K, will support 7-bit words, and will use one stop bit and odd parity.

The above discussion focused on how bits are coded onto a serial wire but said nothing about the rest of the UART (specifically where the bytes it is to transmit come from and where it sends the bytes it receives). A very high-level block diagram of a complete UART is shown in Figure 28.6.

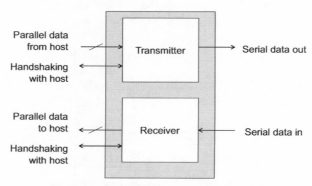

Figure 28.6: Block Diagram of a UART

The UART consists of two major sections - a transmitter and a receiver. The transmitter accepts parallel data (seven bits at a time) from a host and transmits them over the serial line. The receiver monitors a separate serial line and packages up groups of seven bits it receives and hands those off to the host. Thus, a complete UART has two serial lines and two host interfaces (in reality it may not be a host computer that interfaces with the UART but rather can be any digital circuit but, for purposes of this discussion, we will call it the host). These two major sections (transmit and receive) can be designed independently of one another since they do not interact with one another at all. That is the approach we will take.

28.3 Design of a UART Transmitter

We will start with the transmitter. Requirements for its design include the following:

1. The rate at which bits are transmitted is a part of the specification. It is important to know what clock rate the transmitter will run at compared to the BAUD rate desired. Counters will then be used to count down clock cycles to determine when a new bit of data should be sent down the serial line. In our case, the transmit rate will be 256K BAUD. We will further choose that our entire system will be clocked with a system clock of 4 MHz. This means that a serial bit time is equal to 16 clock cycles.

2. A handshaking protocol needs to be designed so that the host and transmitter can communicate.

3. The specification requires that odd parity is to be used.

28.3.1 Host-UART Handshaking

A simple handshaking protocol which is often used in digital circuits is shown in Figure 28.7. This is called a 4-cycle request/acknowledge handshake. When the sender (the host in this case) is ready to send something to the receiver (the transmitter in this case), it performs the following steps: (1) it drives the data to be sent onto the data lines, (2) it then raises the *REQ* signal. It will then hold the data value and the *REQ* signal steady until the receiver acknowledges receipt of the data by raising its *ACK* signal. The sender can then remove the data and its *REQ* signal at any time after this. In response the receiver then lowers its *ACK* signal and the system is ready to initiate another transaction. The letters A-D in the figure mark the four phases of the protocol, which are: A (Sender): "I have data for you", B (Receiver): "Got it", C (Sender): "Goodbye", D (Receiver): "Goodbye".

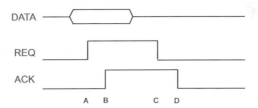

Figure 28.7: Handshake Timing Diagram: Host to UART

Importantly, there are no timing requirements on when the phases occur other than that they occur *in order*. Thus, the receiver can delay acknowledging the data for as long as it desires (if it is busy doing something else, for example). Further, the only requirement on the data is that it appears *prior* to *REQ* going high and is held steady until *after* the *ACK* signal has gone high. Thus, the receiver can either (a) latch the data into its own register for safekeeping and then immediately acknowledge its receipt or (b) process the data and only acknowledge after it is done processing it. We will use the second approach in our final design.

With this settled, we can draw a top-level block diagram for the UART transmitter. The creation of such a diagram helps to cement in our minds what the external interfaces for the transmitter will be and is a necessary first step in starting to create a design for it. This block diagram is shown in Figure 28.8.

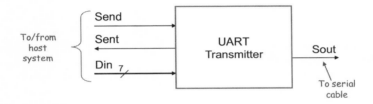

Figure 28.8: UART Transmitter Top Level Diagram

On the left, the top two inputs correspond to the *REQ* and *ACK* signals from Figure 28.7. Below them is the parallel data from the host (seven bits wide).

The transmitter section can be further decomposed into a controller and a datapath. This is a very common way to subdivide a circuit design. The datapath is the portion for the circuit that actually operates on the input data and produces output data. The role of the controller is that of control — both interacting with other circuitry as well as controlling the operation of the datapath. The transmitter section decomposed in this way is shown in Figure 28.9.

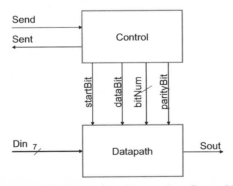

Figure 28.9: UART Transmitter Datapath + Control Diagram

The controller is responsible for handshaking with the host as well as instructing the datapath when to send a start bit, when to send a data bit, and when to send the parity bit. In this case, we will make the decision that the controller will take care of all timing issues and the datapath will basically consist of a registered multi-way MUX, selecting the desired bit for output.

28.3.2 The Transmitter Datapath

The code for the transmitter datapath is given in Program 28.3.1 and is essentially a MUX, selecting either a start bit, one of the data bits, the parity bit, or a '1' bit to output.

Program 28.3.1 UART Transmitter Datapath Code

```
always_ff @ (posedge clk)
  if (startBit)
    Sout <= 0;
  else if (dataBit)
    Sout <= Din[bitNum];
  else if (parityBit)
    Sout <= ~^Din;
  else
    Sout <= 1;
```

This code reflects a number of assumptions made about how the rest of the system is supposed to work that are important to understand:

1. As can be seen, various bits of *Din* are selected for output in the second clause of the *if-then-else*. This requires that the *Din* values need to be valid during the entire transmission period. This, in turn, then suggests that the transmitter is not going to acknowledge receipt of the data to the host by raising the *Sent* signal until *after* it has transmitted it. This ensures that the data remains constant during the entire transmission.

2. Note that there is no *stopBit* signal sent to the datapath from the controller. The reason for this is that the default value on the line is a '1' bit and so when not sending a start bit, data, or the parity bit the default output is a '1' bit, satisfying both the need for a stop bit as well as subsequent idle values on the line.

3. The parity generation expression may be a bit confusing to you at first. Recall that for odd parity, we want to make sure that the transmitted word has an odd number of '1' bits in it. Thus, if the original word has an even number of '1' bits, a '1' bit should be appended (and a '0' bit appended if the original word already had an odd number). The expression used in the code first calculates the parity of the original word using an XOR reduction operation (the "^" operator). It then inverts that bit using the "~" operator. The result is the parity bit. The best way to convince yourself that this works is to apply it to the word '0000000' and to the word '0000001'. You will see that the parity bit, when appended to the other bits ensures that an odd number of '1' bits will be transmitted.

4. It is up to the controller to instruct the datapath on which data bit should be transmitted using the *bitNum* signal.

5. It is important that the *Sout* signal not have any false outputs (glitches). That is why an *always_ff* block was used to generate it — the resulting register created to hold the *Sout* signal will ensure a clean *Sout* signal in spite of glitching in the combinational logic of the datapath.

There are other ways the datapath could have been formulated instead of as a MUX as shown. For example, the controller could have used signals to instruct the datapath to transmit a start bit and the datapath could have done the timing itself to send it for the proper number of cycles. However, that would then have required the datapath to have its own timers as well. It seems more appropriate in this case to have the controller handle all timing functions.

A second and more interesting method, however, is shown in Figure 28.10. Here, the datapath is a shift register. When the host's data is loaded into the shift register, a start bit is loaded on the right end and a parity bit is loaded on the left end. Then, as the shift register is shifted, the exposed bit on the right will be the *Sout* signal. Note that '1' bits are shifted into the shift register from the left so that once the word has been transmitted, a '1' bit is guaranteed to be output on the *Sout* line for both stop bit and idling purposes. The controller in this case need not even know what data bit is being transmitted at any given time — it merely needs to generate a load signal followed by shift signals with the proper timing. Whether this is preferable to the original transmitter design of Program 28.3.1 would be, perhaps, a matter of personal preference unless one was significantly smaller than the other (but they look to be pretty close in complexity).

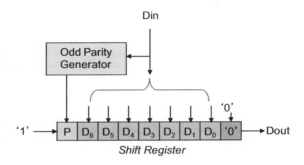

Figure 28.10: UART Transmitter Datapath - Alternate Design

For purposes of the remainder of this case study, we will focus on using the first datapath as shown in Program 28.3.1. However, the design and implementation of these two alternate designs and comparing their relative complexities would be a good exercise.

28.3.3 The Transmitter Control Section

The transmitter control section will need to contain at least a state machine and two counters. The first counter will count data bits transmitted and therefore will need to count at least from 0 to 6. The second counter will be a timer so that each transmitted bit is multiple clock cycles in length. As mentioned above, the desired BAUD rate is 256K bits per second. The system clock rate will be 4MHz and so each bit time will be 16 clock cycles, requiring a 4-bit timer. A block diagram of the control section based on this is shown in Figure 28.11.

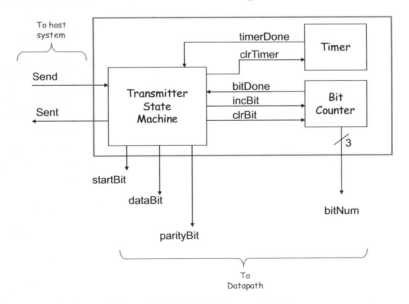

Figure 28.11: UART Control Section

The needed functionality should be somewhat obvious at this point. The state machine needs to have states to implement the handshaking with the host described above. It also needs to transmit: (a) a start bit, (b) the 7 data bits, (c) the parity bit, and (d) a stop bit. The state graph to implement this is shown in Figure 28.12. Reducing that to SystemVerilog code is a fairly straightforward exercise as is designing the bit counter and the timer.

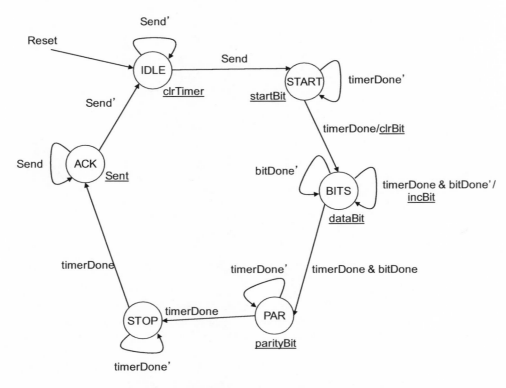

Figure 28.12: UART Finite State Machine Controller

The state machine contains mostly Moore outputs. One Mealy output is in the *BITS* state (the *incBit* signal). A Mealy output is used here to avoid wasting cycles going to an extra state just to assert an *incBit* signal. If you look carefully you will see that multiple things are happening in the *BITS* state. It is waiting for the timer to expire, signifying the end of a bit time. When that happens, it either increments the bit count or it leaves the state to output the parity bit.

The other Mealy output is asserted on the transition from state *START* to state *BITS* and is the *clrBit* signal. It is asserted here to assure that once the machine gets to the *START* state that the bit counter is reset.

Note that the *bitCnt* signal appears nowhere in the finite state machine. Rather, it is an output of the bit counter used by the datapath. However, detecting that its value equals '110' does need to be accomplished somewhere to generate the *bitDone*) signal for the state machine to monitor. Thus, the Bit Counter module would have OFL which would compare the bit count value to '110' and generate the *bitDone* signal. Similarly, the Timer would have OFL to detect that the timer value equals '1111' to generate the *timerDone* signal.

Verilog code to implement the IFL and OFL of the state machine is is a direct translation of the state graph and is given here:

Program 28.3.2 UART Transmitter State Machine

```
always_comb
begin
  // Default values
  Sent = 0;
  clrTimer = 0;  clrBit = 0;  incBit = 0;
  startBit = 0;  dataBit = 0;  parityBit = 0;
  ns = ERR;

  if (Reset)
    ns = IDLE;
  else case (cs)
    IDLE:   begin
              clrTimer = 1;
              if (Send) ns = START;
              else ns = IDLE;
            end
    START:  begin
              startBit = 1;
              if (timerDone) ns = BITS;
              else ns = START;
            end
    BITS:   begin
              dataBit = 1;
              if (timerDone & ~bitDone)
              begin
                incBit = 1;
                ns = BITS;
              end
              else if (timerDone & bitDone) ns = PAR;
              else ns = BITS;
            end
    PAR:    begin
              parityBit = 1;
              if (timerDone) ns = STOP;
              else ns = PAR;
            end
    STOP:   if (timerDone) ns = ACK;
            else ns = STOP;
    ACK:    begin
              Sent = 1;
              if (~Send) ns = IDLE;
              else ns = ACK;
            end
  endcase
end
```

28.3.4   An Alternate Transmitter Coding Style

There is one simple change to this transmitter state machine design which can be done. While quite simple, it represents another approach which is commonly employed. A block diagram of the transmitter for this is shown in Figure 28.13 — the change is small enough you might not even notice it. It consists simply of bringing the Timer and Bit Counter outputs directly into the state machine rather than *timerDone* and *bitDone*. The state machine then contains the code to check the timer count value and decide if it is rolling over. Similarly, the state machine would have code to check the *bitNum* value to see when it was equal to '110'.

The advantage of this is that it eliminates the need for the Timer and Bit Counter modules to declare those two signals and then to generate values on them. Imagine the case where you later decide that you want the state machine to react to additional timer values beyond just '1111'. With the original design, additional signals would need to be defined and generated in the Timer module and then connected to the state machine. With this modified style, however, the state machine code simply check for the new values, a minimal disruption to the existing design.

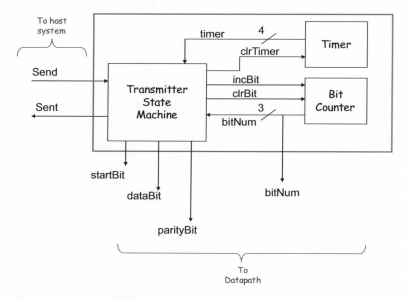

Figure 28.13: UART Transmitter - Alternate Version of Control Section

With this change, the complete transmitter control section SystemVerilog code is given in Programs 28.3.3 and 28.3.4. Note in the FSM's *case* statement that the values of the *timer* and *bitNum* signals are directly compared to constants rather than relying on *timerDone* and *bitDone* signals.

Program 28.3.3 UART Transmitter Control - Part 1 of 2

```
module xmitControl(
      input logic clk, Reset, Send,
      output logic startBit, dataBit, parityBit,
      output logic[2:0] bitNum
      );

   typedef enum logic[2:0] {IDLE, START, BITS, PAR,
                            STOP, ACK, ERR='X} StateType;
   StateType cs, ns;

   logic[3:0] timer;
   logic clrTimer, clrBit, incBit;

   // The timer
   always_ff @(posedge clk)
     if (clrTimer)
       timer <= 0;
     else
       timer <= timer + 1;

   // The bit counter
   always_ff @(posedge clk)
     if (clrBit)
       bitNum <= 0;
     else if(incBit)
       bitNum <= bitNum + 1;

   // The state register for the state machine
   always_ff @(posedge clk)
     cs <= ns;

   ...
```

Program 28.3.4 UART Transmitter Control - Part 2 of 2

```
  ...

  // The IFL/OFL for the state machine
  always_comb
  begin
    // Default values
    Sent = 0;
    clrTimer = 0;   clrBit = 0;   incBit = 0;
    startBit = 0;   dataBit = 0;   parityBit = 0;
    ns = ERR;

    if (Reset)
      ns = IDLE;
    else case (cs)
      IDLE:    begin
                  clrTimer = 1;
                  if (Send) ns = START;
                  else ns = IDLE;
               end
      START:   begin
                  startBit = 1;
                  if (timer==15) ns = BITS;
                  else ns = START;
               end
      BITS:    begin
                  dataBit = 1;
                  if (timer==15 & bitNum!=6)
                  begin
                    incBit = 1;
                    ns = BITS;
                  end
                  else if (timer==15 & bitNum==6) ns = PAR;
                  else ns = BITS;
               end
      PAR:     begin
                  parityBit = 1;
                  if (timer==15) ns = STOP;
                  else ns = PAR;
               end
      STOP:    if (timer==15) ns = ACK;
               else ns = STOP;
      ACK:     begin
                  Sent = 1;
                  if (~Send) ns = IDLE;
                  else ns = ACK;
               end
    endcase
  end
endmodule
```

28.4 Design of a UART Receiver

The UART receiver shown in Figure 28.6 is the mirror image of the transmitter. It receives bits serially on the *Sin* line, assembles them into a parallel word, and transfers them to the host using a handshake similar to that used by the transmitter with the host.

Figure 28.14 shows a high level block diagram of the receiver. It contains one additional signal compared to the transmitter, the *parityErr* signal. When a word is received, the receiver checks the parity of the word (including the parity bit). If the parity is not odd, then we know that one or more of the received bits are wrong. In response, the *parityErr* signal will be raised concurrently with the *Receive* signal. The host may then decide what to do with the received word (not the concern of this design).

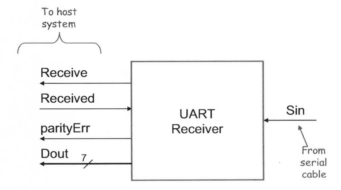

Figure 28.14: UART Receiver Top Level Diagram

Figure 28.15 shows a typical received word. The best place to sample the individual bits will be right in the middle of the bit period (as shown by the arrows overlaid on the diagram). Why? It is possible that the receiver's clock and the remote transmitter's clock may not be at identical frequencies. Thus, the bit periods may be a bit different than expected. By sampling in the middle of each bit time, we maximize that chance that the receiver will sample the actual bit value.

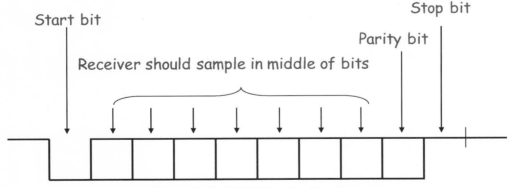

Figure 28.15: UART Receive Waveform

Figure 28.16 shows what happens if the clock of the remote transmitter is too different from the clock of the receiver. Even though the receiver is sampling what it believes is the middle of each bit period, by the end of the word the clock rate discrepancy has cause the sampling to be off. This is one of the reasons why UART transmissions are fairly short (usually only 7 or 8 bits) — every time a new start bit arrives the receiver gets to recalibrate on where the bit boundaries are.

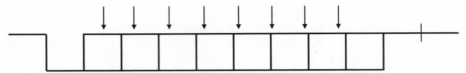

Figure 28.16: UART Receive Waveform - Receiver and Remote Transmitter Clock Rate Mismatch Effects

As with the transmitter, the receiver will contain both a datapath and a control section. Upon seeing the serial line go low to signal a new start bit, the controller will use a timer to count over into the middle of the first data bit's location and then instruct the datapath when to sample the serial line. This would profitably benefit from the alternate controller design seen for the transmitter — the state machine would first count up to 23 (to get to the middle of the first data bit), reset the counter, and then count up to 15 repeatedly to get to the middle of the other bit locations.

The datapath will load the received bits into a register (a shift register would seem most appropriate here). The datapath would further have a parity generator circuit which would output a '1' on *parityErr* if the contents of the shift register did not have odd parity. A block diagram of the contents of the receiver is given in Figure 28.17.

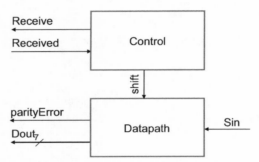

Figure 28.17: UART Receiver Datapath + Control Diagram

The communication between the control and datapath is very simple in this case — the controller simply tells the datapath when to shift in a new data bit (the start bit is not shifted in - only the actual data bits and the parity bit). The design of both the datapath and control sections of the receiver is very similar to that of the transmitter above and will not be detailed here.

28.5 Summary

A serial communications protocol has been presented. A UART design was developed which allows a host to both send and receive data.

The design was a fairly minimal design. A real UART would have a number of other features which could be readily added to this one:

- It could have additional inputs to tell it what speed to transmit and receive at. These inputs would control the Timer module in both the transmitter and receiver (in our design, the bit rate is 16x slower than the clock rate).

- It could have a control input to tell it whether to transmit and receive either 7 or 8 bit words.

- It could have control inputs to instruct it whether to use odd parity, even parity, or no parity.

- It could have a control input to instruct it to work with two stop bits instead of one.

- It could have a framing error output to the host. This is an output that tells the host whether the stop bit was really a '1' bit. BAUD rate setting mismatches between sender and receiver can result in a '0' appearing during the stop bit period, and this would be signalled to the host as another form of error detection in addition to parity errors. The rare bit flip will manifest itself as a parity errors but BAUD rate mismatches would likely result in a steady stream of framing errors. That could be very useful information for the communicating parties to know.

Finally, a discussion about design approach and the use of hierarchy is in order. The diagrams presented in this chapter show a variety of blocks (datapath, control, Timer, Bit Counter etc). One way to approach the design of a complete UART would be to (1) design a separate module for every one of these blocks, (2) combine them into separate transmitter and receiver modules, and (3) then combine the transmitter and receiver modules into a final UART design in a top-level module. This is a perfectly valid approach and is the recommended approach when you are beginning to learn to design. It allows you to design and verify the correctness of the various sub-modules before everything is combined into a complete UART design.

As shown, however, the entire UART is not overly complex (or would not be to an experienced designer). Another approach would be to use less hierarchy (which results in less typing overhead to create module definitions, to define communicating signals, etc). Along these lines perhaps the entire transmitter would be one module and the entire receiver a separate module. Those would then be combined into a top-level module for the UART as a whole. Or, the extreme approach would be to have one module only with all of the transmitter and receiver circuitry inside it.

The choice of how to do it is up to you as a designer. As your design expertise grows, you will develop a design style of your own (and which will likely lead to fewer hierarchical divisions than are shown in this chapter). The important thing is that the style you choose is consistent and clear to you and others (since you and others will have to maintain your code). It should also be easy to debug and should result in correctly functioning circuitry.

Chapter 29

Tri-State Drivers and Buses

This entire book has focused on the use of basic gates and flip flops which all have one characteristic in common. That is, the outputs of those gates and flip flops can only take on two values: a high voltage (a binary '1' value) or a low voltage (a binary '0' value). An important corollary of this is that any given wire in the circuits shown previously can only be driven by a single gate or flip flop. Otherwise, contention will occur. For example, the circuit of Figure 29.1 shows a problem where this is violated.

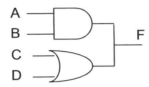

Figure 29.1: A Problematic Circuit Where Two Gates' Outputs are Wired Together

If the output of the top gate is different than the output of the bottom gate then the voltage on the output wire will be indeterminate. In Chapter 17, we described this problem, noting that when this happens 'X' values will show up in your logic simulations. There, however, we noted that this cannot happen when using the *logic* type for signals in your circuit because the compiler will flag any instances of structures such as that shown in Figure 29.1 as errors in your design.

However, in the design of digital systems you will often want to violate these rules and create such *wired logic* structures. In fact, a large class of digital systems do so (specifically, those with bus structures). This chapter describes this, how it works, when you might want to do so, how to code it in SystemVerilog, and how to understand your simulation results when you do so.

Imagine you have a single wire that want to use to communicate between many (most) of the different circuit modules in your system. In particular, you want each of these different circuit modules to be able to drive this wire as well as read the value on the wire. One way to accomplish this is shown in Figure 29.2, where the common wire is called a *bus*.

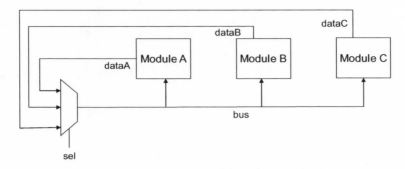

Figure 29.2: A Bus Implemented With a MUX

Here, the signals that might need to be driven onto the bus are brought to a single location in the circuit and fed into a MUX to select between them. In this case (where the bus is a single-bit wire) this does not seem to be a huge problem. But, imagine how many wires would need to converge at one point in the circuit if the bus were 64 bits wide and if the number of modules the bus needed to connect to was very high! You would potentially need to bring hundreds of wires together into the needed MUX structure. Then, the output of the MUX (the bus) would need to be distributed throughout your entire circuit. Such a structure is unwieldy and would take up significant amounts of silicon area in a circuit.

An alternative to this is shown in Figure 29.3. Here, the single bus wire simply runs throughout the circuit. Any module desiring to drive the bus wire does so using something called a *tri-state driver*. These are the triangle gates shown in the circuit.

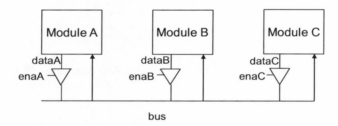

Figure 29.3: A Bus Implemented With Tri-State Drivers

A tri-state driver is a non-inverting buffer whose output has three states and which is controlled by an enable signal. Like any other gate, the output of the buffer can be either a '1' or a '0'. However, unlike other gates the output of the buffer can be electrically disconnected from the bus (and therefore not drive it with any value at all).

To understand this, an analogy might be useful. In the early days of telephones (when a dedicated telephone line to your house was expensive), it was common to have a "party line". A party line was a telephone line shared between multiple households. At every household you could both listen to the party line as well as speak on the party line. If you wanted to make a phone call you would have to pick up the phone and then listen to make sure nobody else was using the line. If so, you would then make your call. But if you failed to check that the line was empty and made a call, your conversation would clash with the one already going on that line. And, interestingly enough, if you were a snoopy kind of person, you could always listen in on your neighbors' conversations!

A bus in this instance is like a party line. It is a shared communication medium that all connected modules can both listen to as well as drive. That is, every module can monitor the values on the bus (just like with the MUX-based version above). But, a module can either be (a) driving the bus with 1's and 0's (talking) or (b) it can disconnect itself from the bus (not talking). That last condition is the tri-state condition. What is needed is a new kind of logic gate which can disconnect itself from its output wire when it does not intend to drive 1's and 0's onto that output wire.

A tristate driver and a truth table of its logic is shown in Figure 29.4. The reason the gates in the combinational logic cloud are not shown is to force you to think about its function rather than merely memorize the gate structure.

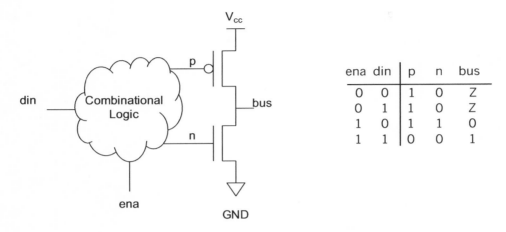

ena	din	p	n	bus
0	0	1	0	Z
0	1	1	0	Z
1	0	1	1	0
1	1	0	0	1

Figure 29.4: A Tri-State Driver

First, note that the right half of the tri-state driver is simply a CMOS inverter as was shown in Section 5.2. However, unlike the inverter shown there, the gates of the p-FET and n-FET transistors are *not* wired together but separately controlled. And, remember how the two types of FET transistors work. A '1' on the gate of an n-FET (the bottom transistor) will turn it on and a '0' will turn it off. Conversely, a '0' on the gate of a p-FET (the top transistor) will turn it on and a '1' will turn it off.

Now, note the bottom two rows in the truth table for the combinational logic. Here, the *ena* signal is true, meaning the driver is to drive values onto the bus wire. In this case if *din* is '0' then a '1' will be driven onto both gates of the FETs. This will turn ON the n-FET and turn OFF the p-FET, driving a '0' value onto the bus. Conversely, if *din* is '1', then '0' values will be driven onto the FET gates, turning ON the p-FET and turning OFF the n-FET — this will drive a '1' value onto the bus. The net effect is that when *ena=1*, *bus=din*.

Now consider the top two rows of the truth table. Here, the *ena* signal is false. In both cases a '1' value is driven onto the gate of the p-FET, turning it OFF and a '0' value is driven onto the gate of the n-FET, turning it OFF also. Thus, when *ena=0*, the tri-state driver has no effect on the voltage value on the bus because both transistors are turned off. In short, a tri-state driver has three states: (1) driving a '1' onto its output, (2) driving a '0' onto its output, and (3) not driving its output.

A typical use for a bus is shown in Figure 29.5. This is a partial drawing of portions of the datapath of the LC-3 CPU as popularized in the textbook *Introduction to Computing Systems: From Bits and Gates to C and Beyond* by Yale Patt and Sanjay Jeram Patel.

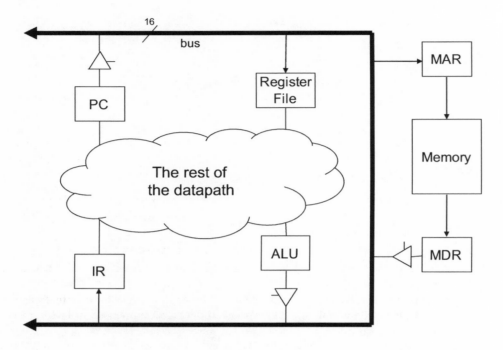

Figure 29.5: A Microprocessor CPU Datapath With Bus and Tri-State Drivers

Here, a 16-bit bus (represented by the heavy dark line) is used to connect the various pieces of other circuitry in the design. These include the program counter (PC), the register file, the arithmetic logic unit (ALU), the instruction register (IR), and the memory. Three different tri-state drivers can be seen. These allow any of the PC, the ALU, and the memory subsystem's memory data register (MDR) register to drive their values onto the bus. A bus such as that shown here is usually known as a *tri-state bus*, implying that it driven using distributed tri-state drivers as shown in the figure above.

A typical operation for such a microprocessor might be to store the results of an ALU operation into a register in the register file. To do so, the tri-state driver below the ALU would be turned on, driving the ALU output values onto the bus. During the same clock cycle the addresses and write enable signals on the register file would be asserted so that on the next rising edge of the clock the value on the bus would be written into the register file.

A more complex operation would be fetching an instruction from memory and placing the instruction thus fetched into the IR. This is an operation that takes three clock cycles:

1. The value of the PC is driven onto the bus using its tri-state driver and, on the clock edge at the end of that cycle, that value (the value of the PC) is loaded into the memory address register (MAR) in the upper right corner of the drawing.

2. The memory is then accessed and the results loaded into the memory data register (MDR) at the lower right of the figure.

3. The value of the MDR is driven onto the bus by the MDR's tri-state driver and that value loaded into the instruction register (IR) in the lower left of the figure.

Thus, to accomplish this multi-step operation, one set of 16 wires (the bus) is used to carry data values first between the PC and the MAR, and then later between the MDR and the IR. This is typical of many digital designs where common communication channels (buses) are used to provide flexible interconnections between a variety of modules in the system.

29.1 SystemVerilog Design for Bus Structures

As mentioned previously, signals can take on any of four different values in SystemVerilog — '0', '1', 'X', and 'Z'. This 'Z' value is the *undriven* logic value. Thus, when in the 3rd state, a tri-state driver will output 'Z' values. In reality, it is outputting nothing at all, but we use the 'Z' value in SystemVerilog to model this.

However, as previously noted, the compiler will flag cases where the outputs of two or more gates are wired together as in Figure 29.1. And, if you carefully look at Figures 29.3 and 29.5 you will see that the outputs of the tri-state drivers are all wired together. So, how do you code such structures?

The answer is that SystemVerilog has another signal type, separate from the *logic* type, that can be used for this purpose. It is the *wire* type. This is a signal which *can* have multiple drivers and therefore is the type of choice for tri-state bus signals.[1] A sample of code representing a tri-state driver is shown here:

Program 29.1.1 A Tri-State Driver in SystemVerilog

```
wire bus;  // Define the bus wire
assign bus = ena?data:'z;  // Describe the tri-state driver
```

This follows directly from the descriptions above — when the enable signal is true the output gets assigned the data input value and when the enable signal is false the output gets assigned nothing (or 'Z' values in this case). Note that 'z or 'Z are shorthand for as many 'Z' values as are needed for the width of the wire being assigned to.

As another example, consider the circuit of Figure 29.3 where three tri-state drivers are shown. A fragment of the code for this is shown here:

Program 29.1.2 A System With Three Tri-State Drivers in SystemVerilog

```
wire bus;  // Define the bus wire
assign bus = enaA?dataA:'z;  // Describe the tri-state driver for Module A
assign bus = enaB?dataB:'z;  // Describe the tri-state driver for Module B
assign bus = enaC?dataC:'z;  // Describe the tri-state driver for Module C
```

This code fragment assumes that the definitions of the three modules (A, B, and C) are also included in the code (but not shown). But, for those three modules, what is the type of the *bus* signal? The code below shows how Module A might be defined:

Program 29.1.3 A Module Which Simply Reads the bus Value in SystemVerilog

```
module A(input wire bus, output logic dataA, ...);
    ...
```

In this code fragment, module A simply reads the bus value and so it is declared to be of type *input wire*. However, another possibility is shown in Figure 29.6. Here, the tri-state drivers are included inside each of the modules and so the *bus* signal is considered a bi-directional signal for the module (the module both reads it and writes it). SystemVerilog code for this structure is shown below the figure.

---

[1]In earlier versions of Verilog there was no *logic* type — everything was of type *wire* (which can have multiple drivers). With these earlier versions of Verilog, the compiler would not flag obvious errors such as Figure 29.1, and thus not notifying you of errors such as the one shown. And, in a complex design, finding such errors could be difficult to do manually.

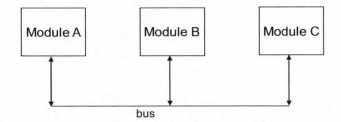

Figure 29.6: A System Where the Tri-State Drivers are Inside the Modules

---

Program 29.1.4 A Module Which Has The Tri-state Driver Inside It in SystemVerilog

```
module A(inout wire bus, ...);
  ...
  assign bus = ena?data:'z;
  ...
endmodule
```

In this code, the *bus* signal has been declared with a direction of *inout*, signifying that this module can both read as well as write the bus signal. Inside the module, the bus value can be read and used in any way desired. And, as shown, a tri-state driver can be included in the module's logic.

The tri-state driver described above *allows* multiple drivers to drive a shared bus but the discussion above provides no information on how to *prevent* multiple tri-state drivers from driving the bus at once. It is up to you as the designer to correctly generate the various enable signals for the tri-state drivers in the circuit and ensure that at most one such tri-state driver is turned on at a time.

When performing a logic simulation of a design such as the ones shown above, you may see four different values on a tri-state bus signal:

- If you see '0' or '1' values, that indicates that either: (1) only one tri-state driver is turned on at that point in time or (2) multiple tri-state drivers are turned on but just happen to be outputting the same '0' or '1' values (and so there is no conflict).

- If you see 'X' values, that suggests that multiple tri-state drivers are turned on at once and they are driving different logic values onto the bus.

- If you see 'Z' values, that indicates that no tri-state drivers are turned on and so the bus is not being driven (we say the bus is *floating* in this case). This is not necessarily an error condition unless you were expecting actual logic values to be driven onto the bus at that point in time (in which case you have an error in the logic that is generating the various tri-state enable signals).

29.2 Summary

The notion of a bus, controlled by tri-state drivers, has been presented and a description of its operation given. A detailed analysis of a tri-state driver circuit was also presented. Finally, a CPU architecture which uses such a tri-state bus was presented.

Chapter 30

SystemVerilog vs. Verilog

30.1 SystemVerilog vs. Verilog

SystemVerilog, in many ways, represents a very significant change from Verilog. Many of the additions to SystemVerilog focus on the addition of an extensive object-oriented (OO) language framework for writing testbenches and circuit verification code. However, none of that is touched on in this book.

In terms of circuit design features, SystemVerilog adds a number of features which simplify the writing of Verilog code. In many cases these features make it possible for a SystemVerilog compiler to flag errors at compile time that with previous versions of Verilog would not have been detected by the compiler. Some of these features (most of which are included in the previous chapters) are described below.

30.2 Data types

SystemVerilog introduces a whole collection of new data types. It also introduces a variety of array and array-like structures. Some of these are there mainly to support simulation and verification while others are synthesizable to hardware. Descriptions of these typically occupy the first few chapters of SystemVerilog reference books and are not covered here.

30.2.1 The *logic* Variable Type

One new type is important for design — the *logic* type which was used in the previous chapters for all signals. It is a four-valued logic type like Verilog originally had, allowing the values 0, 1, X, and Z. Its advantage is that it can be used essentially for everything you do as a beginning designer.

In reality, Verilog has notions of *variable* types vs. *net* types. This text has glossed over those and described everything using the terms *signal* and *variable* interchangeably. In Verilog, the various places where variables vs. net types could be used is confusing at best (at least to beginners and likely to many experienced designers as well). An example of this is learning when to use the original Verilog *reg* keyword and when to not use it. SystemVerilog relaxes most of that by introducing the *logic* type. It is now the universal data type for signals.

The *wire* type (which is the default in Verilog designs) is a tri-state-able wire, meaning it can be driven by multiple drivers. However, the vast majority of wires in digital designs are driven by only one driver and, therefore, wiring up multiple drivers to those wires is an error. The *logic* type can only be driven by a single driver. Thus, if you use *logic* for all wires (*except* those you want to be tri-state), the compiler will then flag any case where you mistakenly wire up multiple drivers to the same logic signal.

In the relatively few cases in your designs where you *do* want tri-state busses, you can then use the *wire* keyword. You should consult other resources for additional details.

30.2.2 Enumerated Types

SystemVerilog's introduction of enumerated data types eliminates the need for *parameter* constant declaration statements. In addition, CAD tools such as simulators can display enumerated values in waveform windows or results listings as text strings (instead of as their equivalent binary encodings).

30.3 Enhanced *always* Blocks

In Verilog there was only the *always* block which was used for both combinational and sequential blocks. As a result, the synthesizer had to guess your intention, based on how you wrote the code. As a result, it was not able to point out some of the mistakes you might make in coding an *always* block.

SystemVerilog introduces three variations: *always_ff*, *always_comb*, and *always_latch* (this last one is not covered in this text). As described in previous chapers, these new flavors of *always* allow the designer to declare her/his intent regarding what circuitry they are attempting to describe. This, then, allows synthesis tools to verify that the circuit described matches the designer's intent and warn the designer if it does not. While the SystemVerilog standard does not require that CAD tools flag such mismatches, most synthesis tools do so.

30.4 Verilog, SystemVerilog, and VHDL Interoperability

It is important to note that SystemVerilog is *backward compatible* with Verilog, meaning that any legal Verilog design code should both simulate and synthesize the same as before. The added features described here are layered on top of the older Verilog standard. CAD tools determine whether your code is SystemVerilog or older Verilog by the filename extension. Use a ".v" for Verilog files and an ".sv" for SystemVerilog files.

Also, you can mix both Verilog and SystemVerilog files in a project. The CAD tools have no problems with this. Thus, older Verilog modules or sub-designs which are known to be correct can be mixed with newer SystemVerilog modules in designs. In fact, today's CAD tools even allow VHDL design files to be mixed into projects with both Verilog and SystemVerilog design files, making the choice of what to use for a given module largely a matter of personal preference!

30.5 Moving Forward

In addition to the features which have been summarized above, SystemVerilog actually adds many other language features. They have not been described in the interest of brevity and simplicity for a beginning digital design textbook. Rather, a subset of the most important features have been touched on to help you as you begin your learning of HDL-based coding using SystemVerilog.

Appendix A

ASCII Table

Table A.1: The Printing Characters from ASCII

Hex Value	Character	Hex Value	Character	Hex Value	Character
20	space	40	@	60	`
21	!	41	A	61	a
22	"	42	B	62	b
23	#	43	C	63	c
24	$	44	D	64	d
25	%	45	E	65	e
26	&	46	F	66	f
27	'	47	G	67	g
28	(	48	H	68	h
29	)	49	I	69	i
2A	*	4A	J	6A	j
2B	+	4B	K	6B	k
2C	'	4C	L	6C	l
2D	−	4D	M	6D	m
2E	.	4E	N	6E	n
2F	/	4F	O	6F	o
30	0	50	P	70	p
31	1	51	Q	71	q
32	2	52	R	72	r
33	3	53	S	73	s
34	4	54	T	74	t
35	5	55	U	75	u
36	6	56	V	76	v
37	7	57	W	77	w
38	8	58	X	78	x
39	9	59	Y	79	y
3A	:	5A	Z	7A	z
3B	;	5B	[	7B	{
3C	<	5C	\	7C		
3D	=	5D	]	7D	}
3E	>	5E	^	7E	~
3F	?	5F	_		